MINDFUL EXPANSION

DAILY INSIGHT | AWARENESS | EMPOWERED EXPANSION

DELIBERATELY CREATED WITH GRATITUDE AND PURPOSE BY...
BRANDON THOMAS

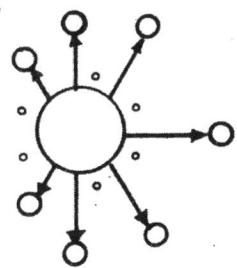

INTROSPECTION THROUGH INTENTION
VOLUME | 01

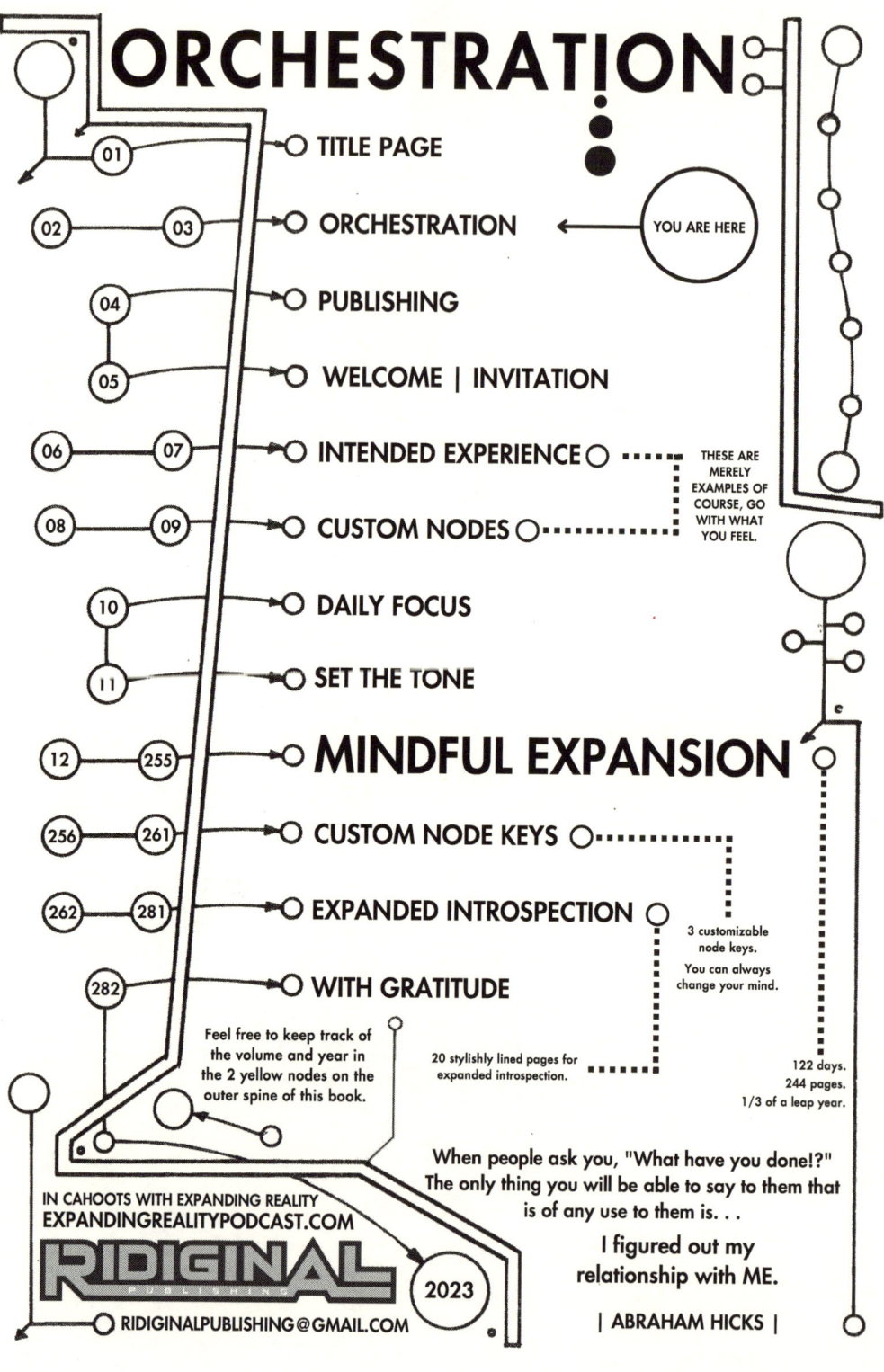

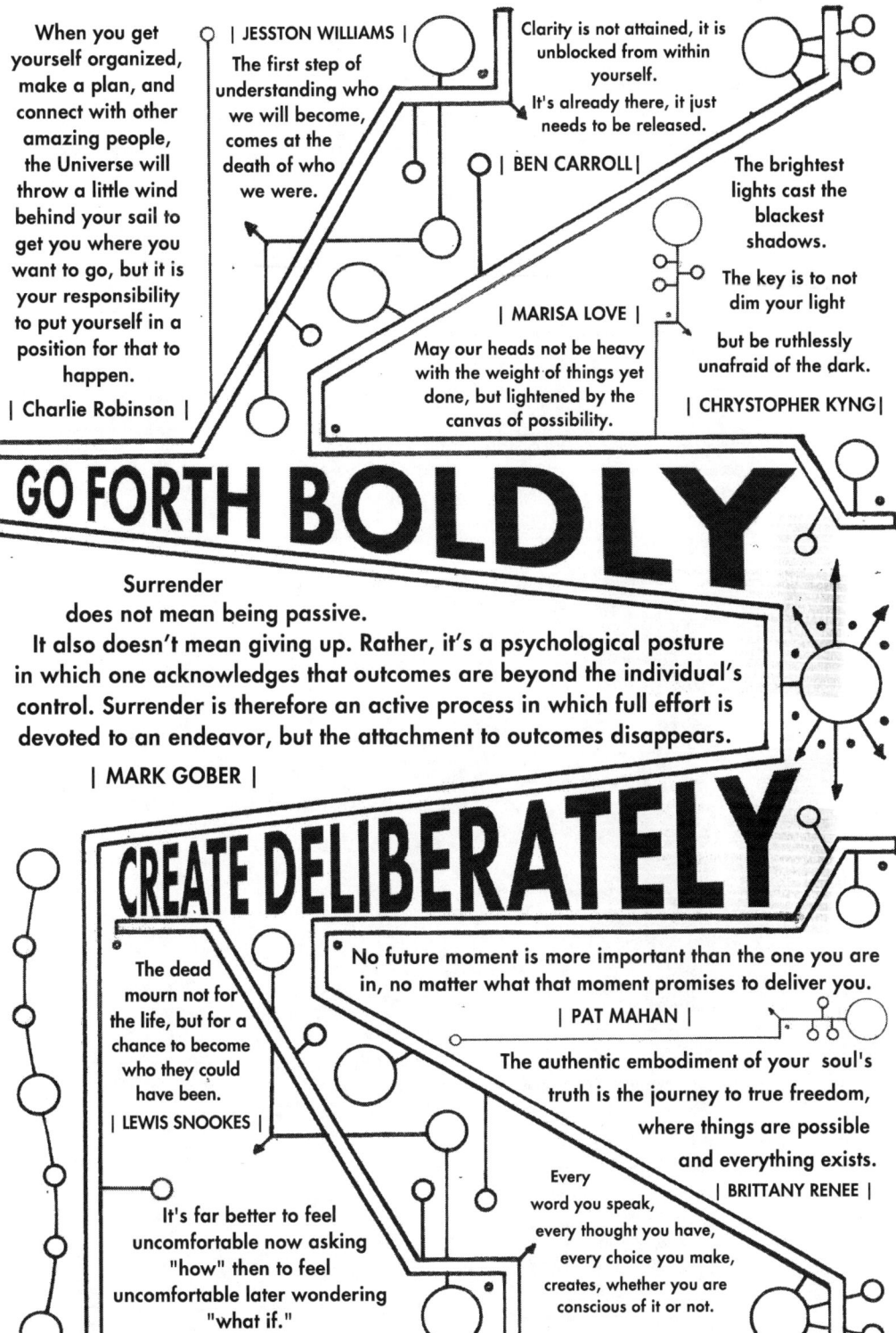

MINDFUL EXPANSION

○ DEDICATION

Dedicated to my perfect wife & partner Mary, who's love and belief in me make every heartbeat better than the last.

Dedicated to the deliberate creator in all of us that is dedicated to our well-being at every level. Empowering life to breathe life into creation's greatest creation-YOU.

Dedicated also to all of the deliberate creators who have moved on and away from us in the physical.
May you find your peace.

RIDIGINAL PUBLISHING

EMPOWERING & AMPLIFYING THE VOICES & VISIONS OF RIDICULOUSLY ORIGINAL AUTHORS.

Deliberate creators! Write us for more information or to set up a meeting to speak about your own ridiculously original creation.
Ridiginalpublishing@gmail.com

ADDITIONAL AWESOMENESS AVAILABLE FROM RIDIGINAL PUBLISHING...

EXPANDING REALITY
EXPANDED INSIGHT & EPISODIC REFLECTION | VOLUME 001

Expanding Reality is The expansion of consciousness cleverly disguised as a podcast. This, is the handbook that accompanies that journey.
Follow along with your favorite show. Noting the wisdom and awesomeness from mind expanding guests & asking larger questions inspired by the insights gleaned from each episode.

AVAILABLE NOW AT EXPANDINGREALITYPODCAST.COM & AMAZON

All rights reserved. This book or any portion thereof may not be reproduced or used in any manner whatsoever without the express written permission of the publisher, except for the use of brief quotations in a book review or other flattering manner.

Copyright © 2023 by
Brandon Thomas

[super official]

EXPAND MINDFULLY

• **WELCOME TO YOU** •

This journal has been one of my greatest allies in the journey of self discovery. As I created, adapted, altered, refined and enjoyed this powerful tool for growth and expansion for myself, I've discovered this to be life-changing and inspiring. I welcome you to expand yourself, becoming mindfully aware of what taking charge of your life actually elicits. . . freedom.

Free from the limitations of the old self.

REMAIN CENTERED

You will only ever find more YOU.
Through all of the shadow work. . . through all of the healing. . .
through all of the manifestation techniques and all of the meditation and
plant medicine journeys. . . you will only ever find more of you.
YOU are the prize.

| AMY BELAIR |

REMAIN FOCUSED

DECIDUOUS : <u>adjective</u> [de·cid·u·ous]
TO SHED THAT WHICH IS NO LONGER NEEDED.

Before you is an invitation to empower the greatest and grandest version of your highest and most insightfully aware self. A reminder to embody the force of that inner voice that beckons you forward. To authentically embrace discipline & ownership. To steer your intergalactic spaceship as the fully capable captain with your once-in-a-lifetime life.

• **INVITATION TO YOU** •

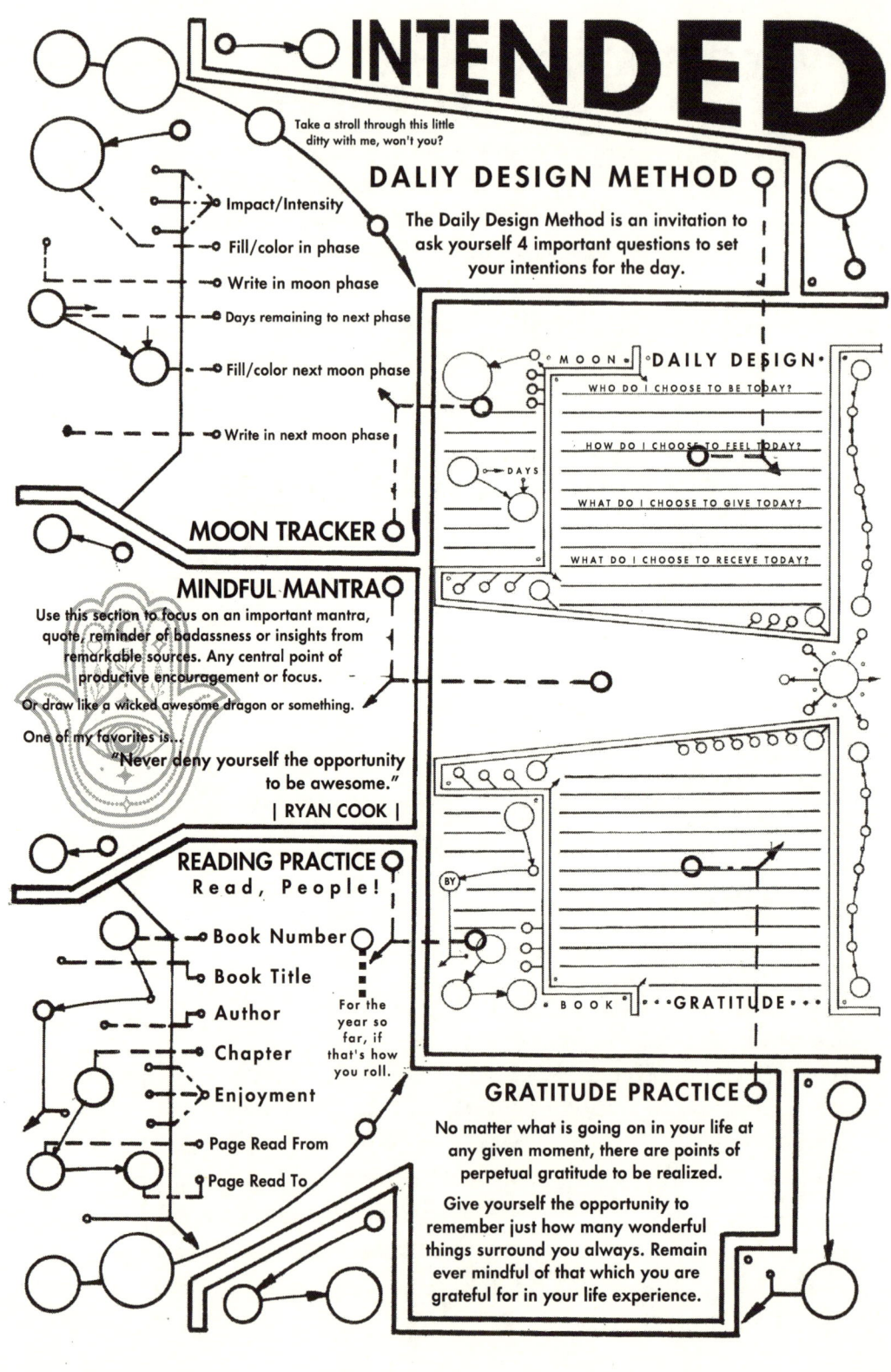

EXPERIENCE

NOW & NOTEWORTHY
What is going on in and around your immediate environment that is of note? What astrological occurrences are on your radar due to their possible impact on your life at the moment?

THOUGHT NINJA
The Thought Ninja is a mindfulness tool given to me in my darkest hour. This gift offered me the insight into why I would sometimes find myself so far out of alignment with my true me. My unaware mind would tumble down the terrifying rabbit holes of former programing that simply has no place in my life moving forward. Cut that nonsense out before it takes root.

By asserting my dominance over my mental temple, the Thought Ninja mercilessly cuts out the fear tentacles before they can root into spirals.

Use this section to release what no longer serves.

RELEASE

CONVERSATION WITH SELF
Use this space for a conversation with yourself. Be open. Be honest. Be REAL.

Note here any and all events, happenings, feelings, emotions, struggles, triumphs, accomplishments, discoveries, goings-on, trauma, feelings of existence and the meaning of life in an inherently meaningless reality...

If you need more room to elaborate., there are 20 pages of "Expanded Introspection" available to you in the back section of this book.

ATTRACT
What'll ya have?

In the reality in which we find ourselves, expansive options of experience are available to us at any given state of our existence. There are "things" that we are bound to desire to experience. In that experience are what we may feel to be located "outside" of our current observable environment.

What is it that you would like to attract into your life experience next? What is it that sounds new, different, exciting, adventurous, elation fueling, fun, peaceful, enjoyable and remarkable that you would like to make yourself a vibrational match for?

Do you know what you want?
Do you know where it is?

GOALS & VISIONS
To have goals is to have glory. With a clear and focused vision, nothing stands in your way. Along this journey you will realize the truth, that it is you who hold the keys to your own personal prison. Liberate yourself with inspired action that has been mindfully oriented to your highest visions for your greatest experience. Do so, one step at a time.

Question: "How do you eat an elephant?"
Answer: "One bite at a time."

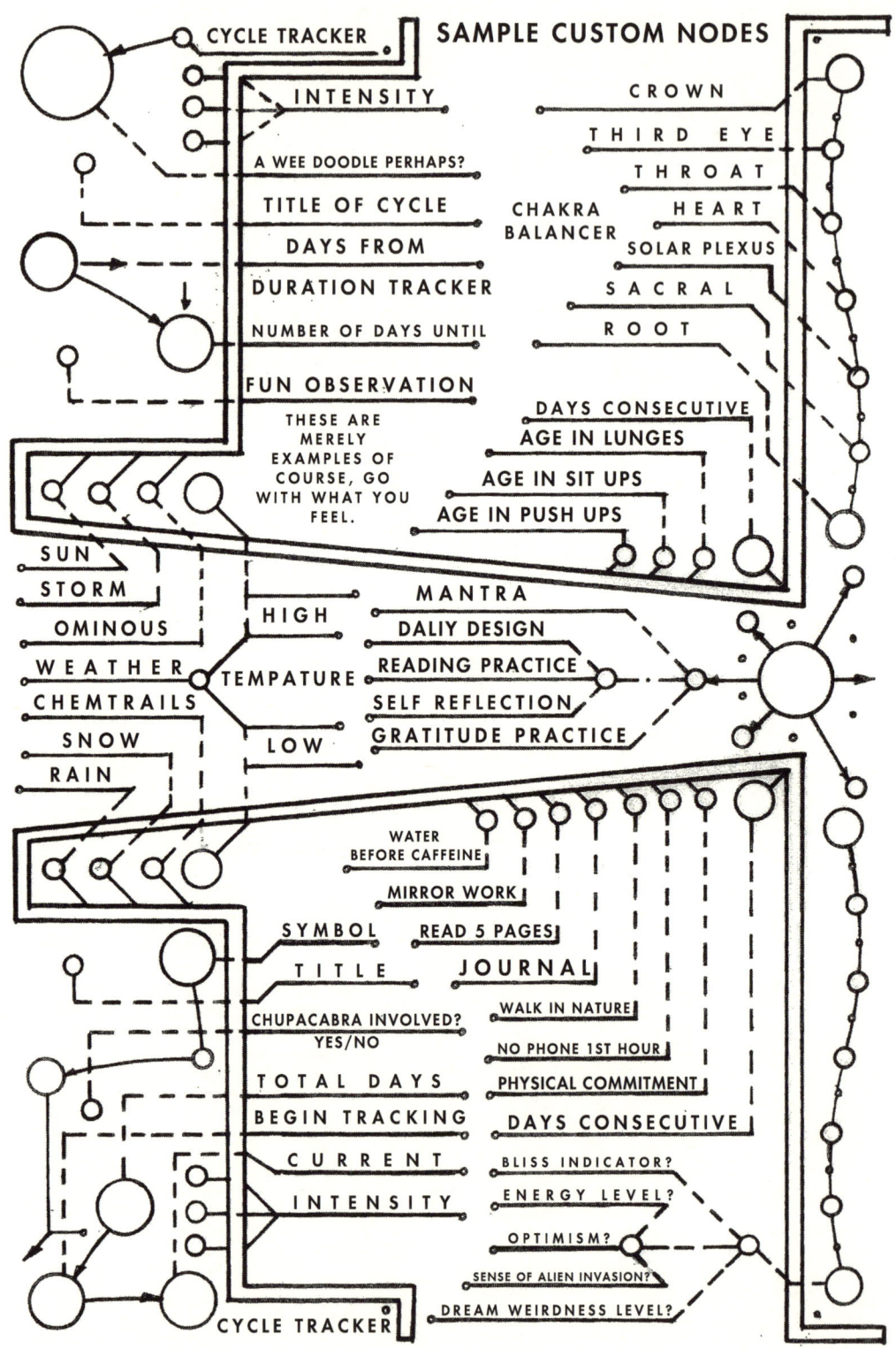

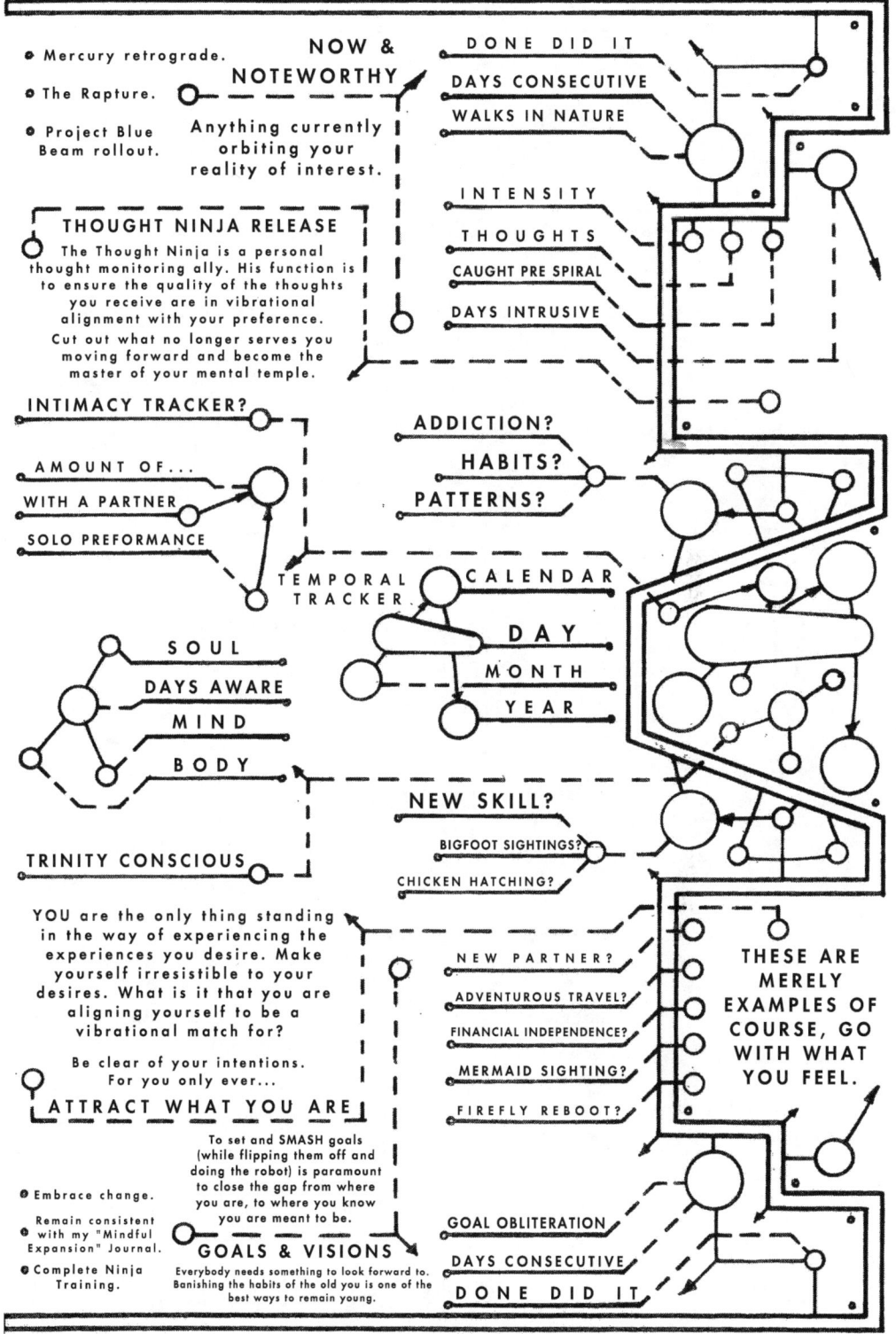

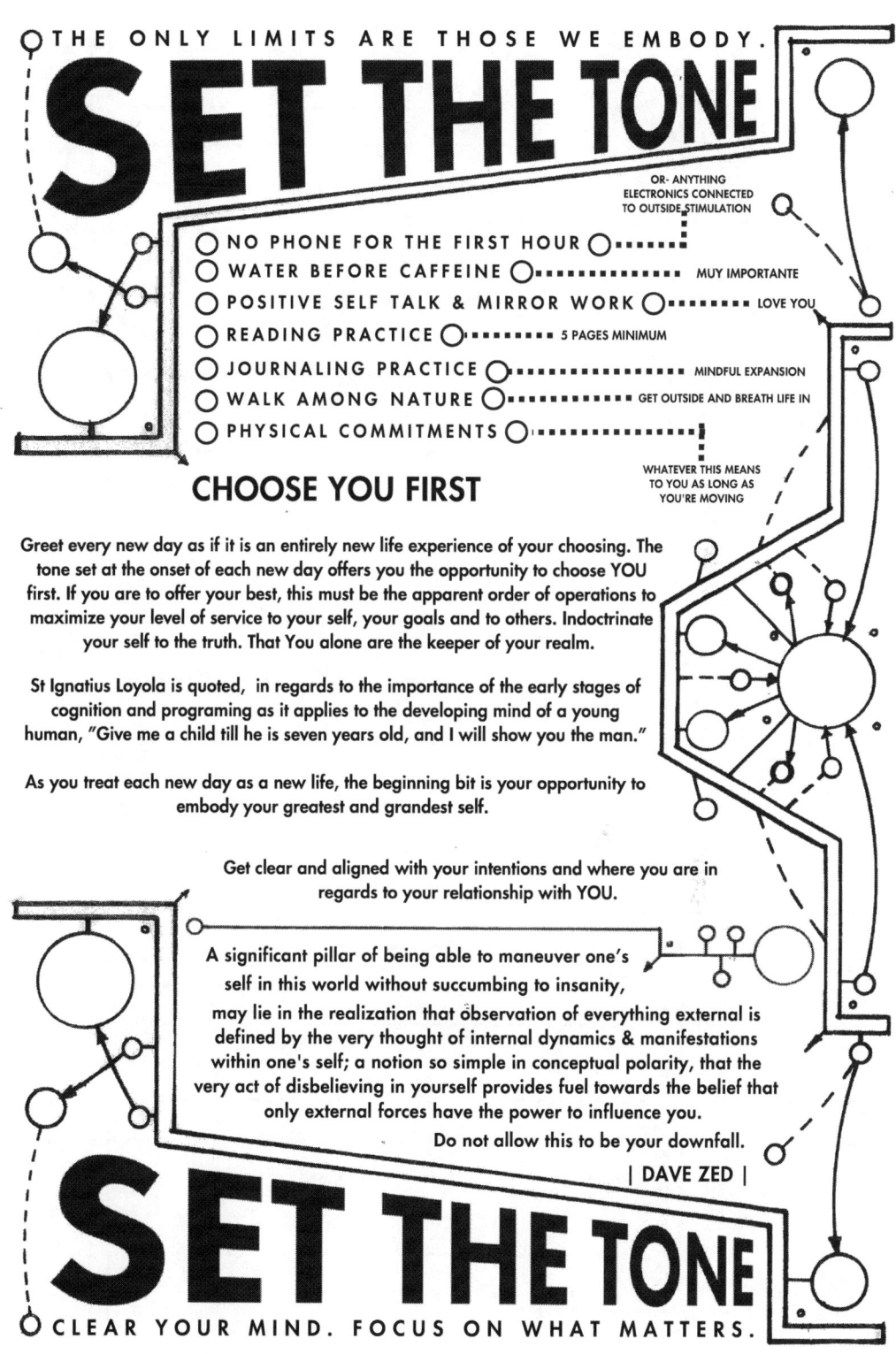

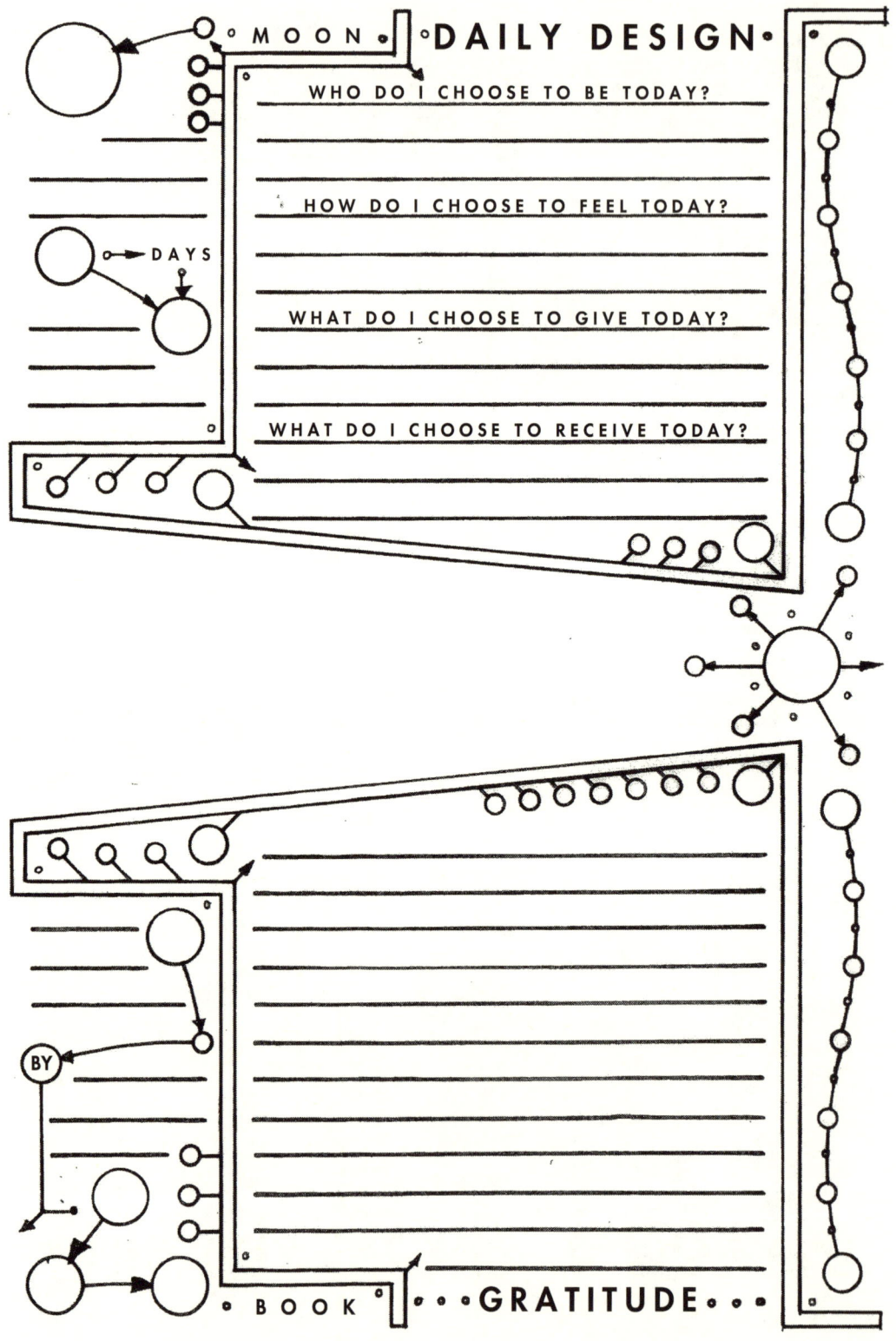

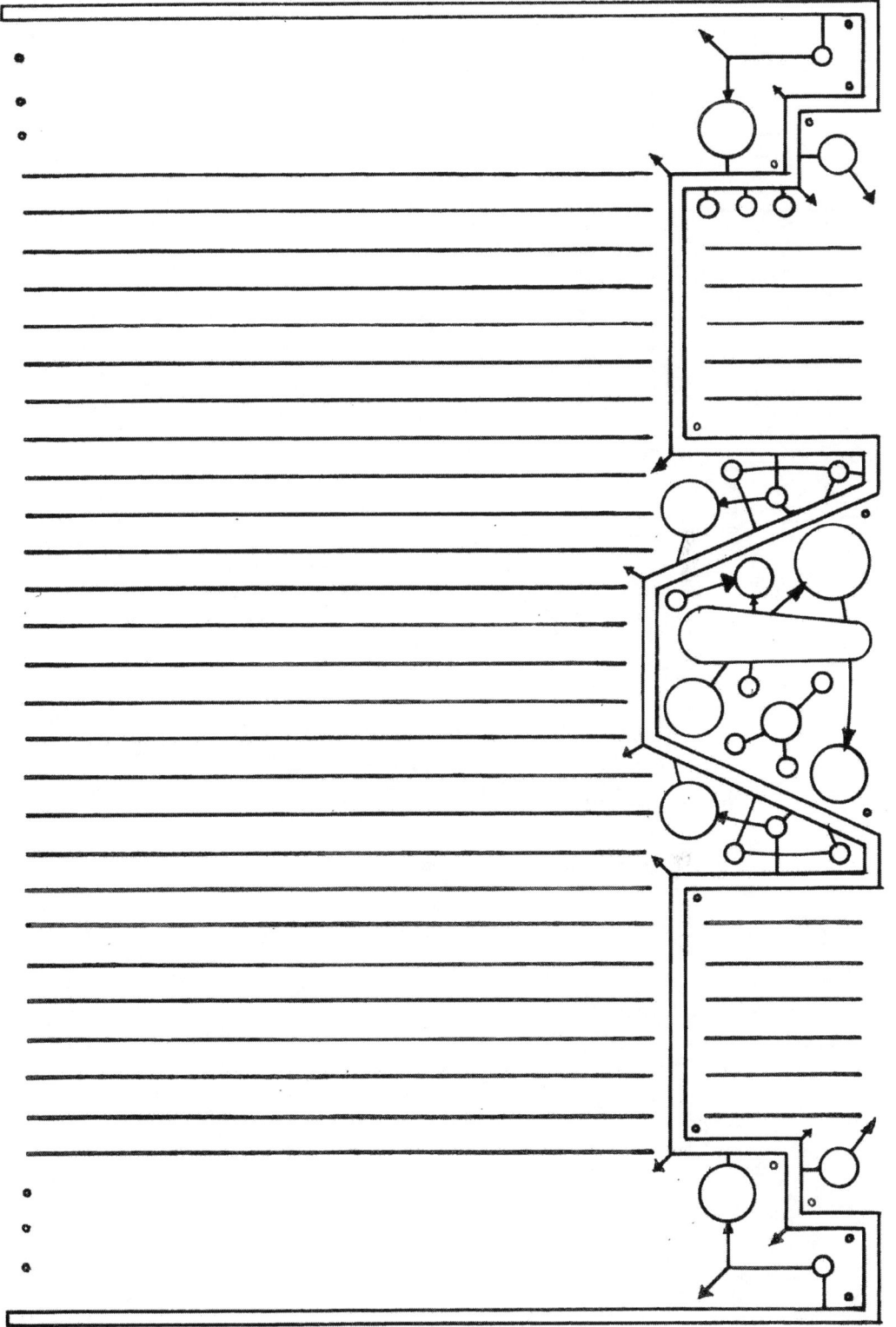

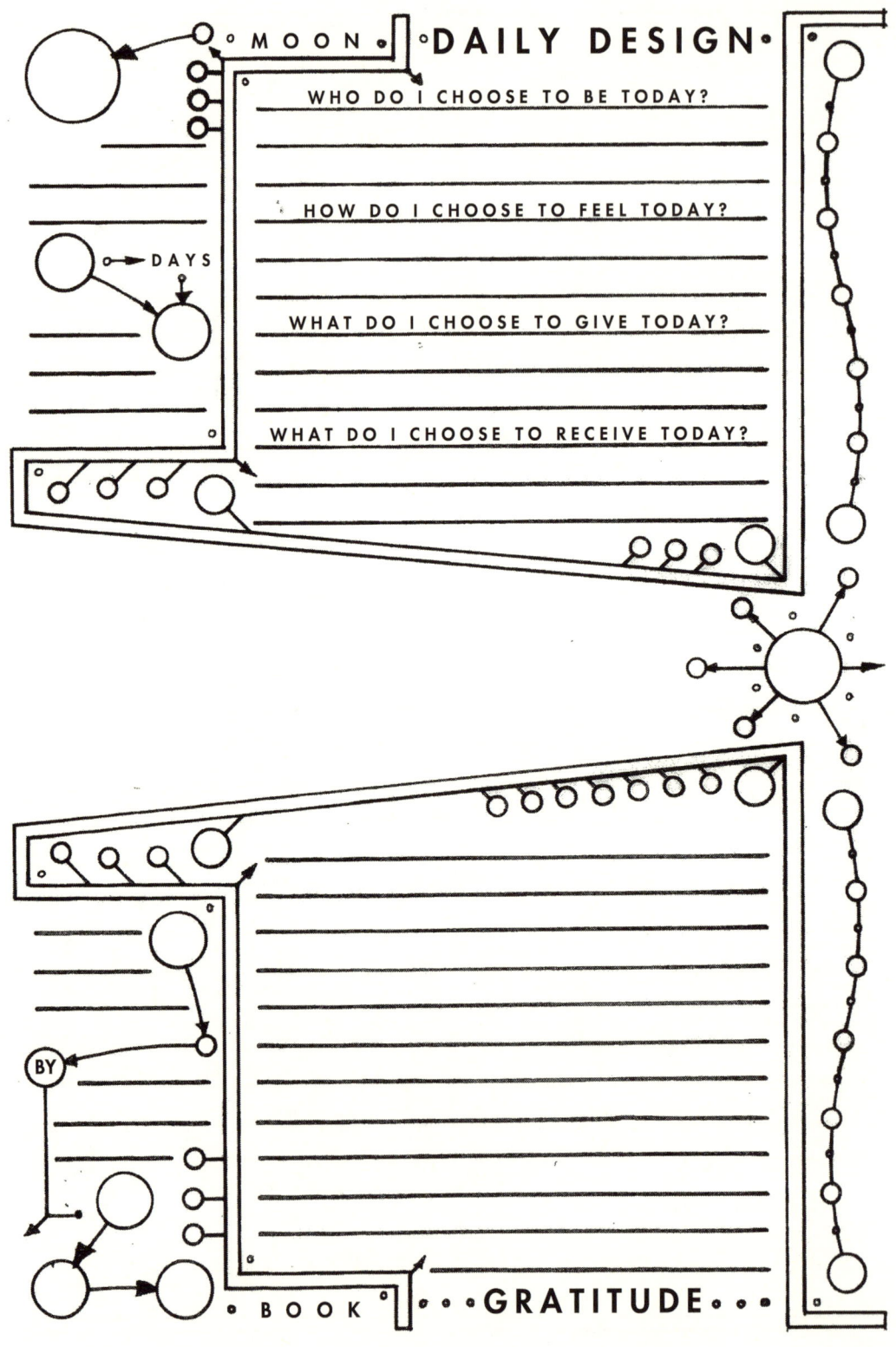

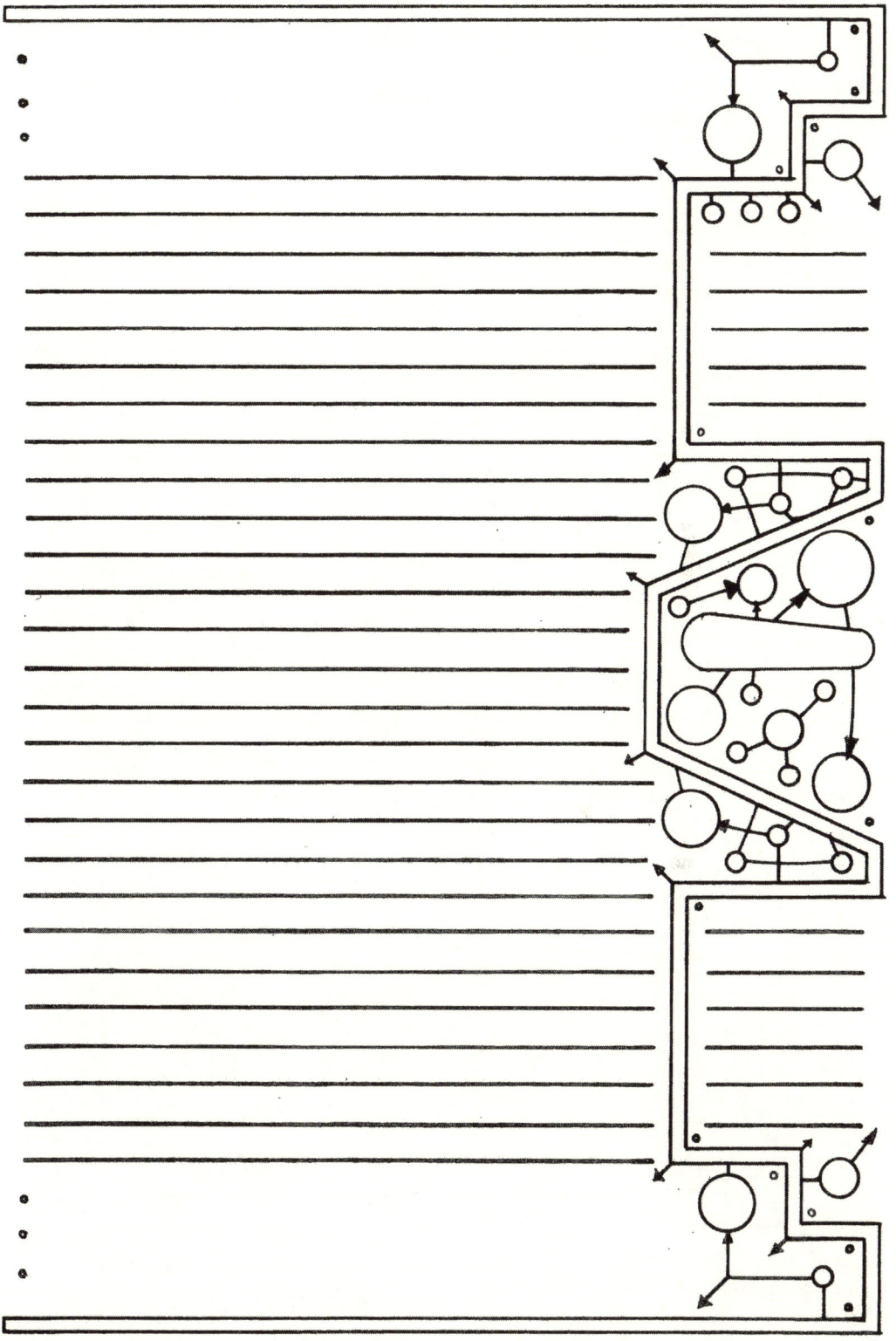

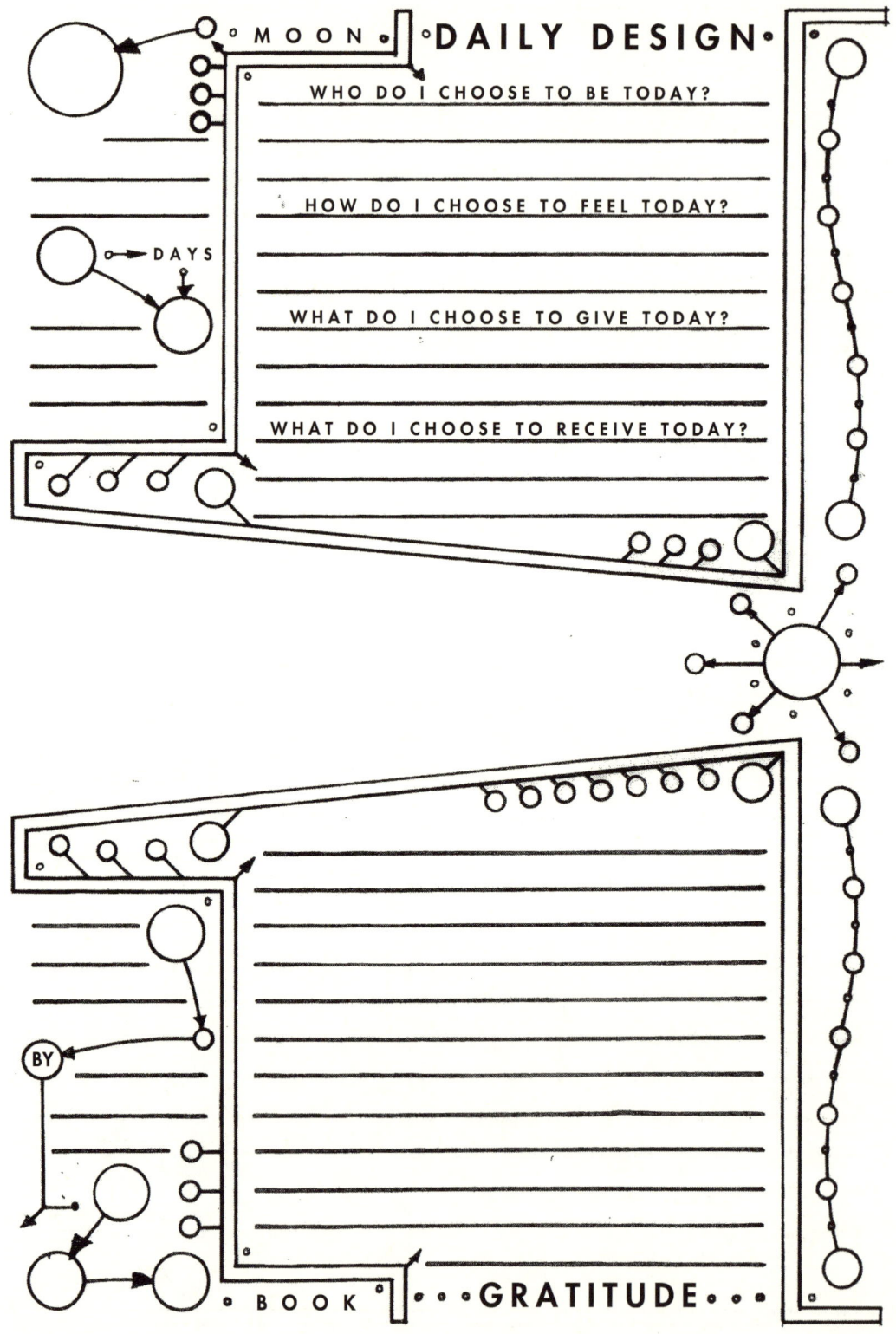

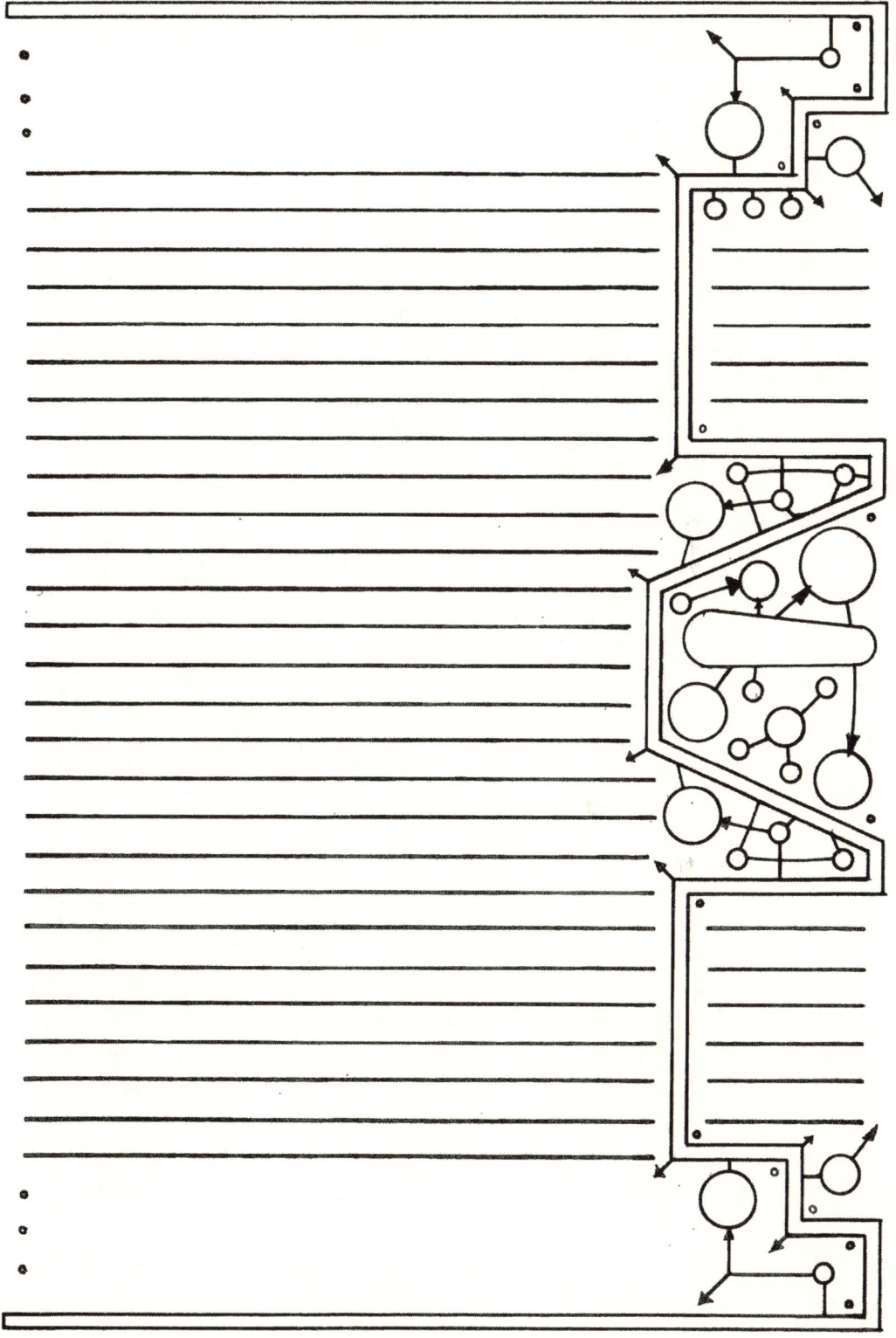

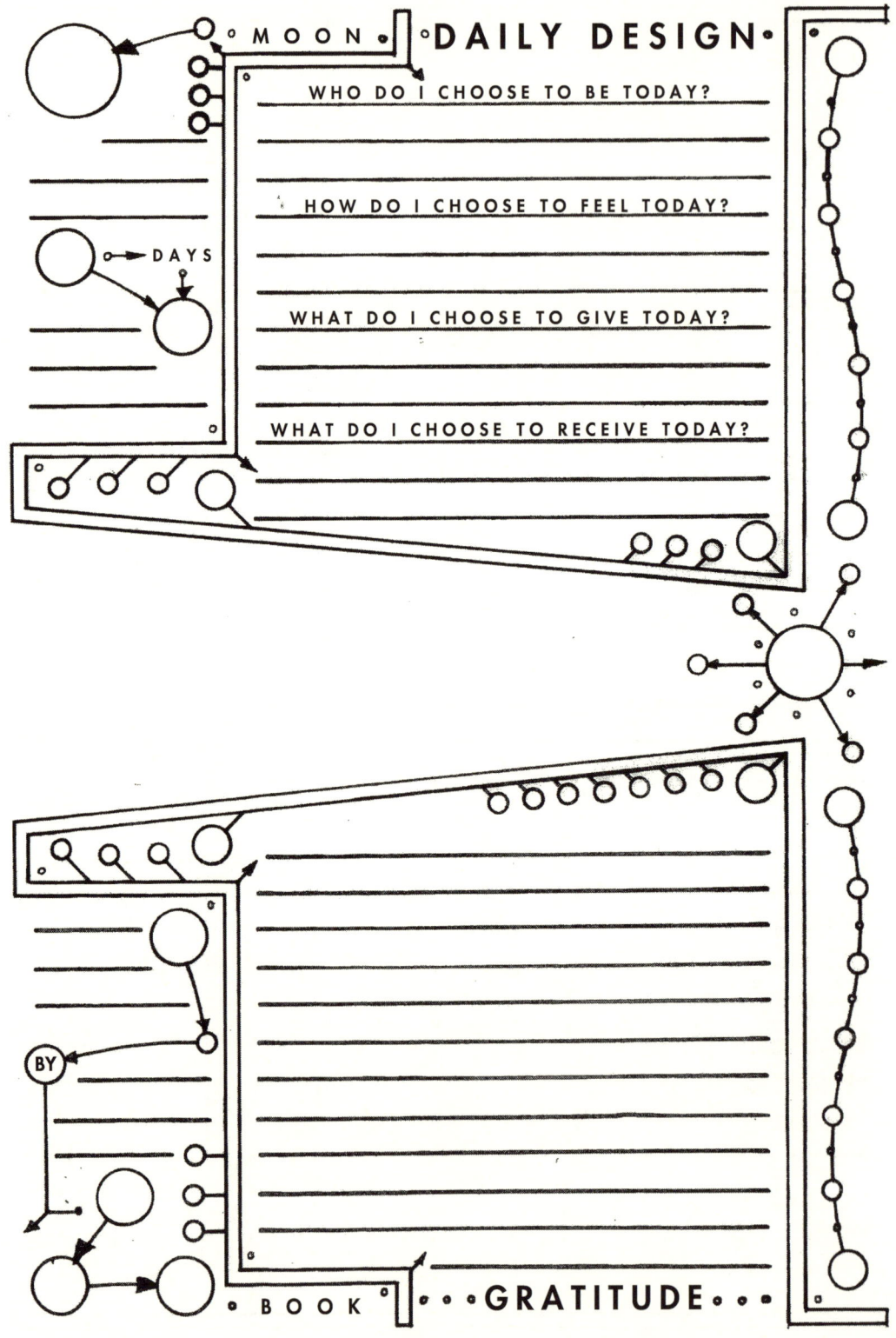

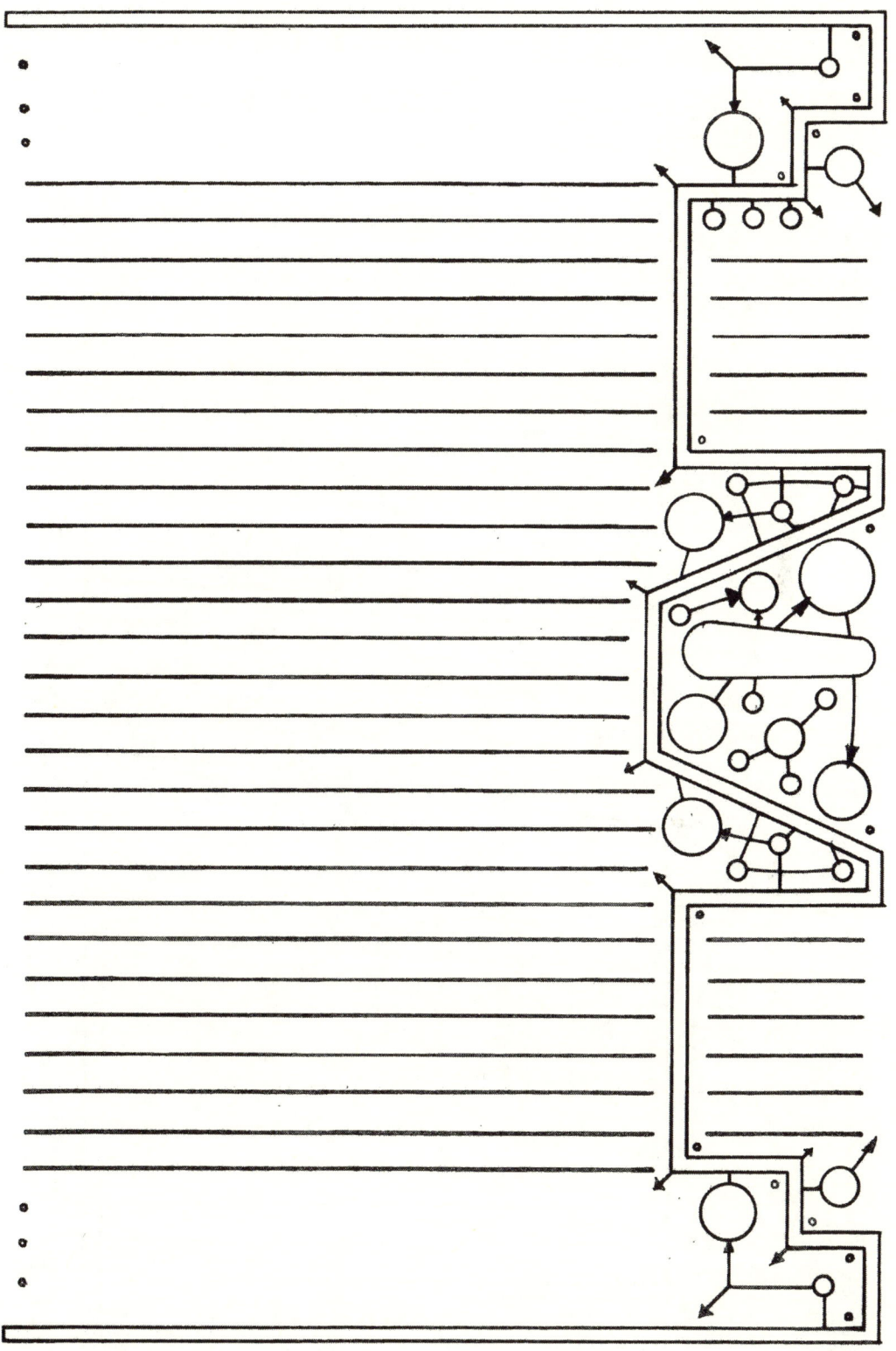

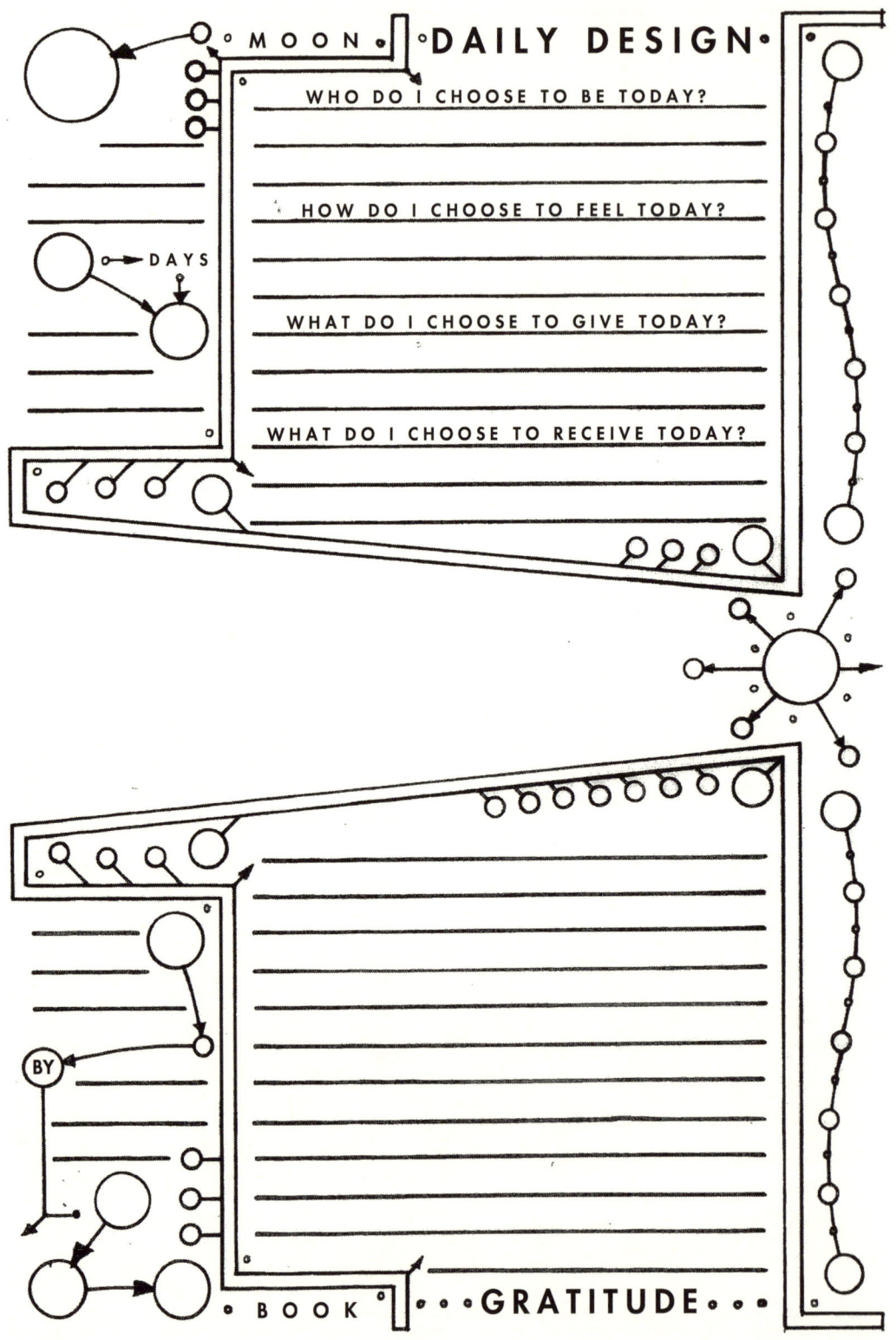

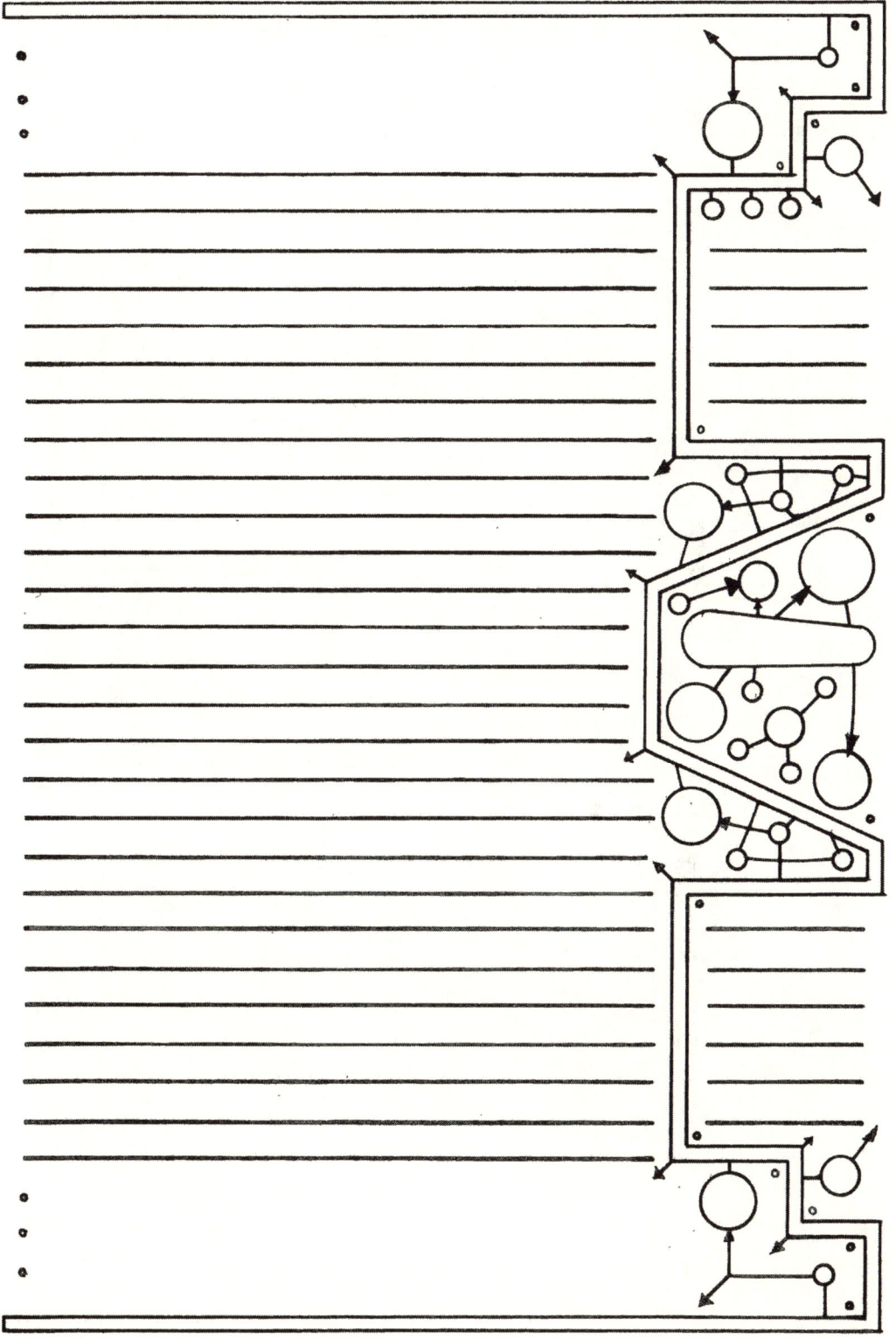

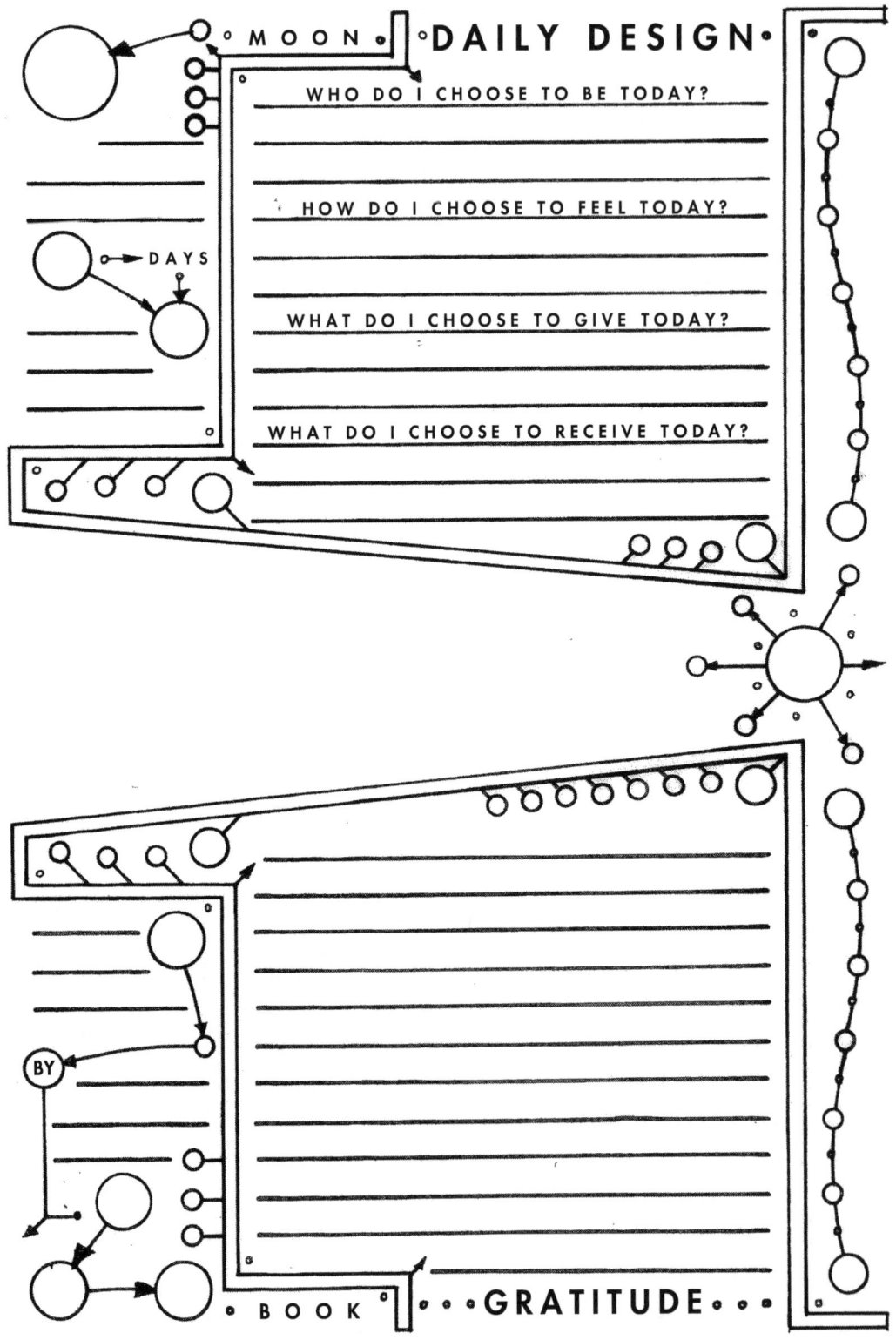

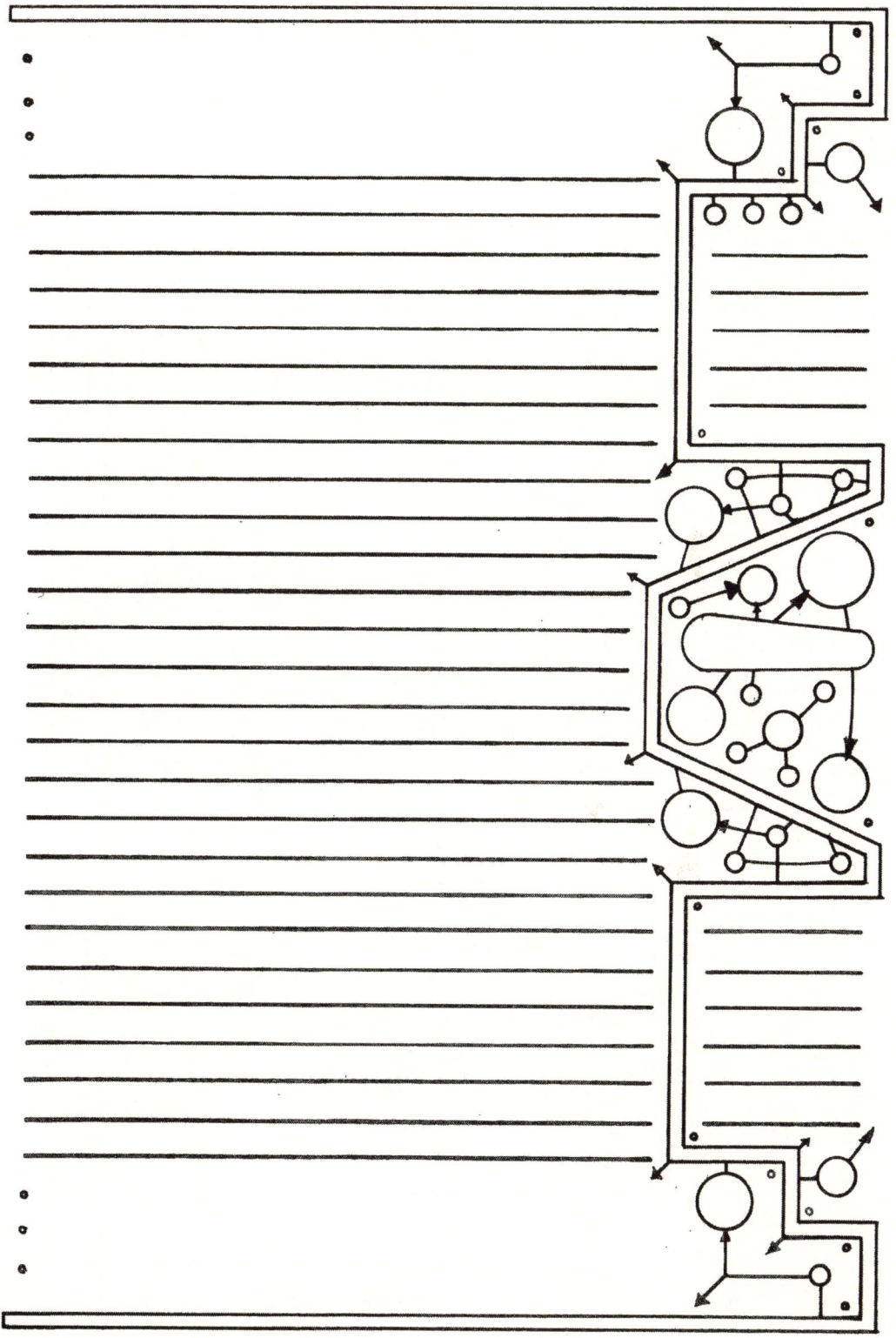

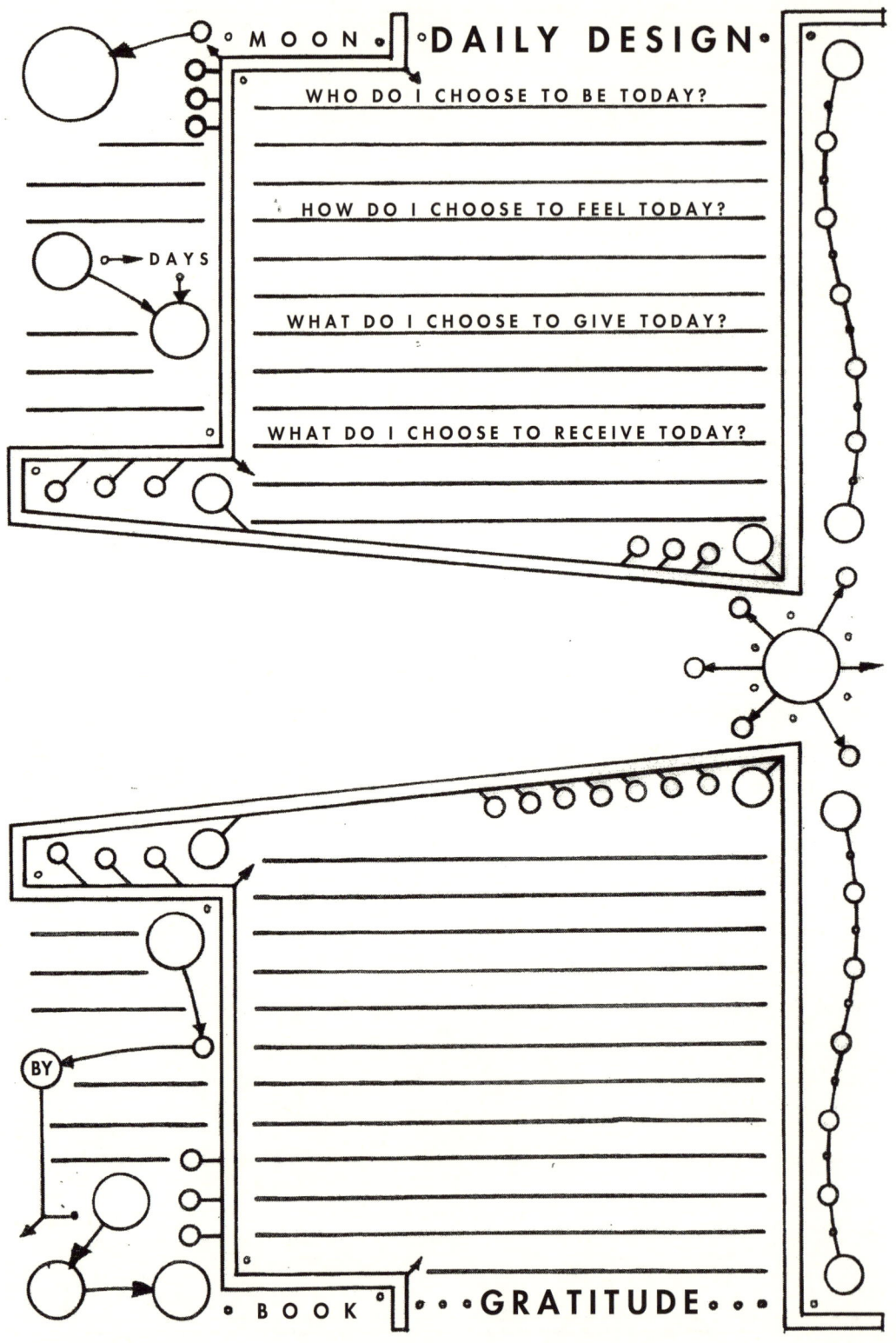

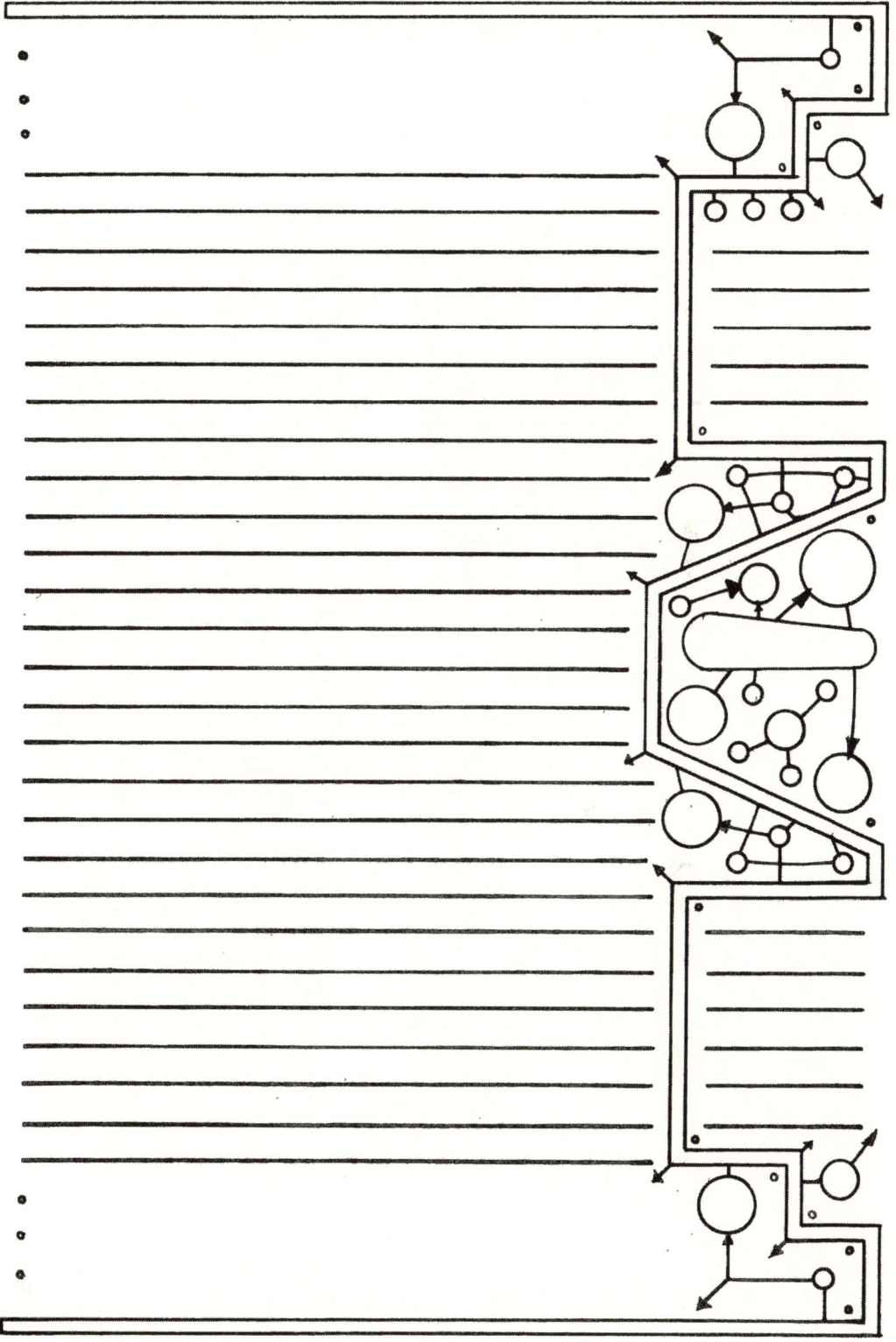

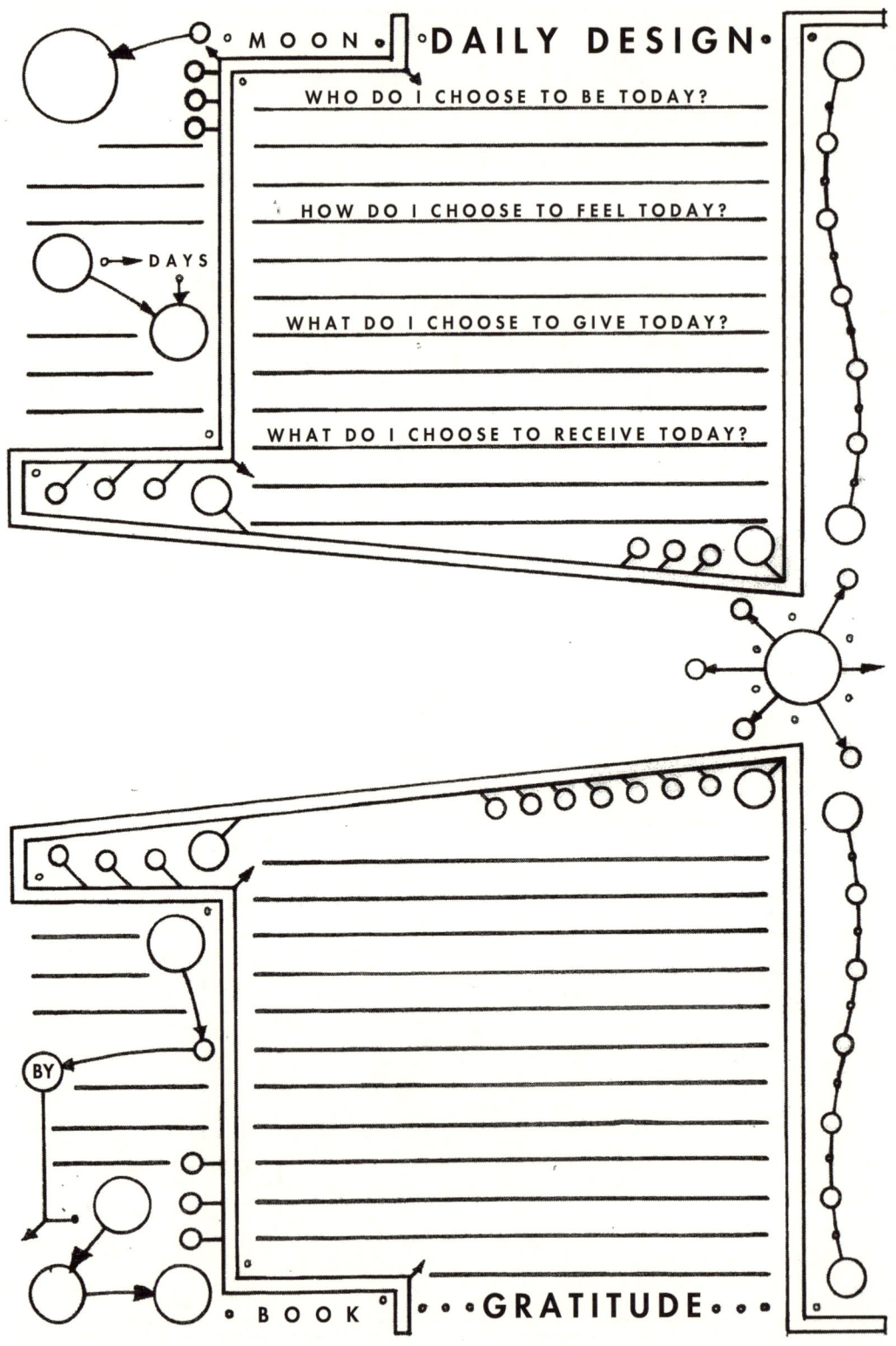

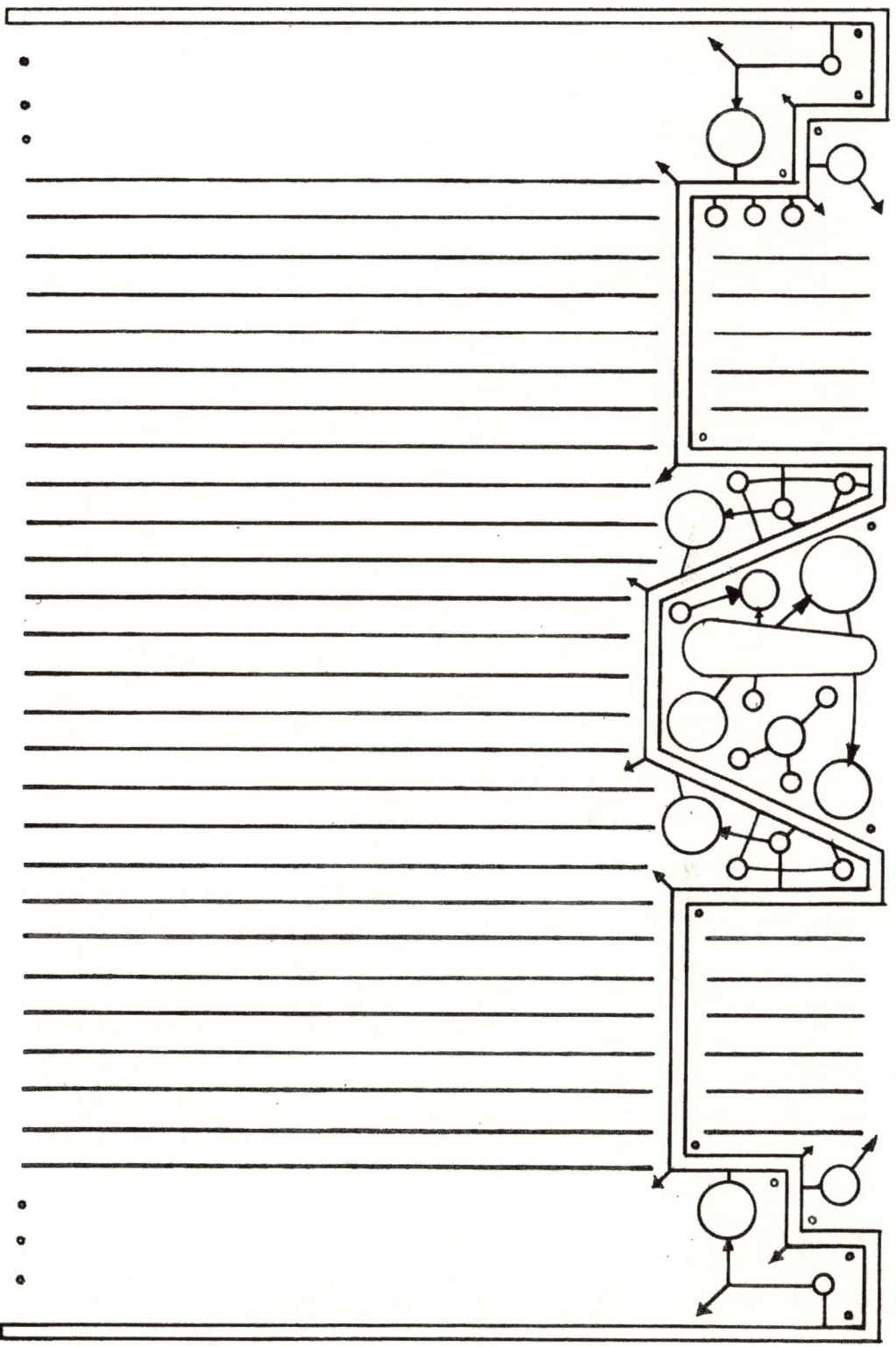

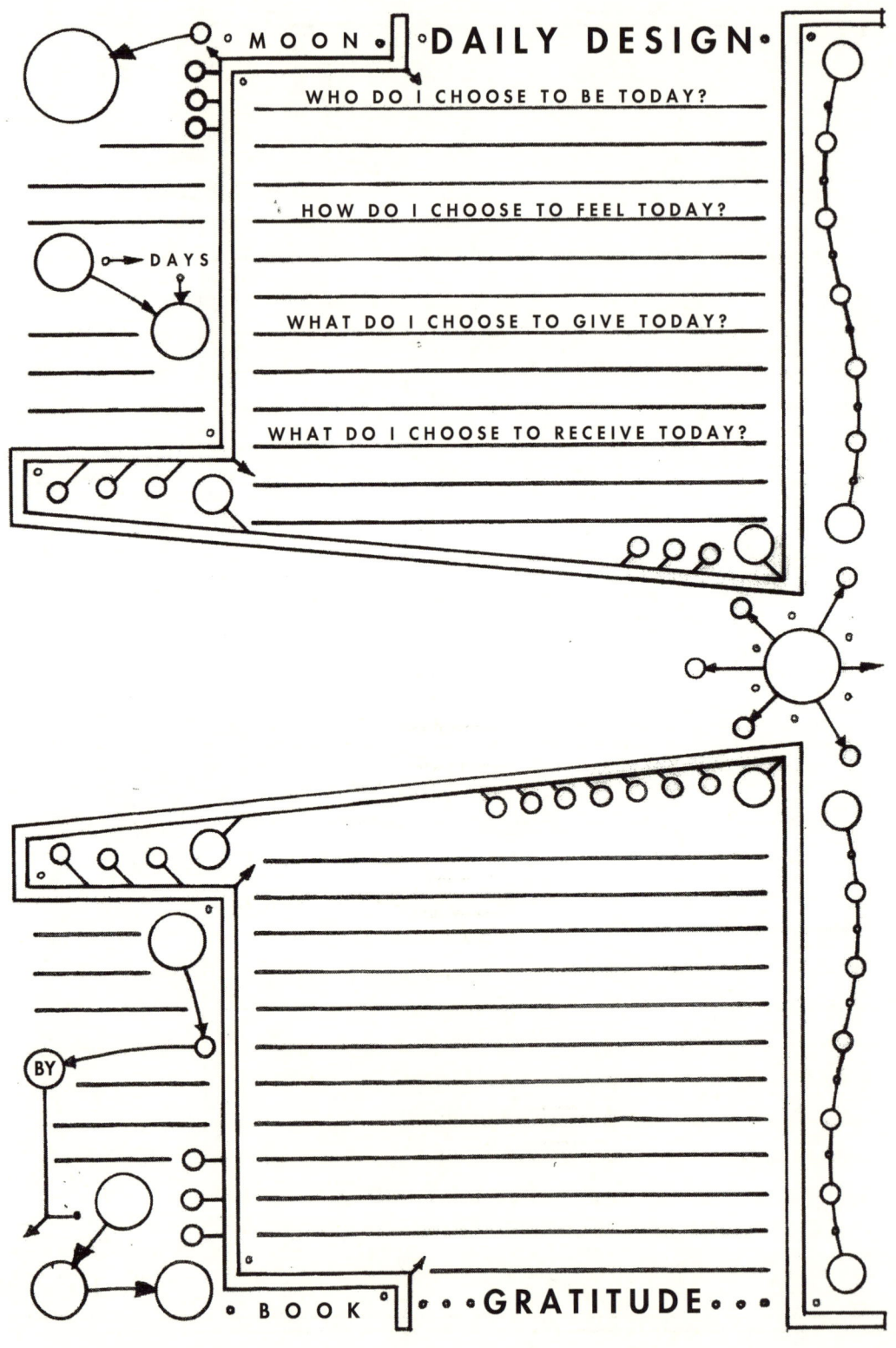

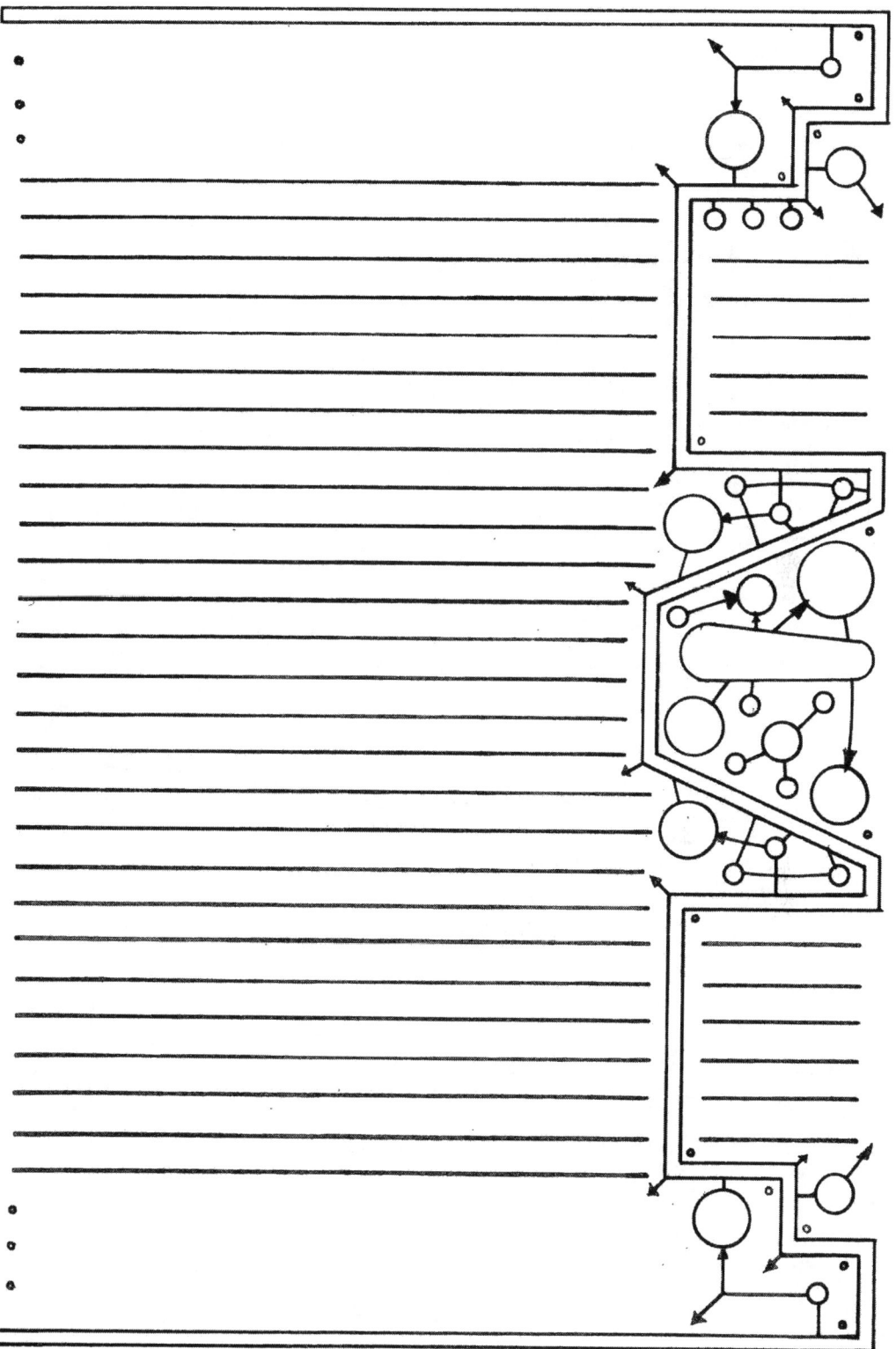

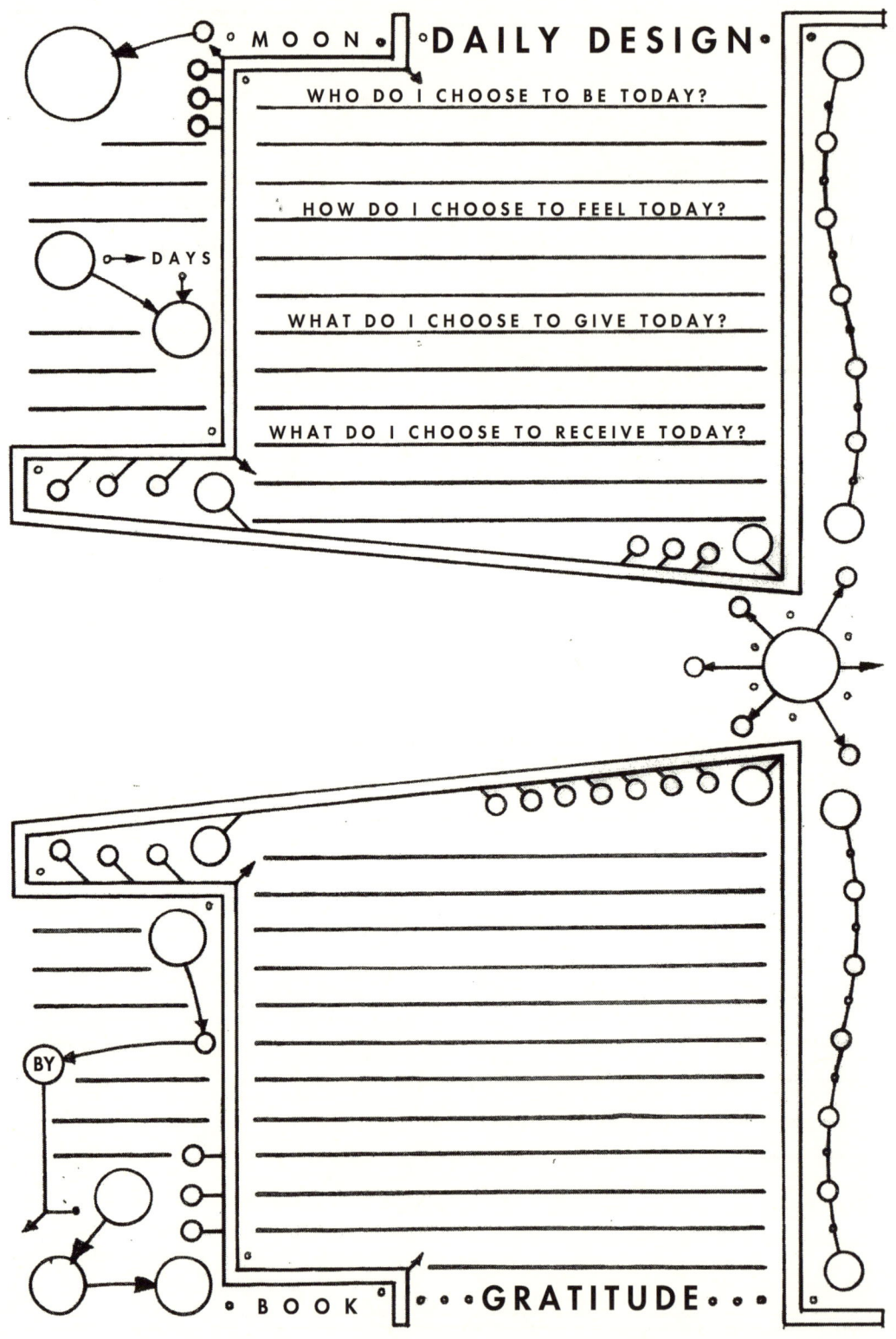

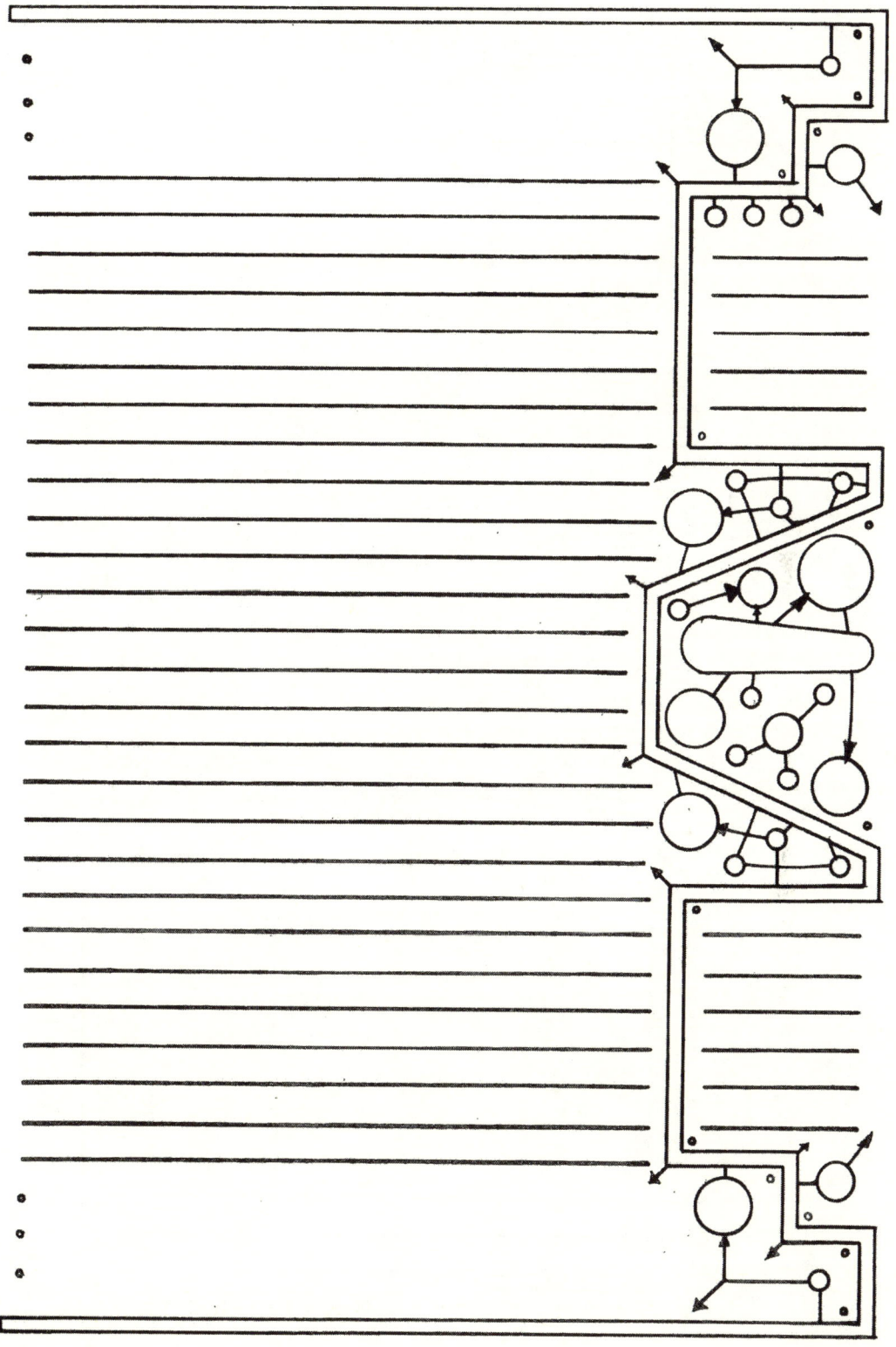

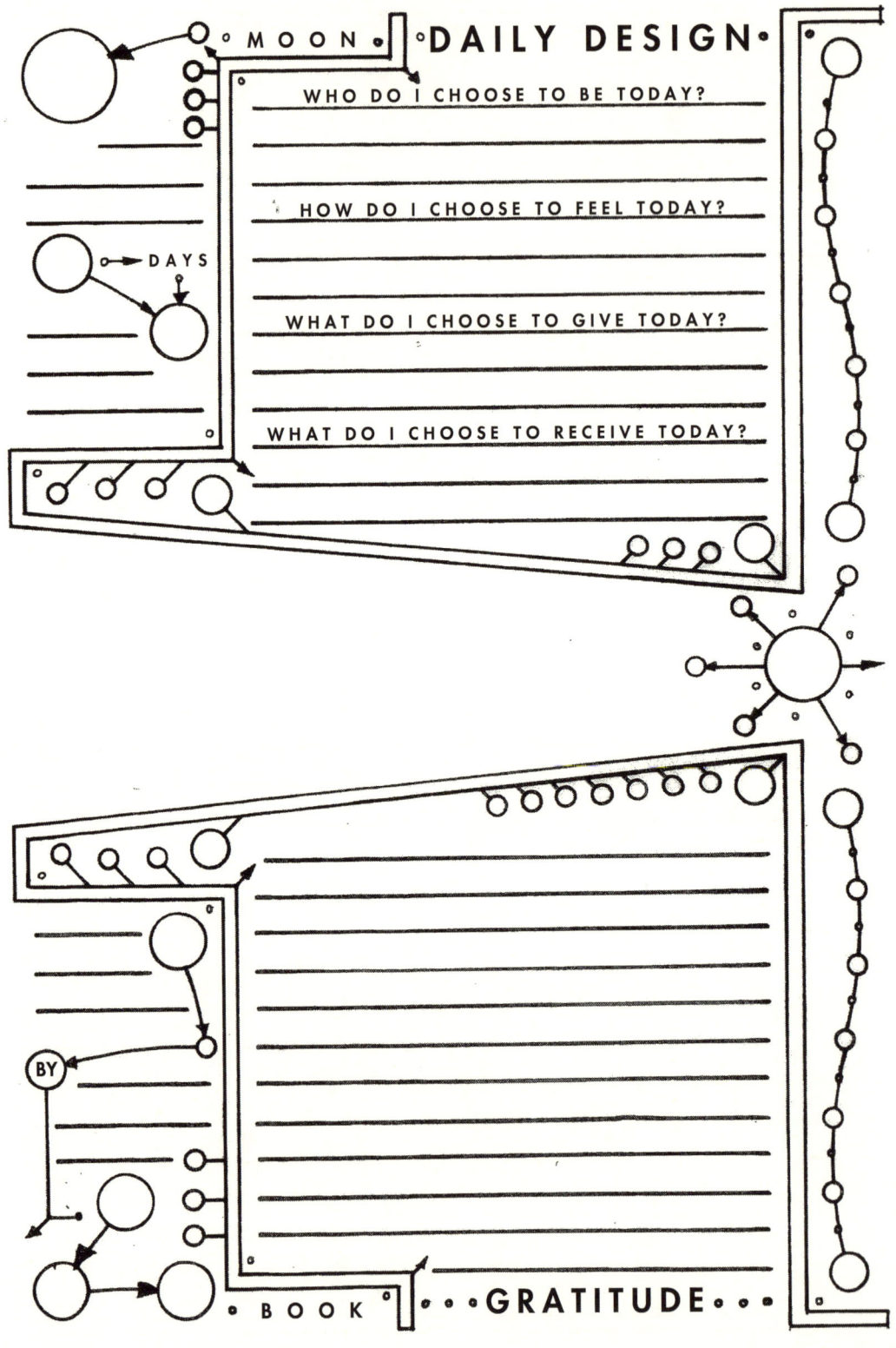

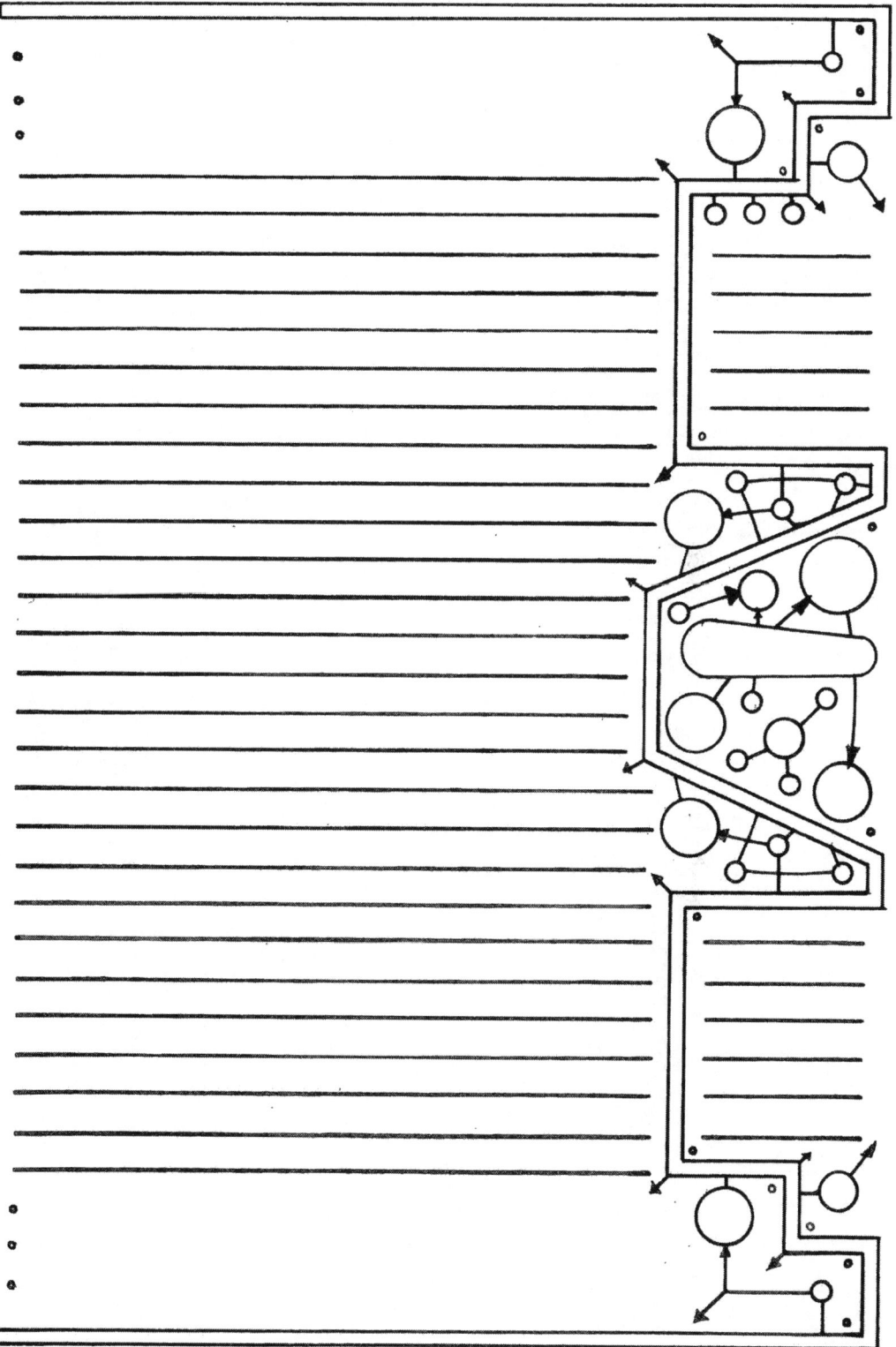

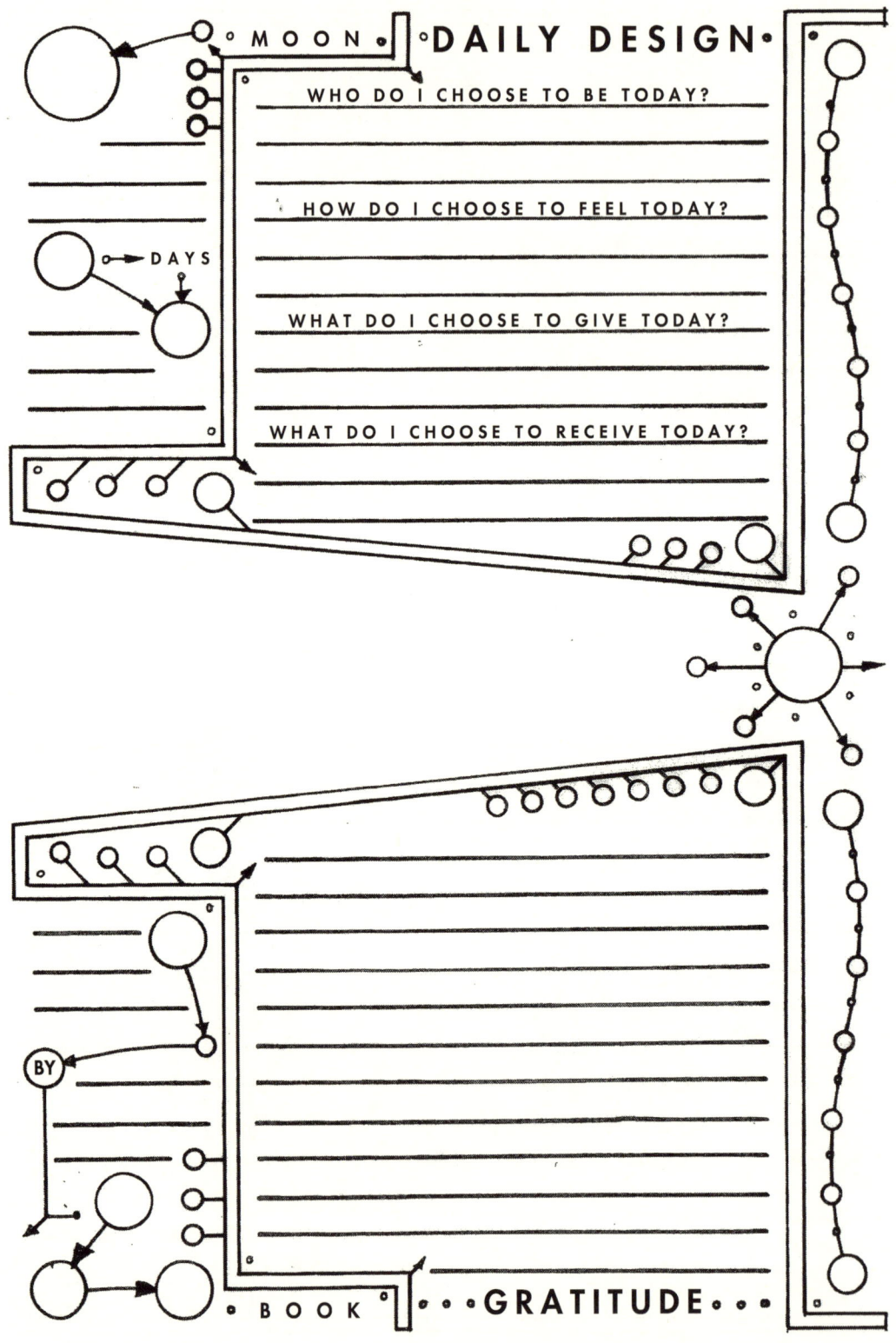

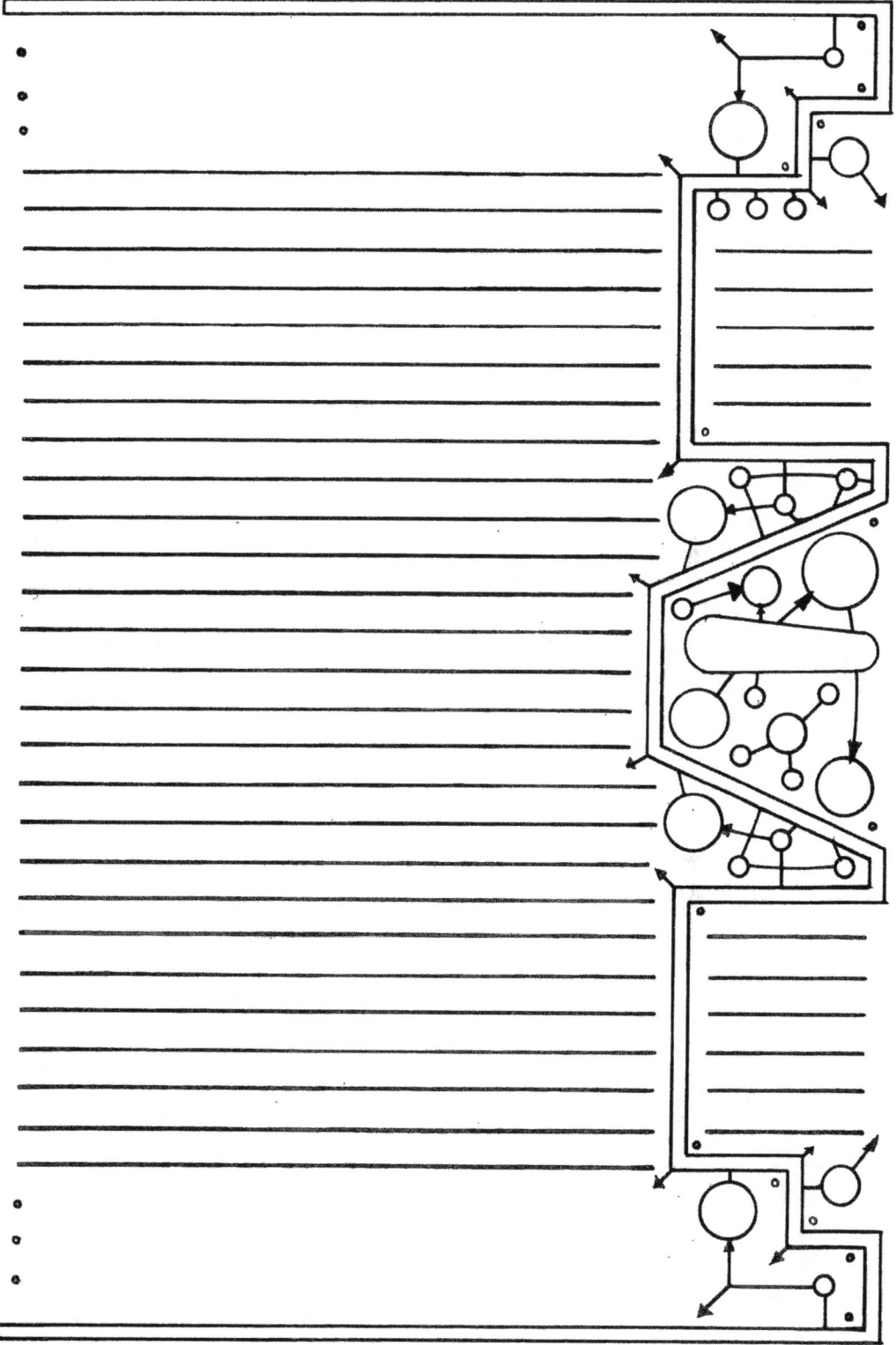

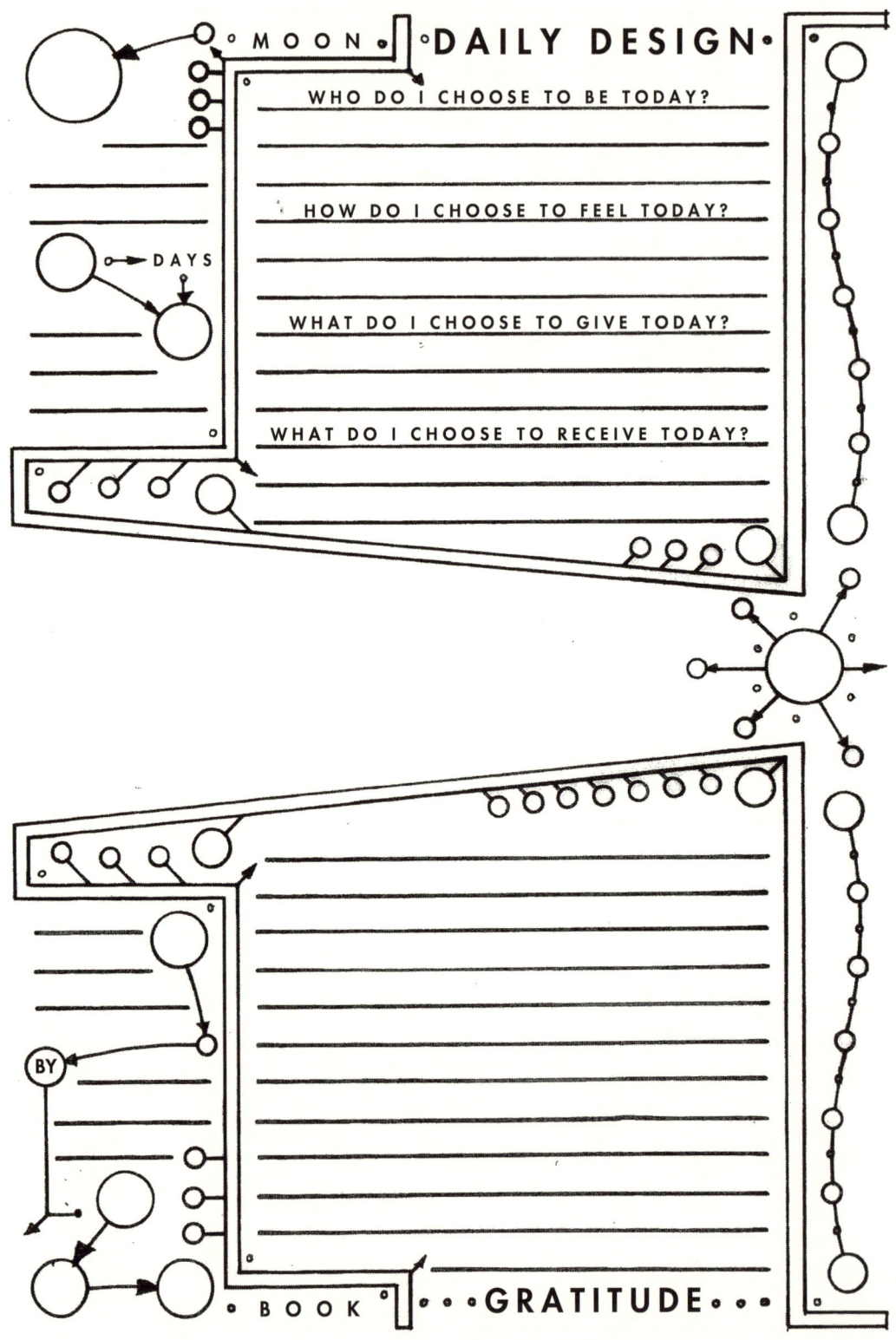

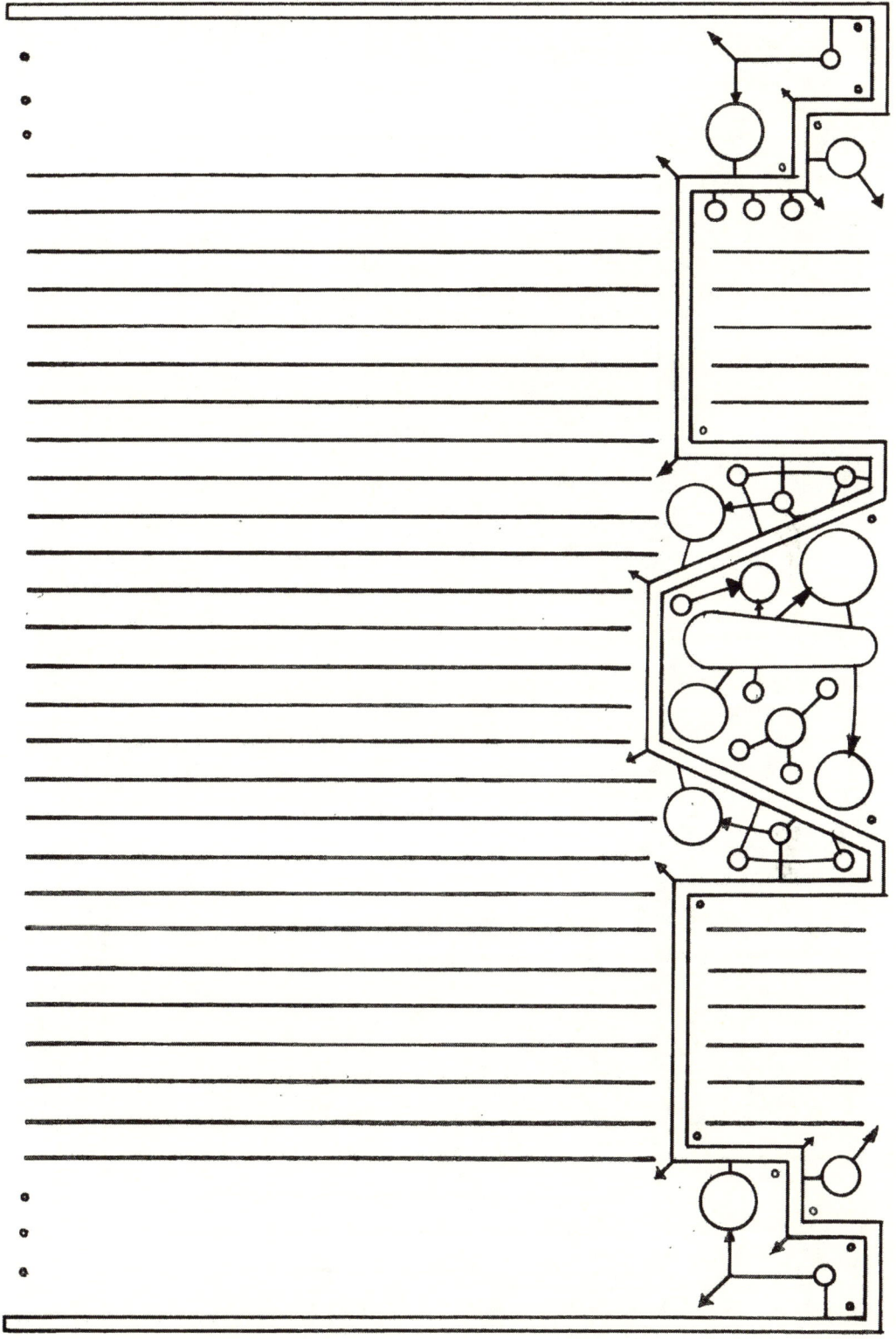

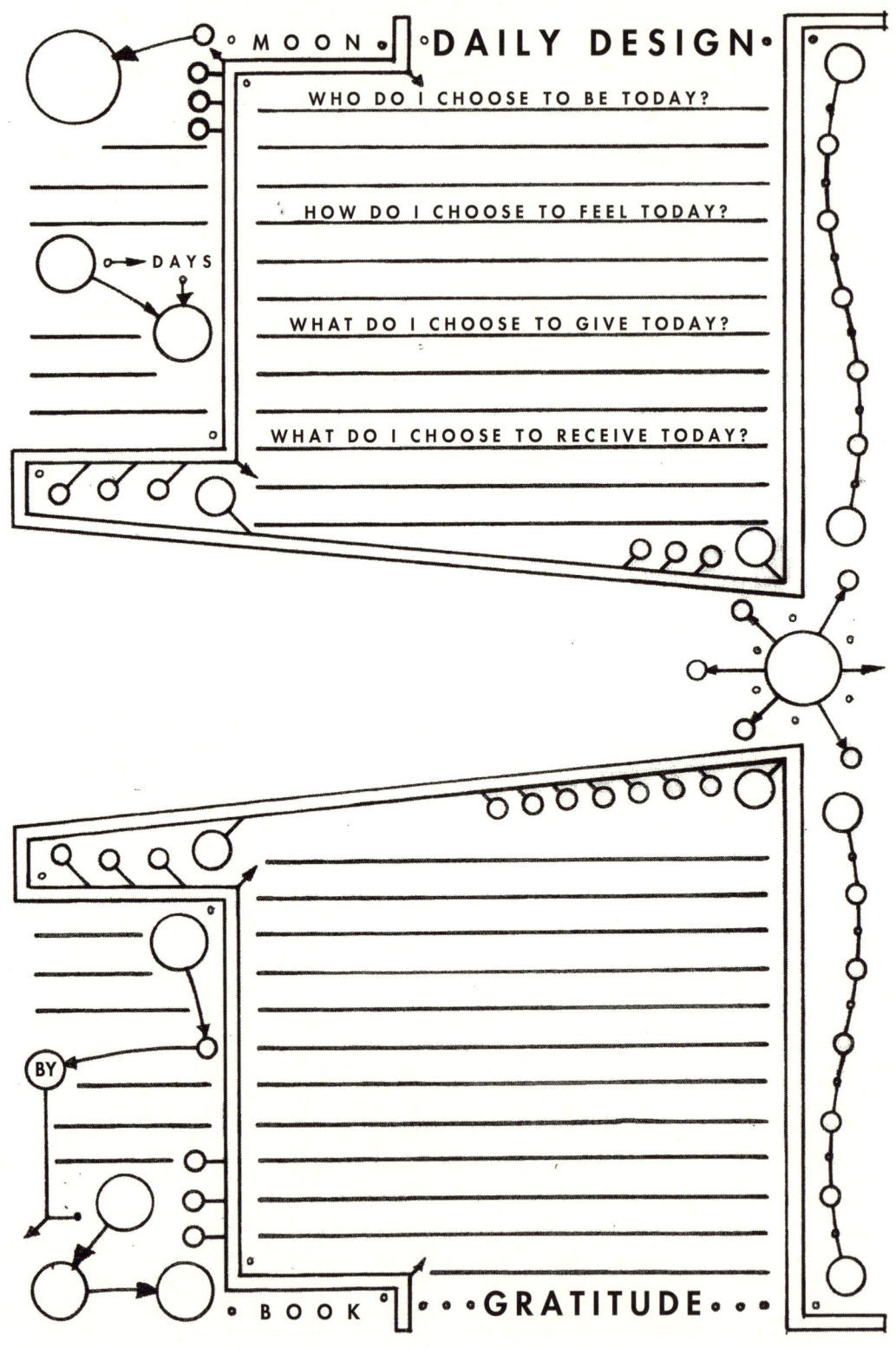

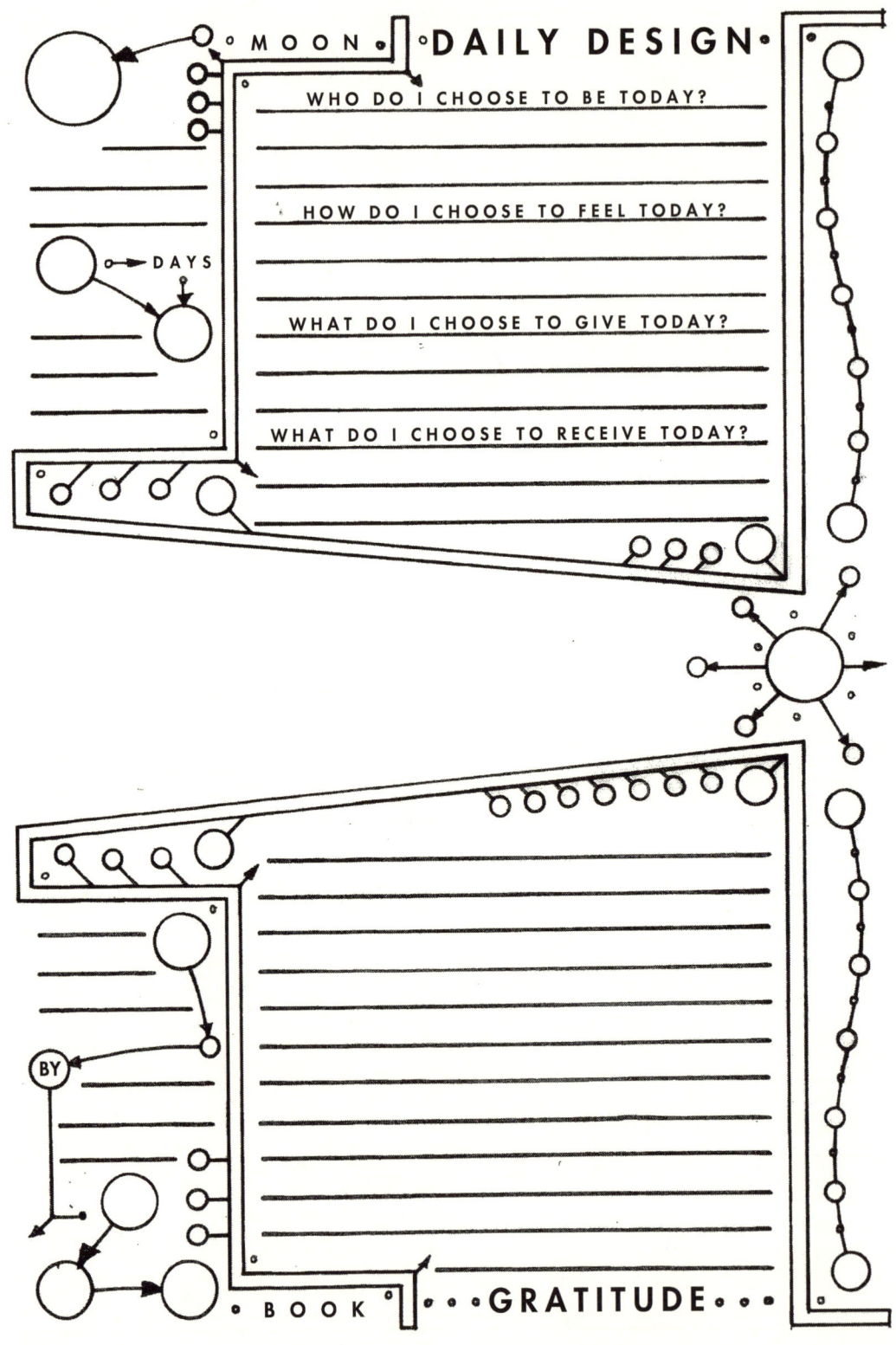

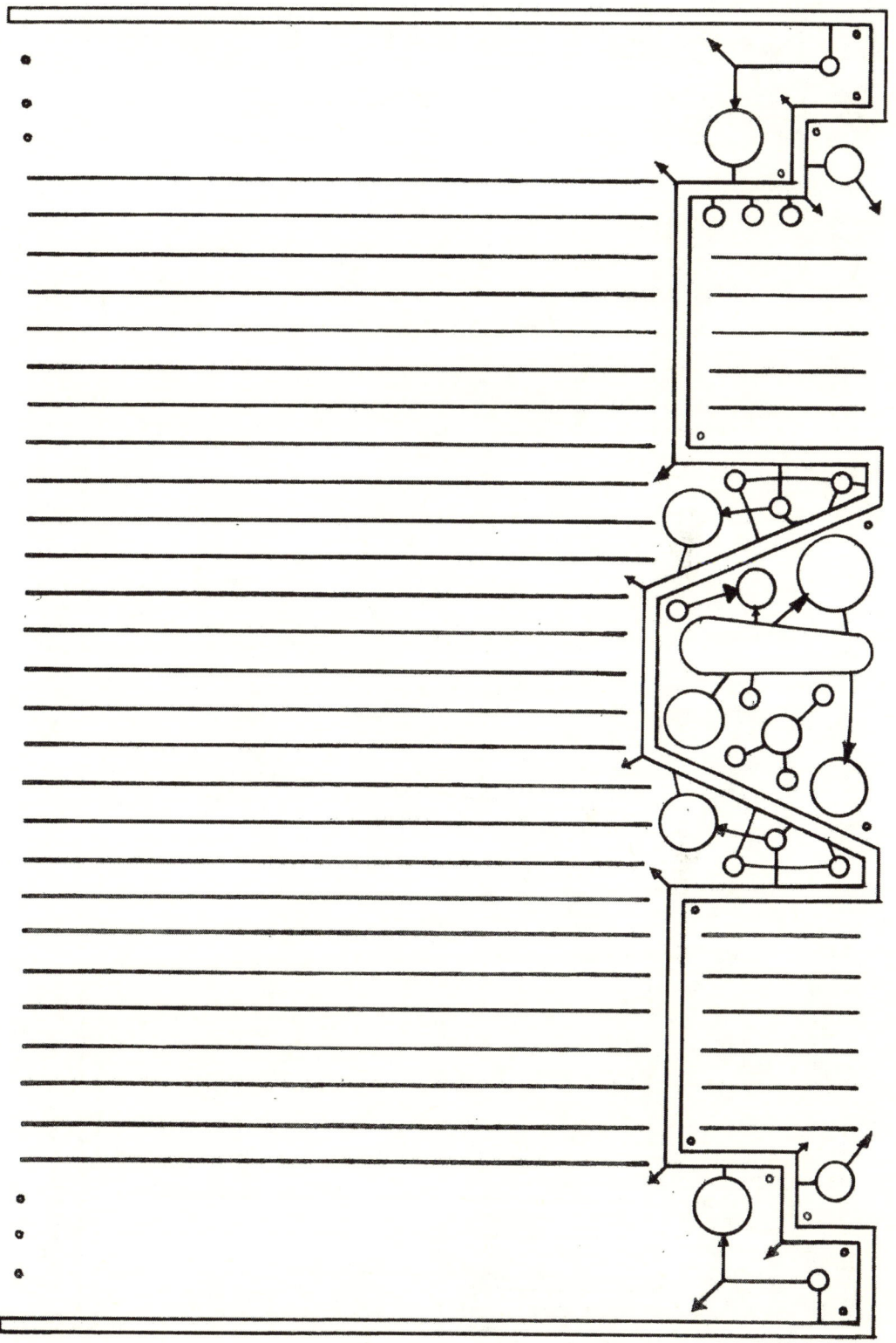

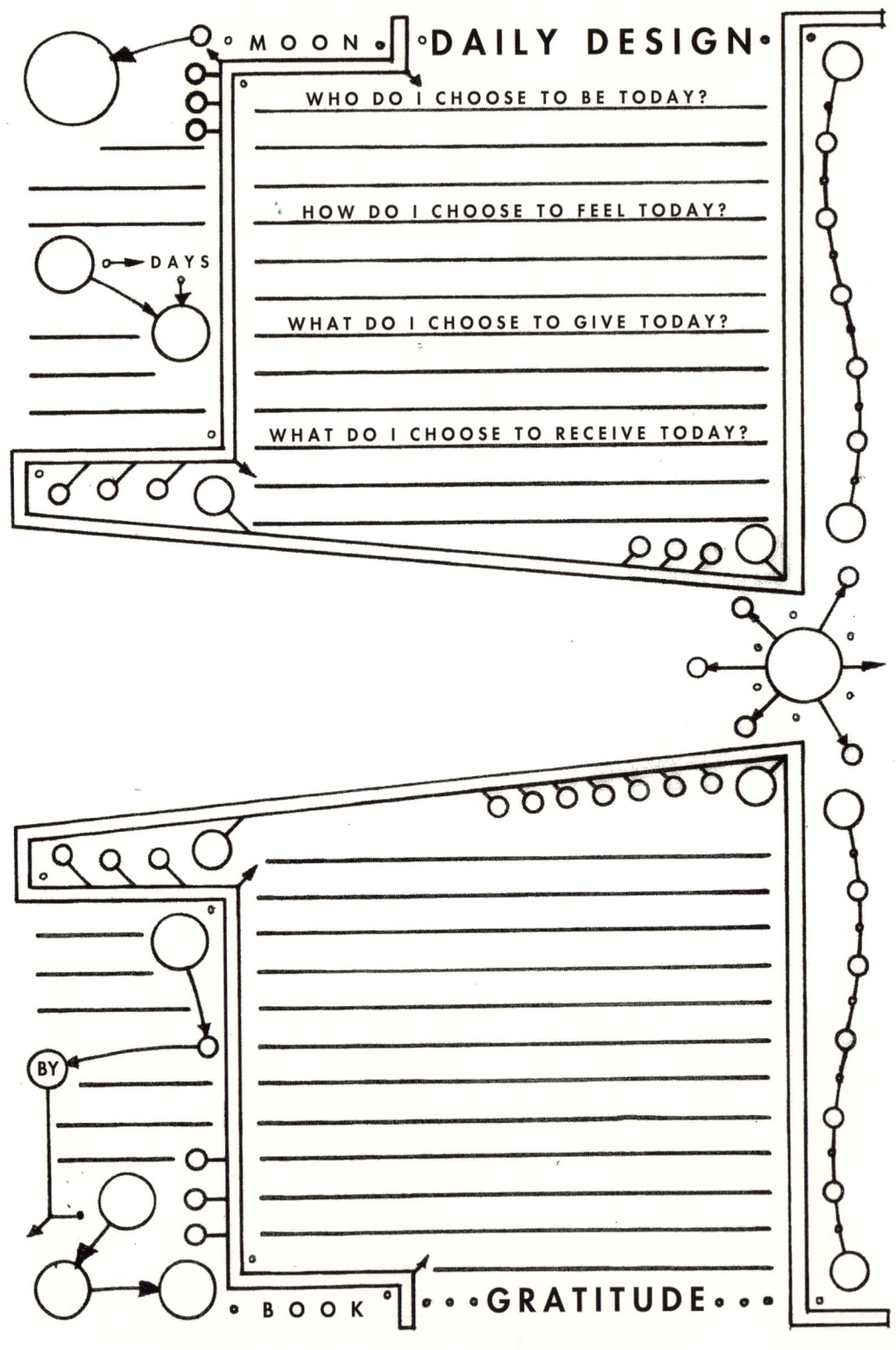

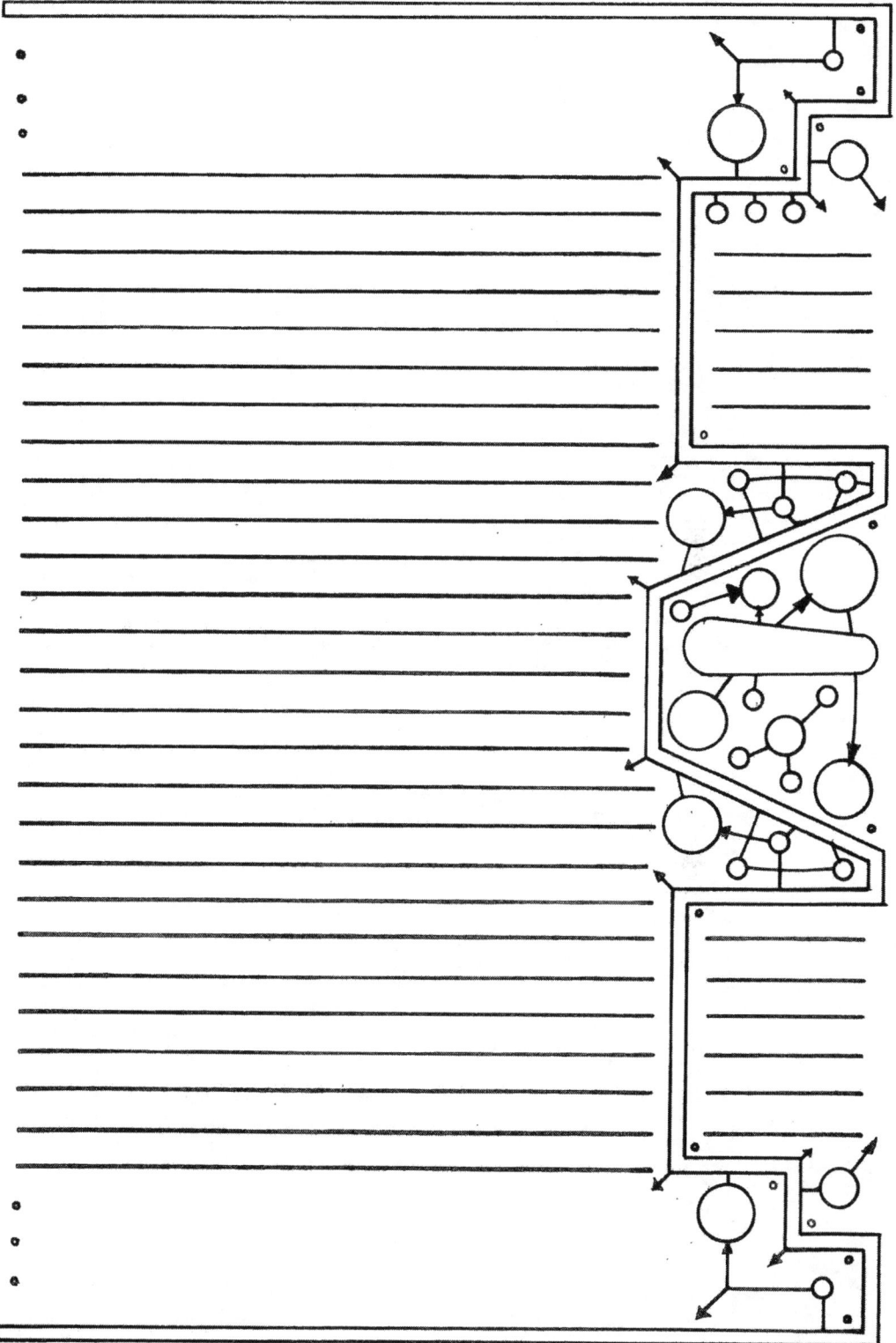

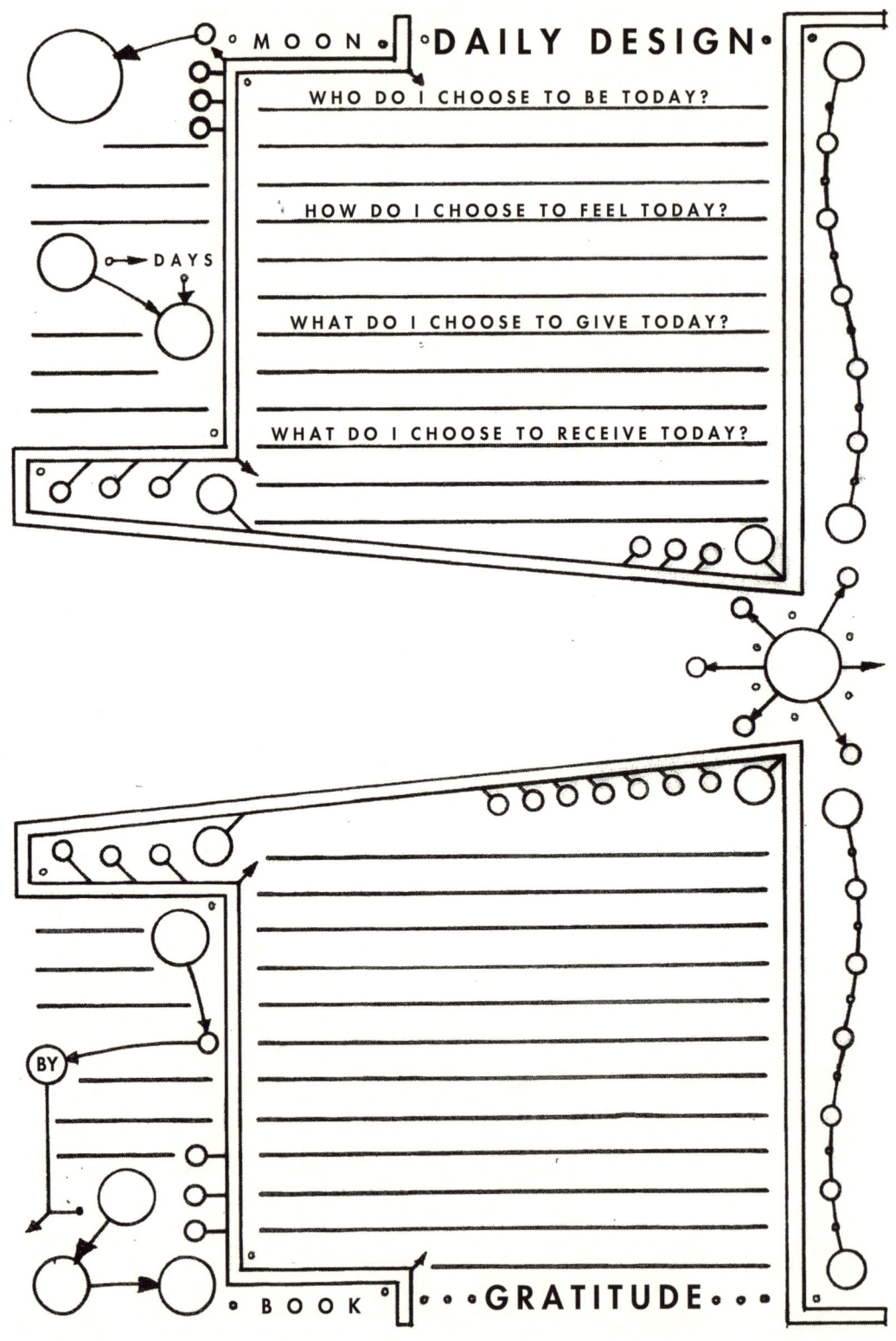

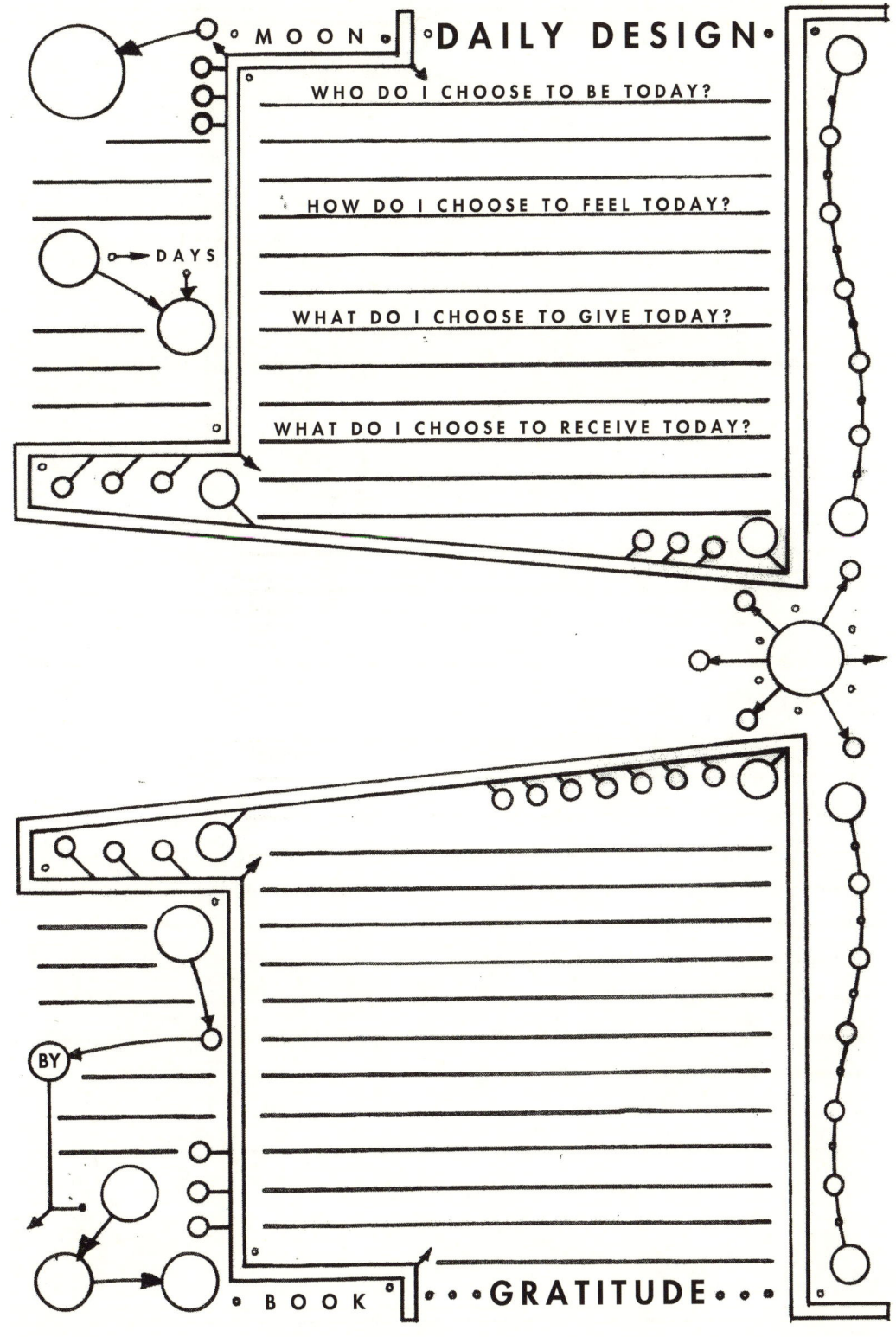

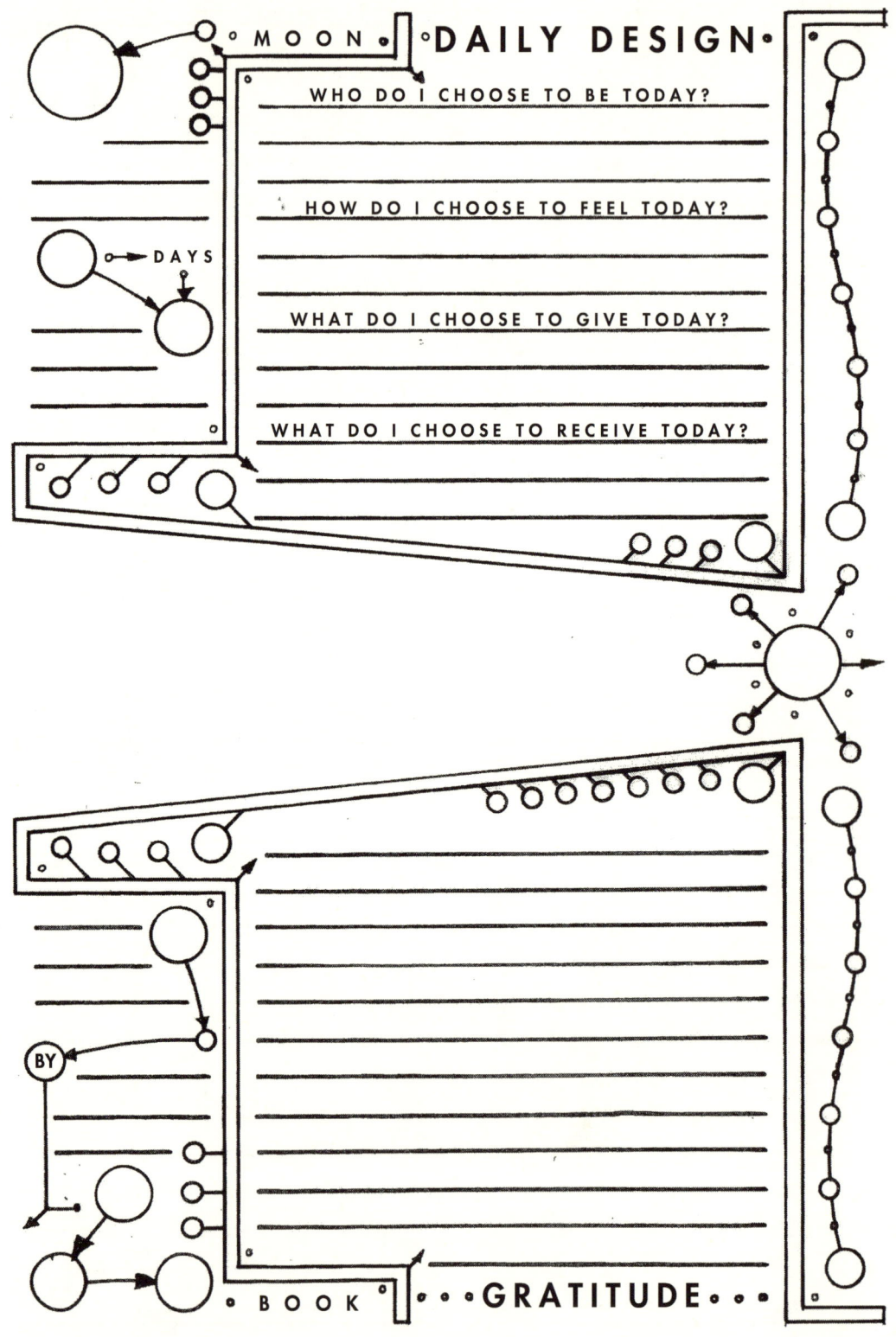

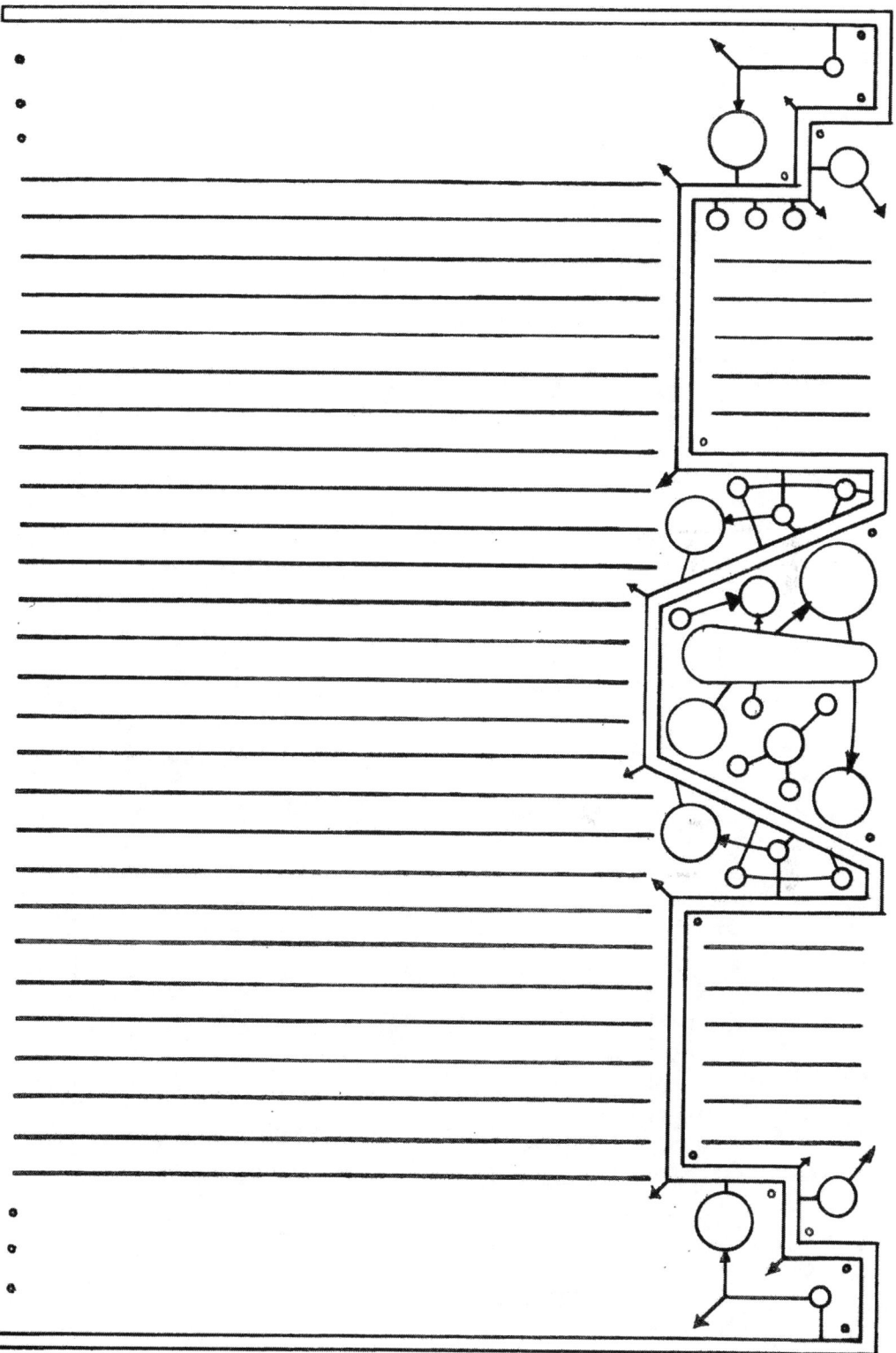

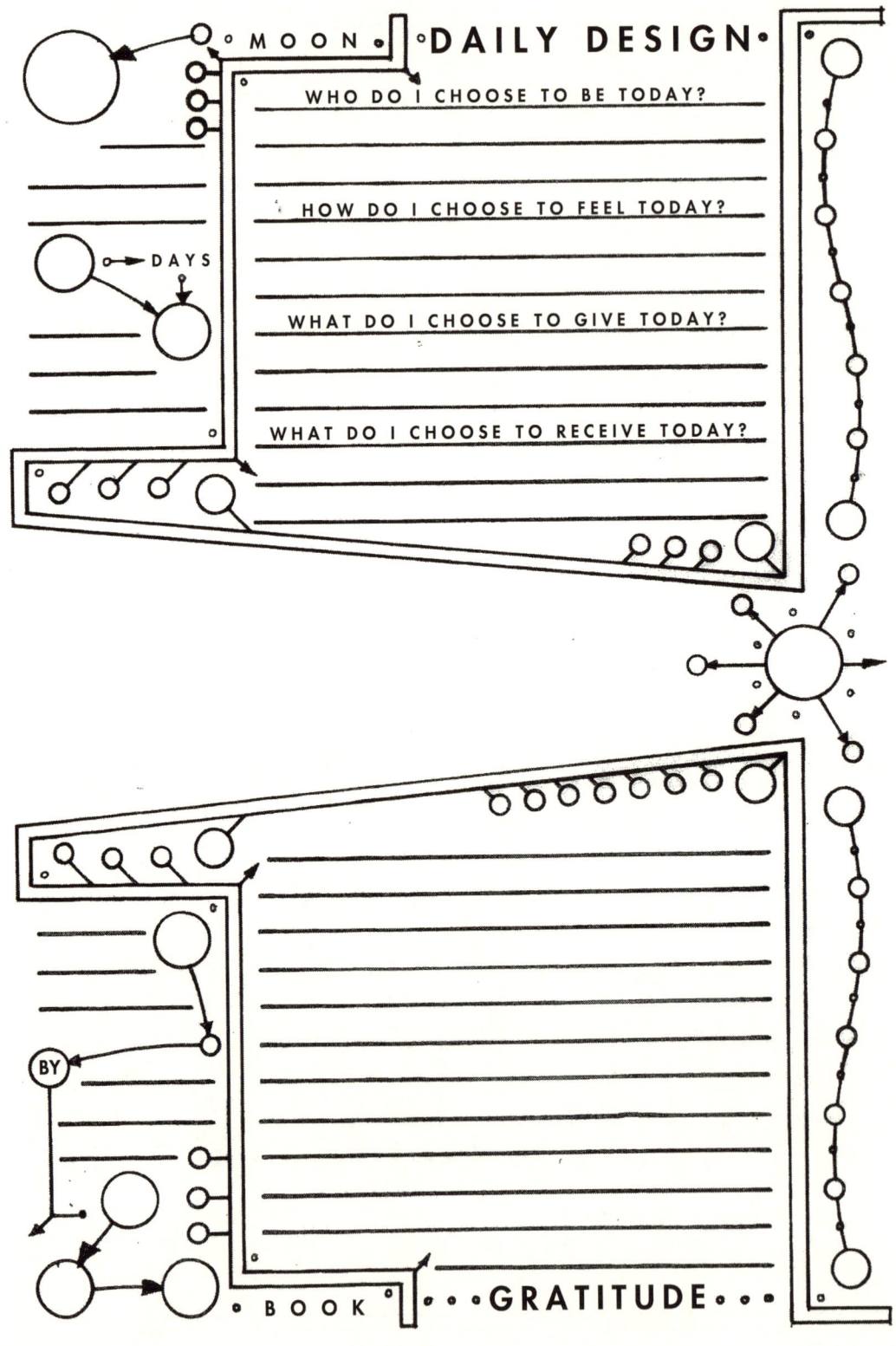

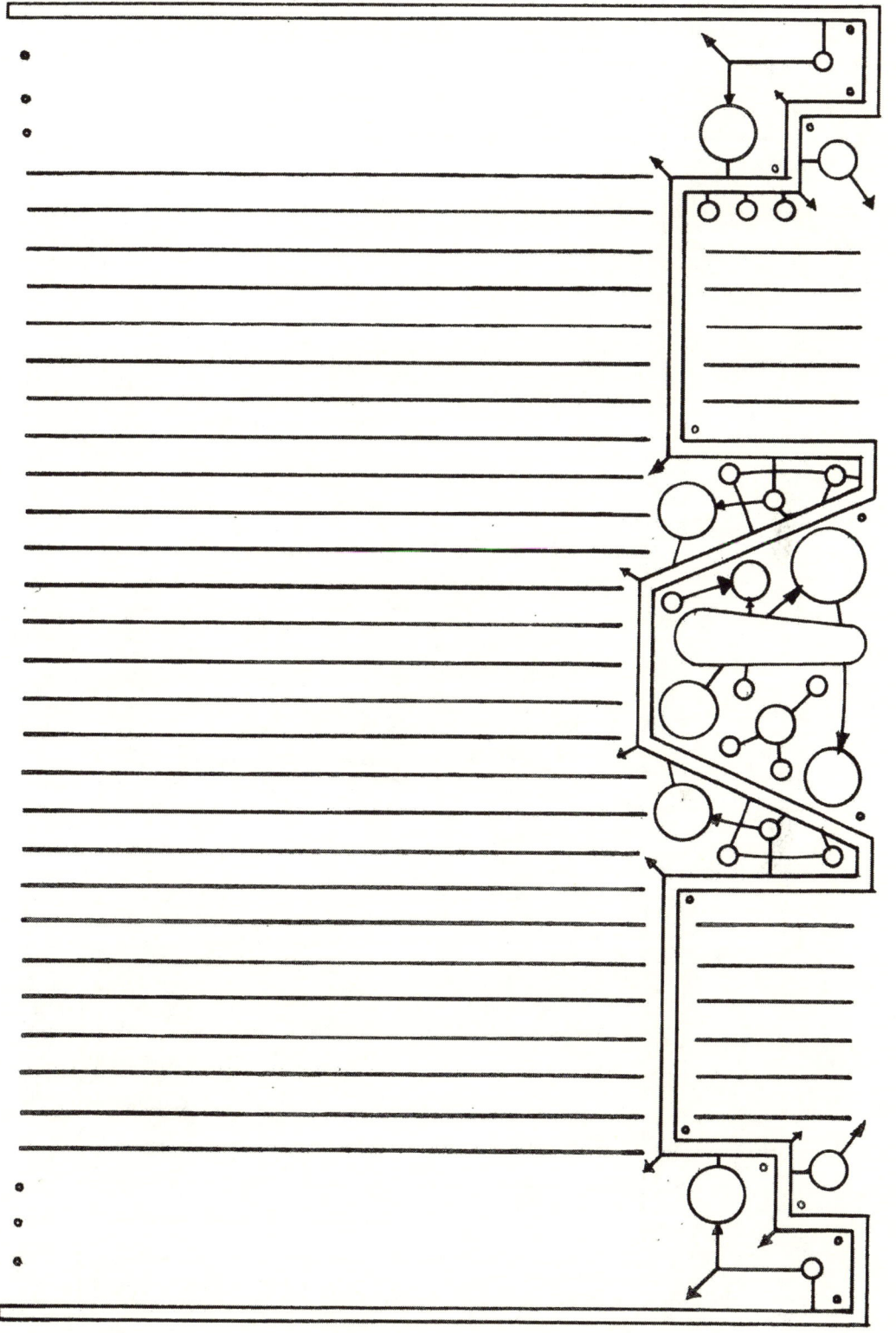

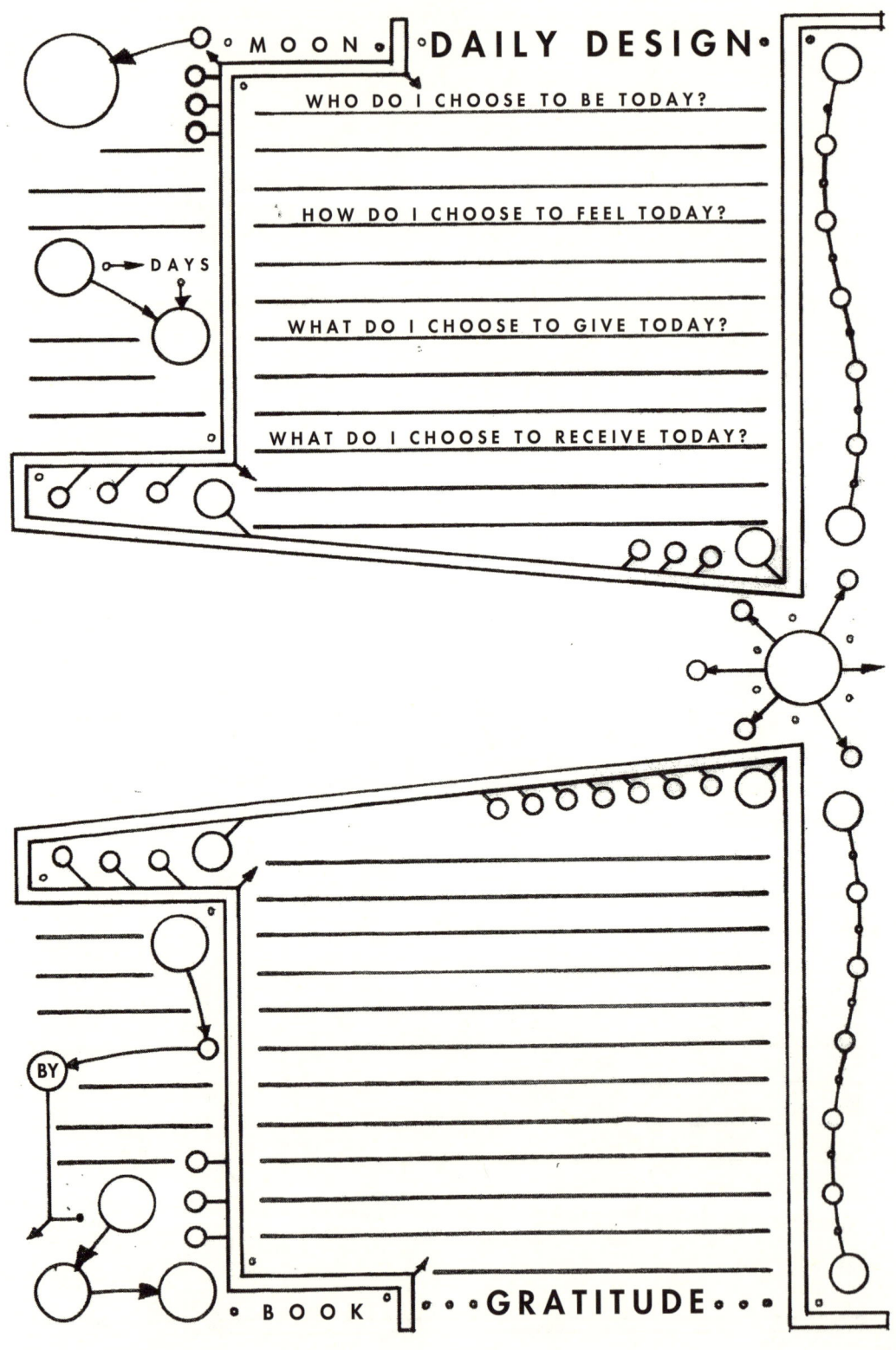

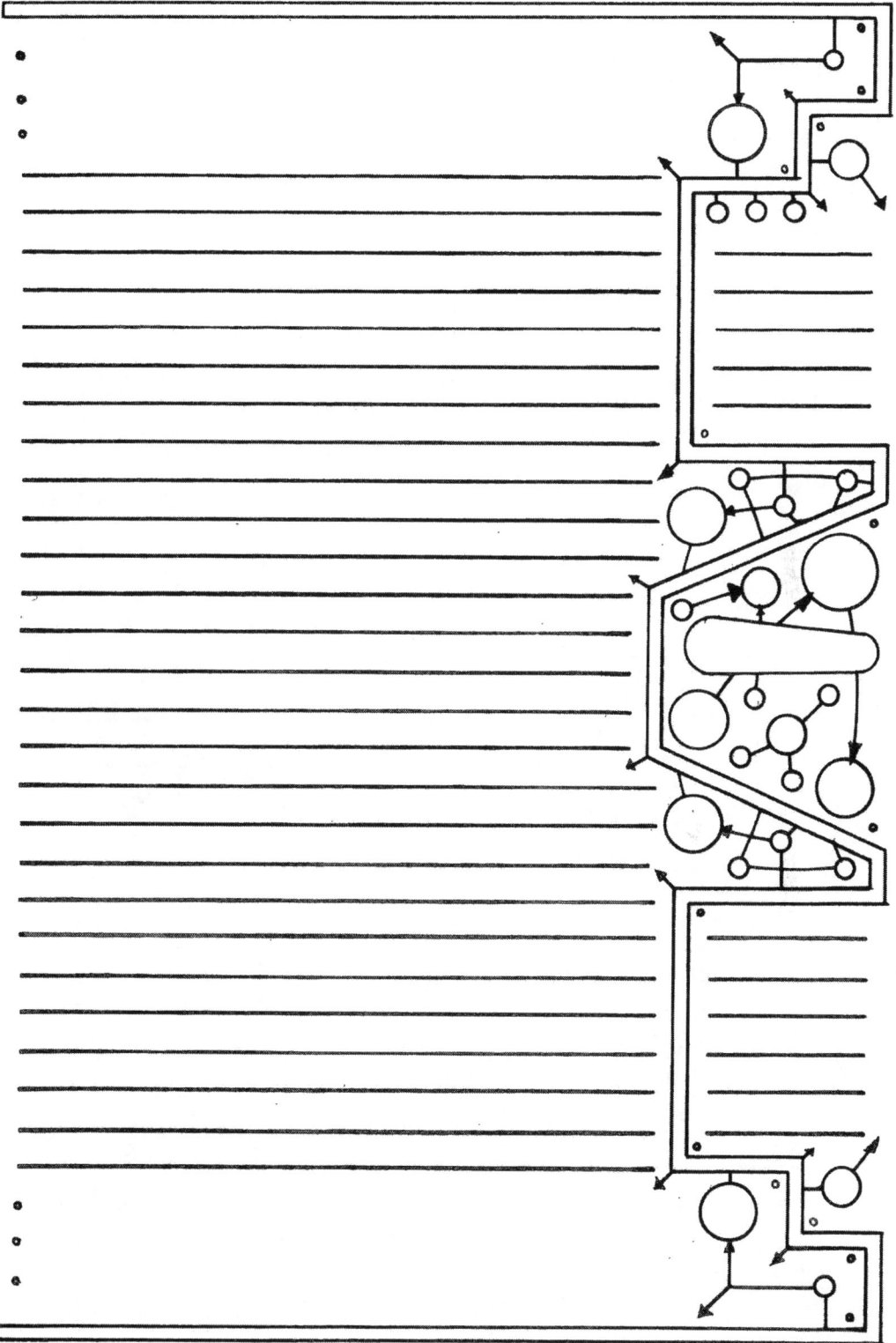

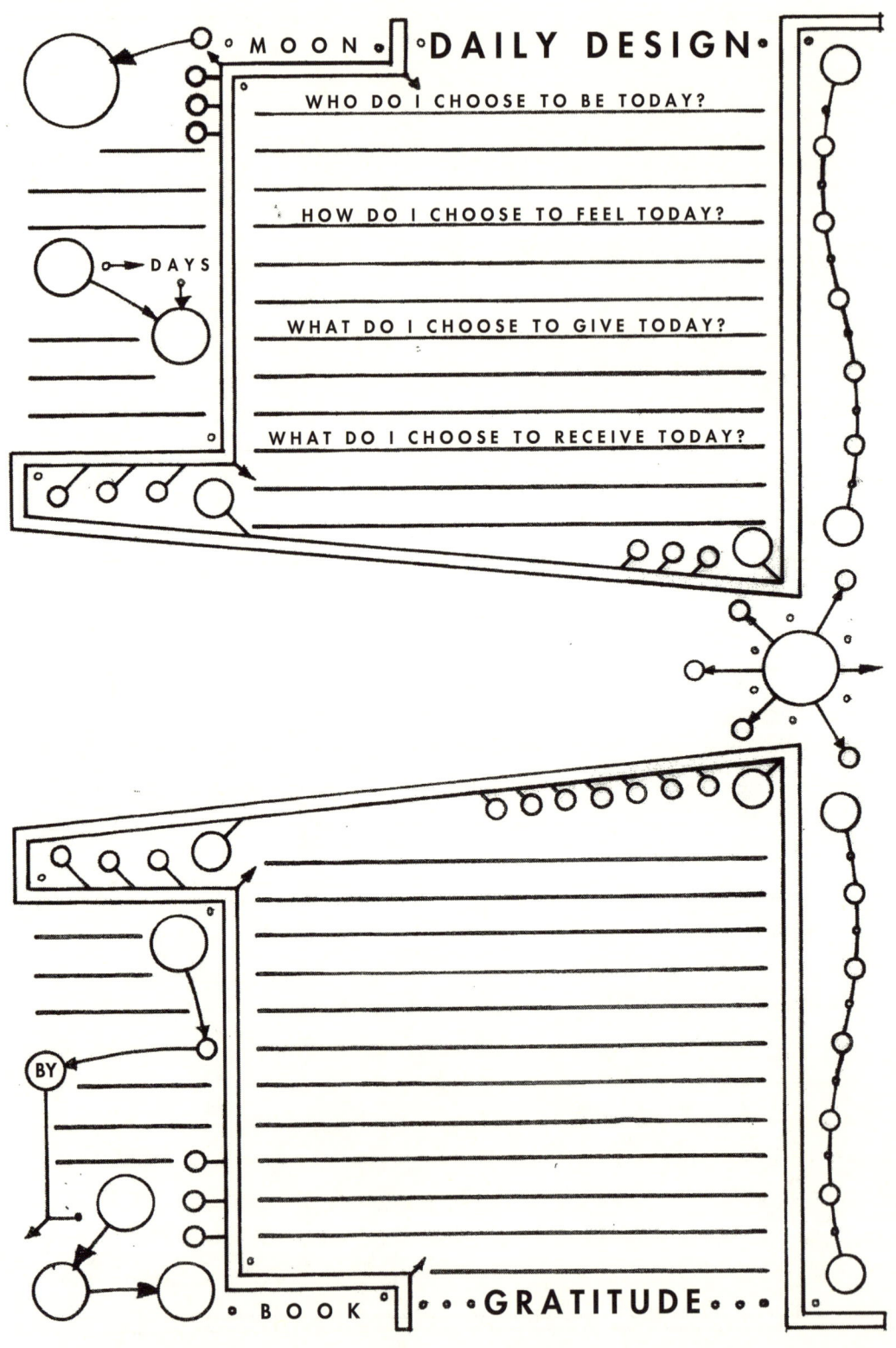

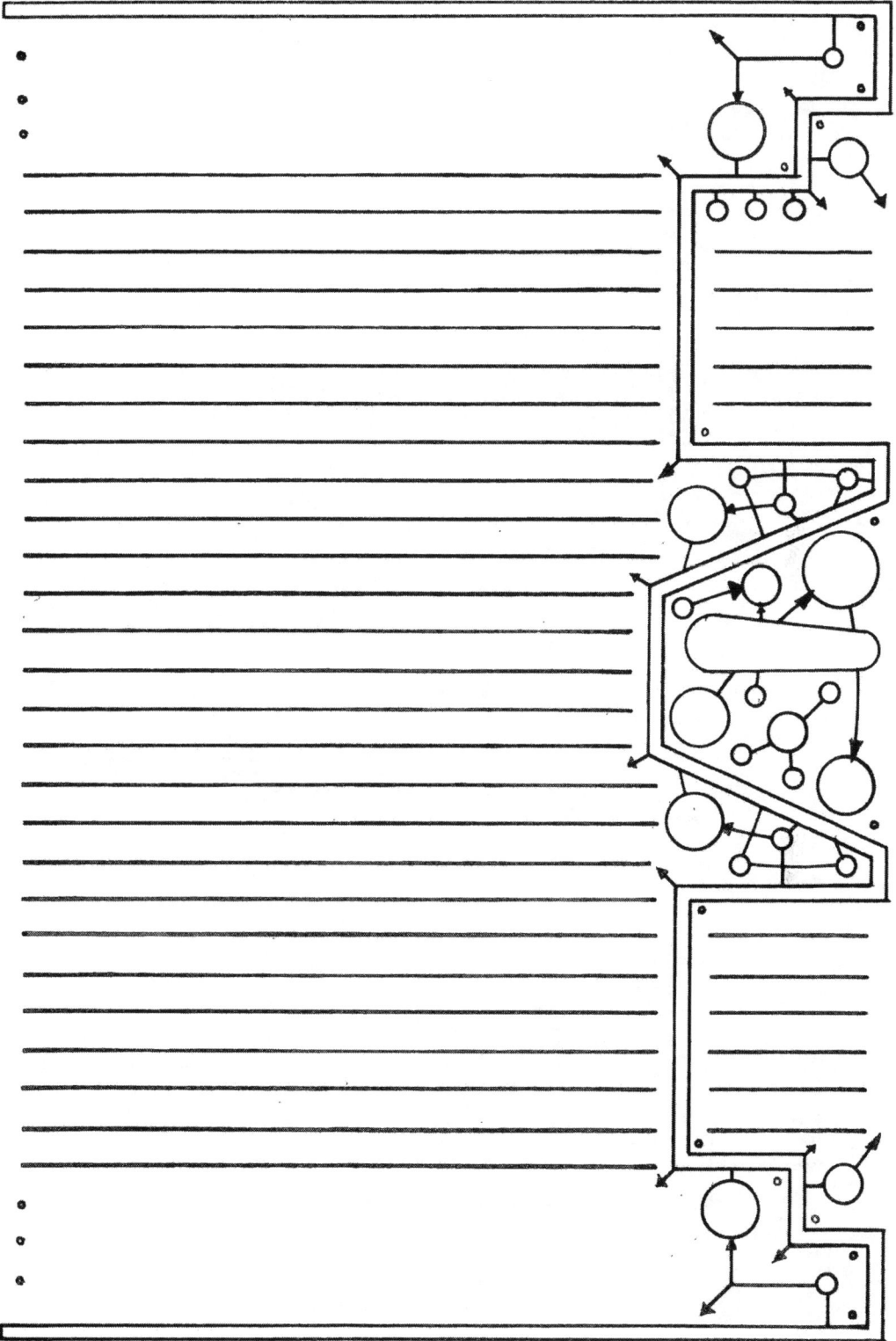

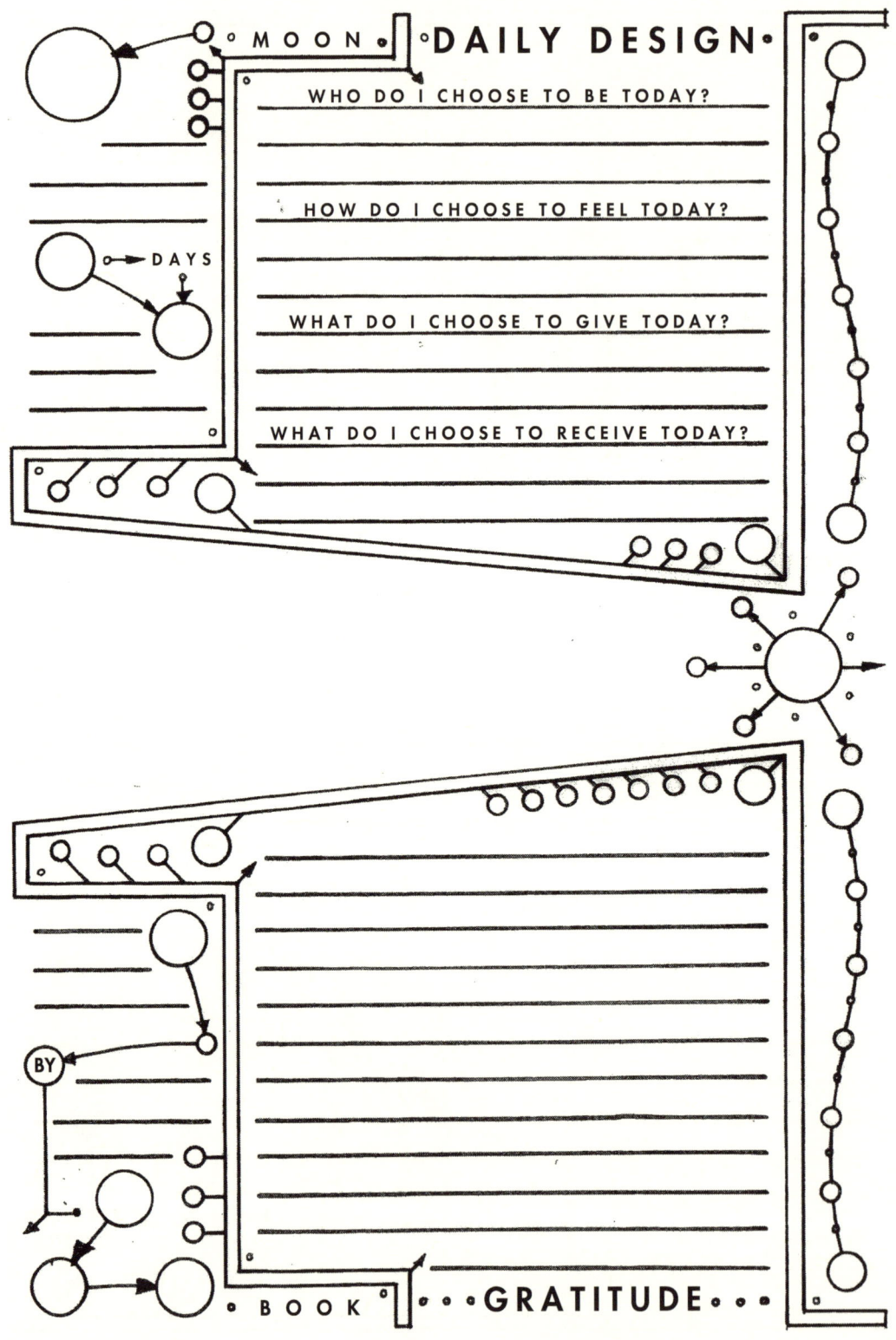

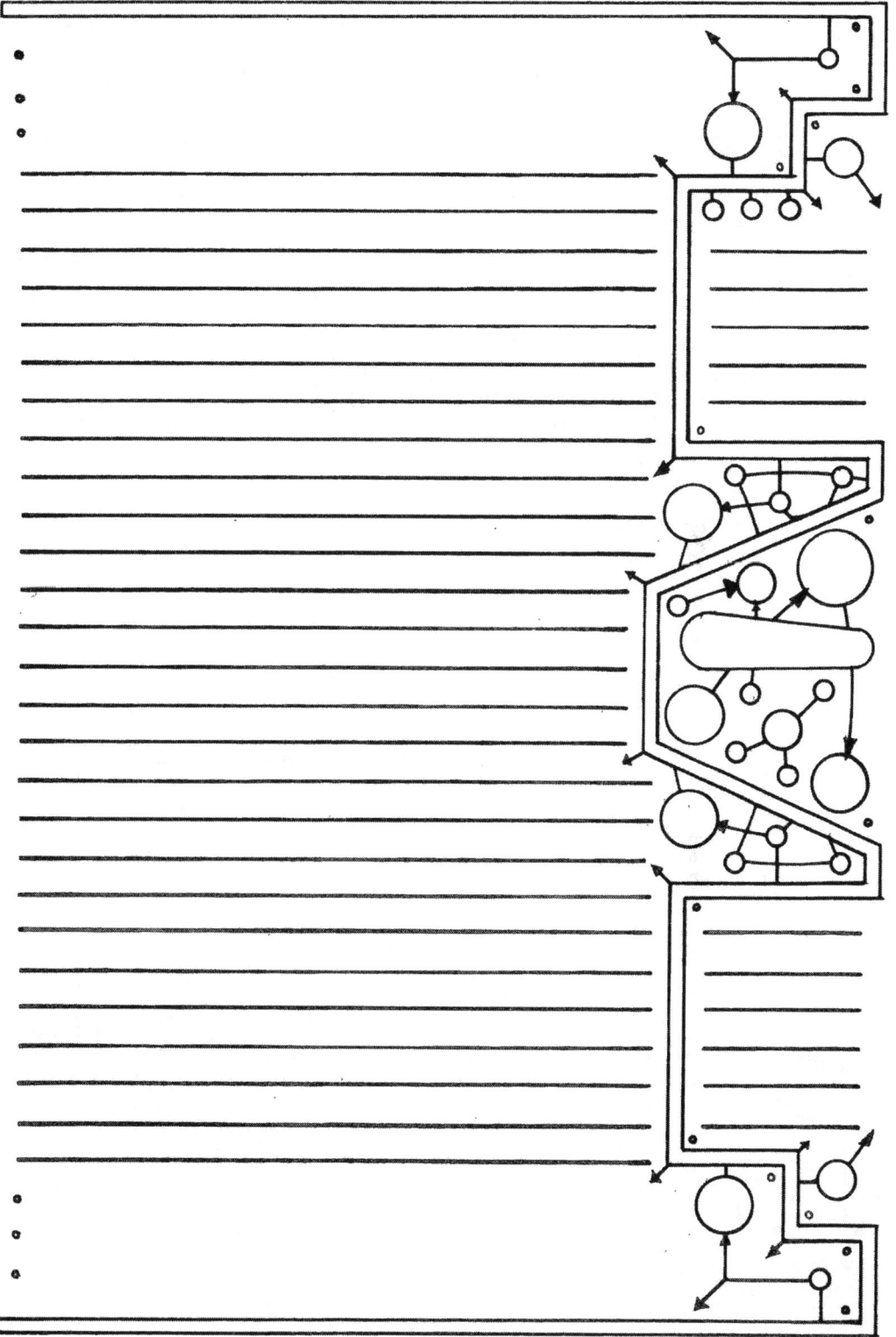

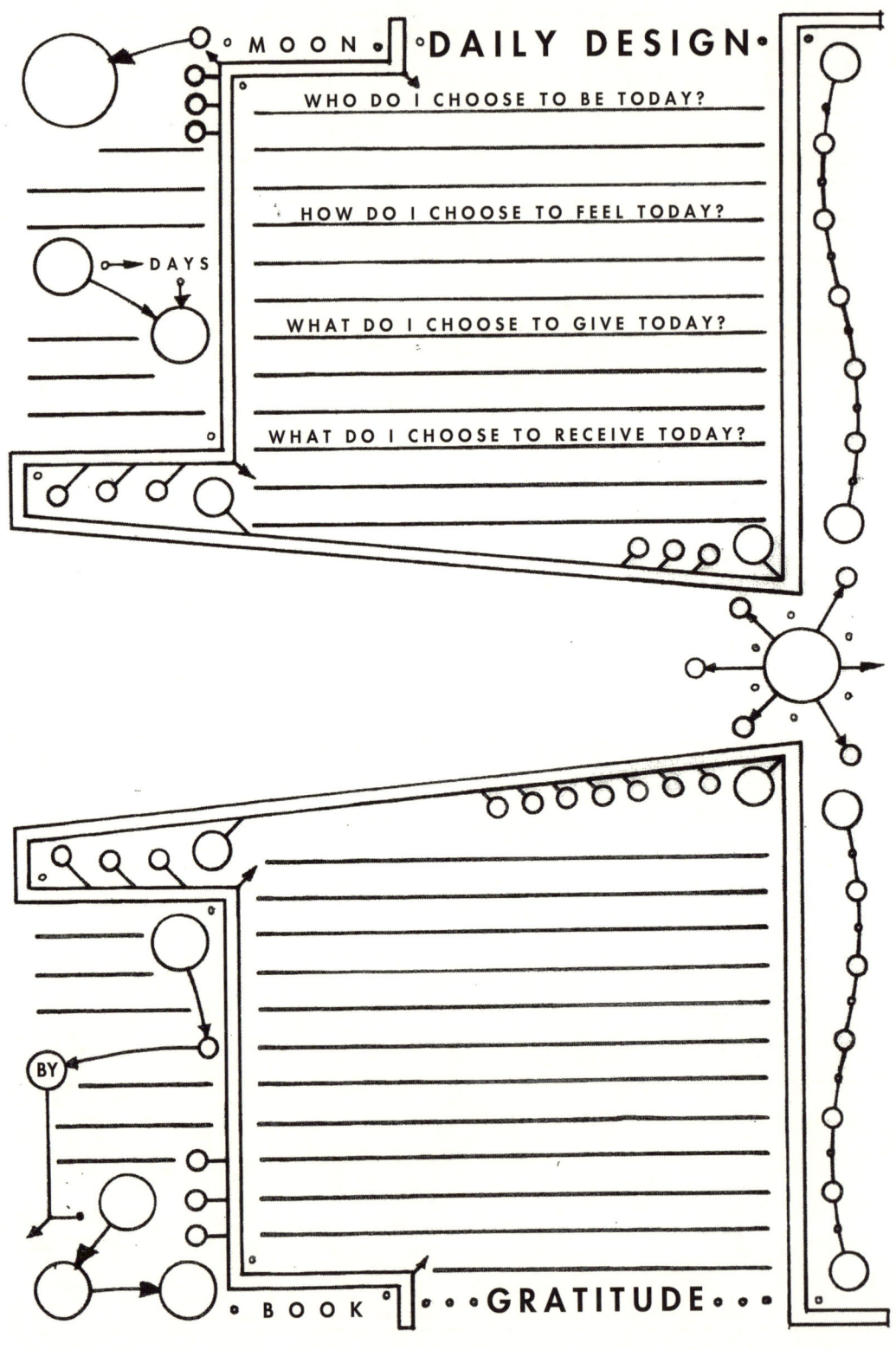

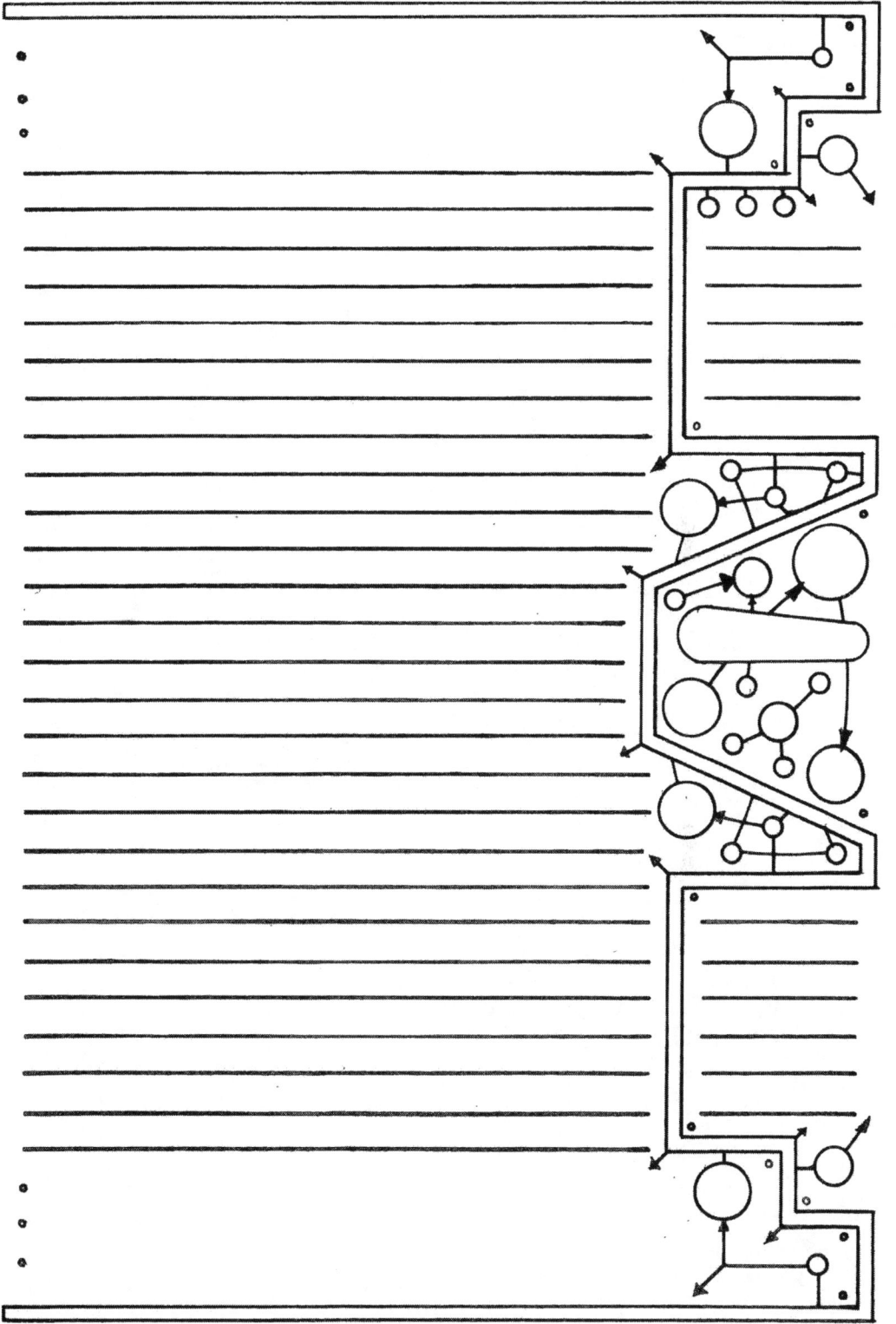

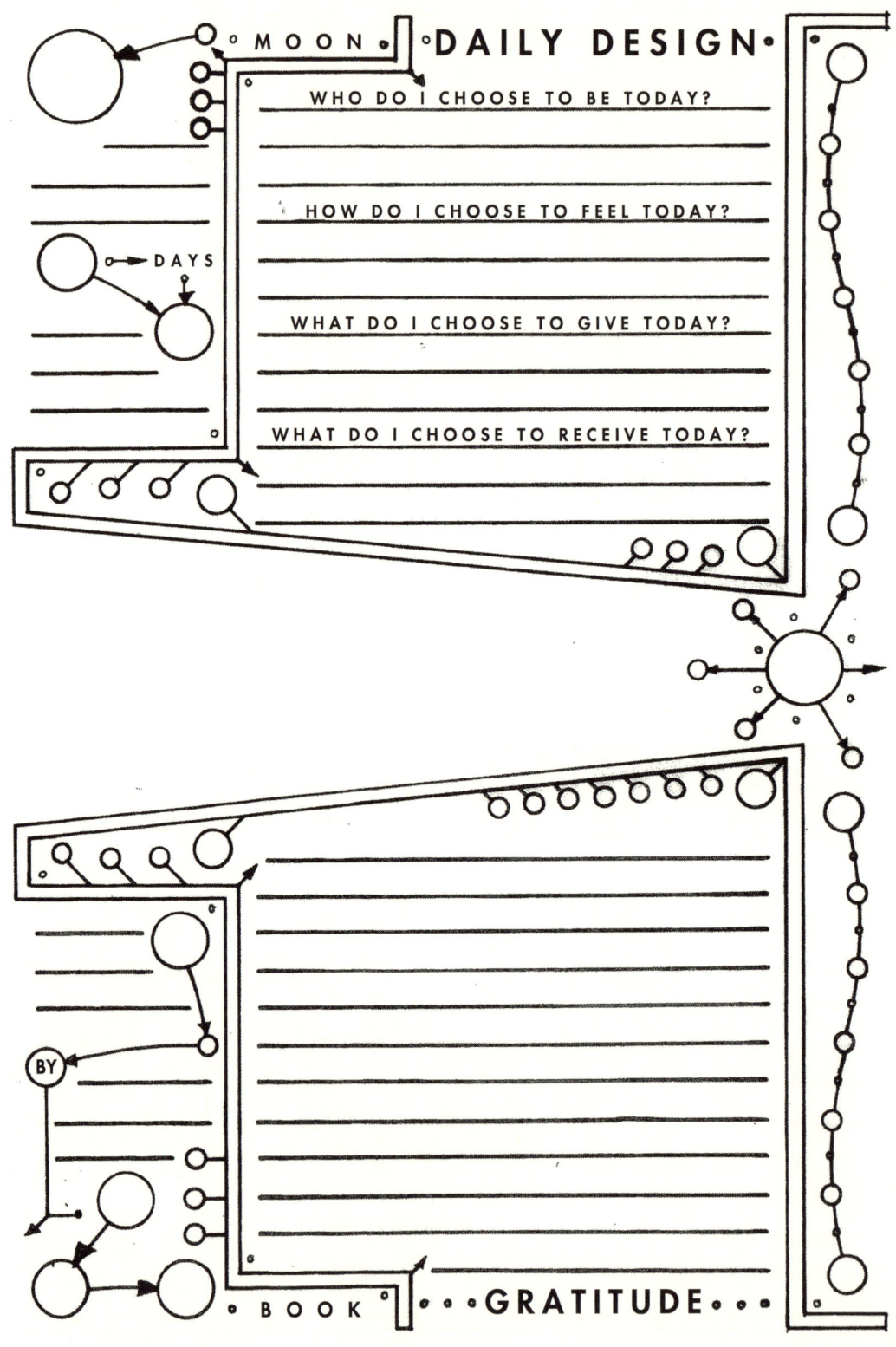

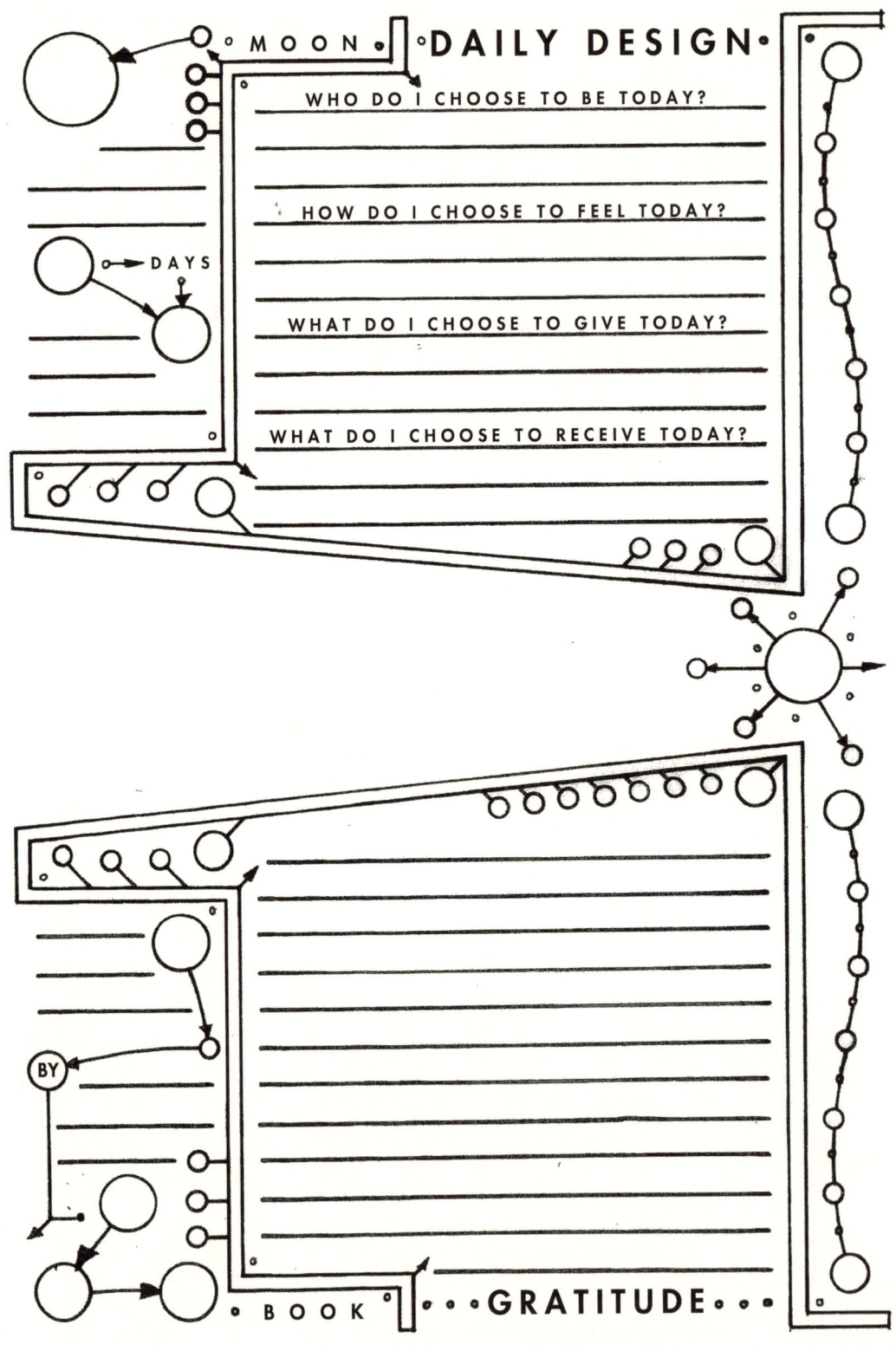

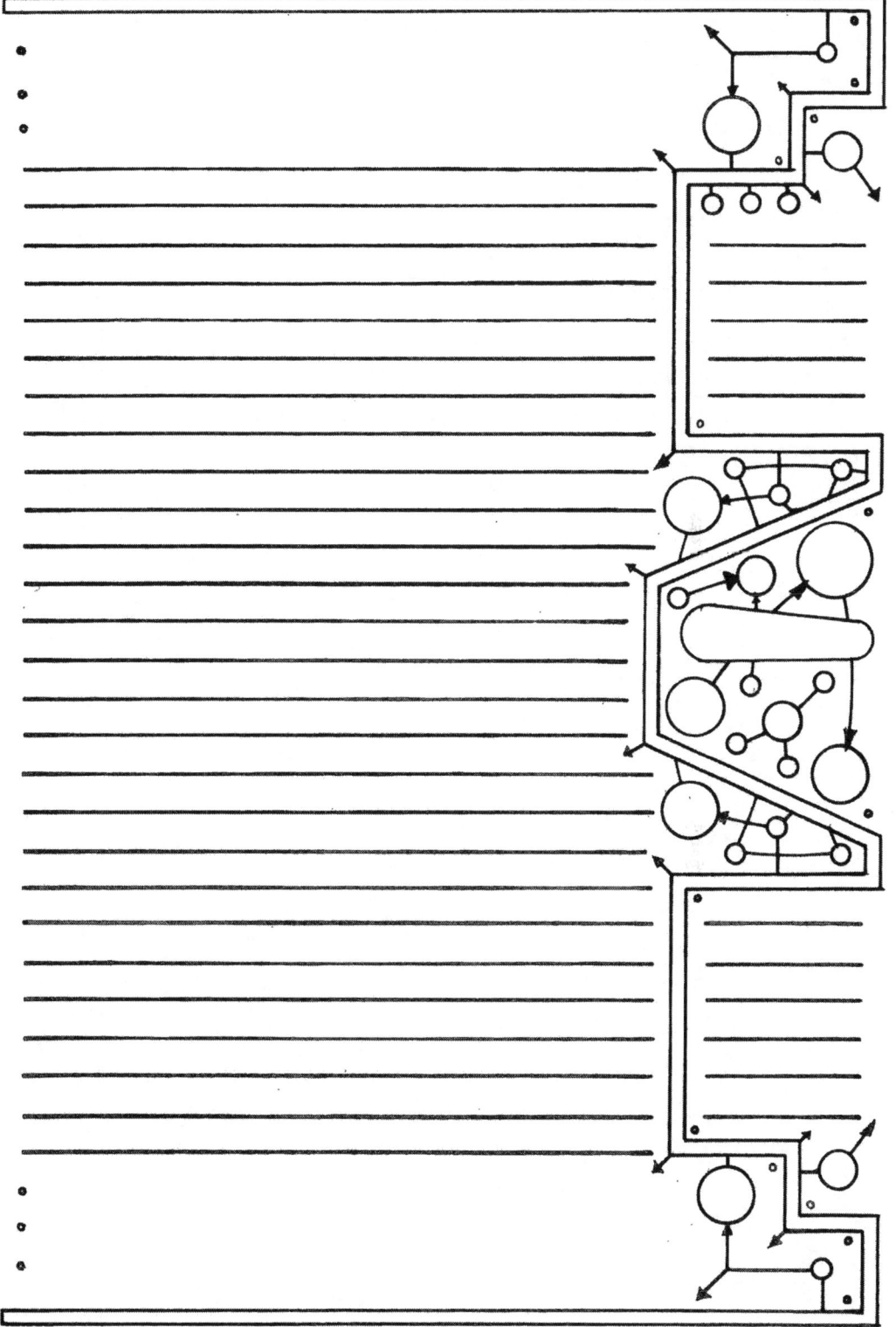

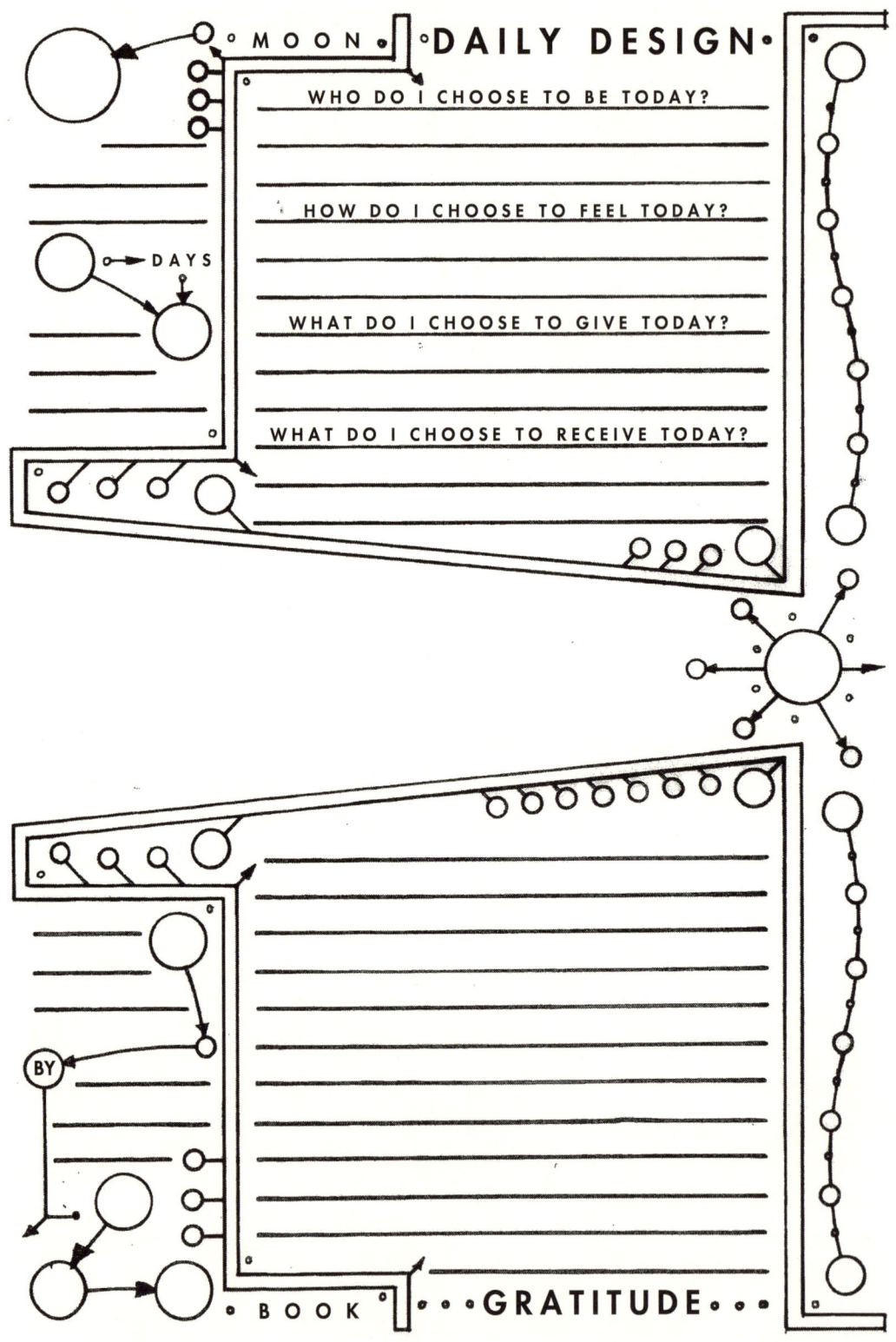

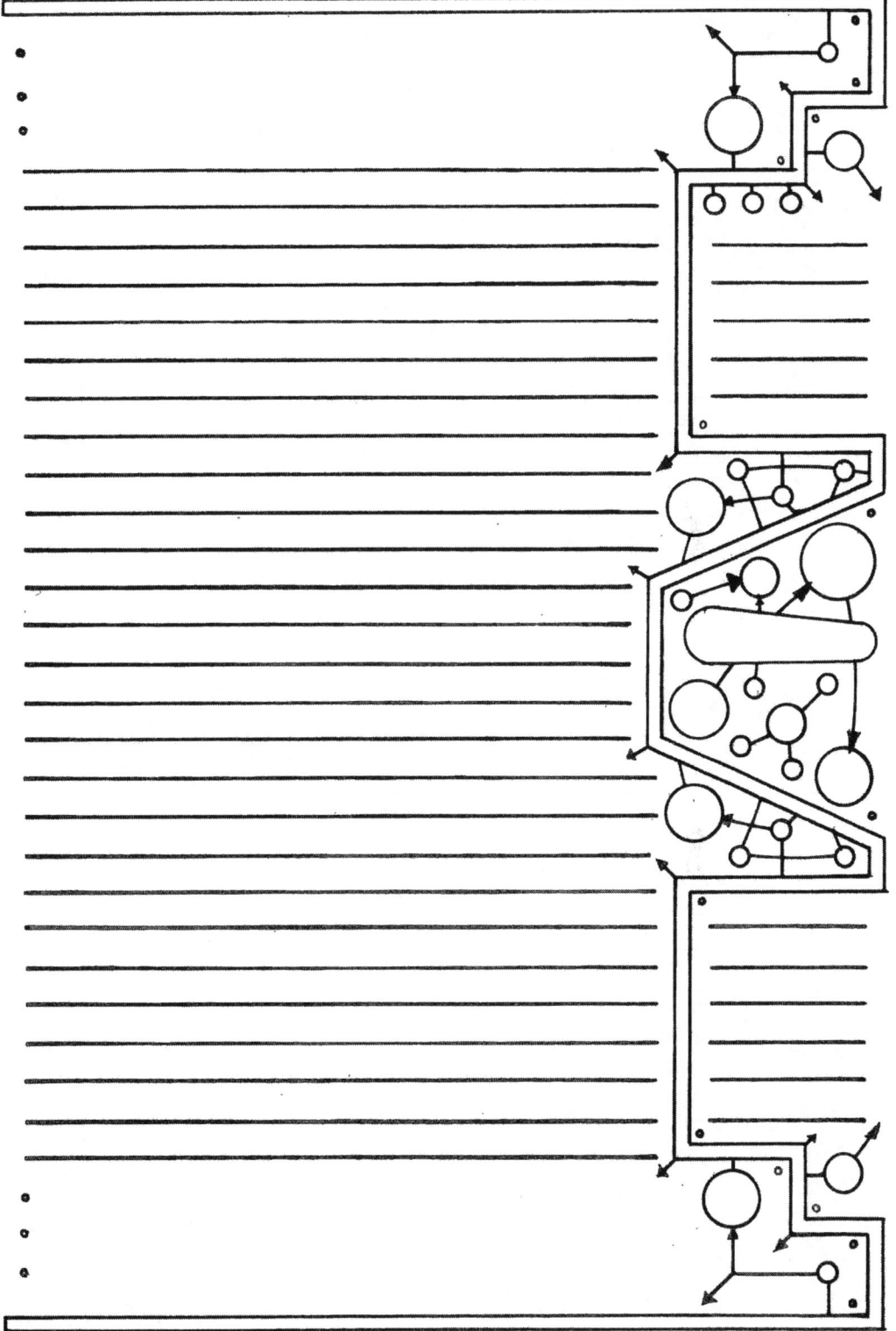

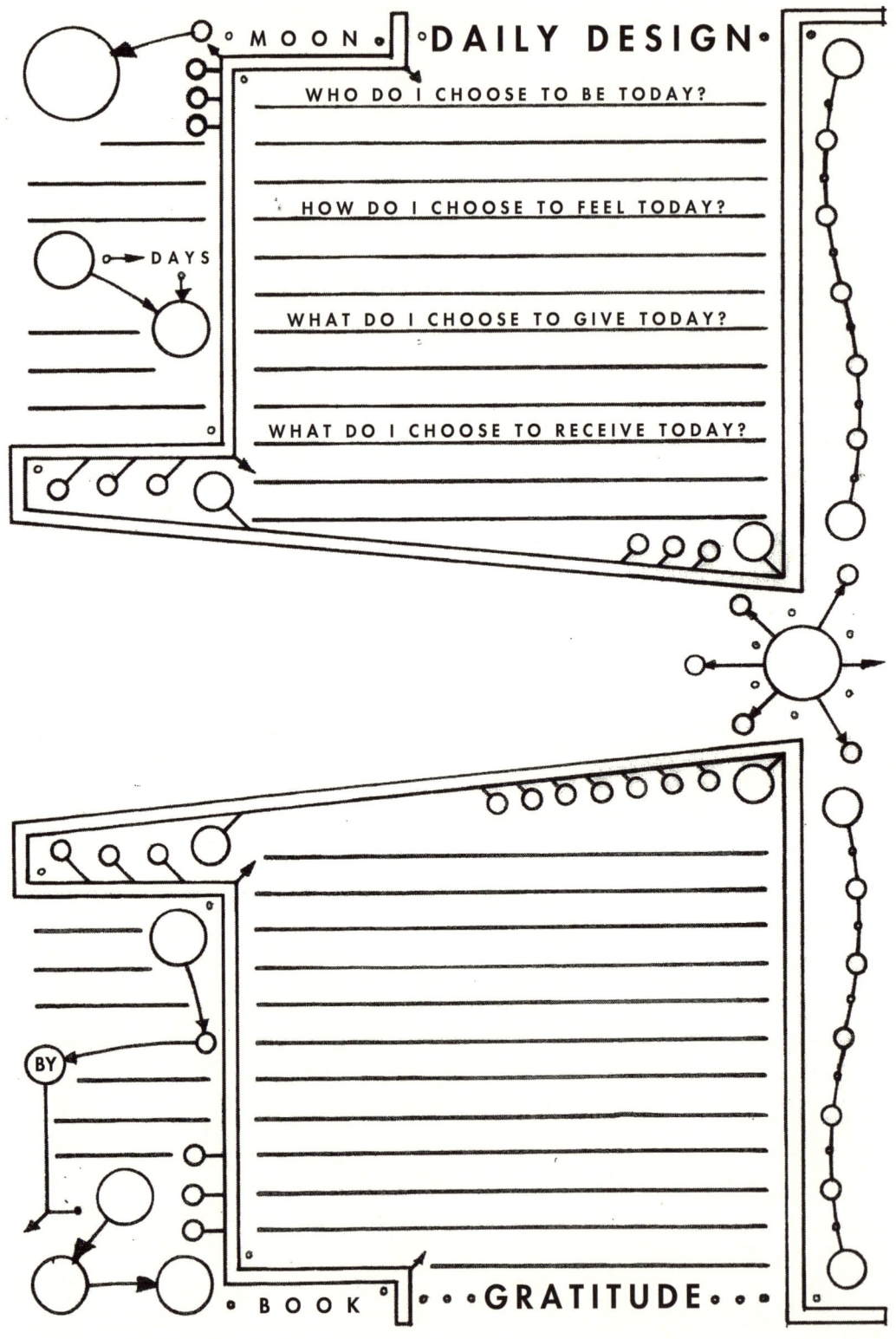

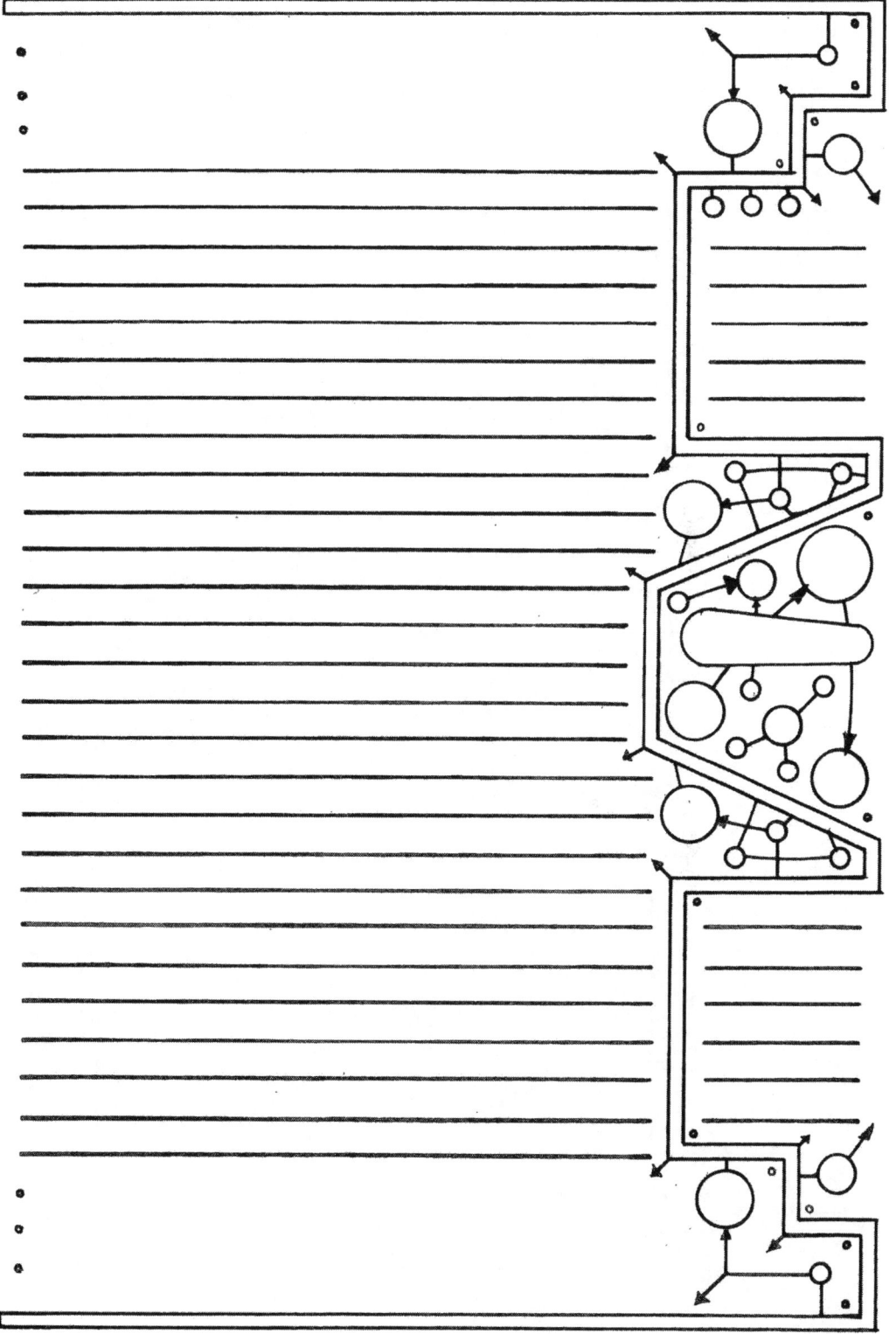

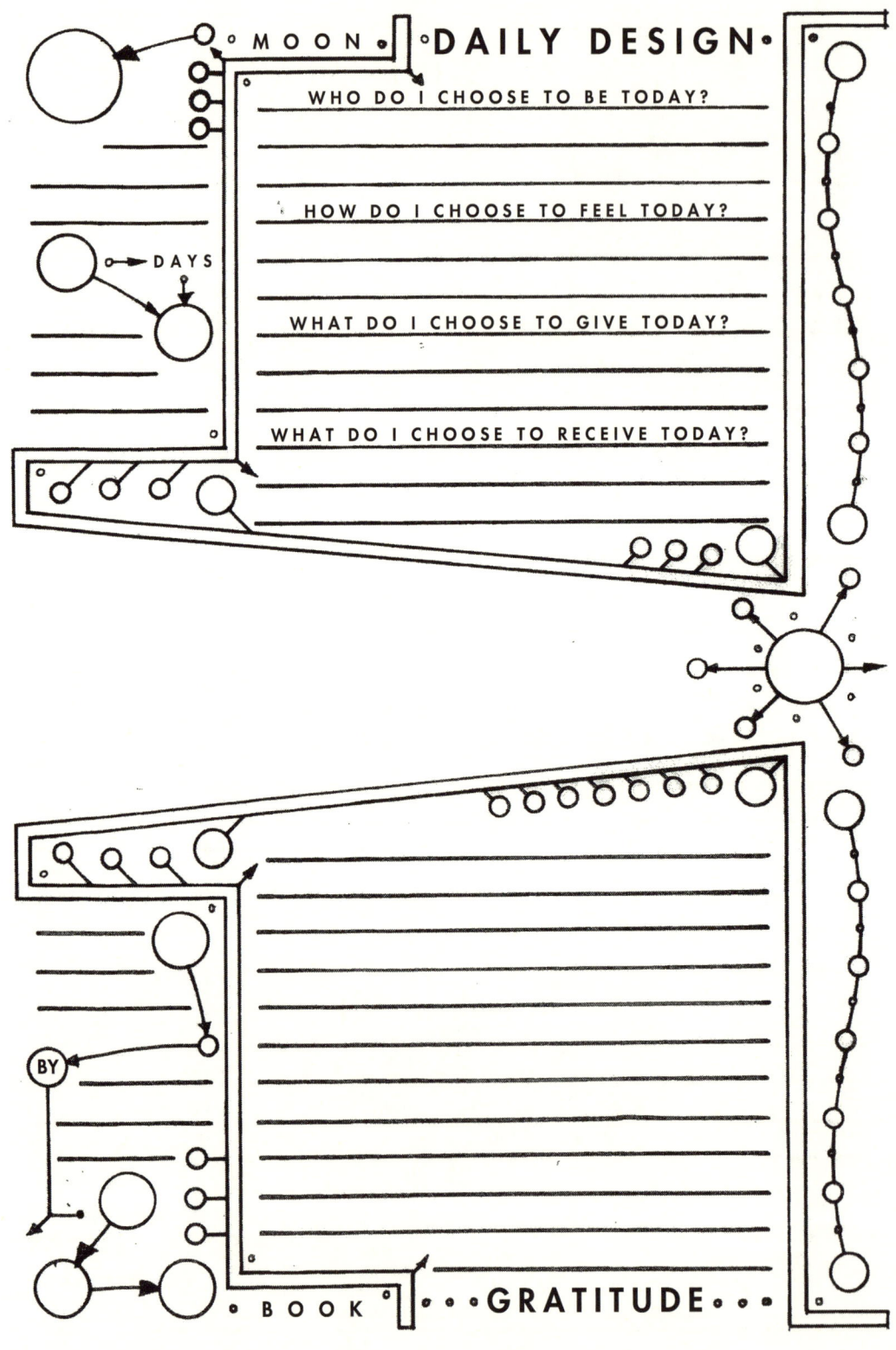

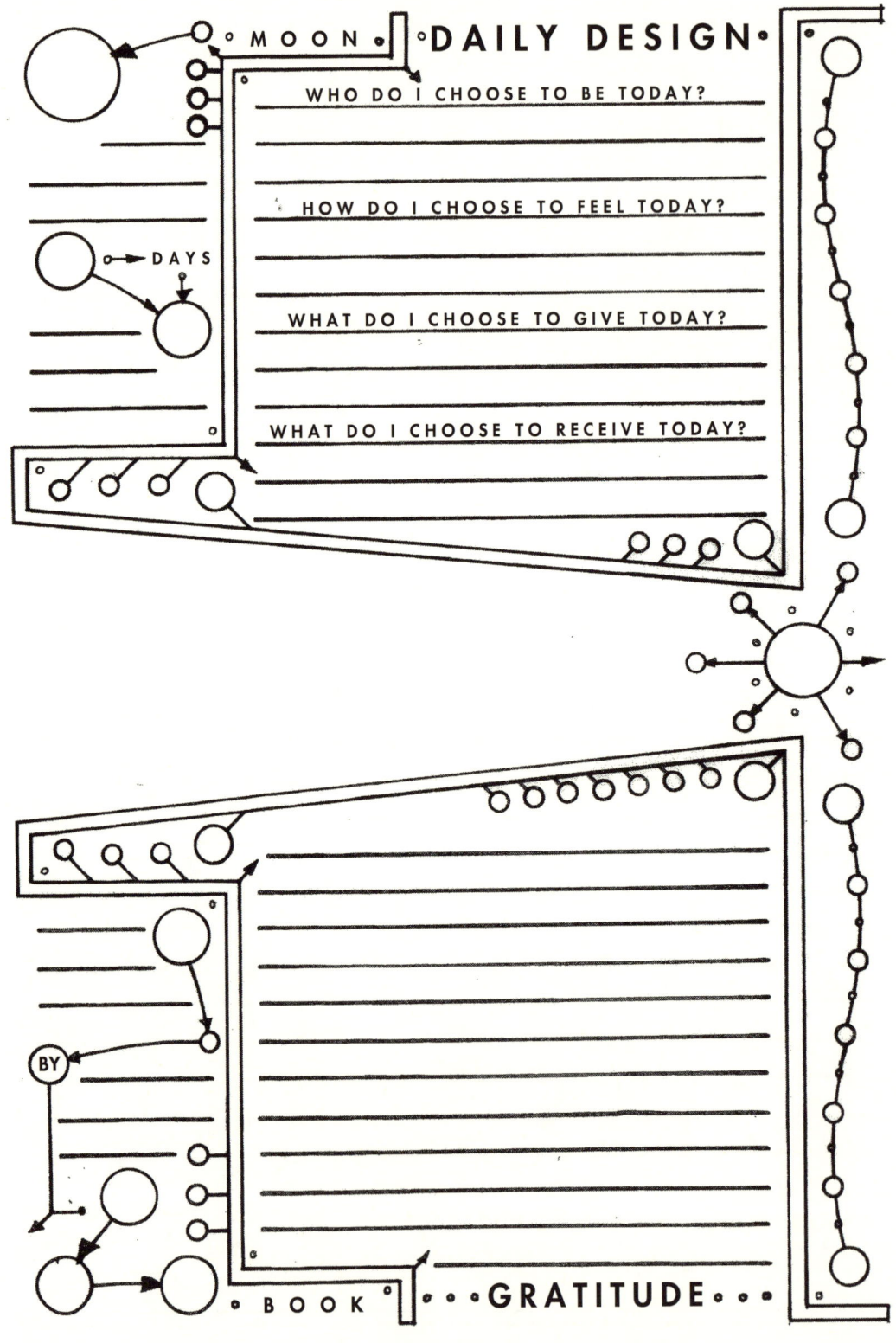

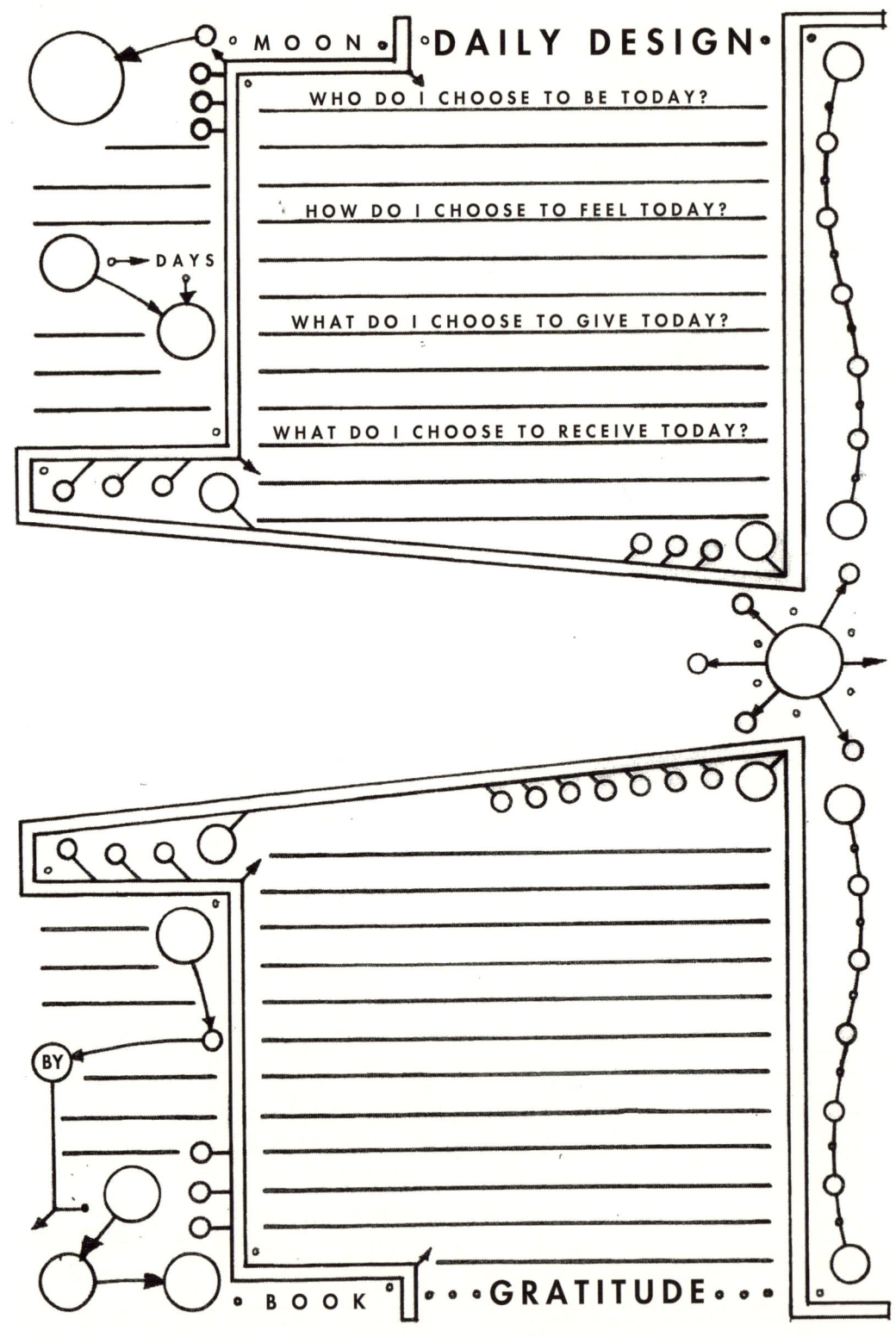

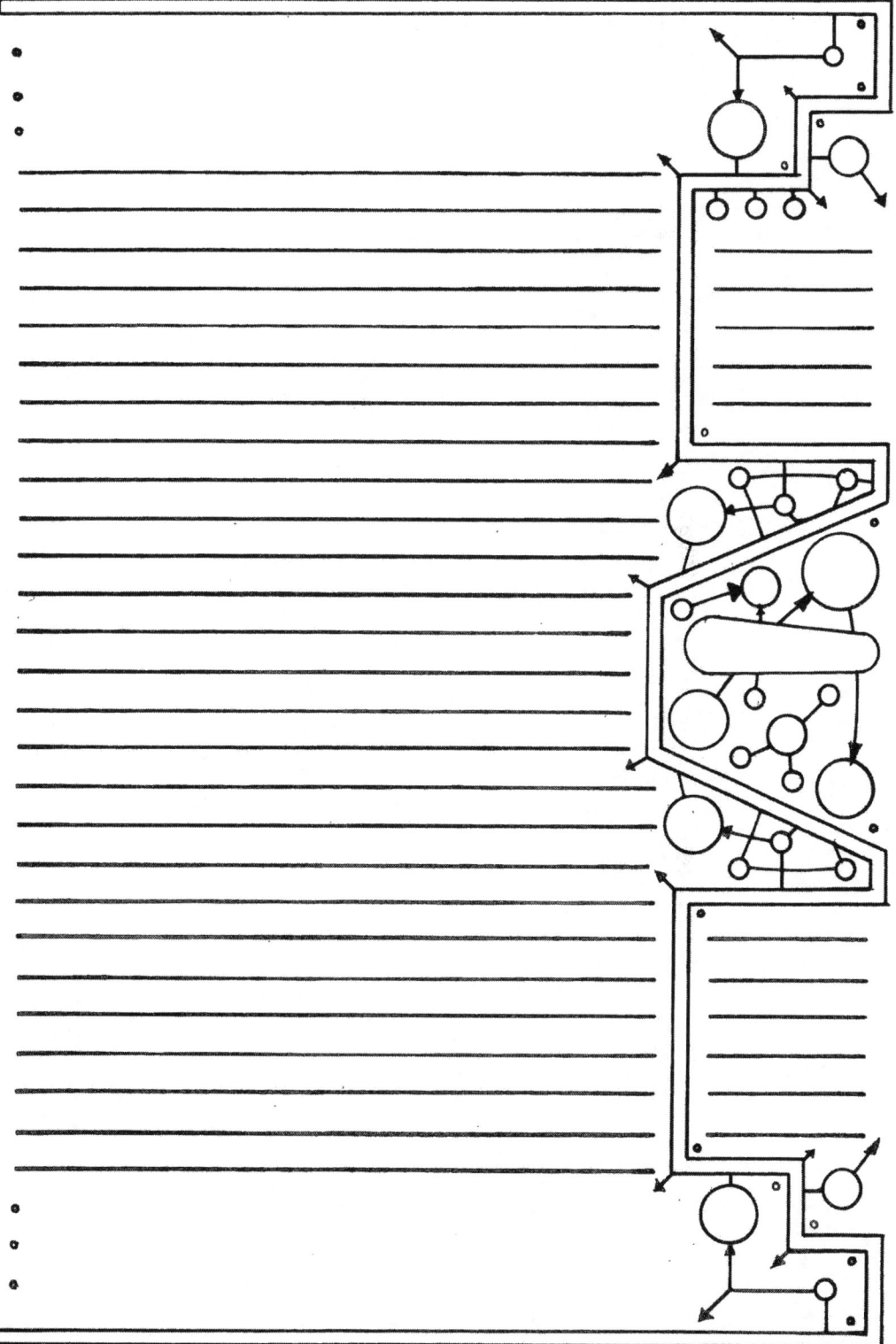

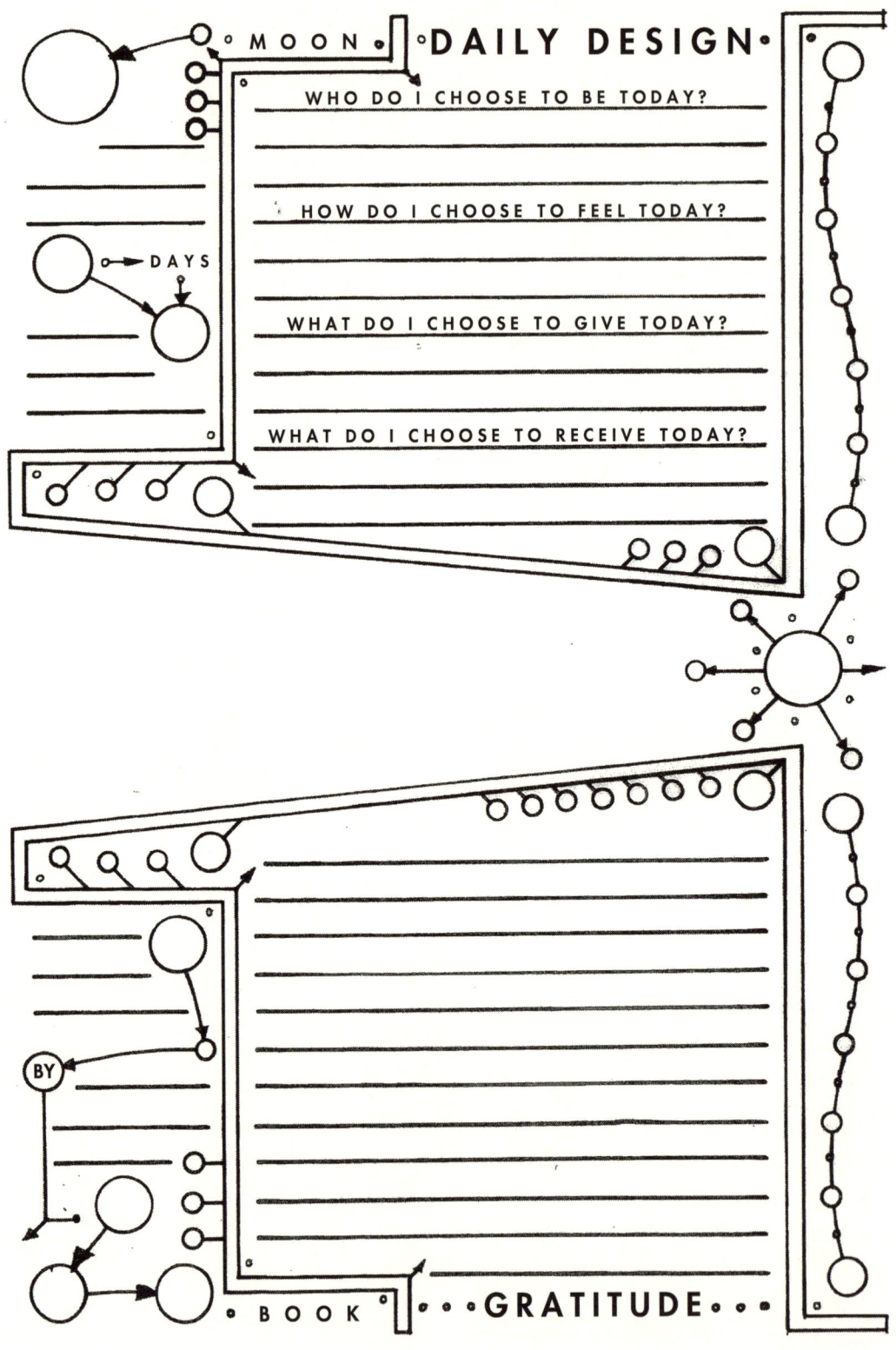

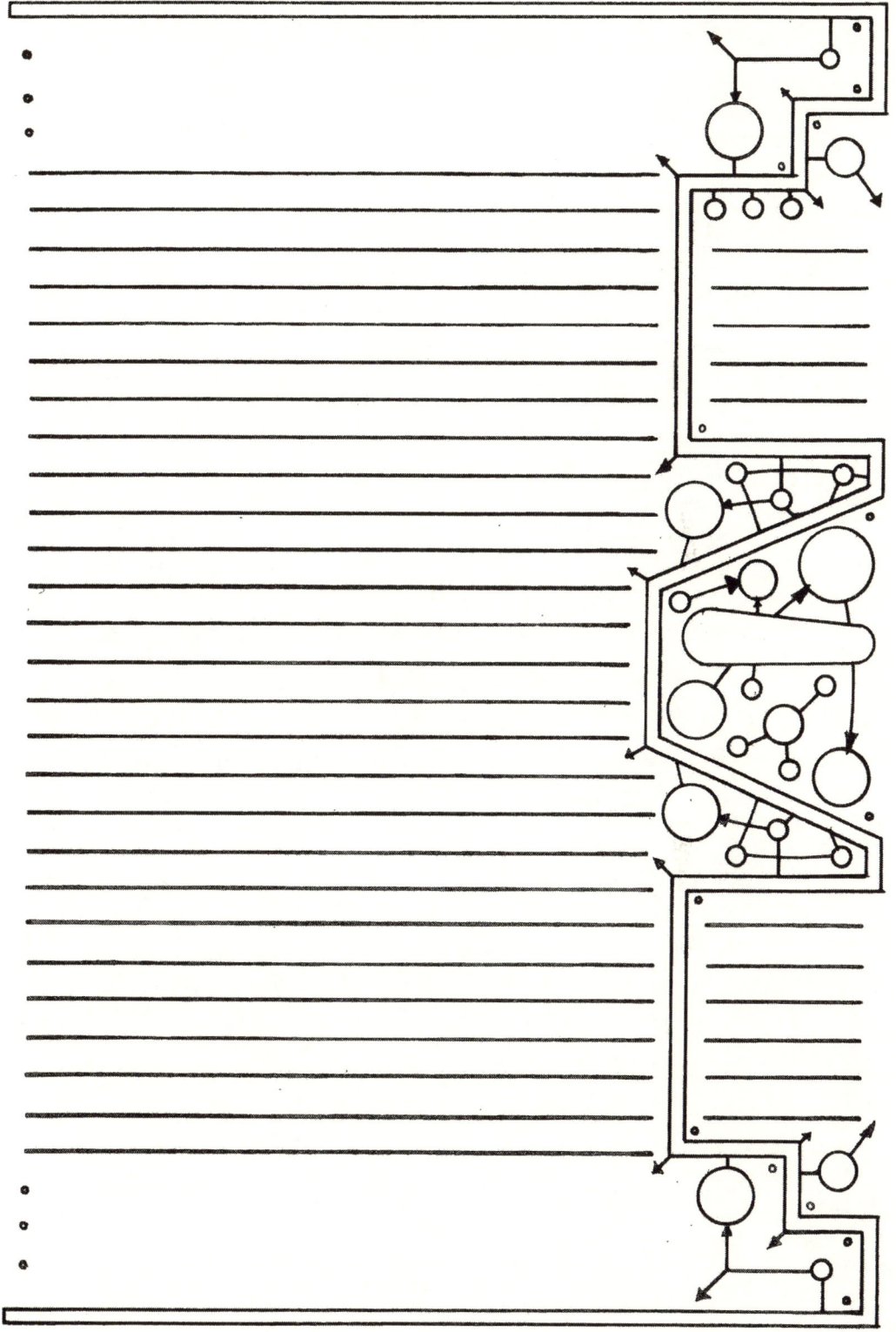

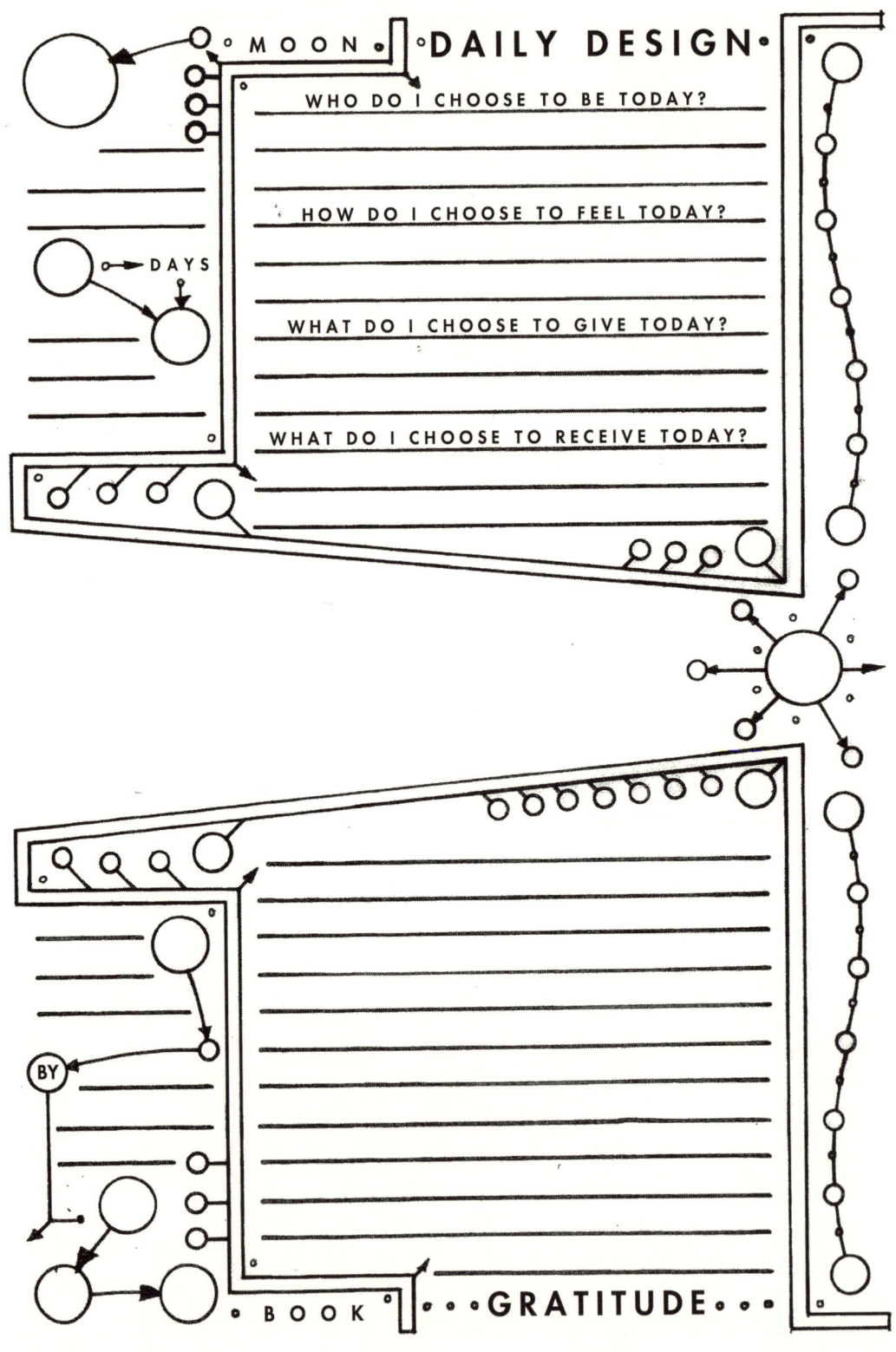

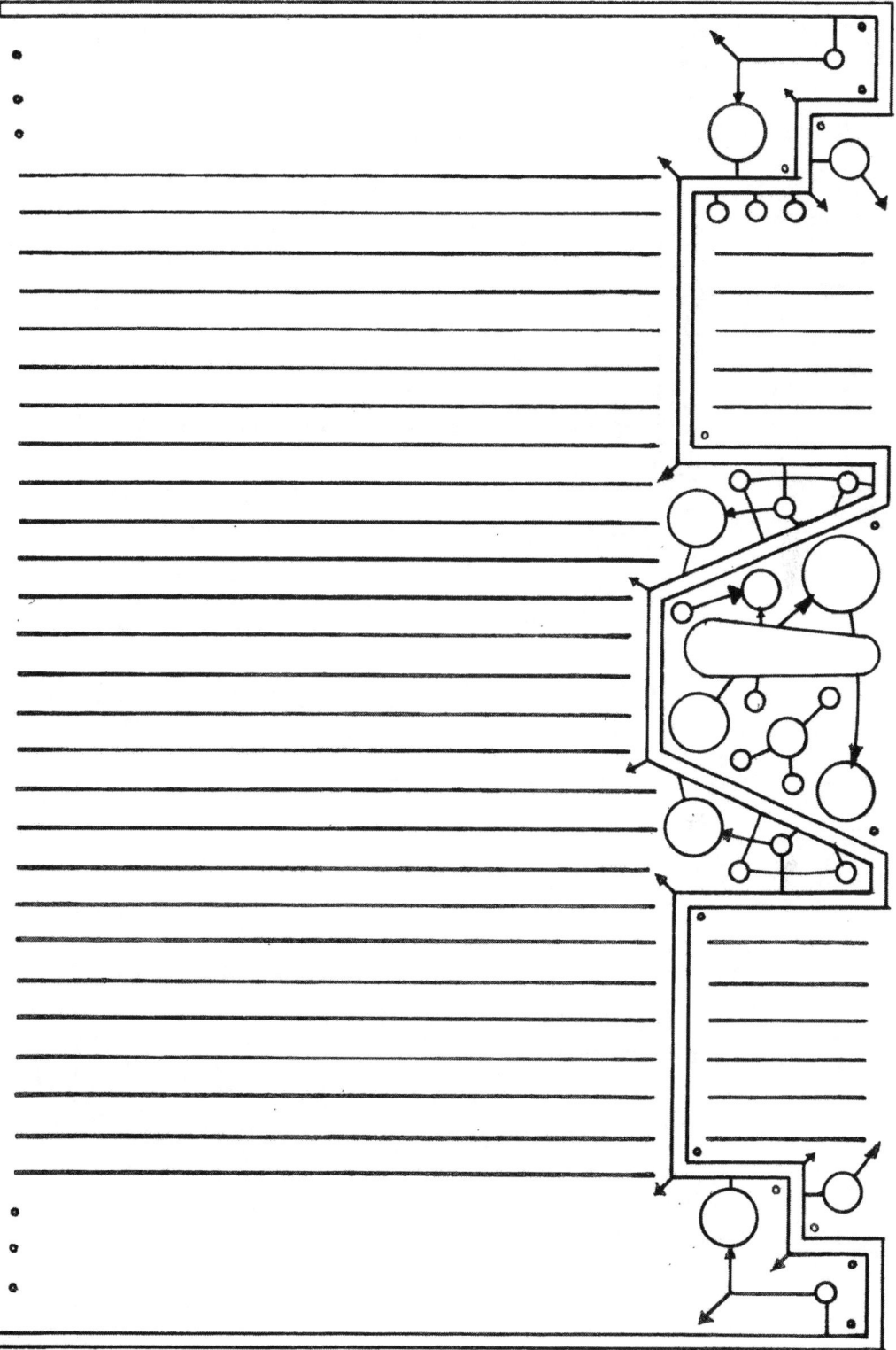

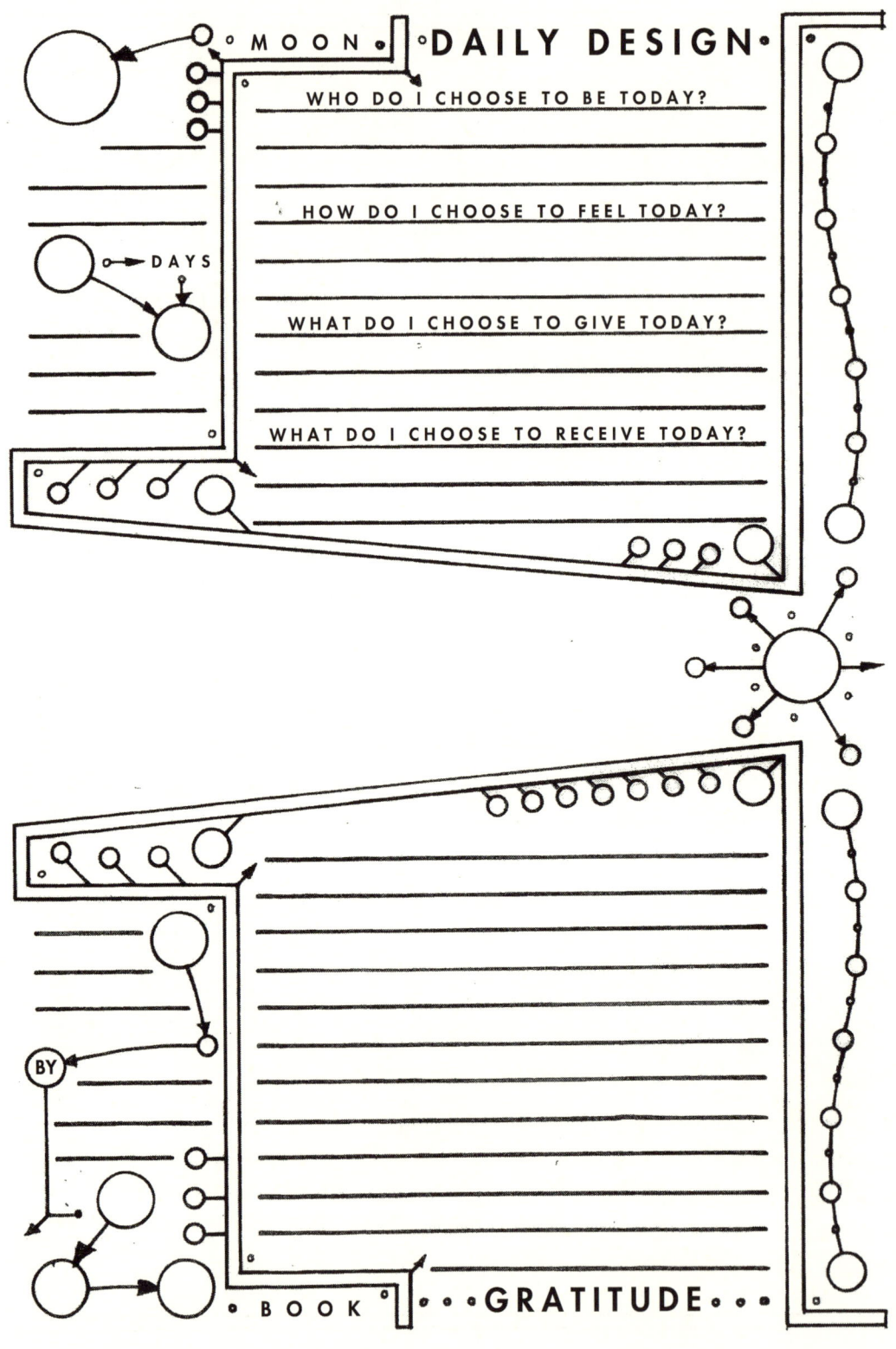

·DAILY DESIGN·

· MOON ·

WHO DO I CHOOSE TO BE TODAY?

HOW DO I CHOOSE TO FEEL TODAY?

DAYS

WHAT DO I CHOOSE TO GIVE TODAY?

WHAT DO I CHOOSE TO RECEIVE TODAY?

BY

· BOOK · ··· GRATITUDE ···

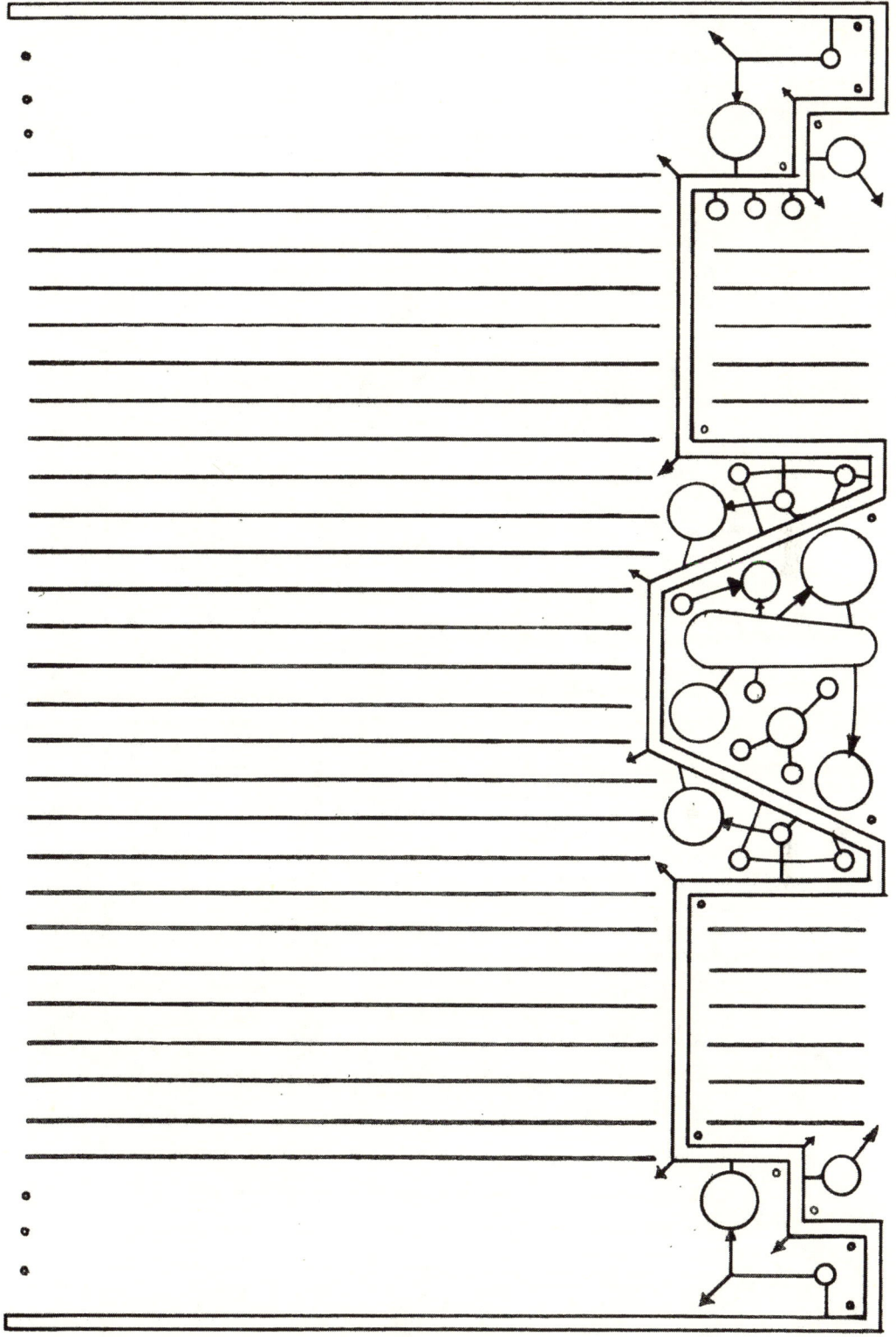

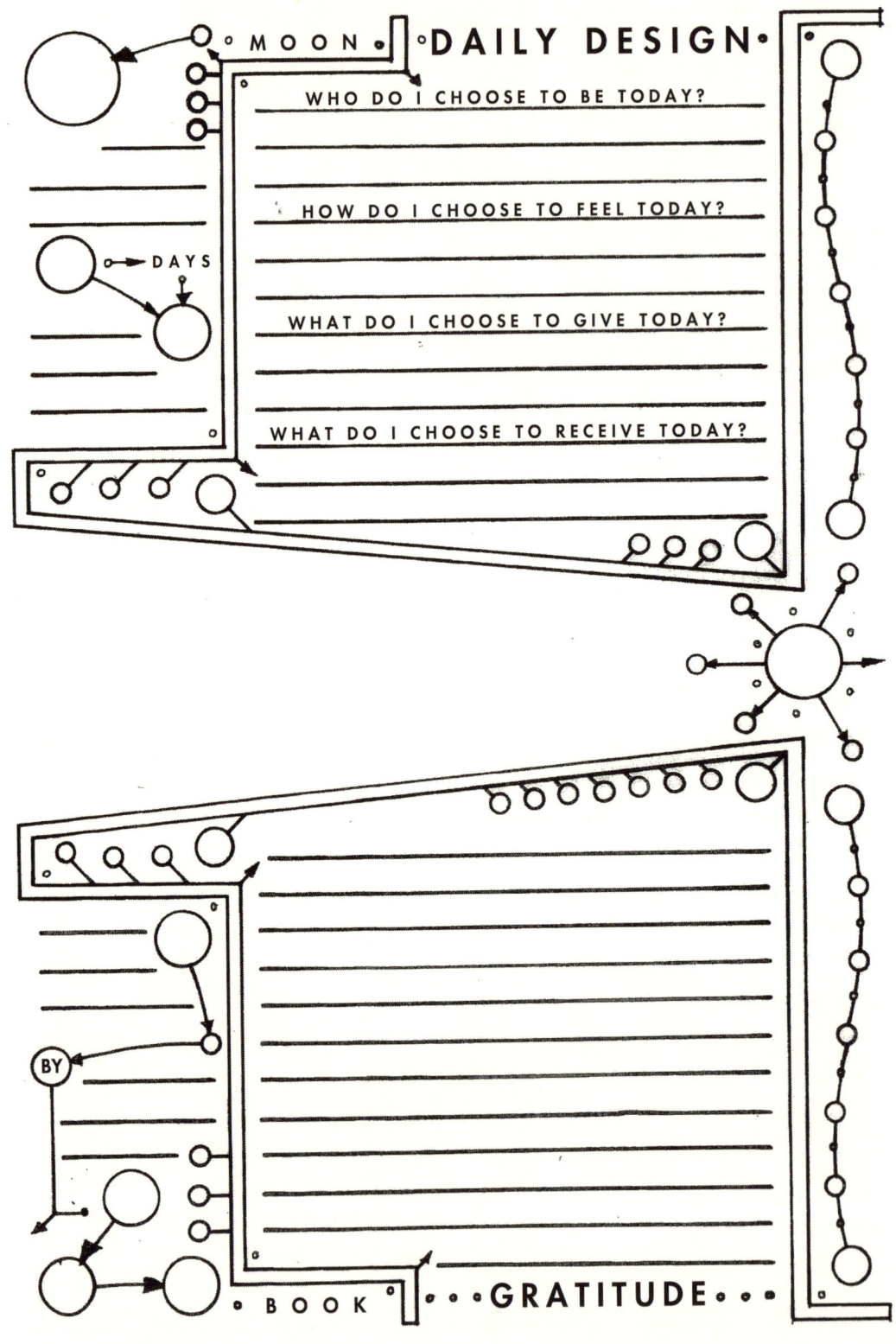

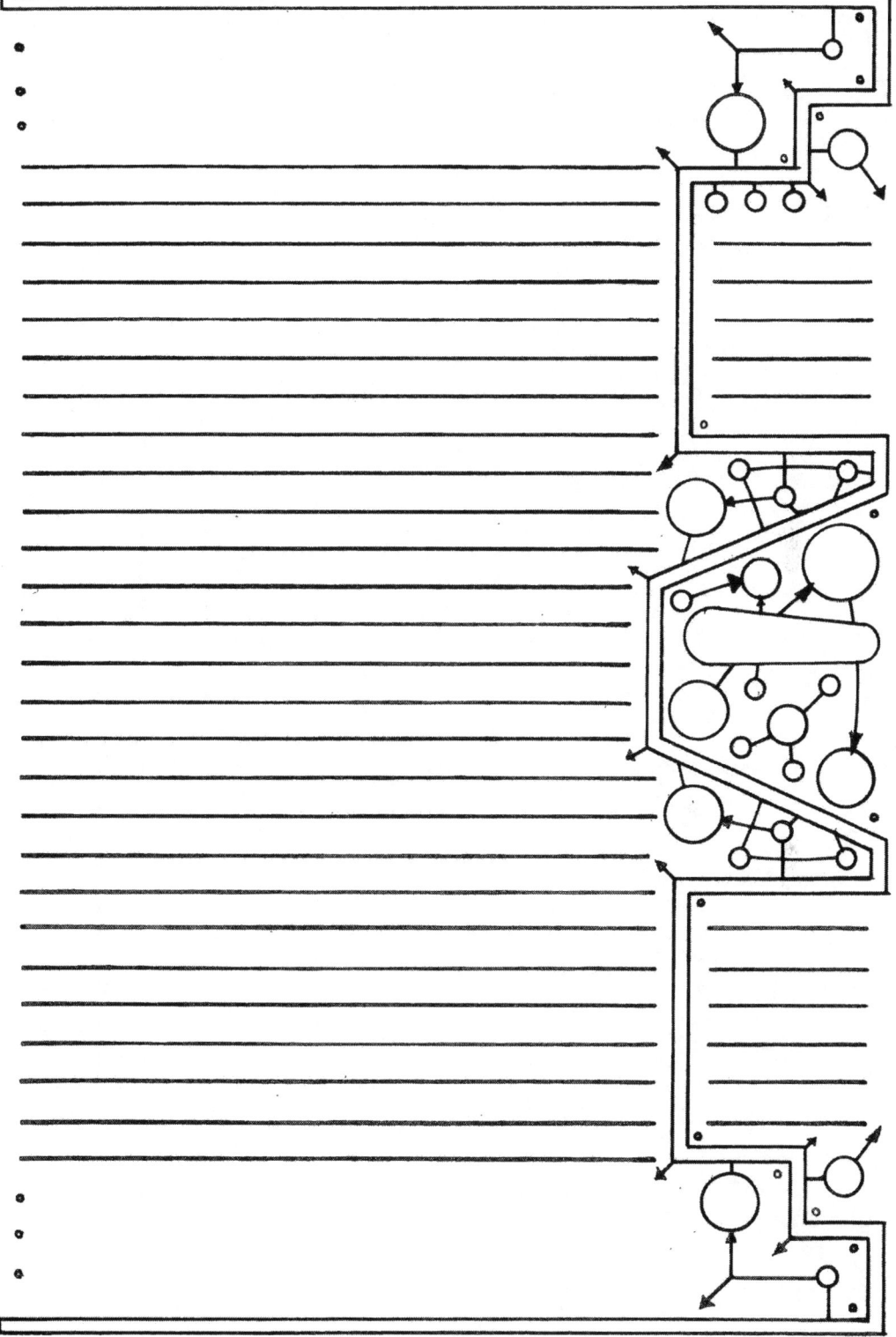

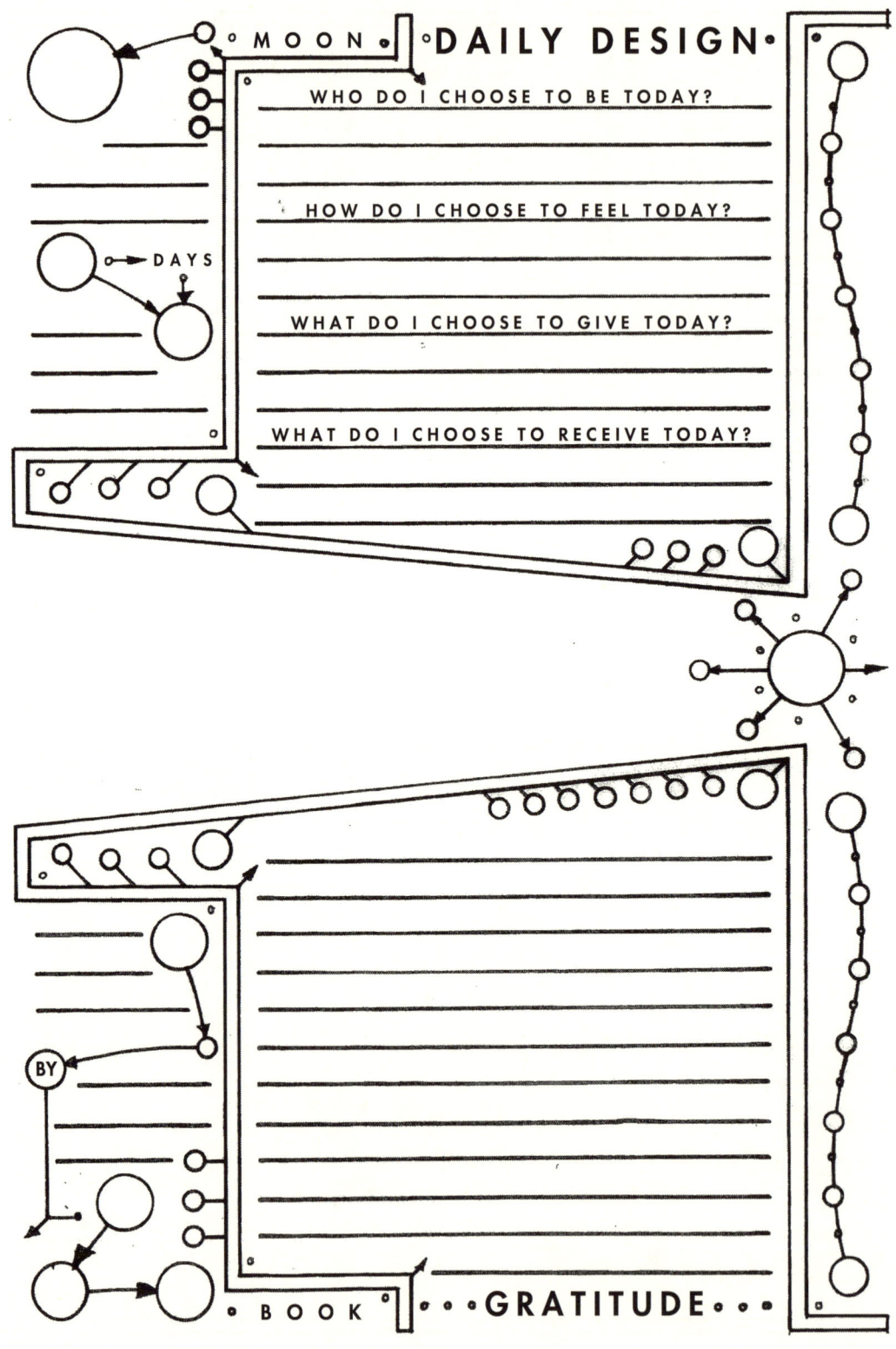

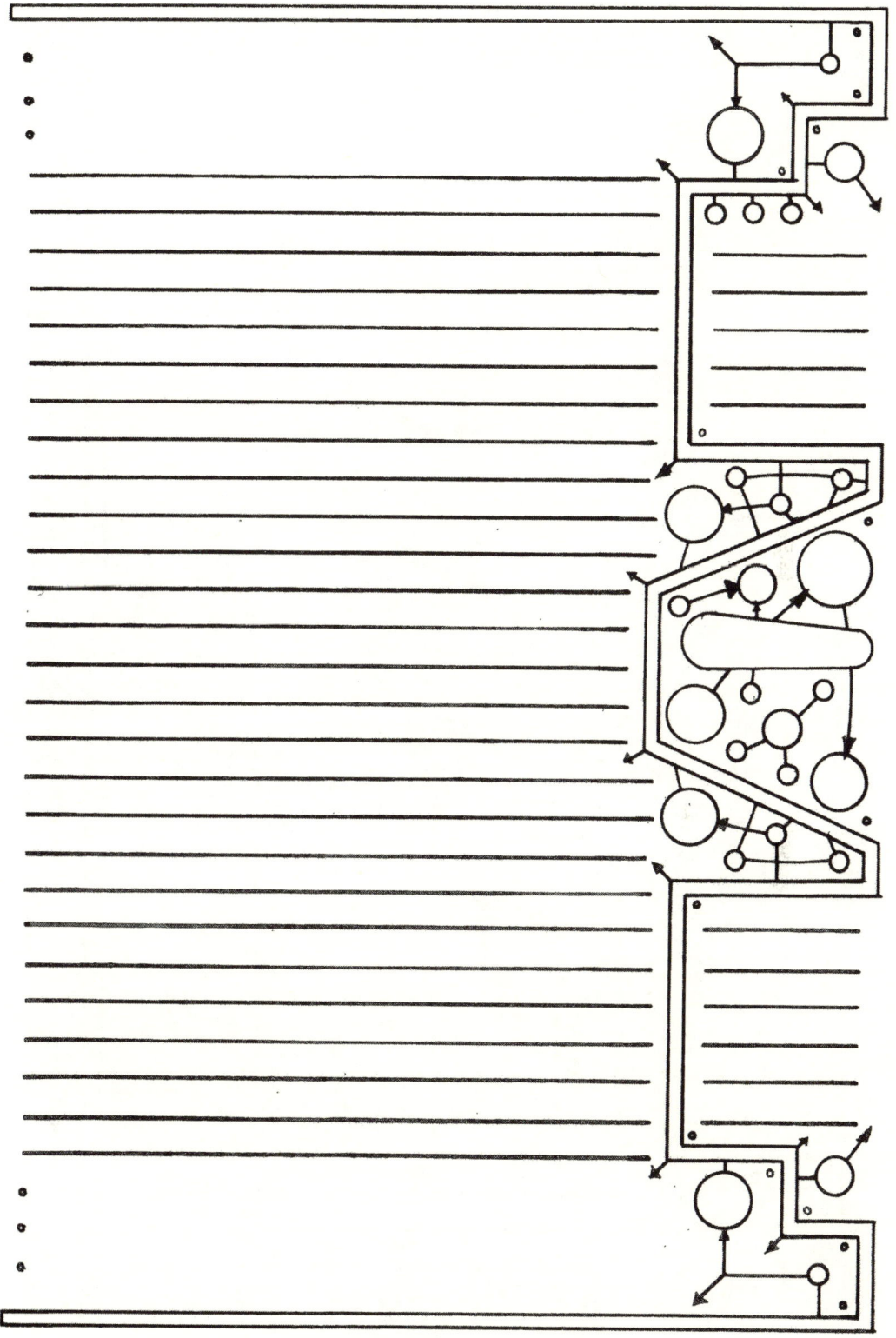

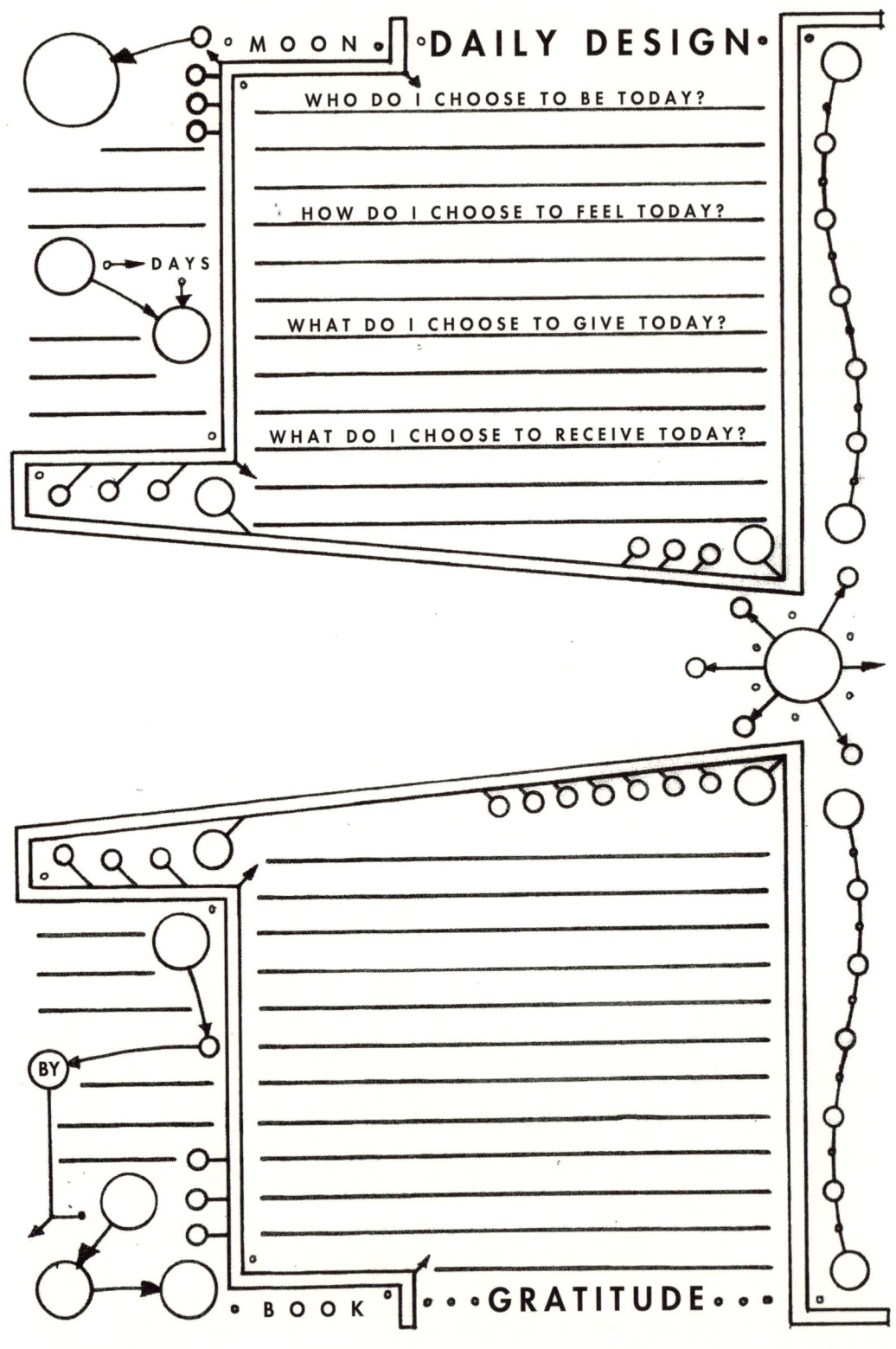

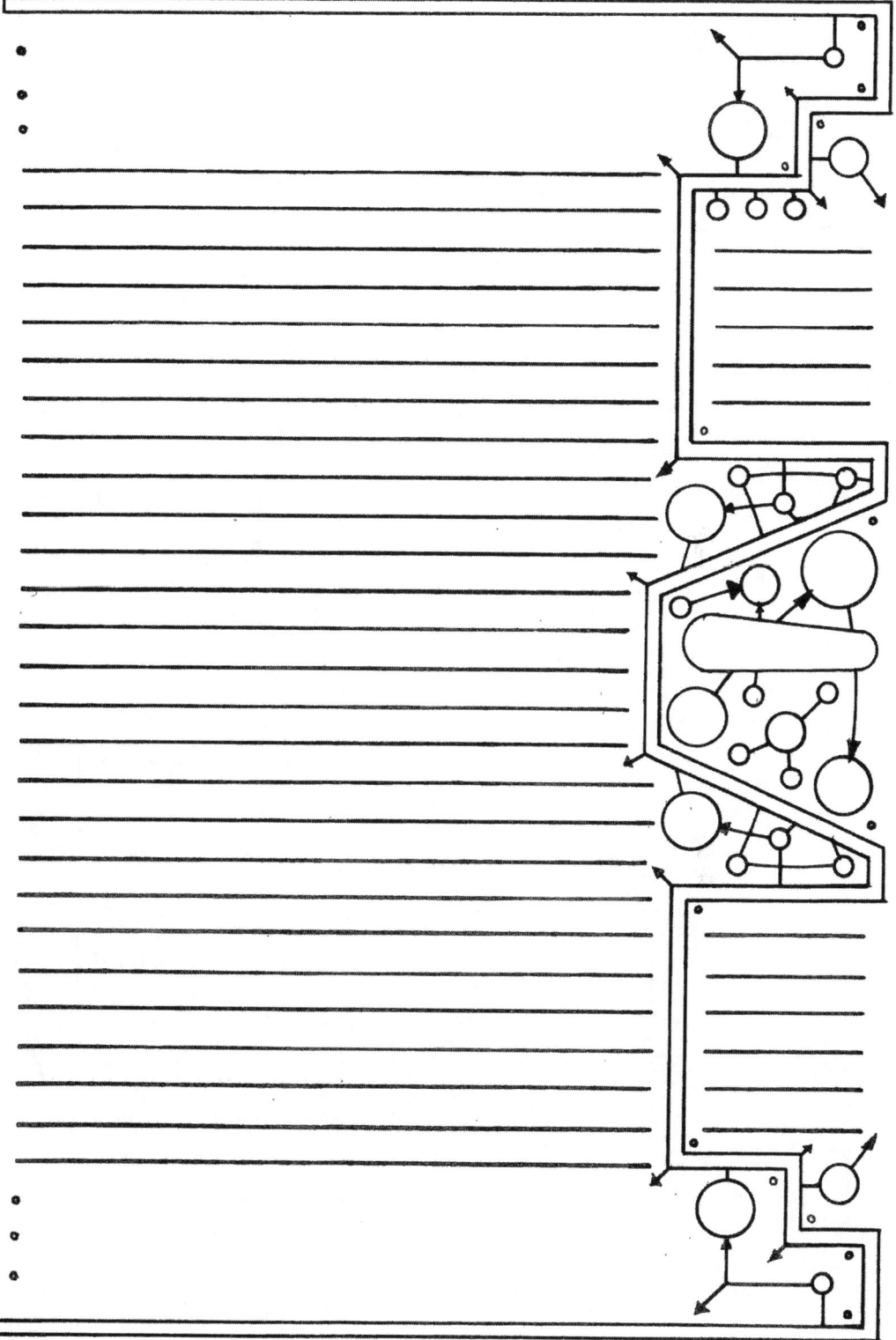

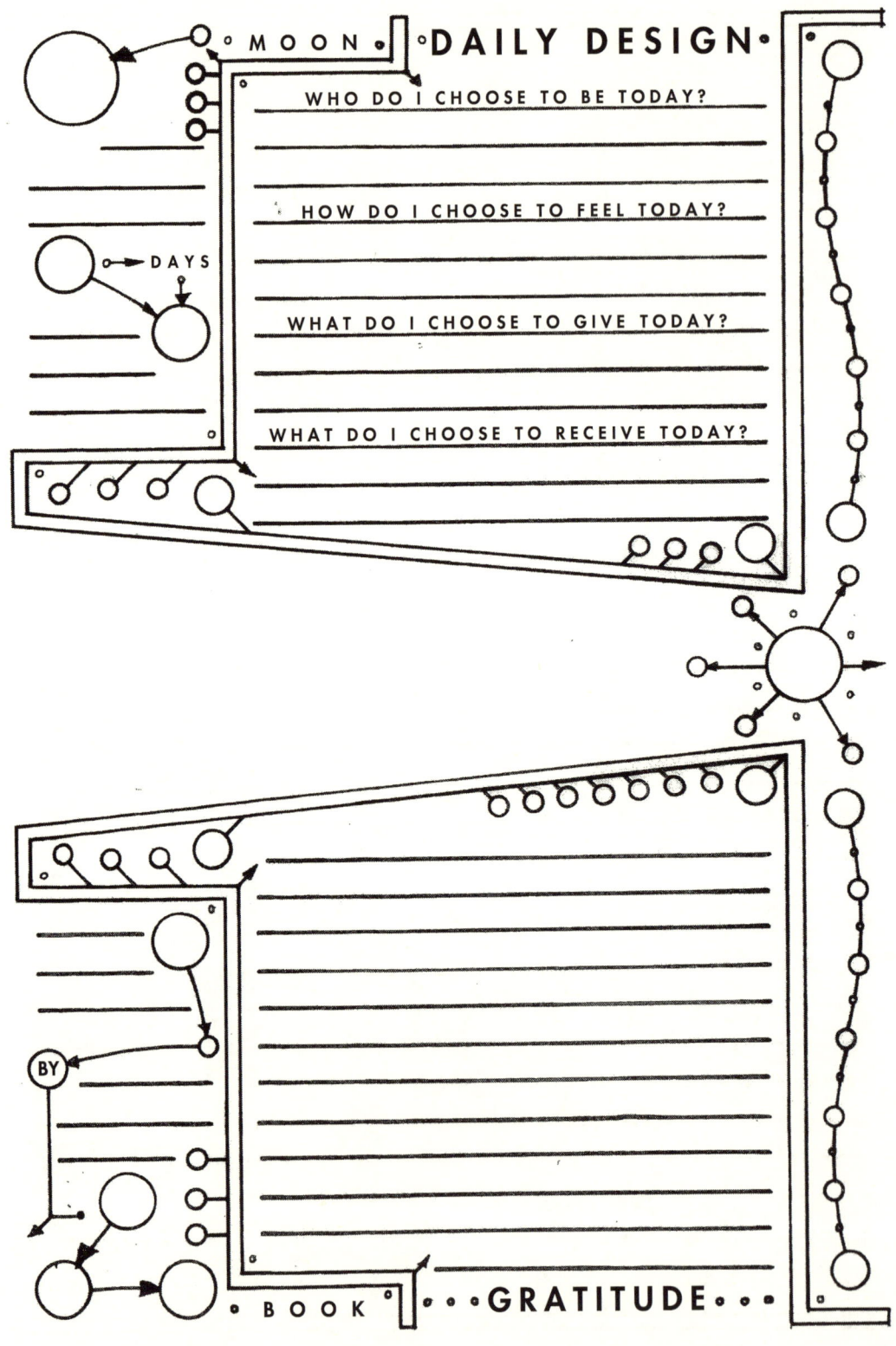

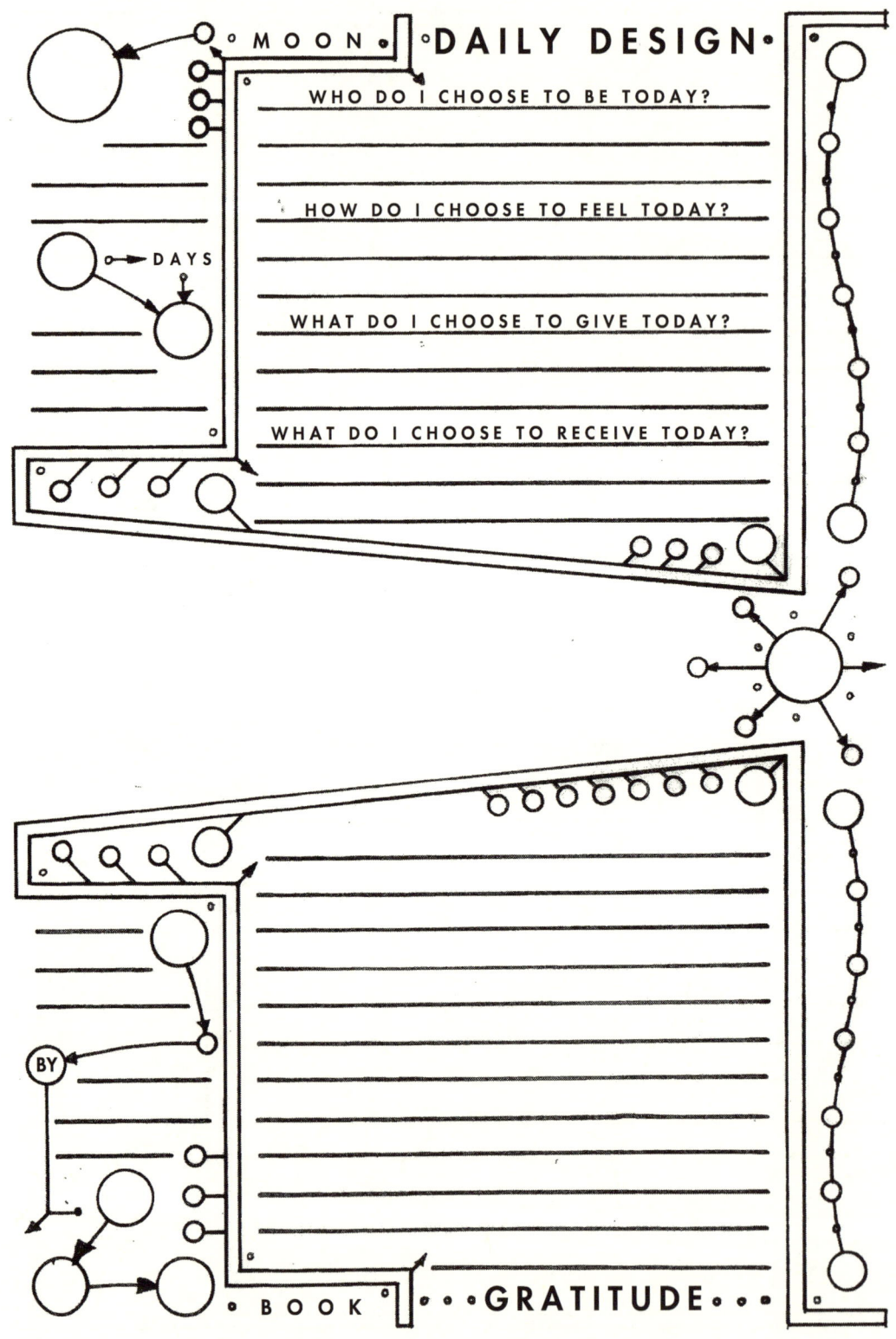

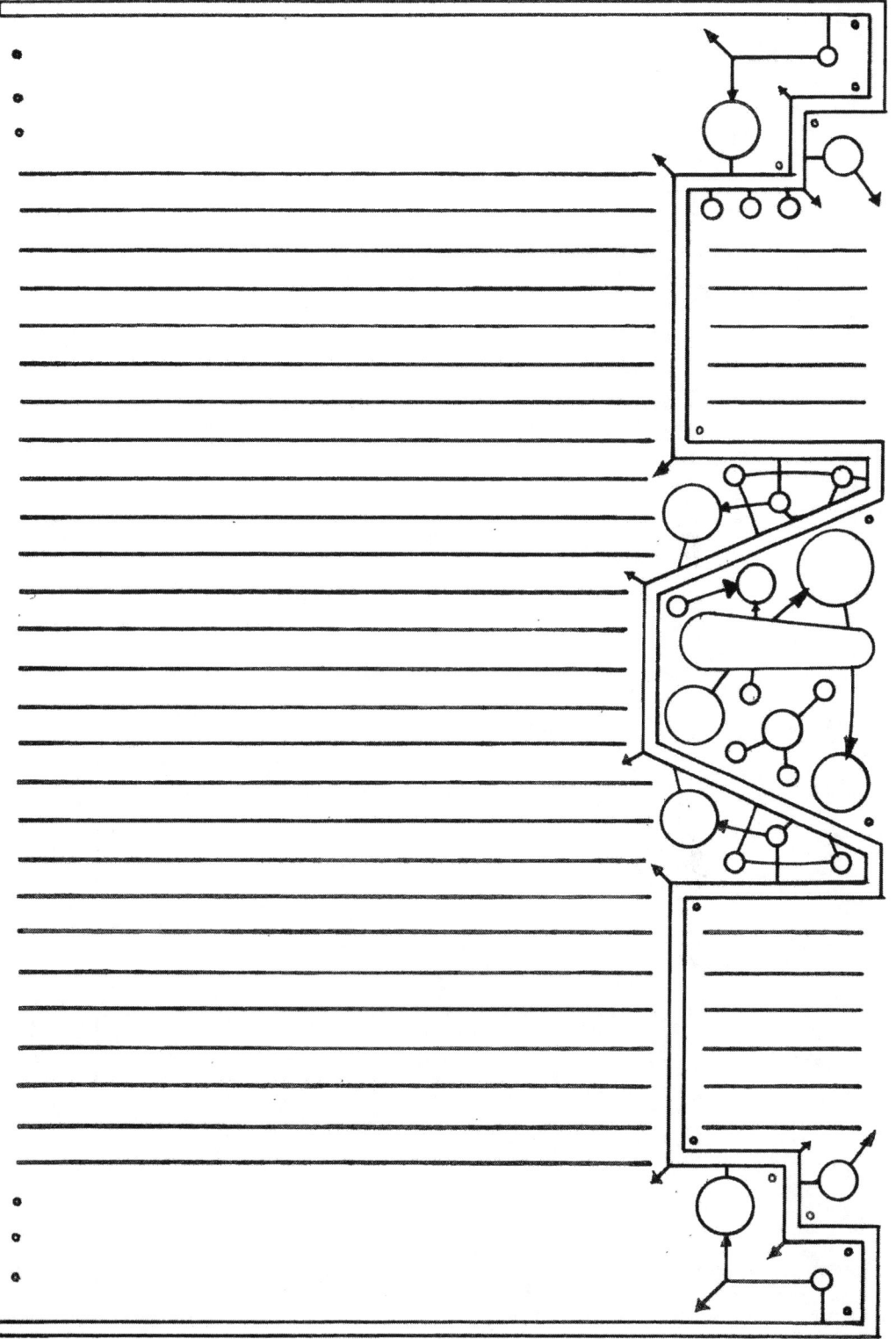

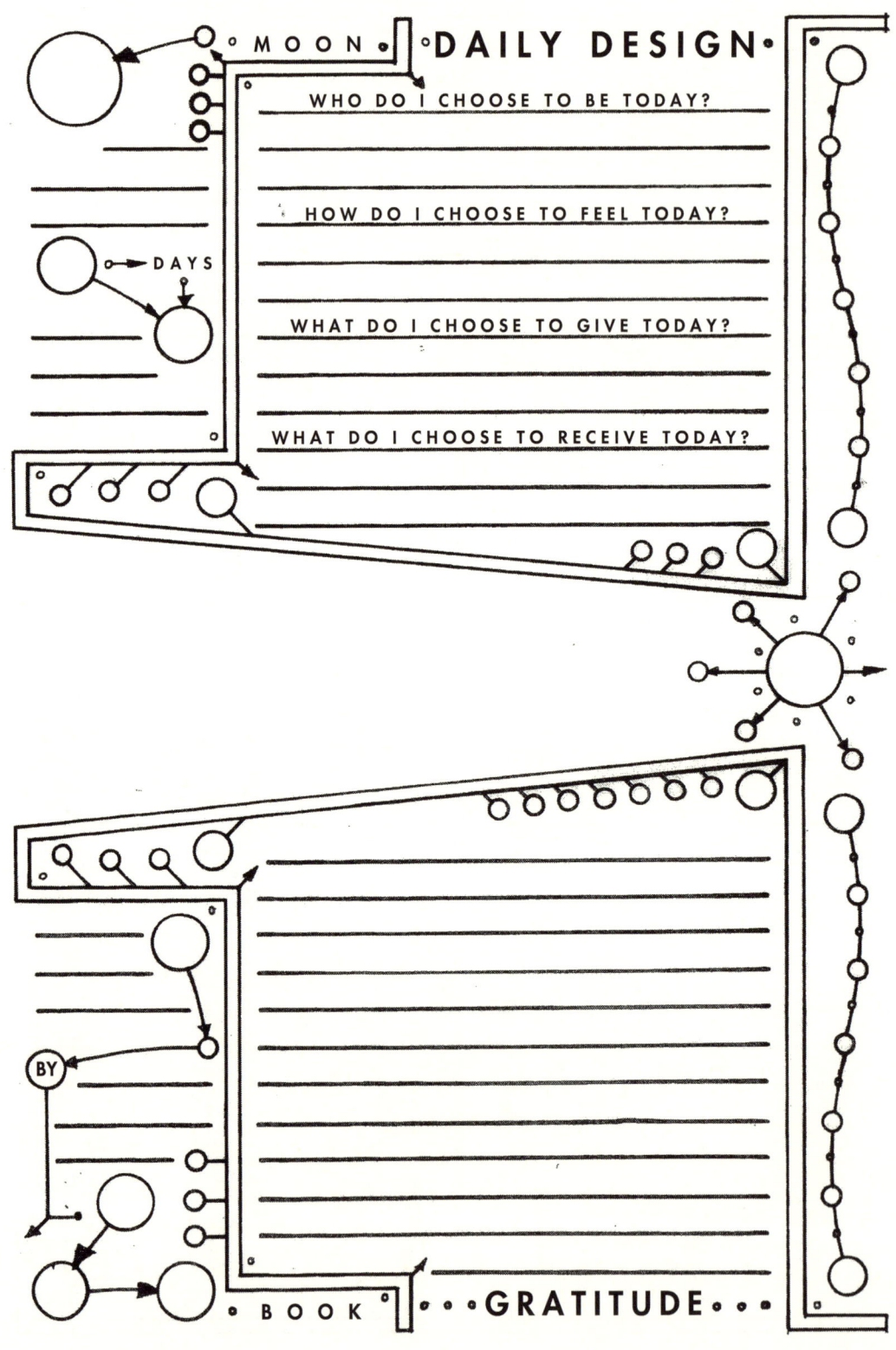

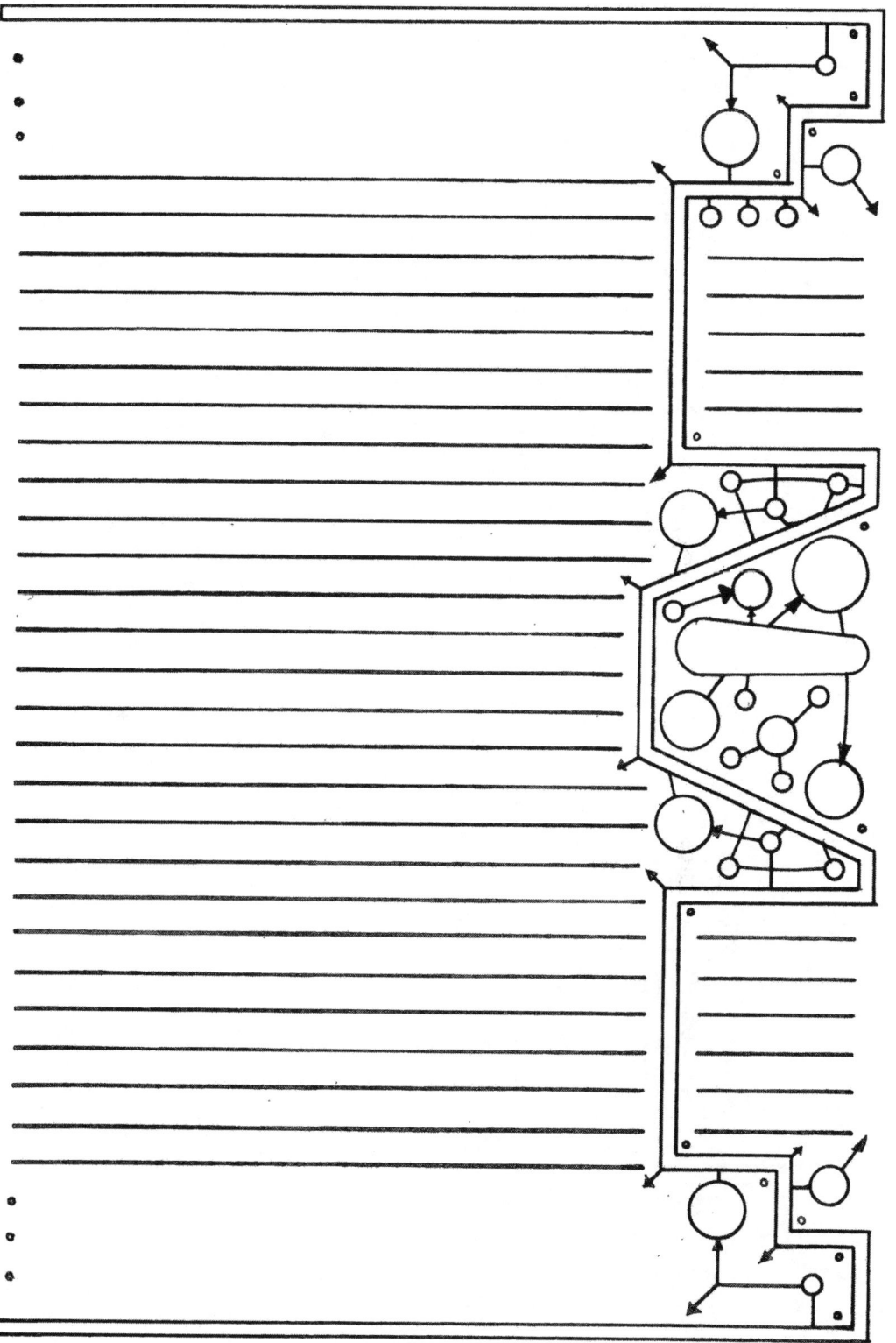

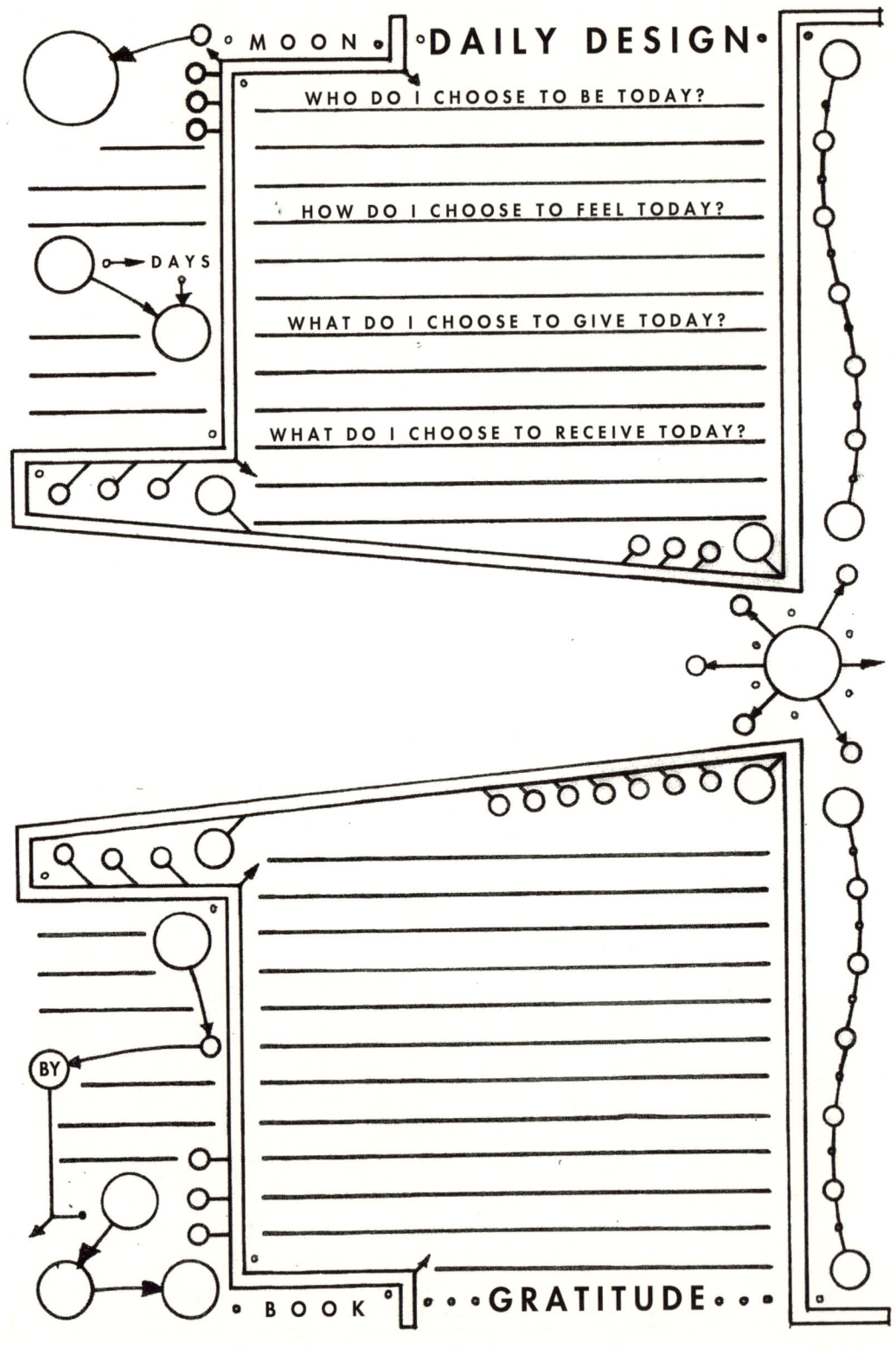

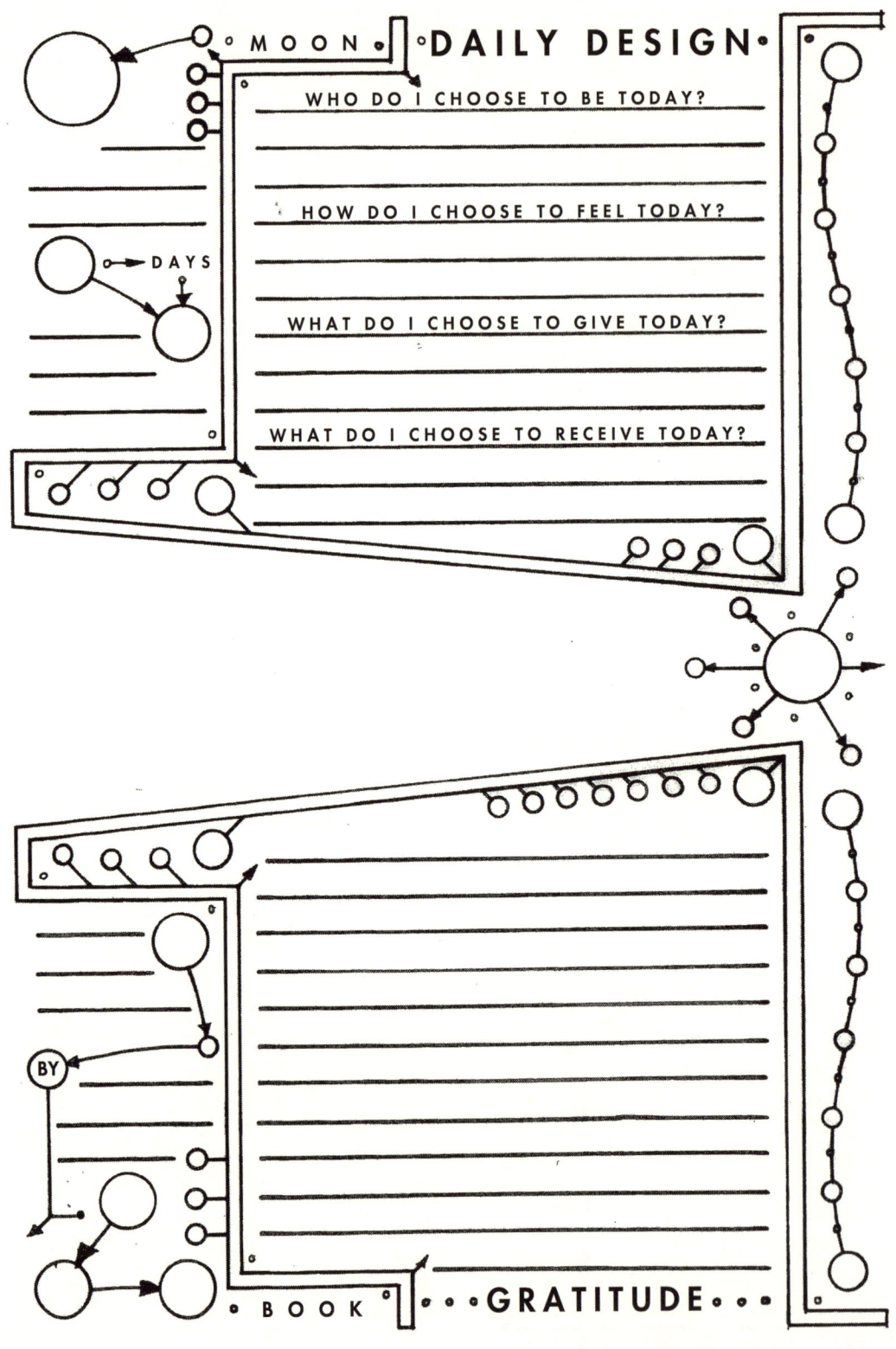

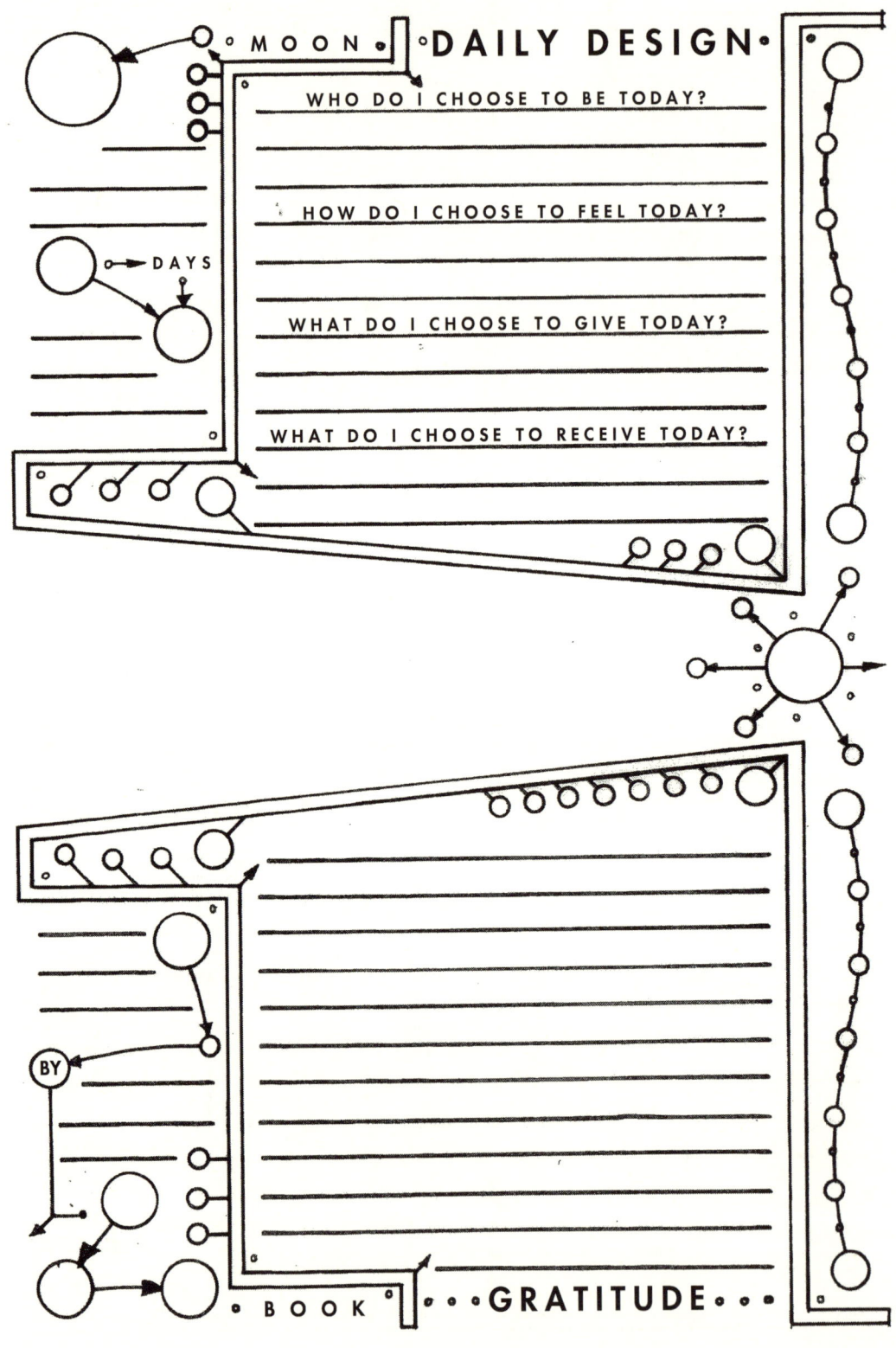

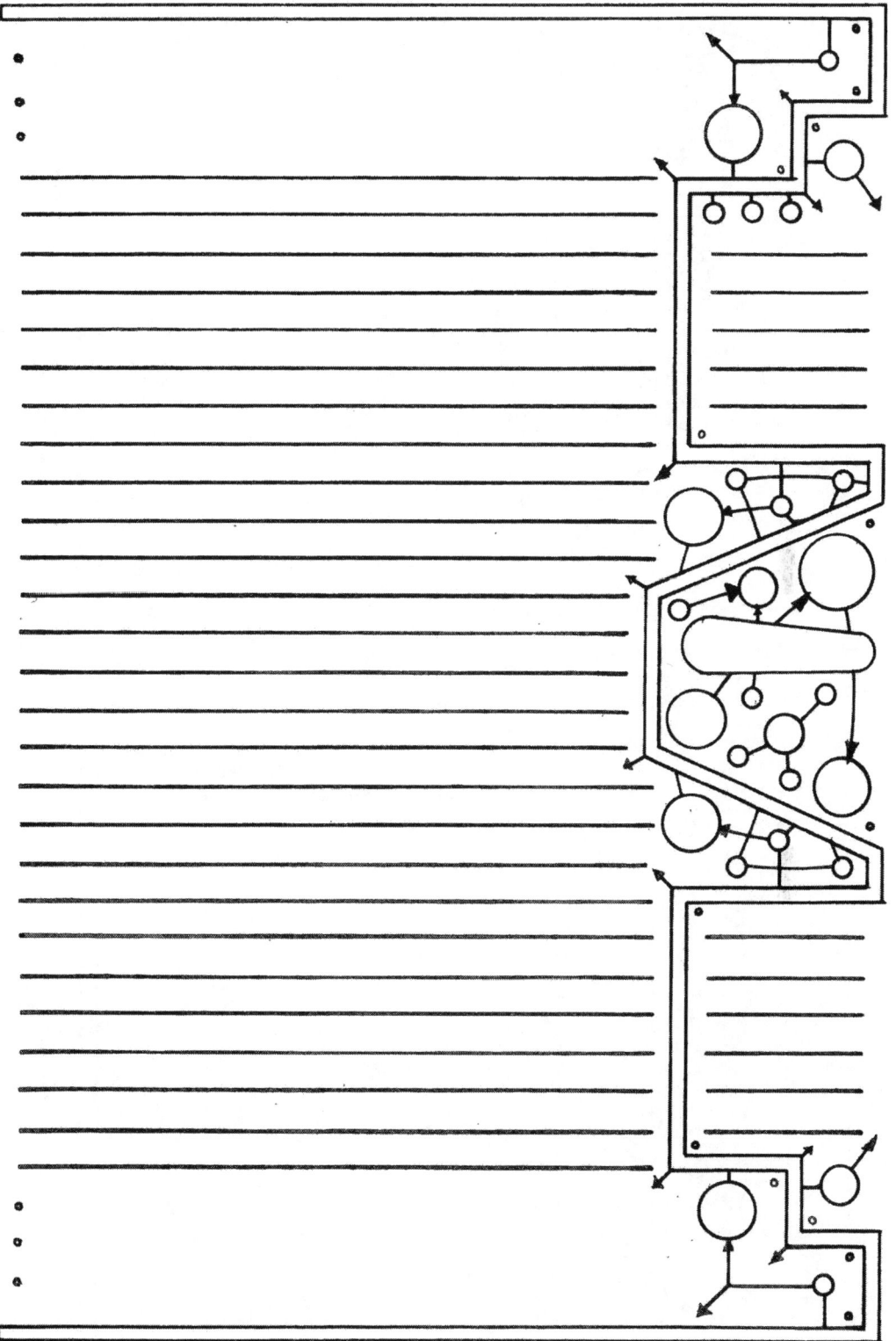

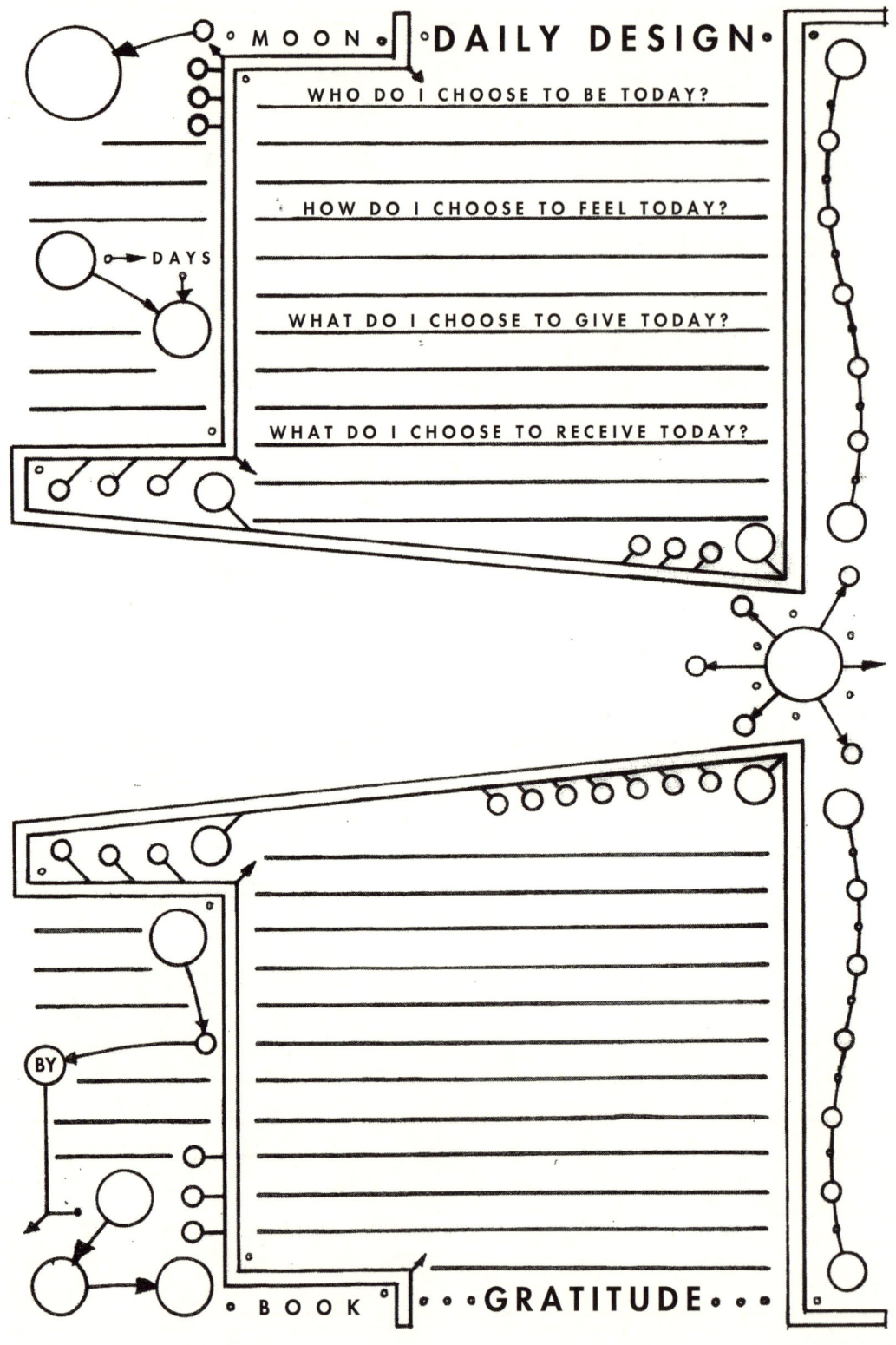

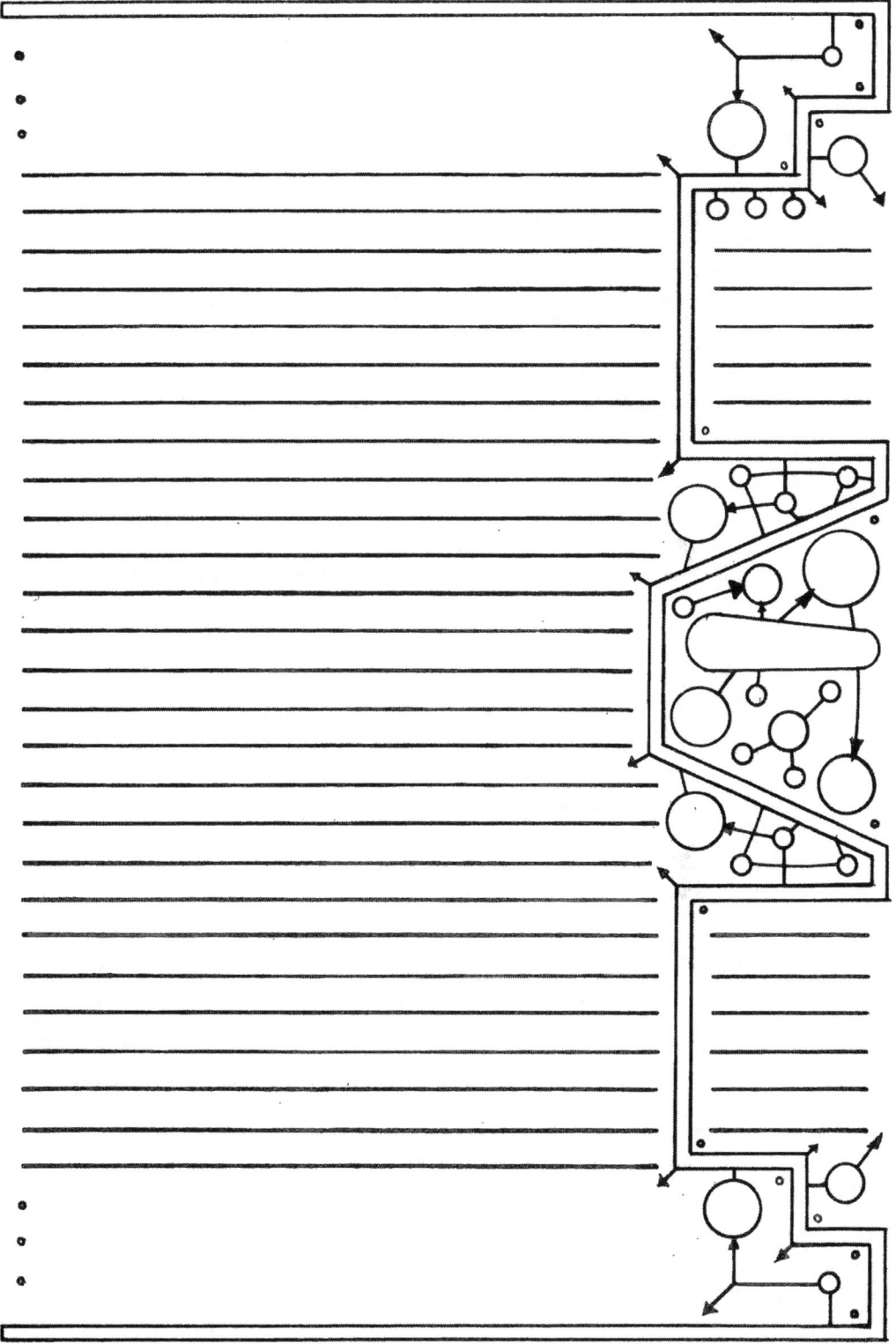

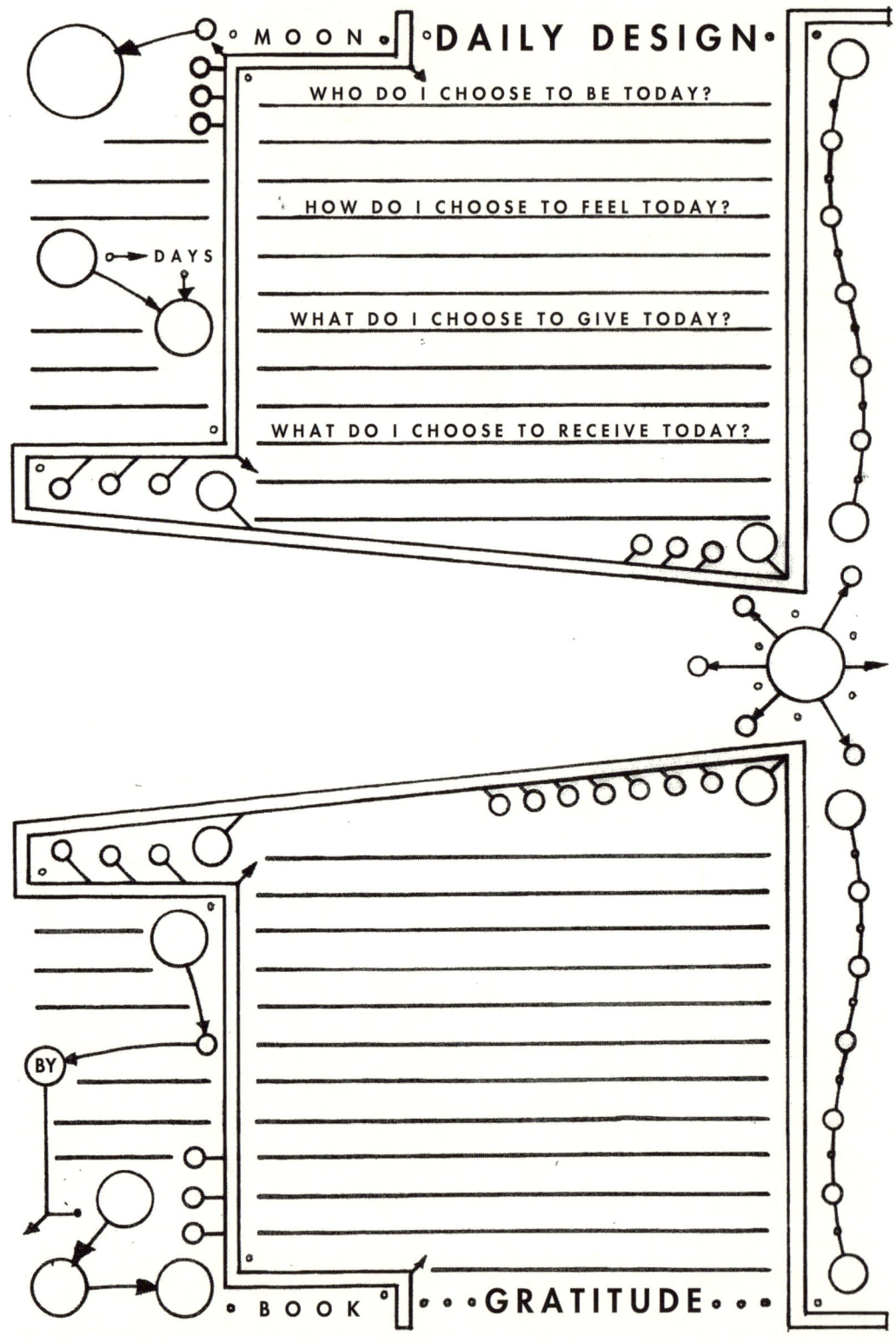

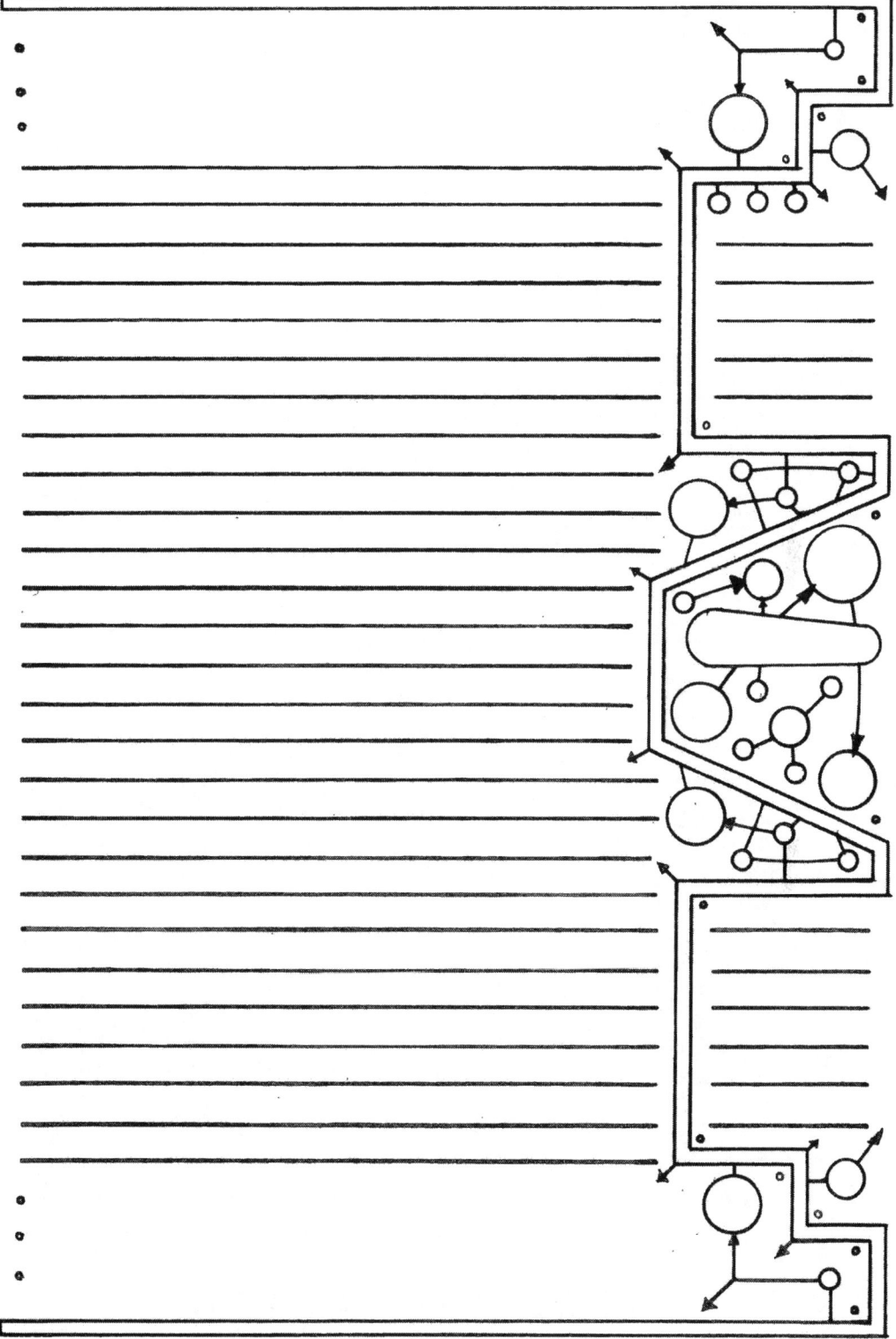

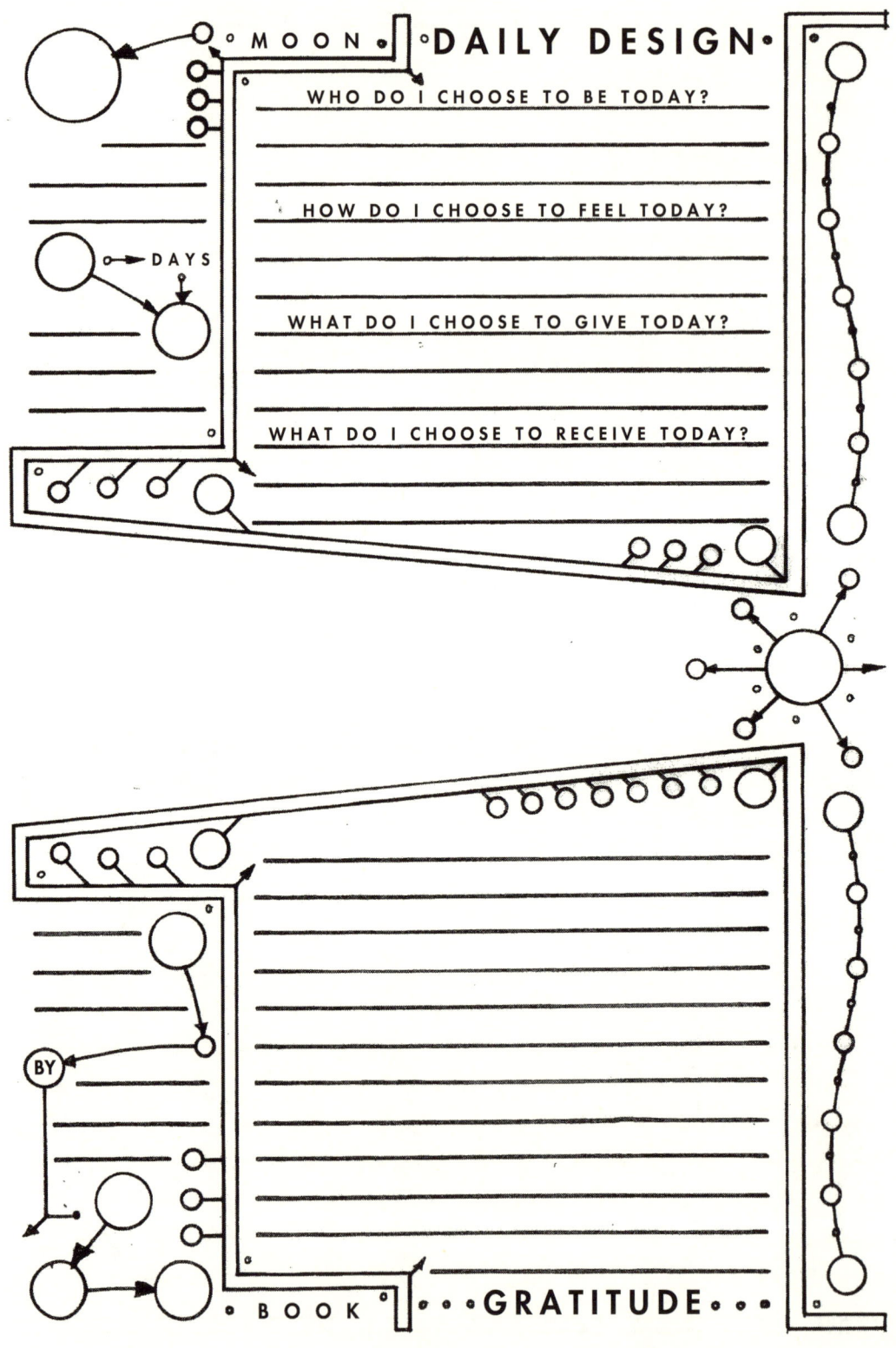

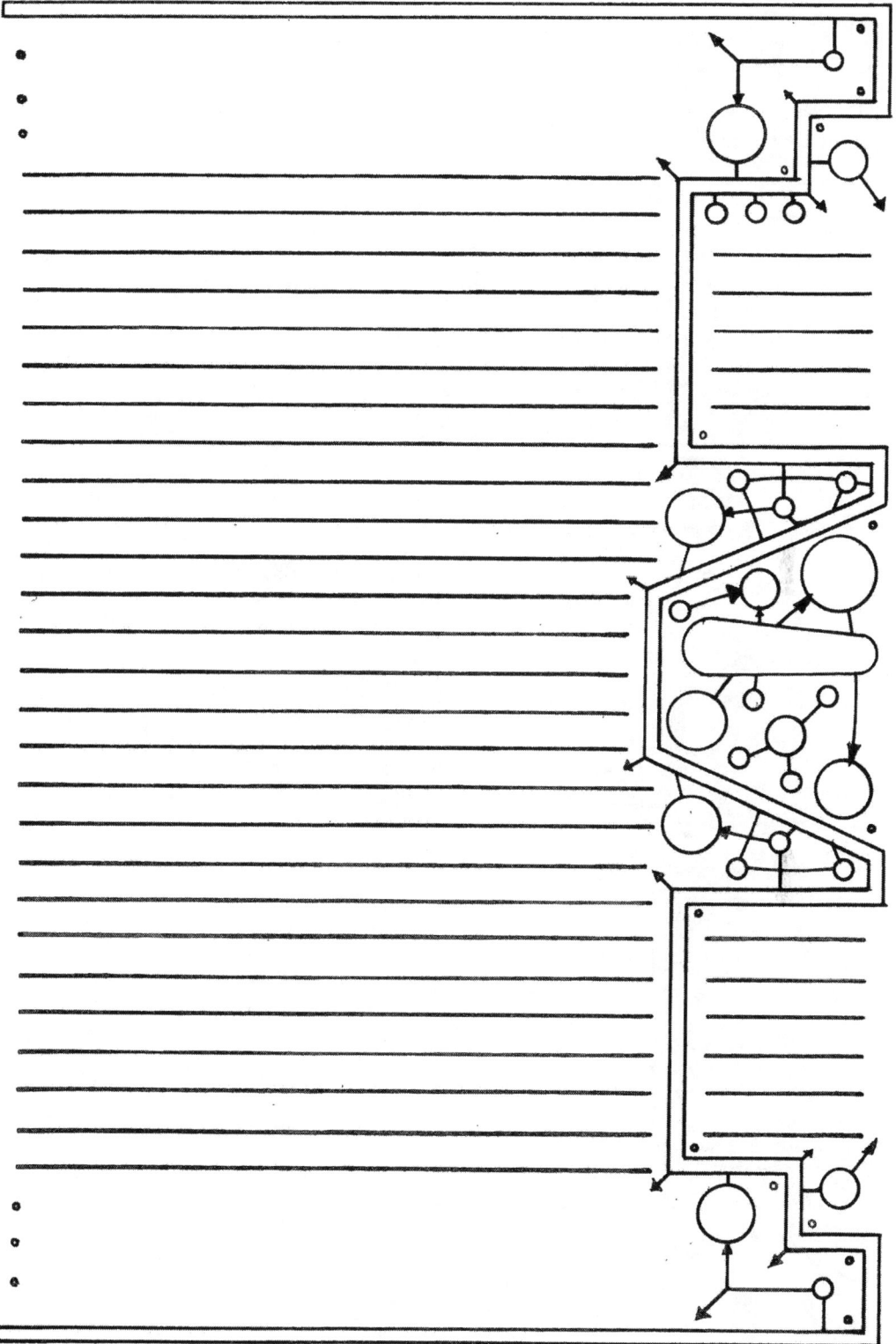

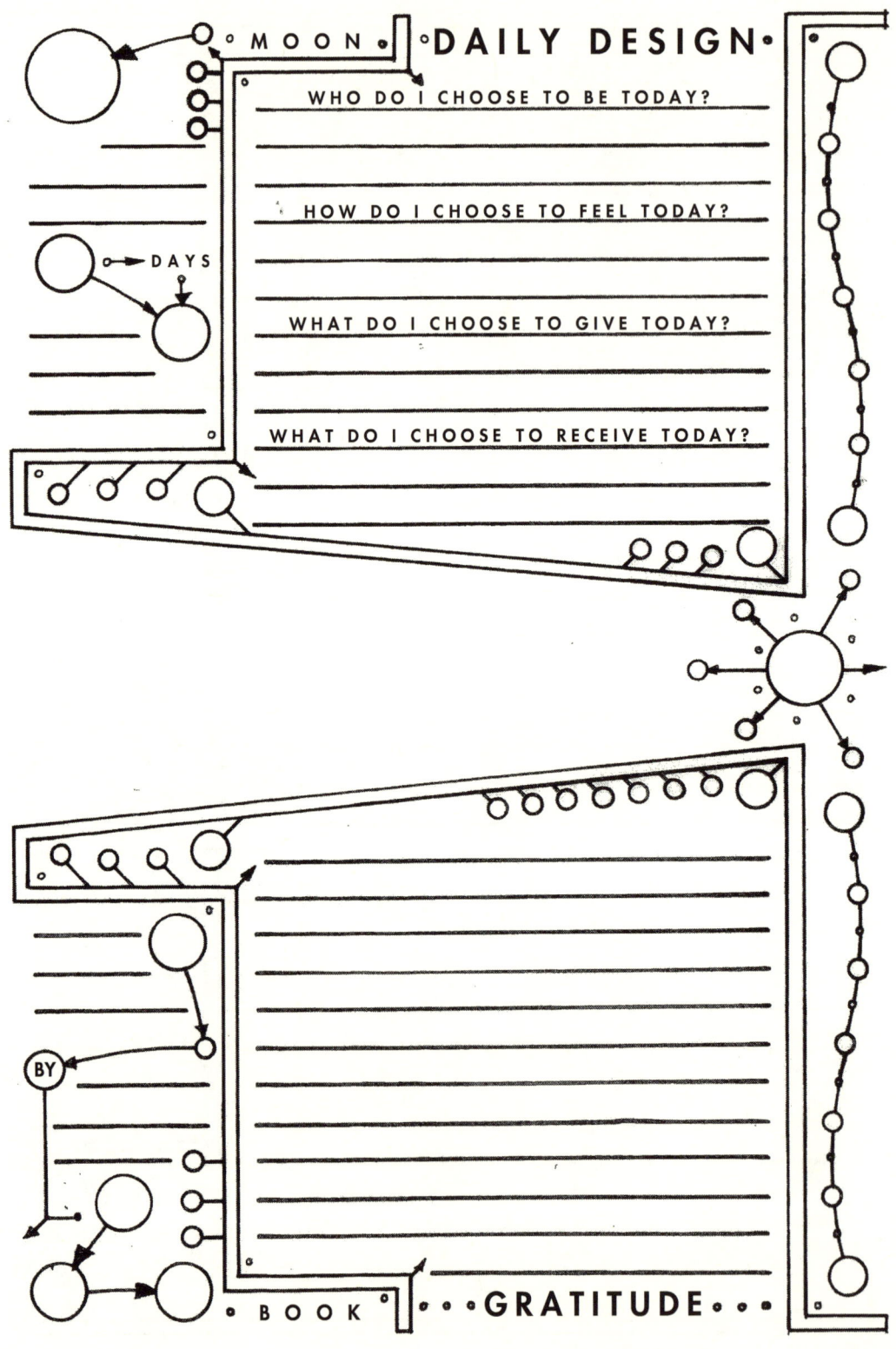

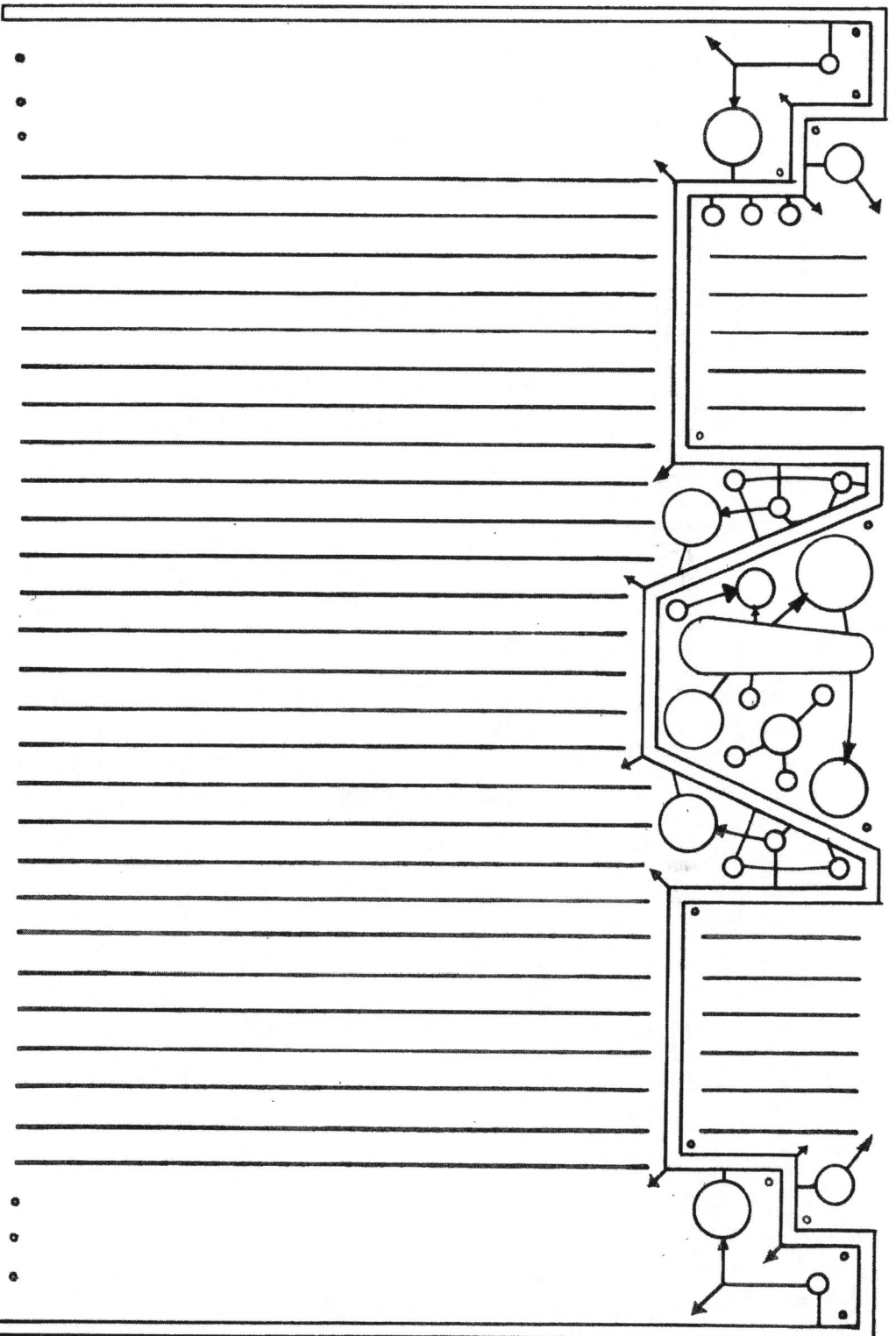

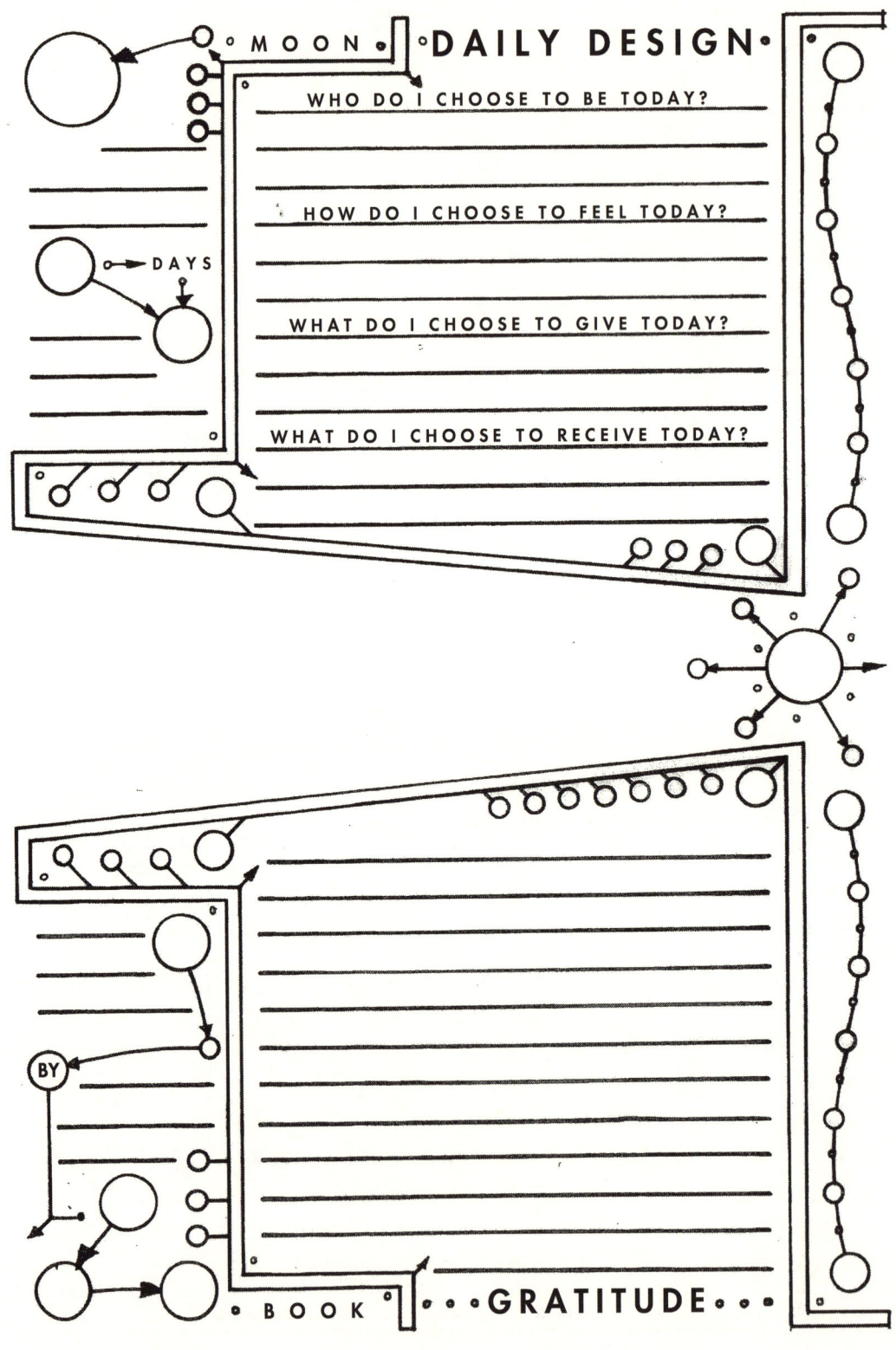

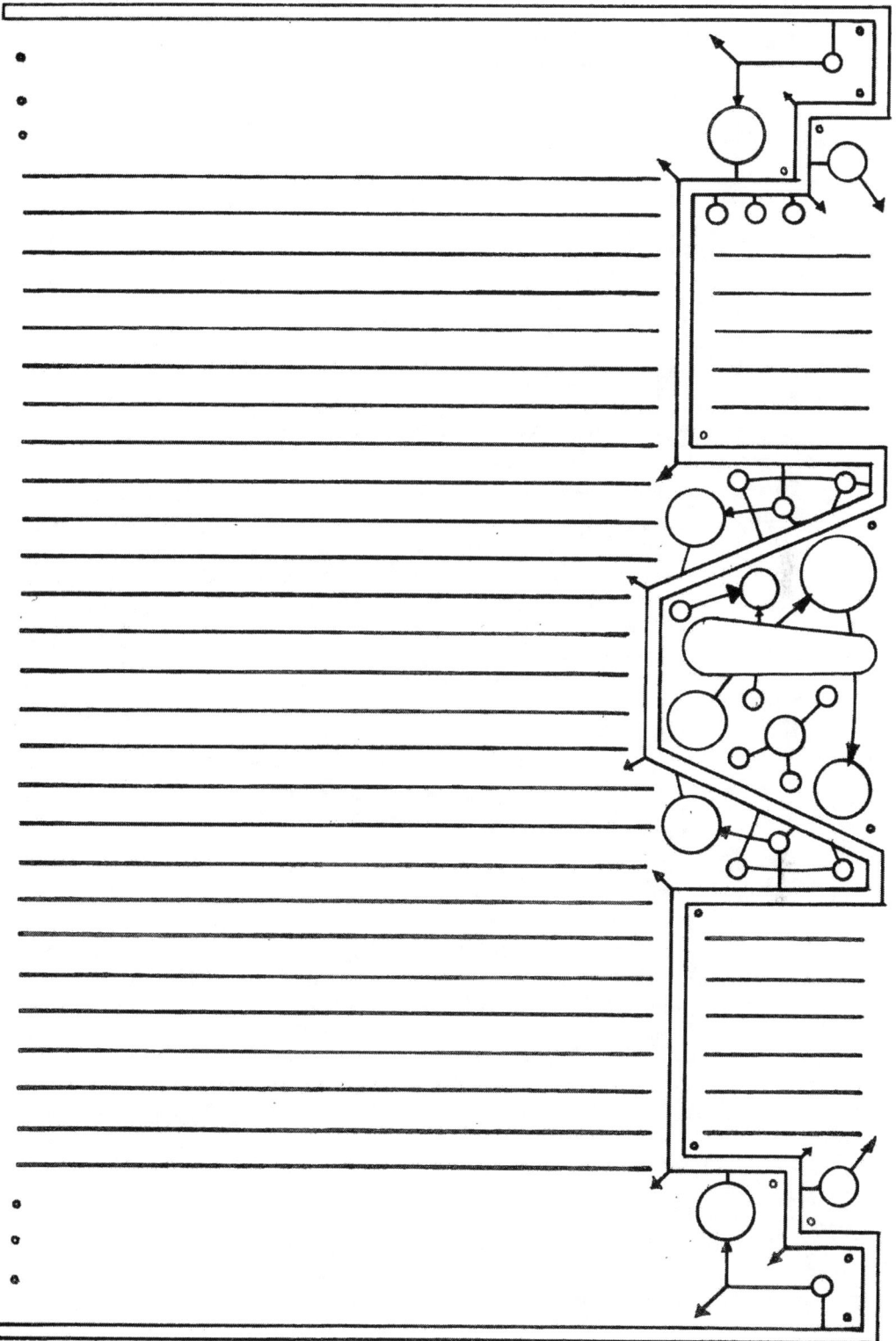

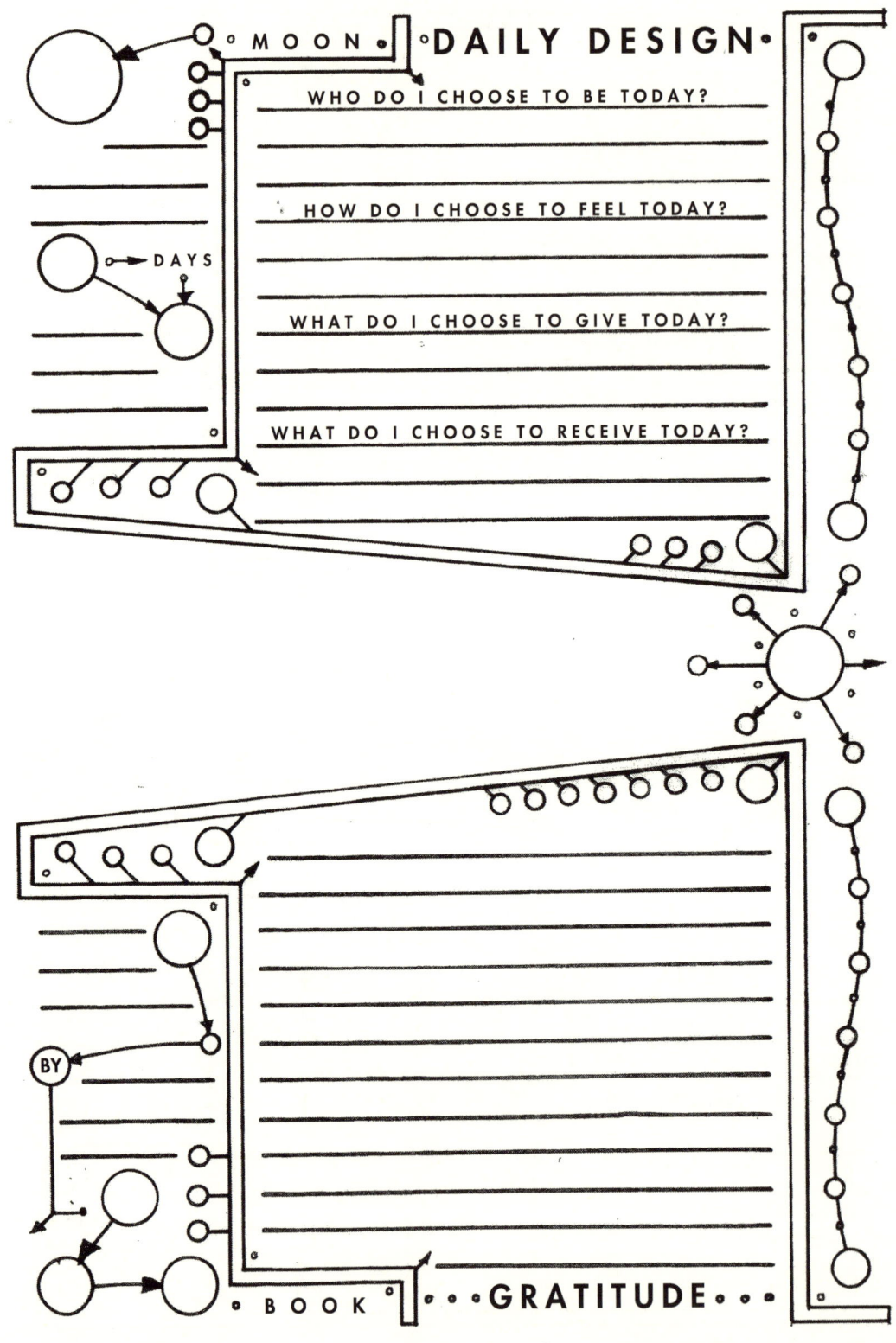

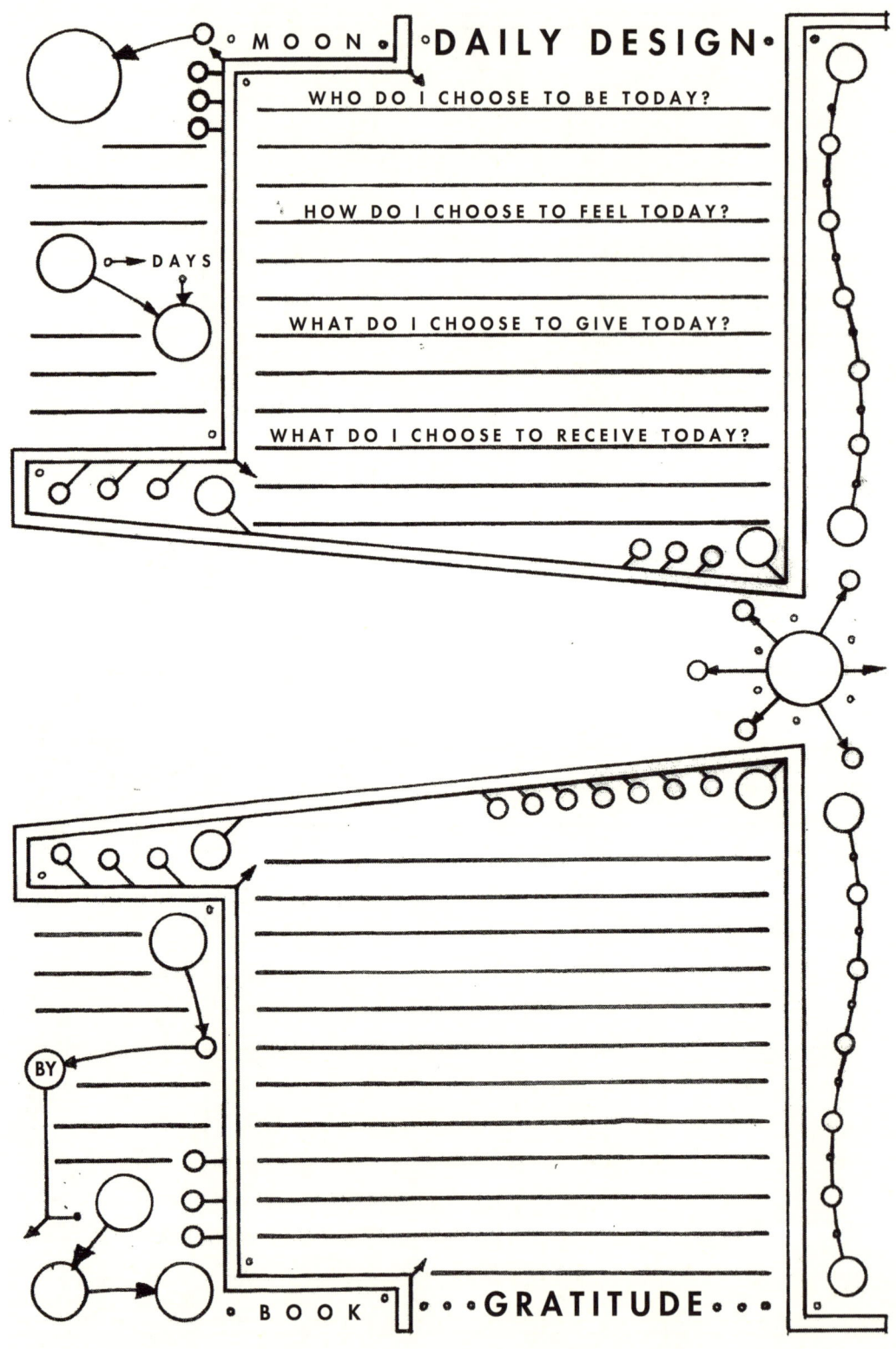

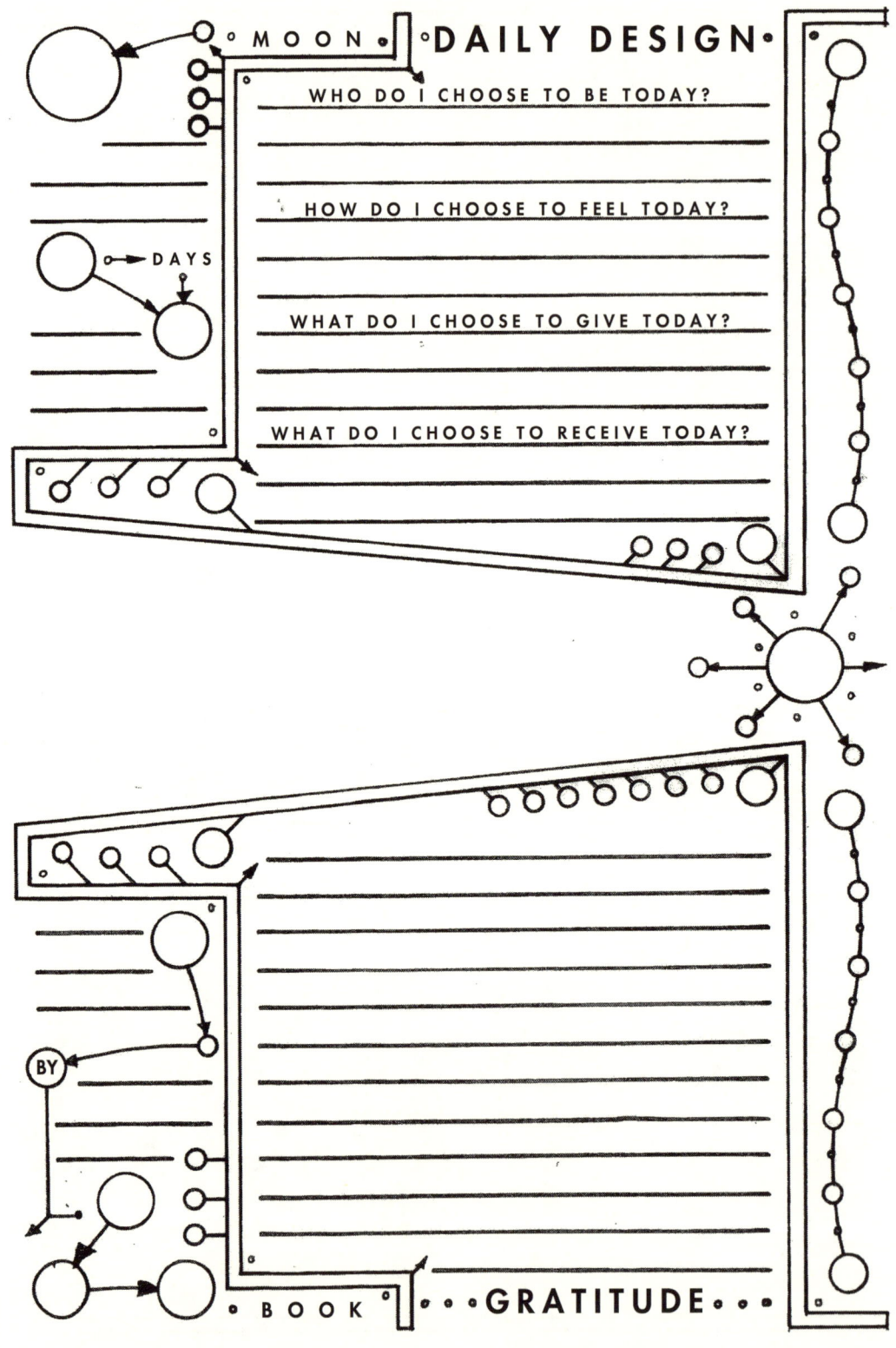

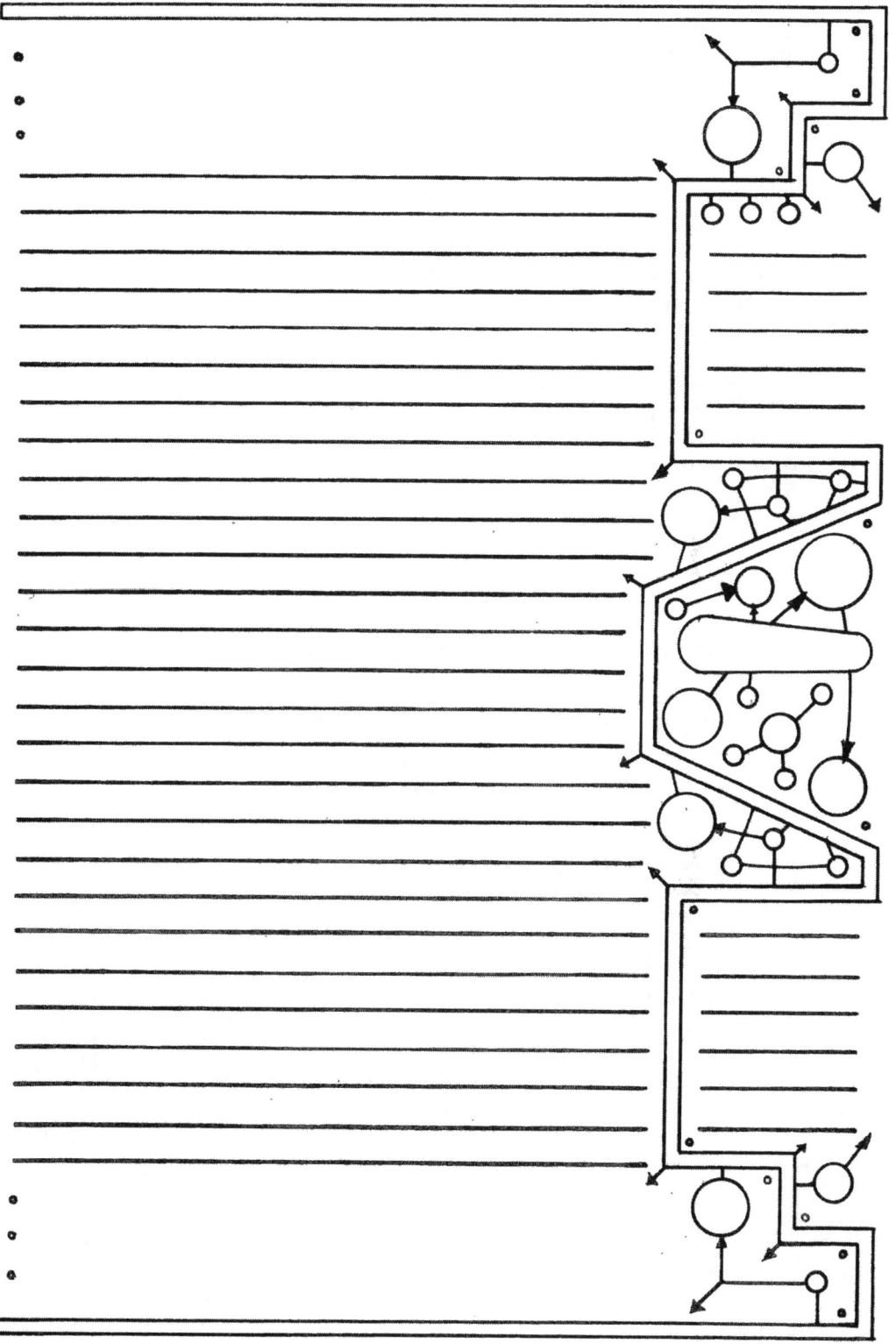

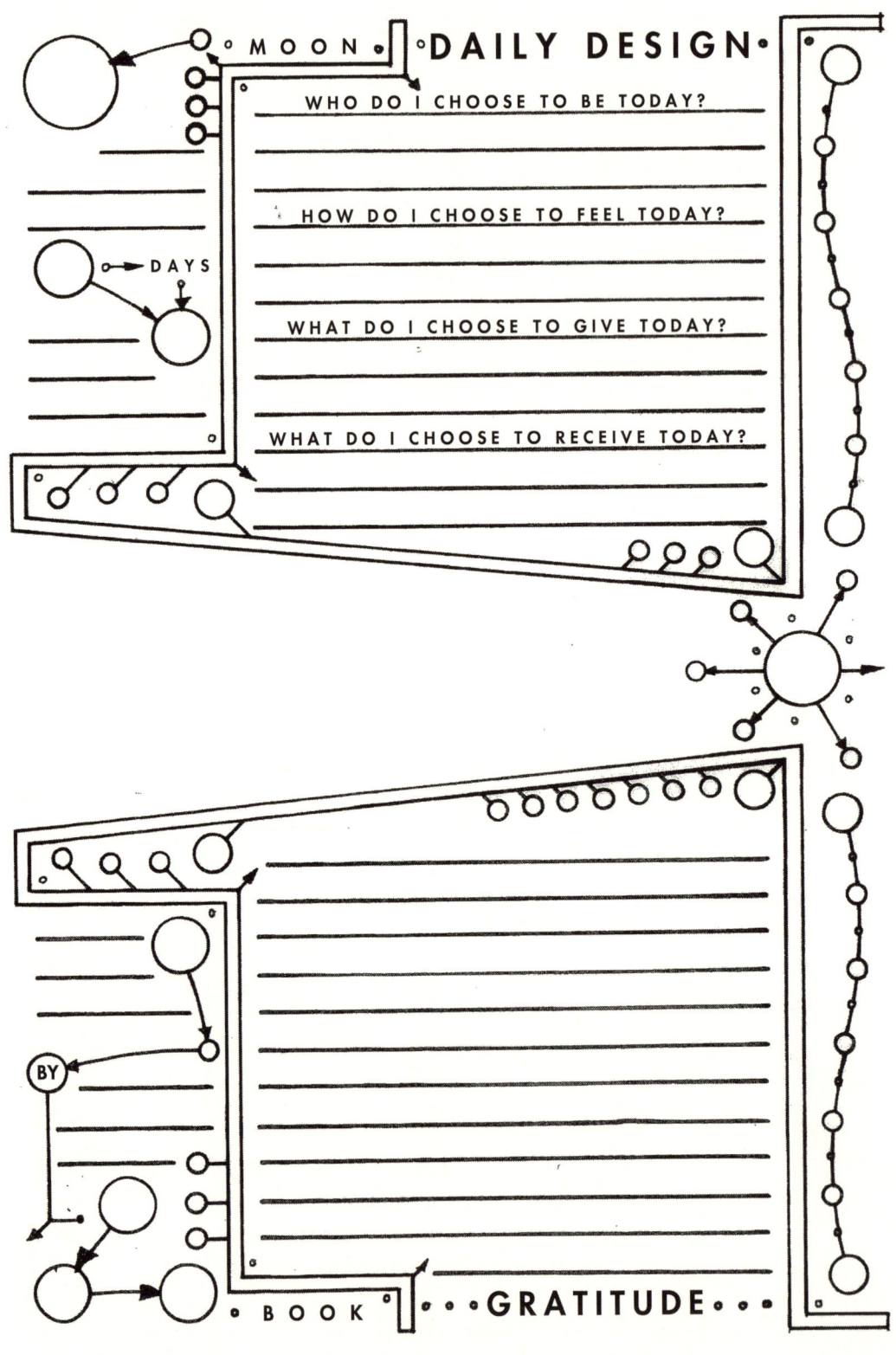

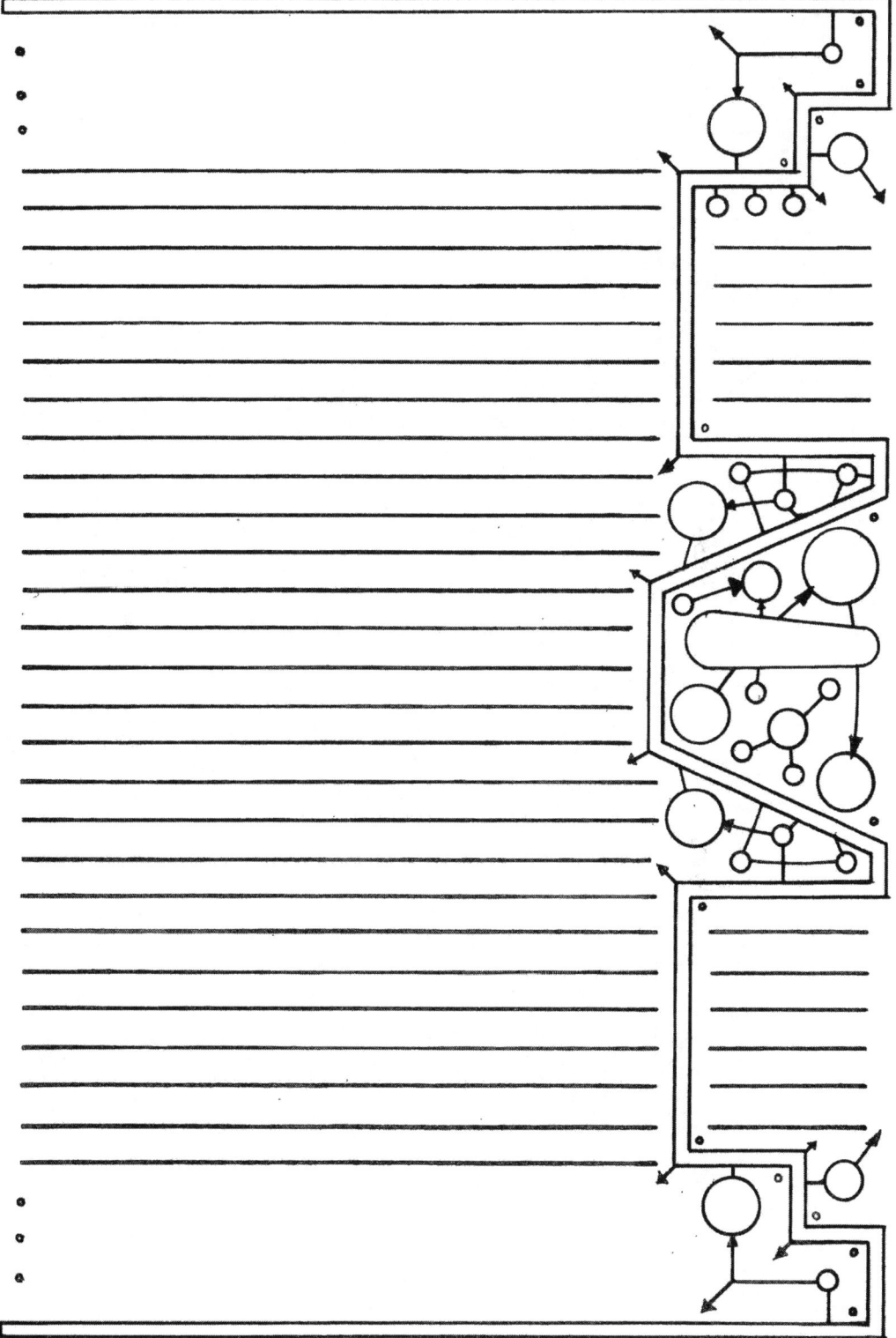

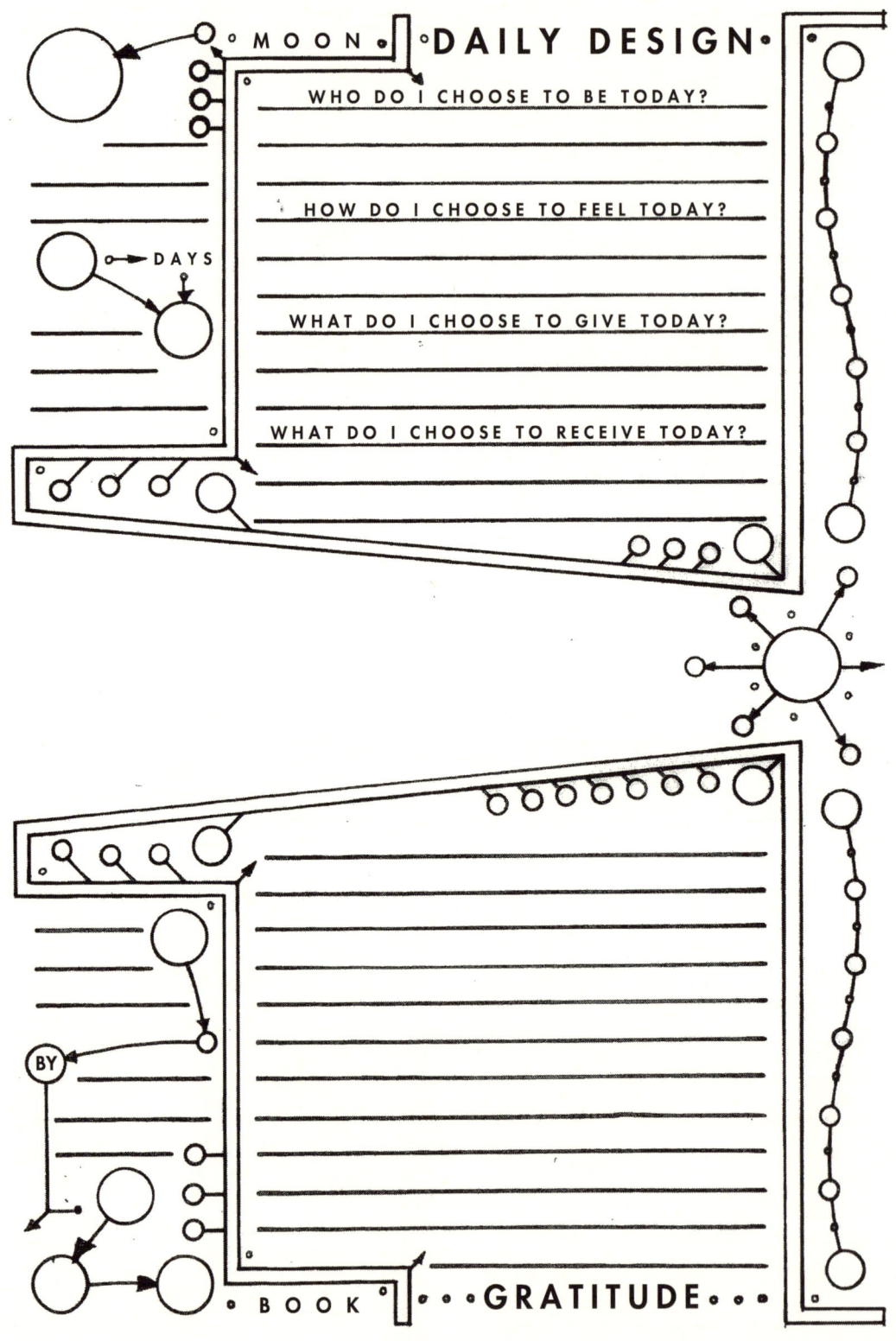

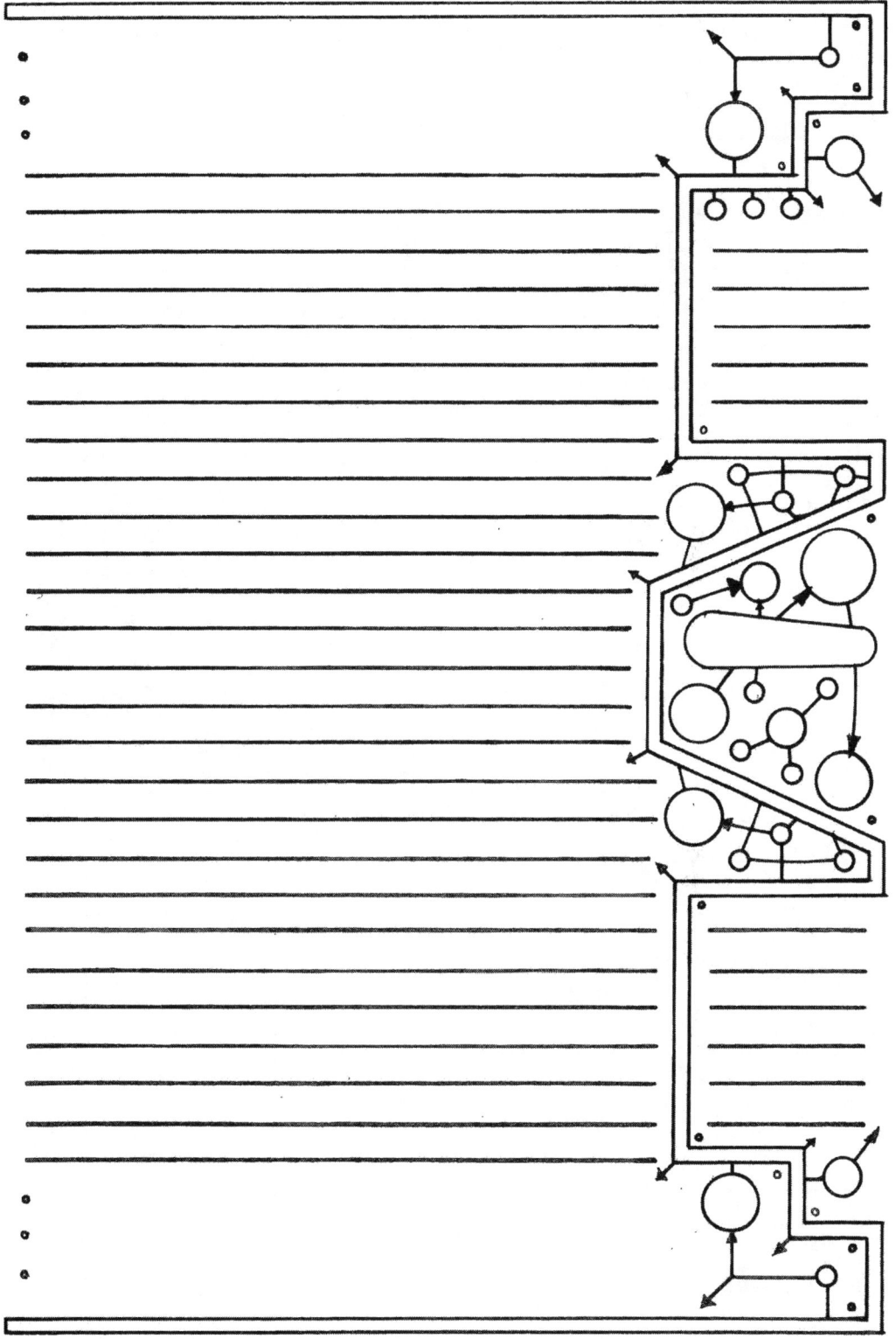

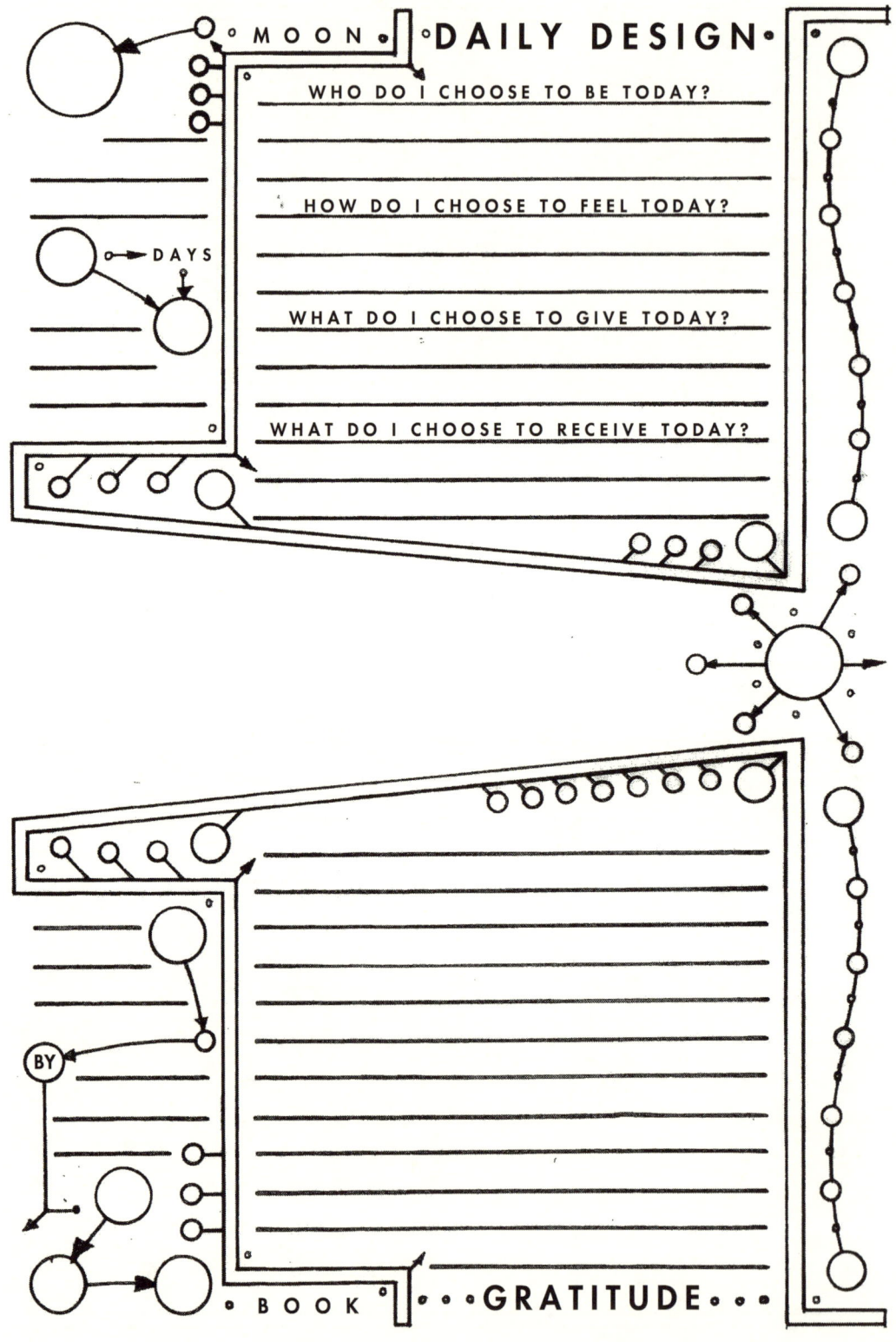

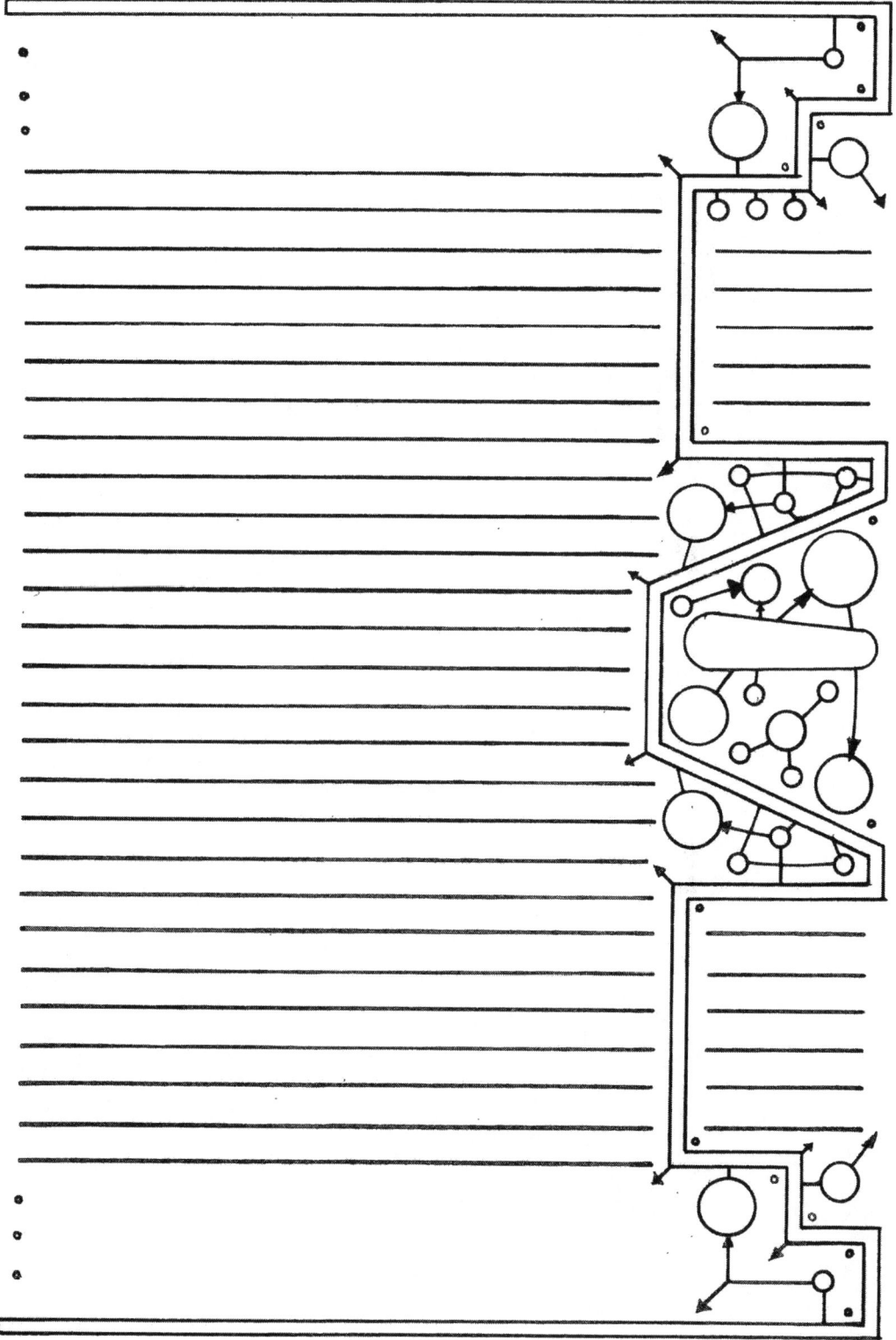

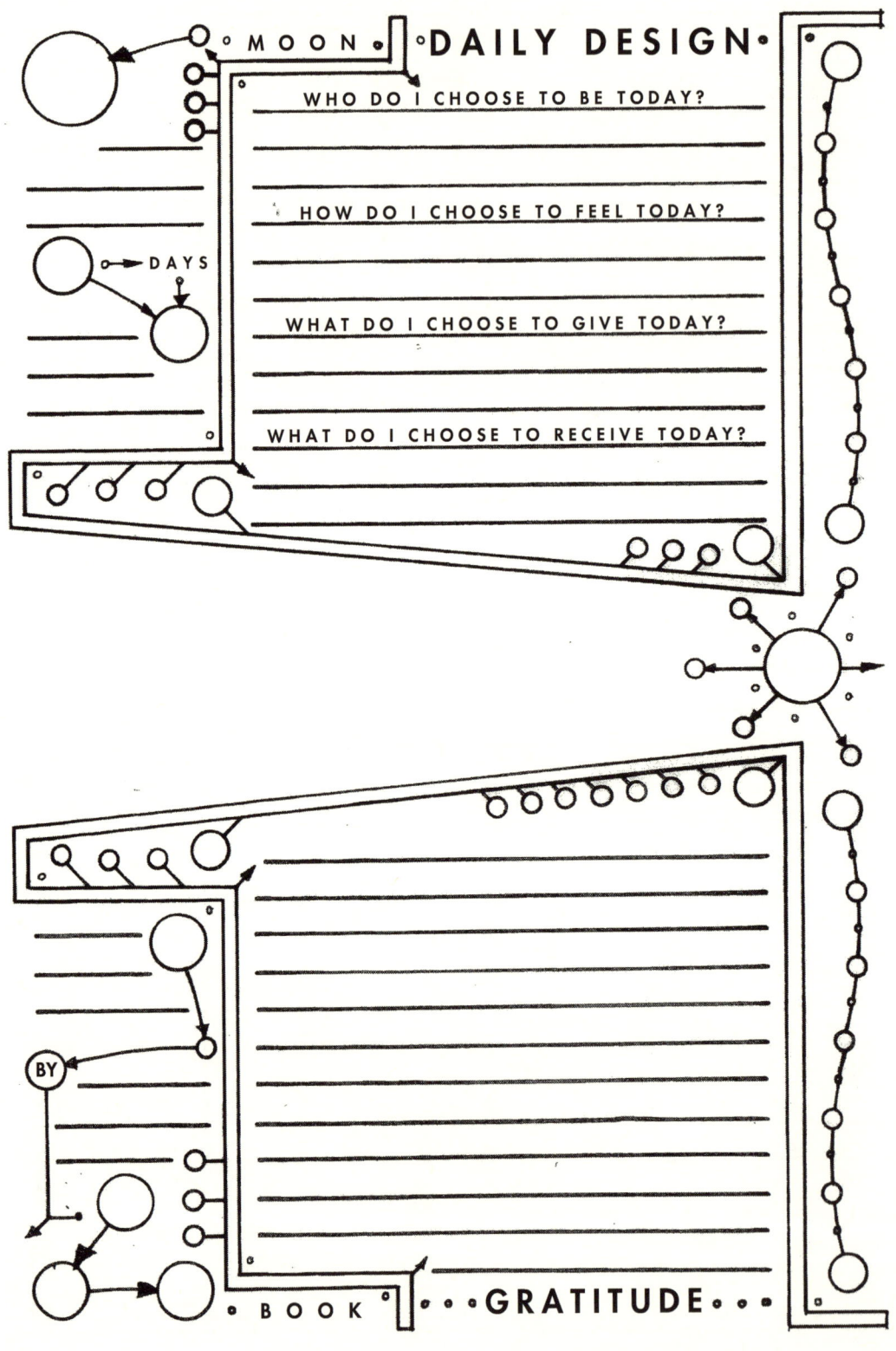

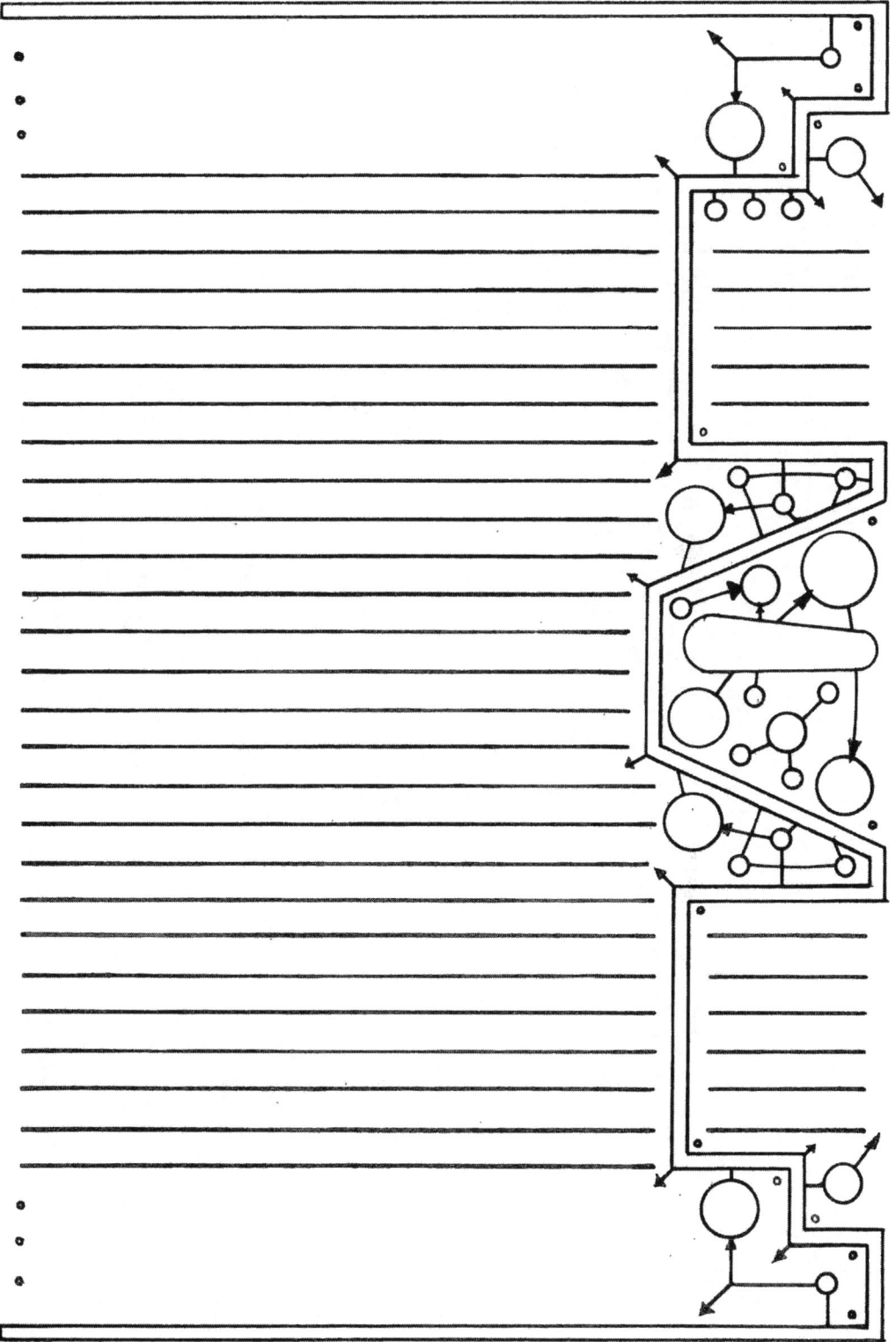

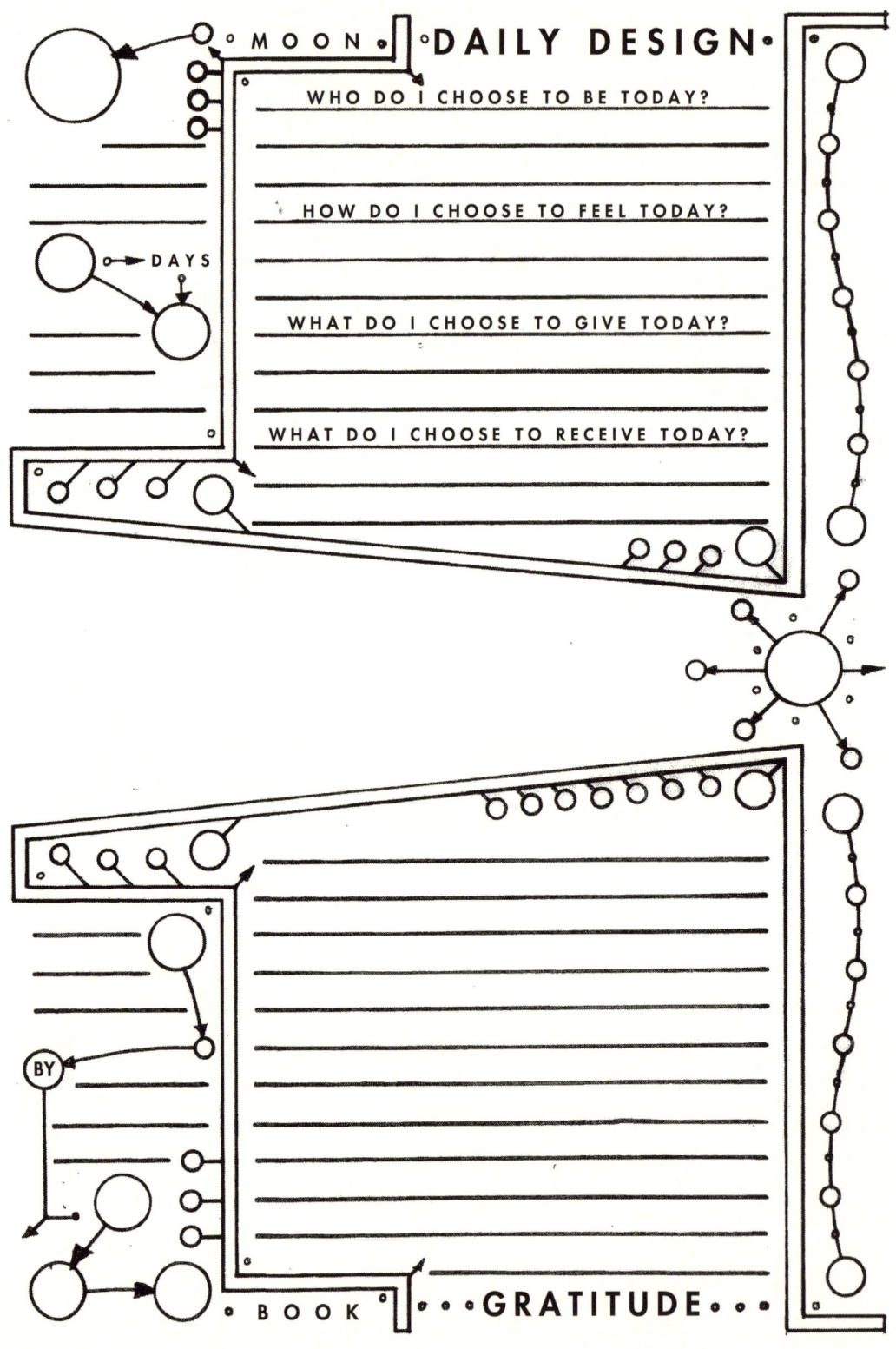

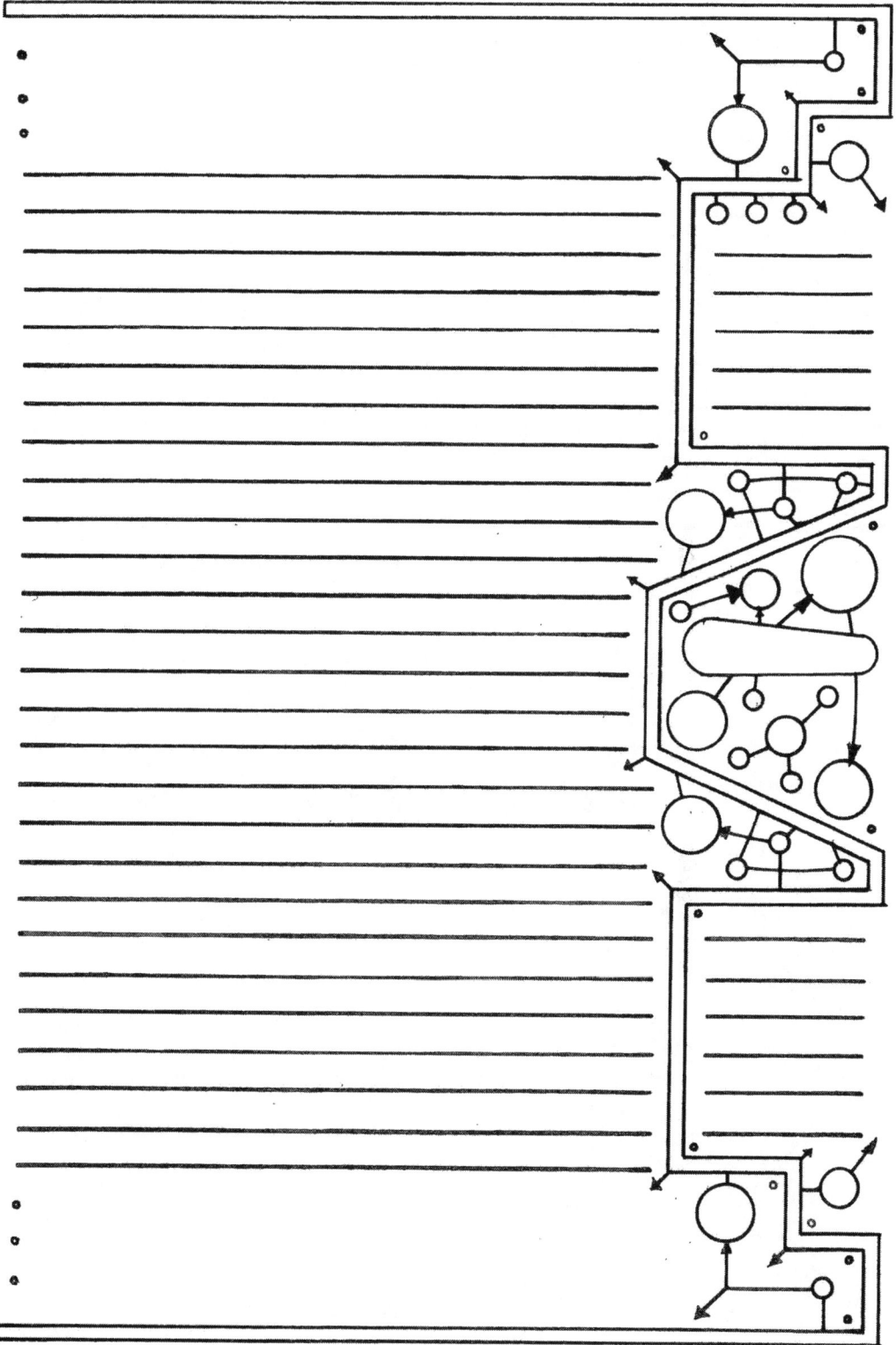

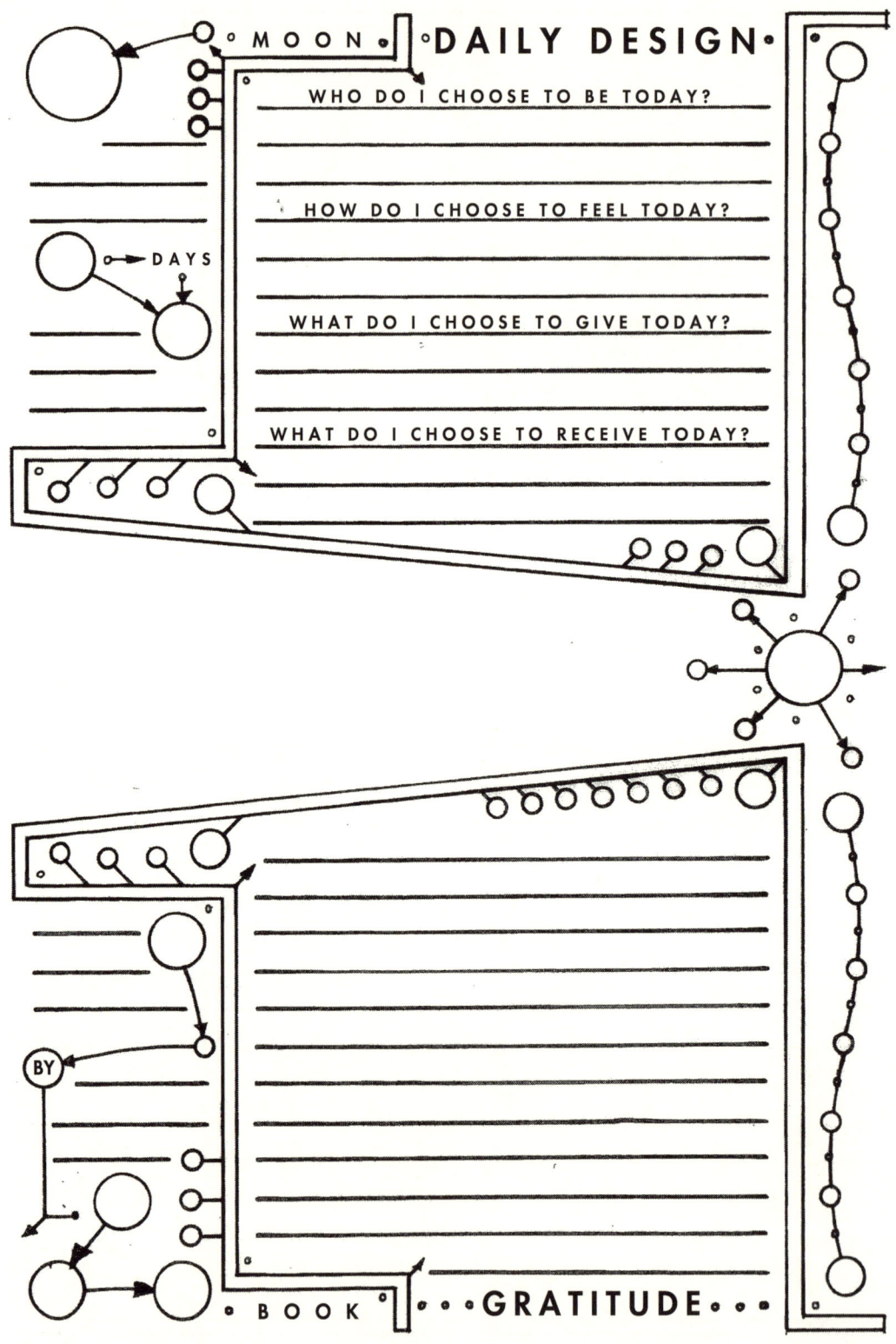

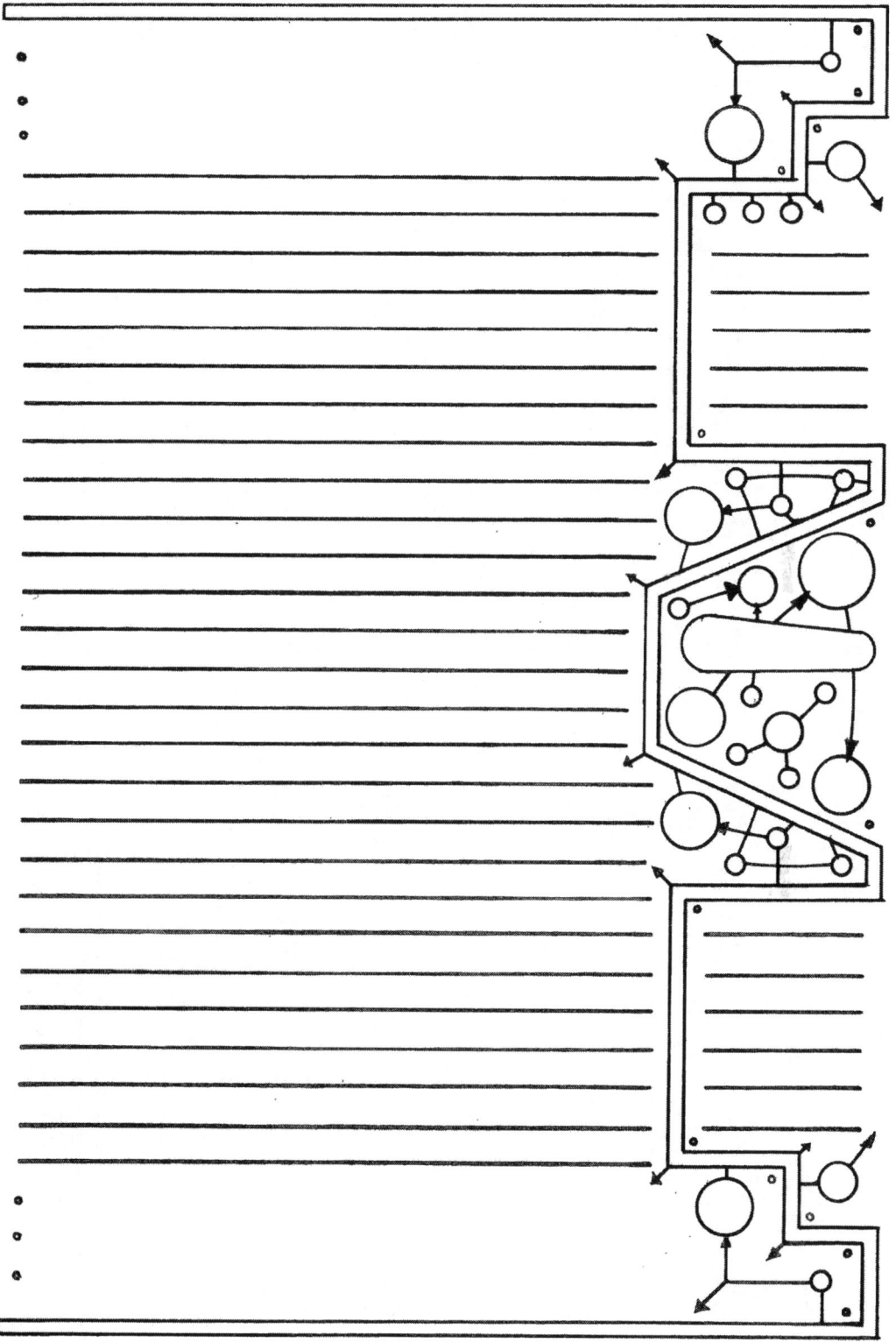

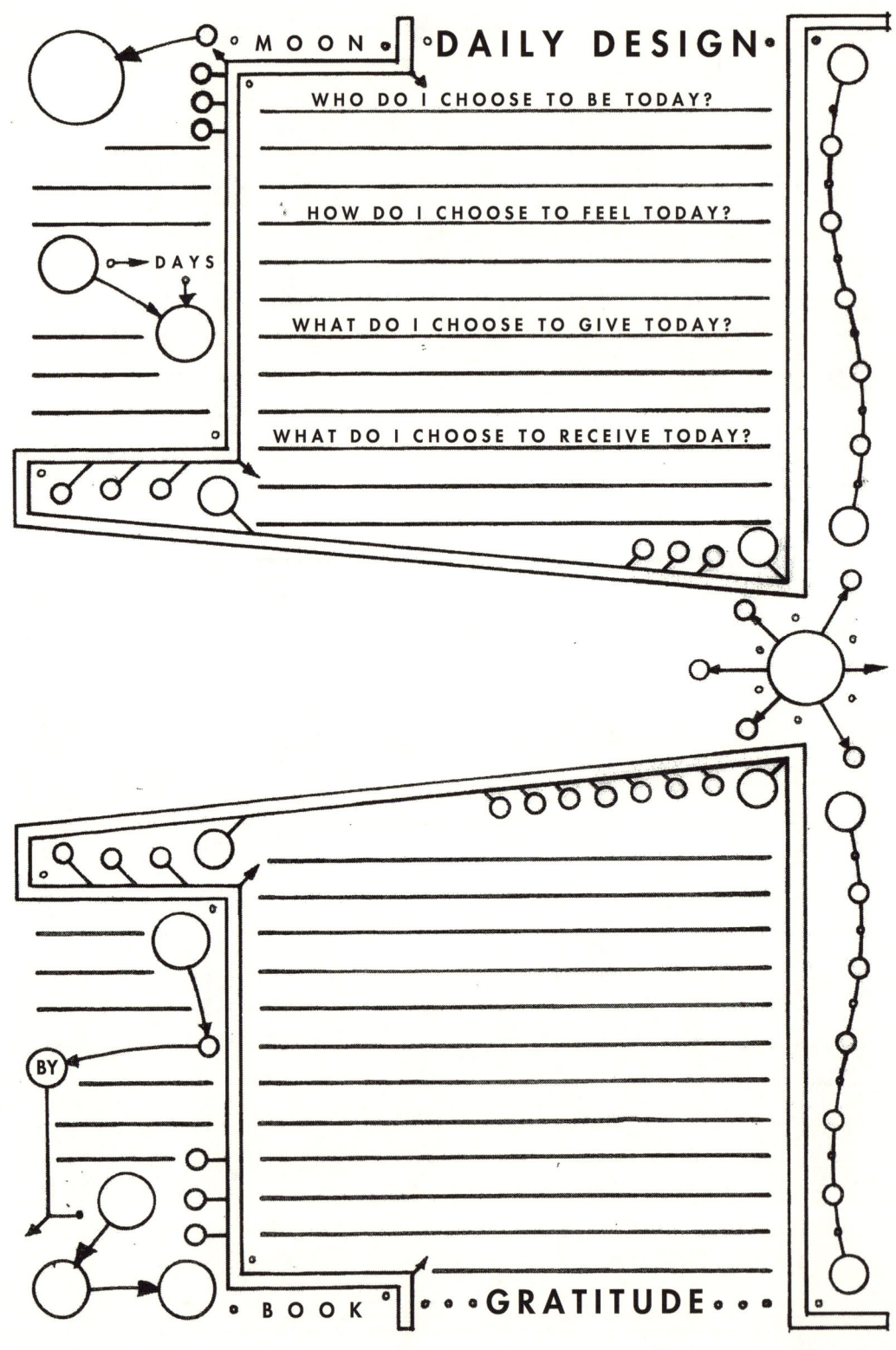

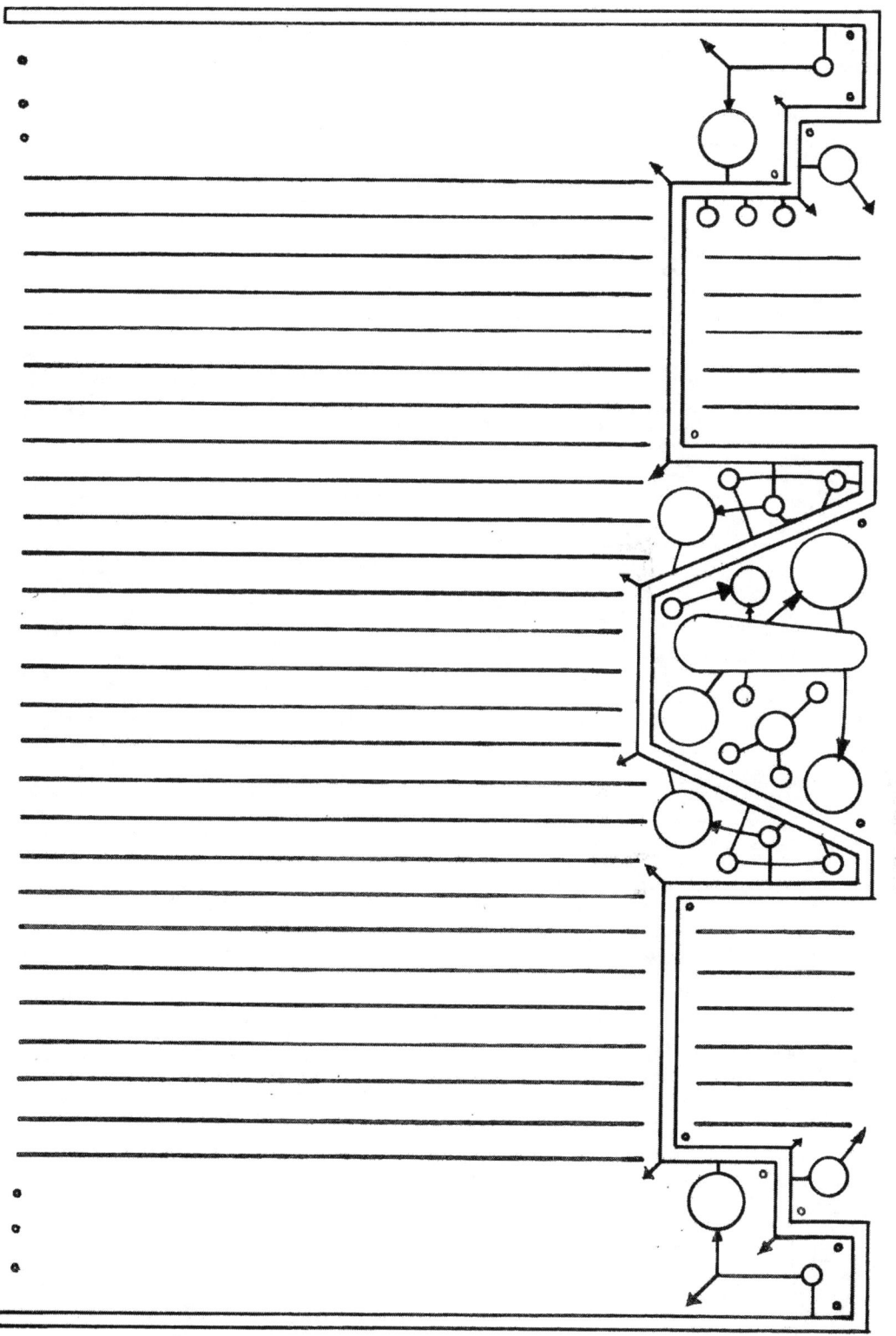

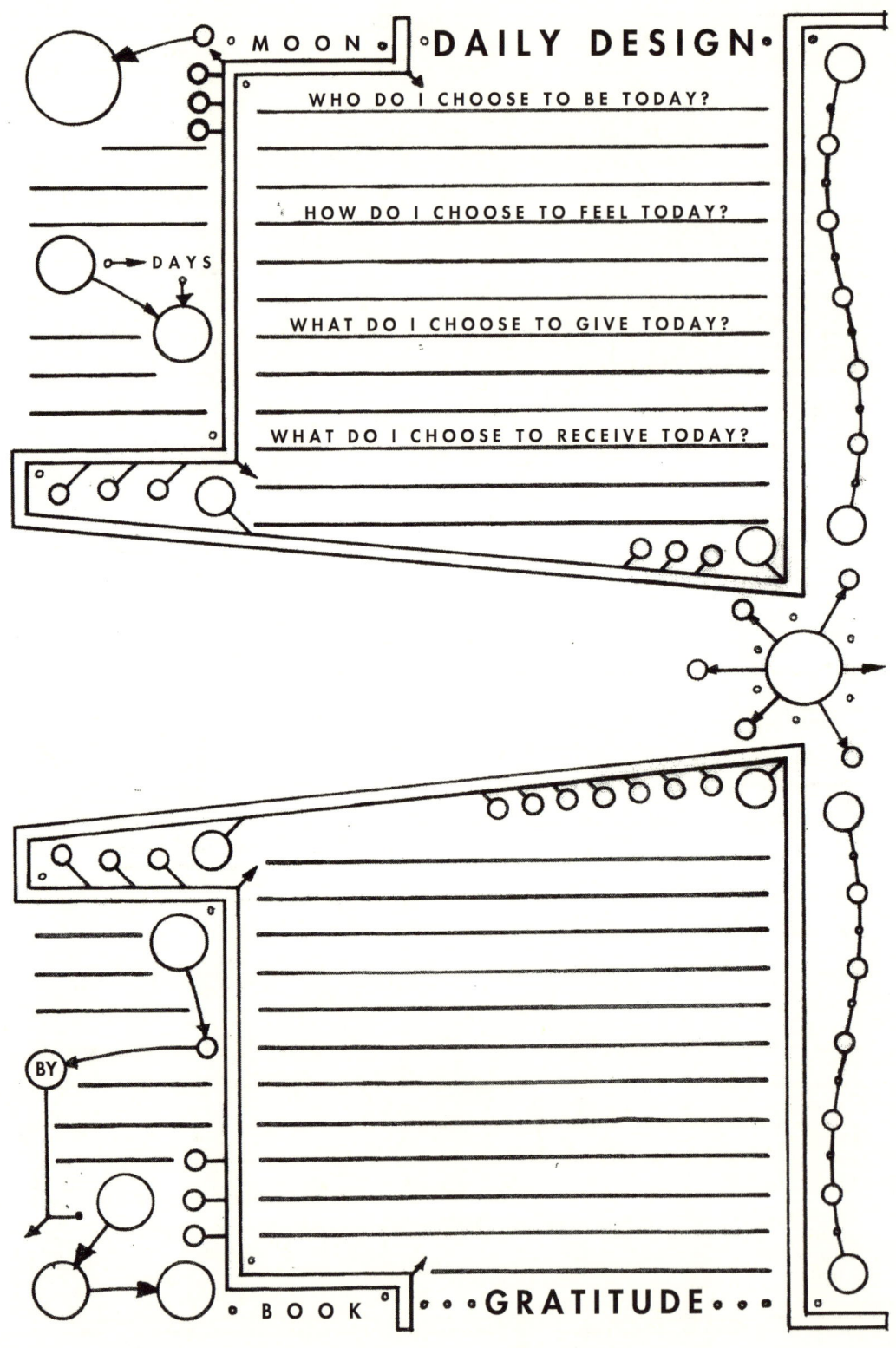

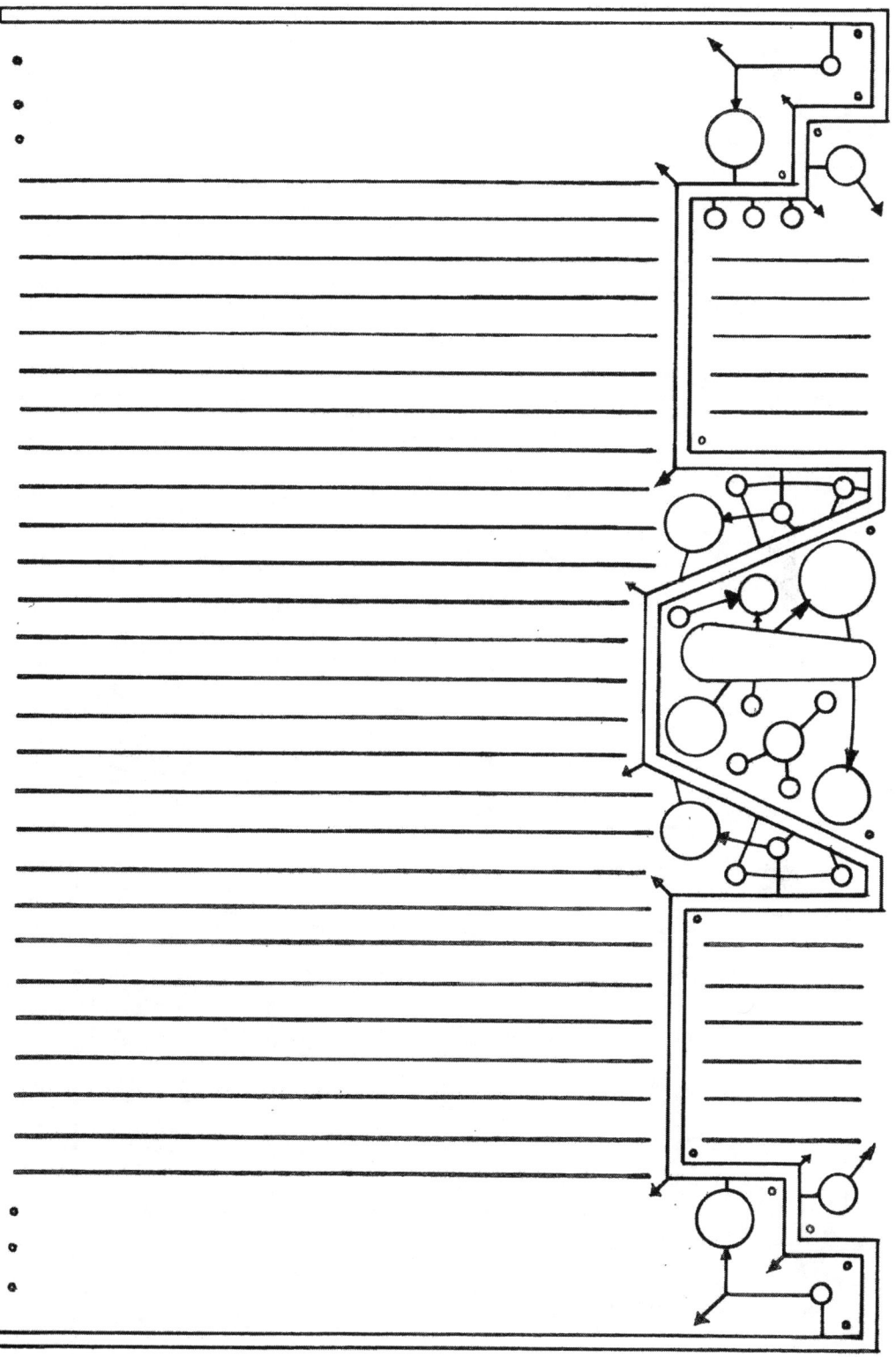

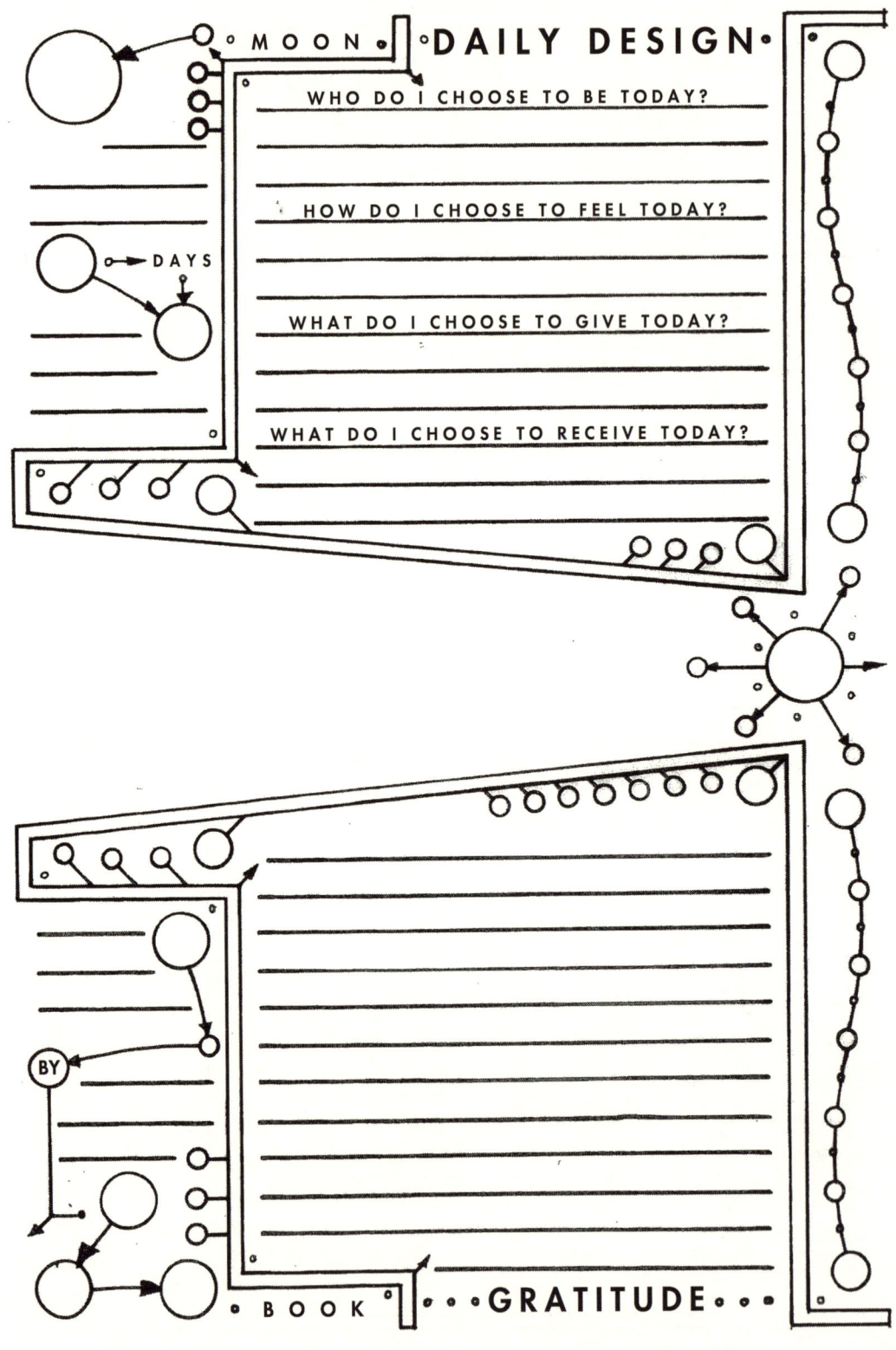

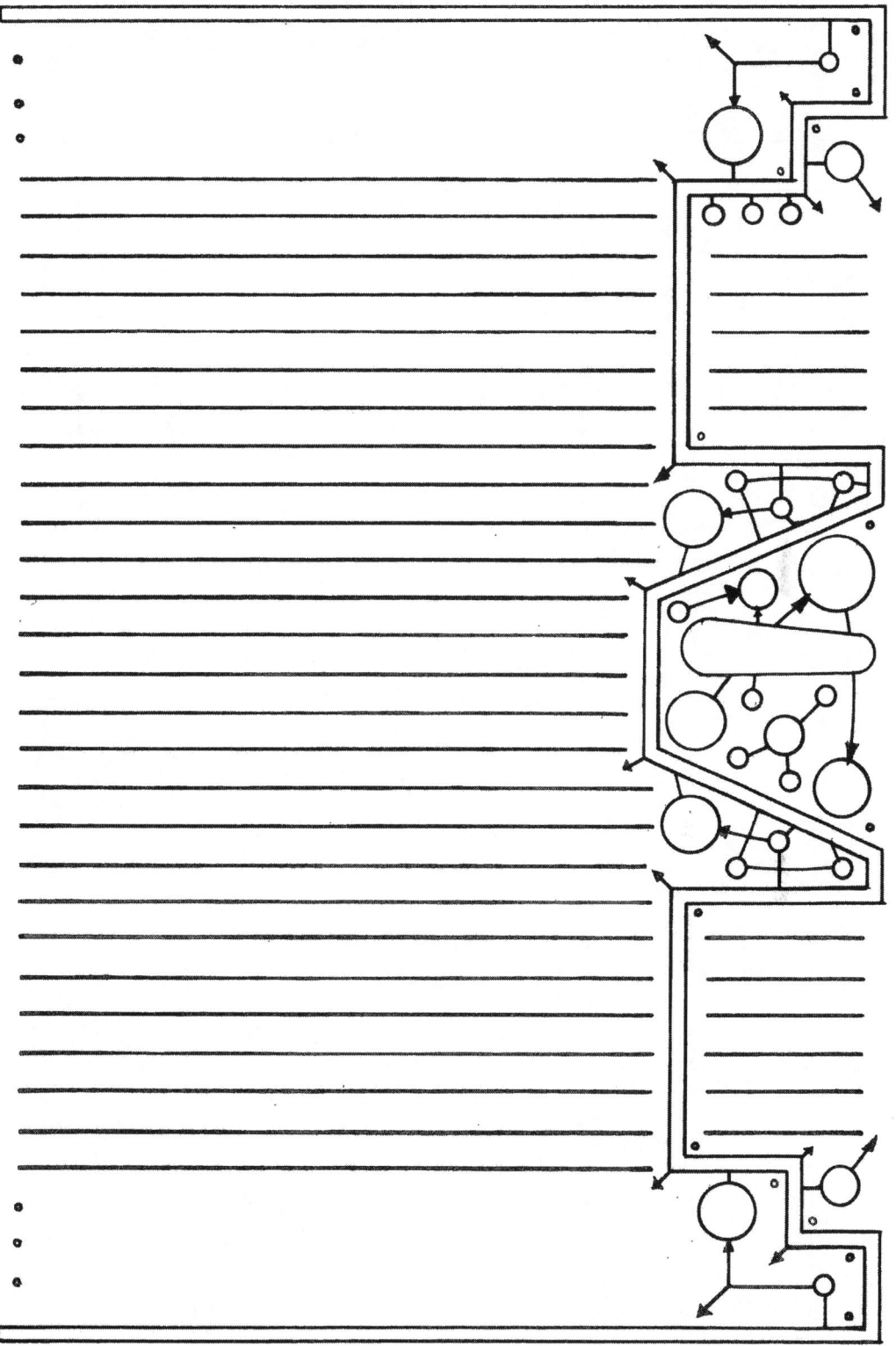

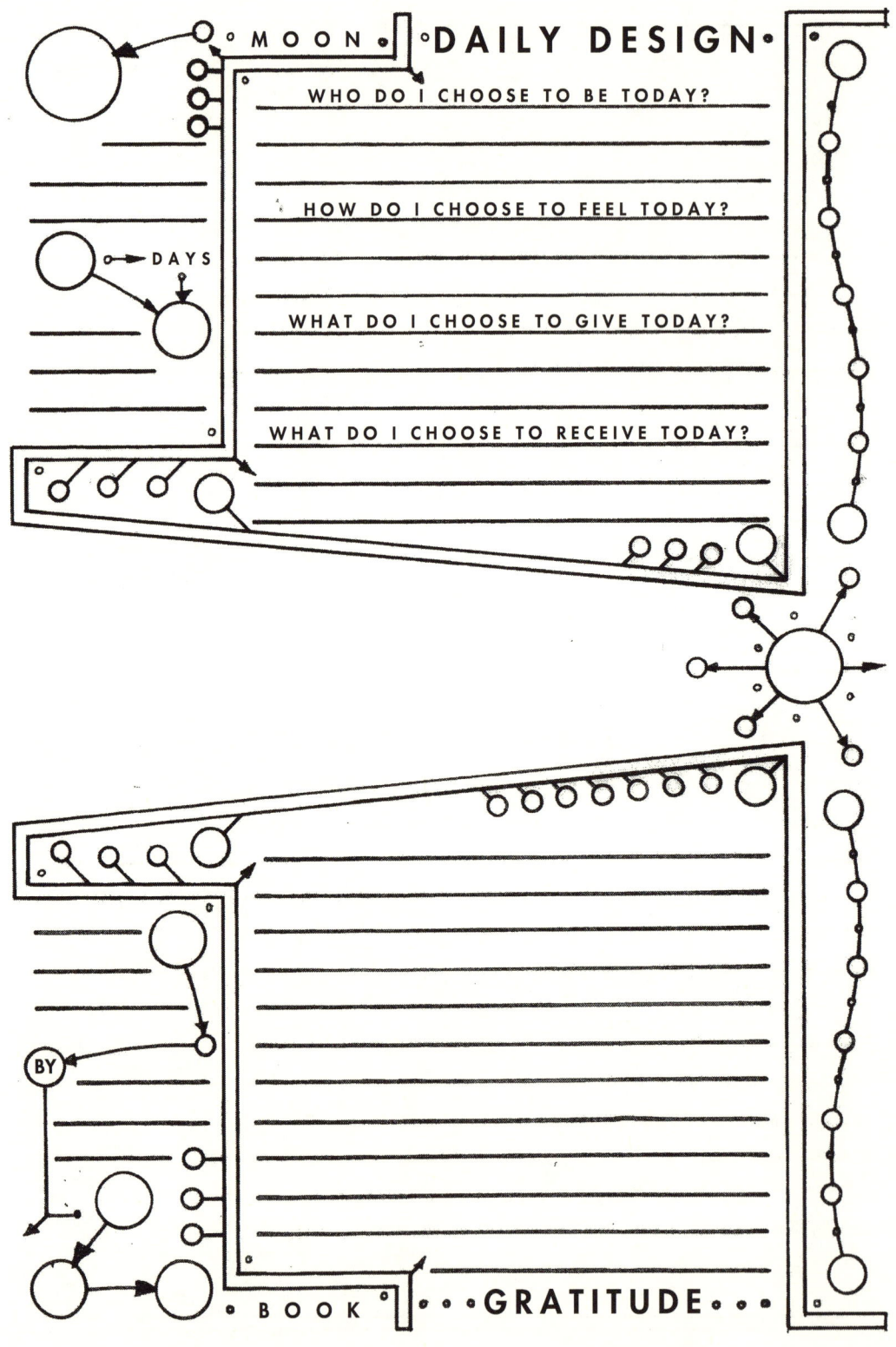

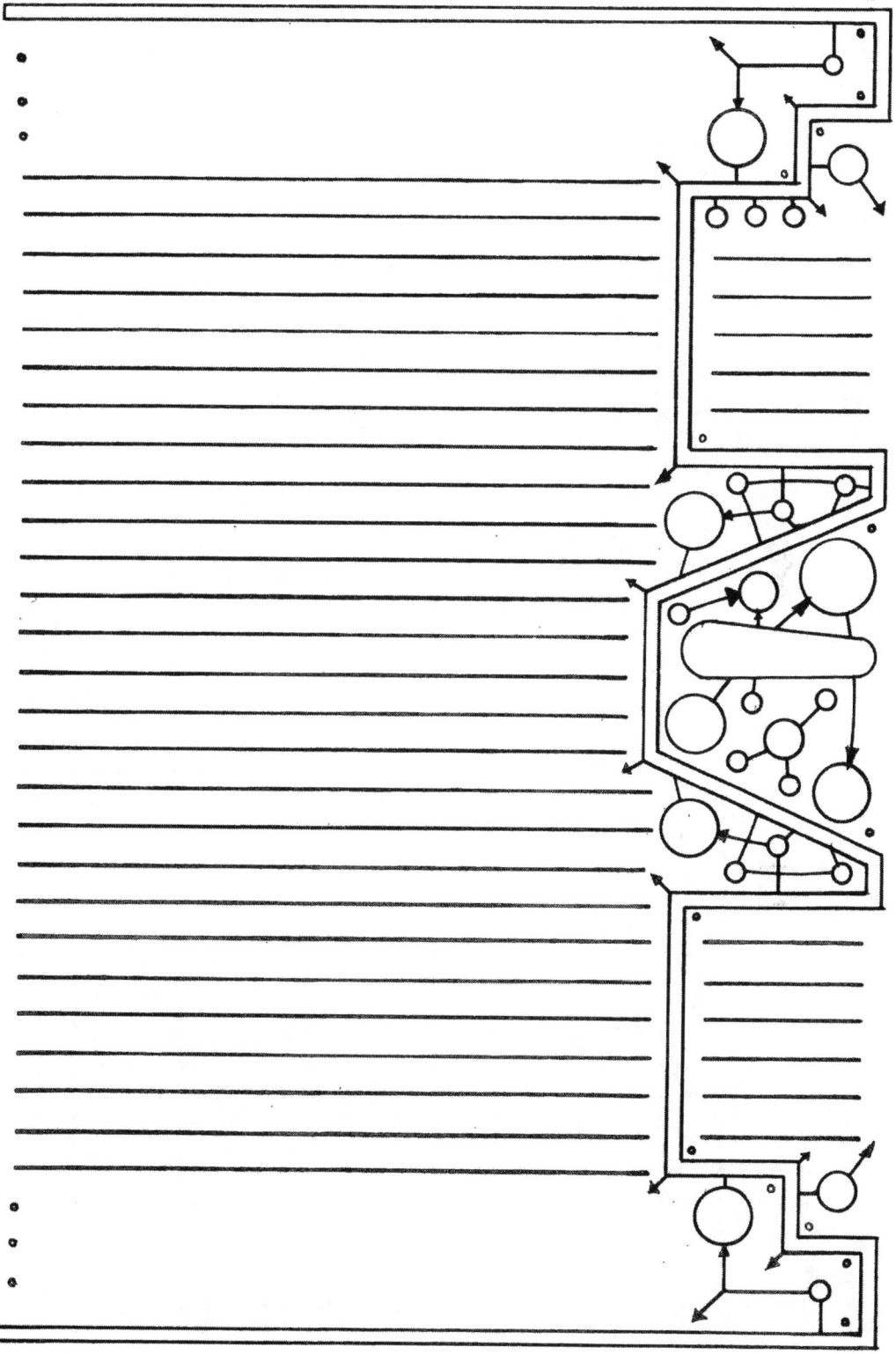

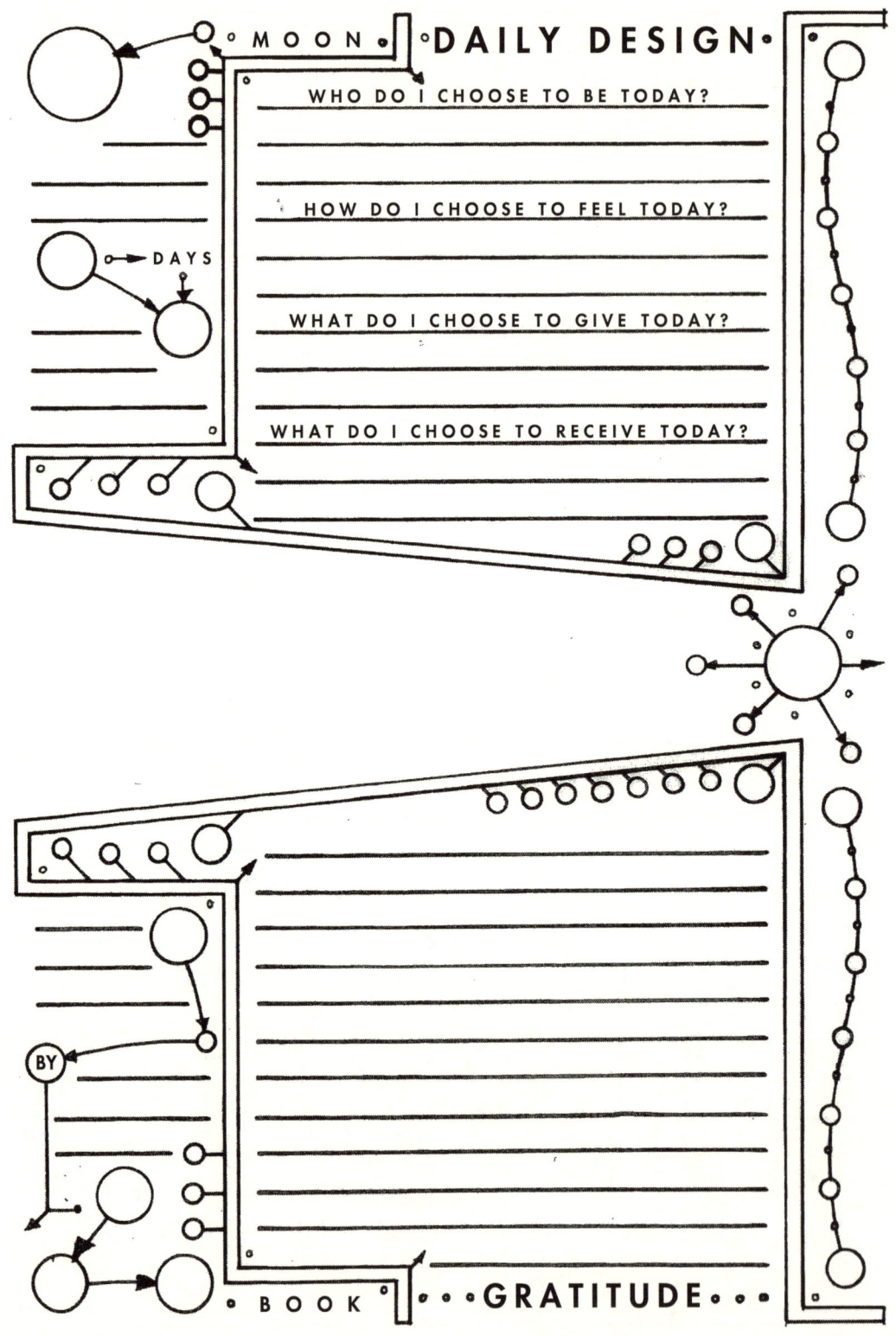

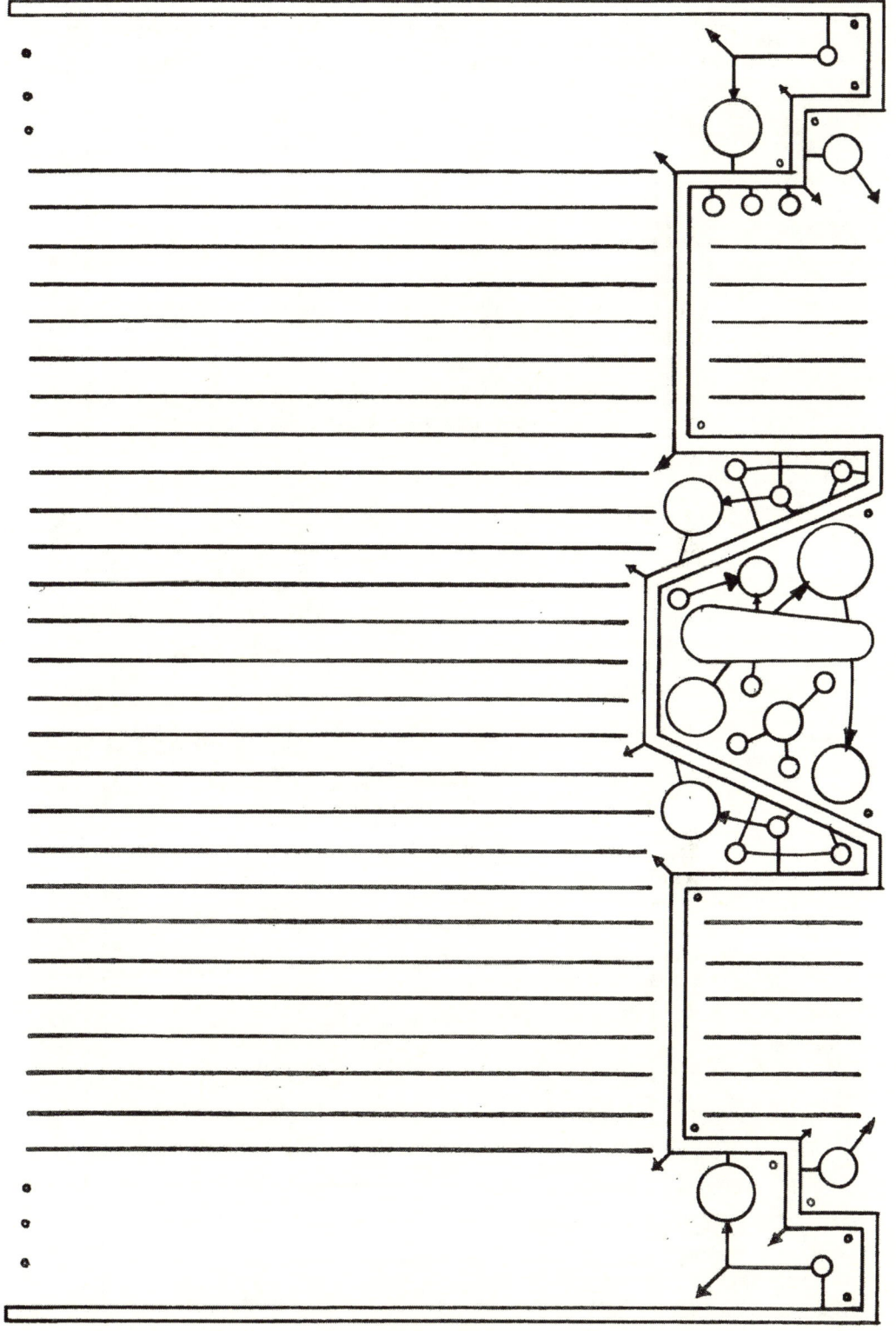

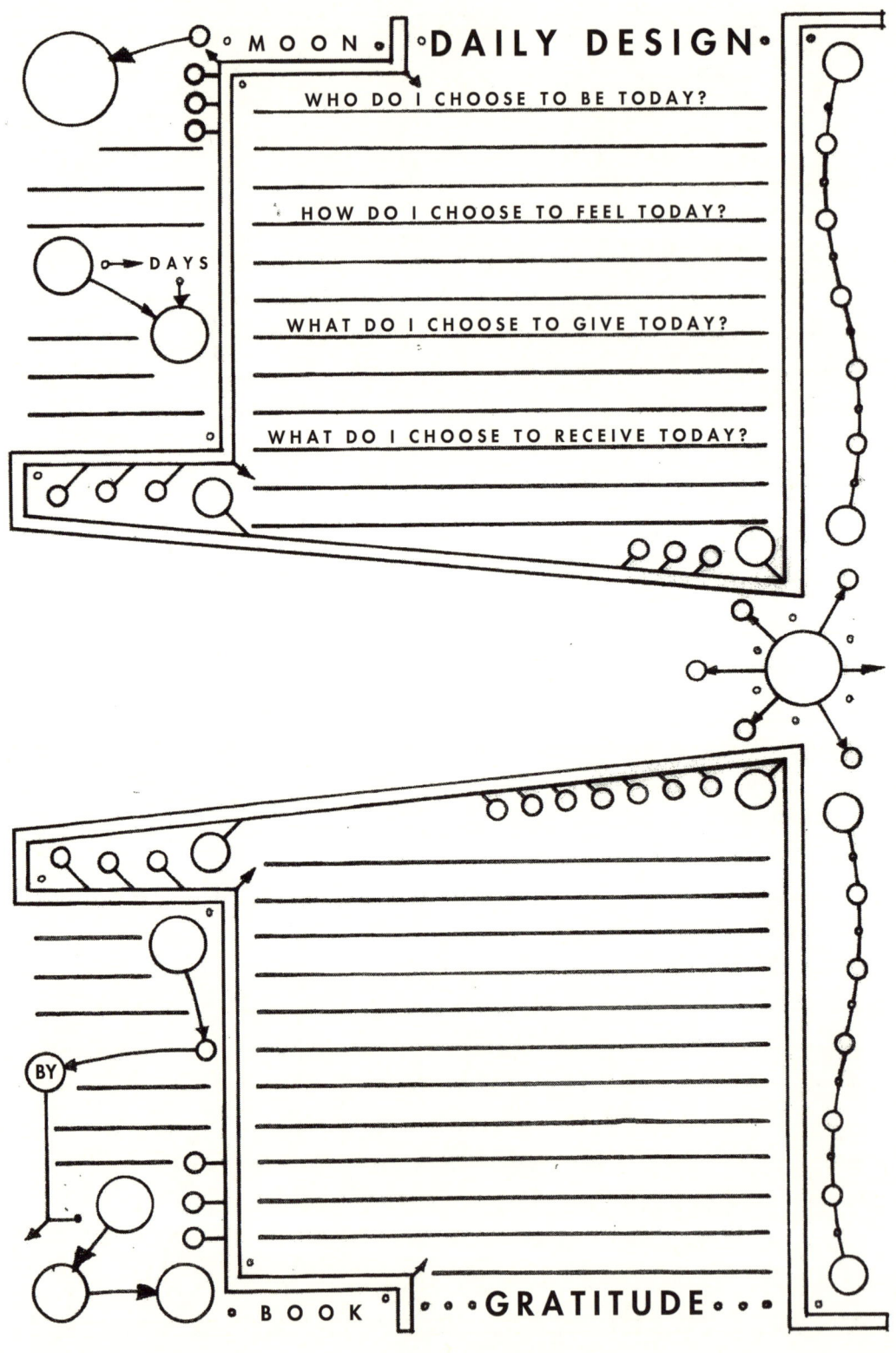

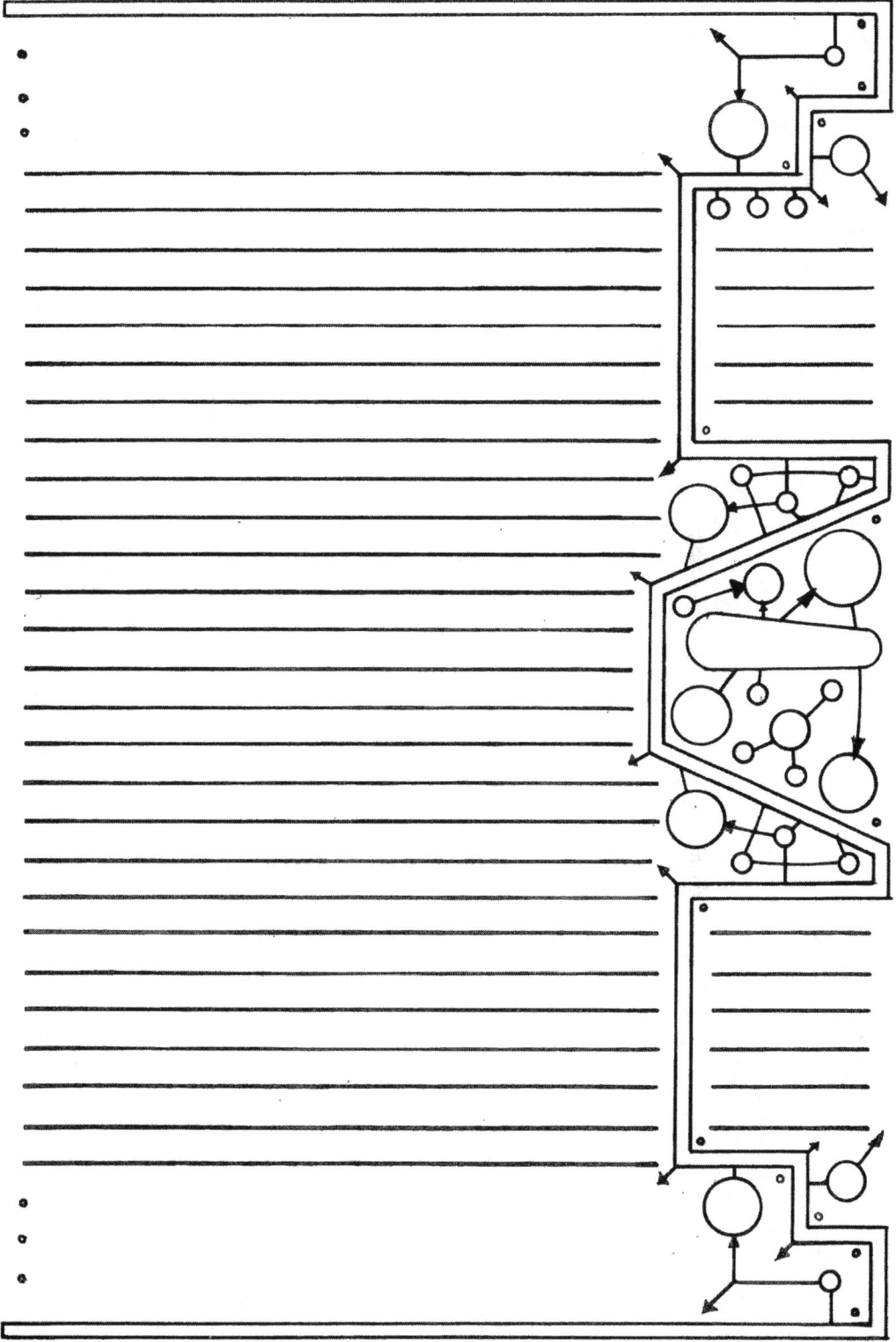

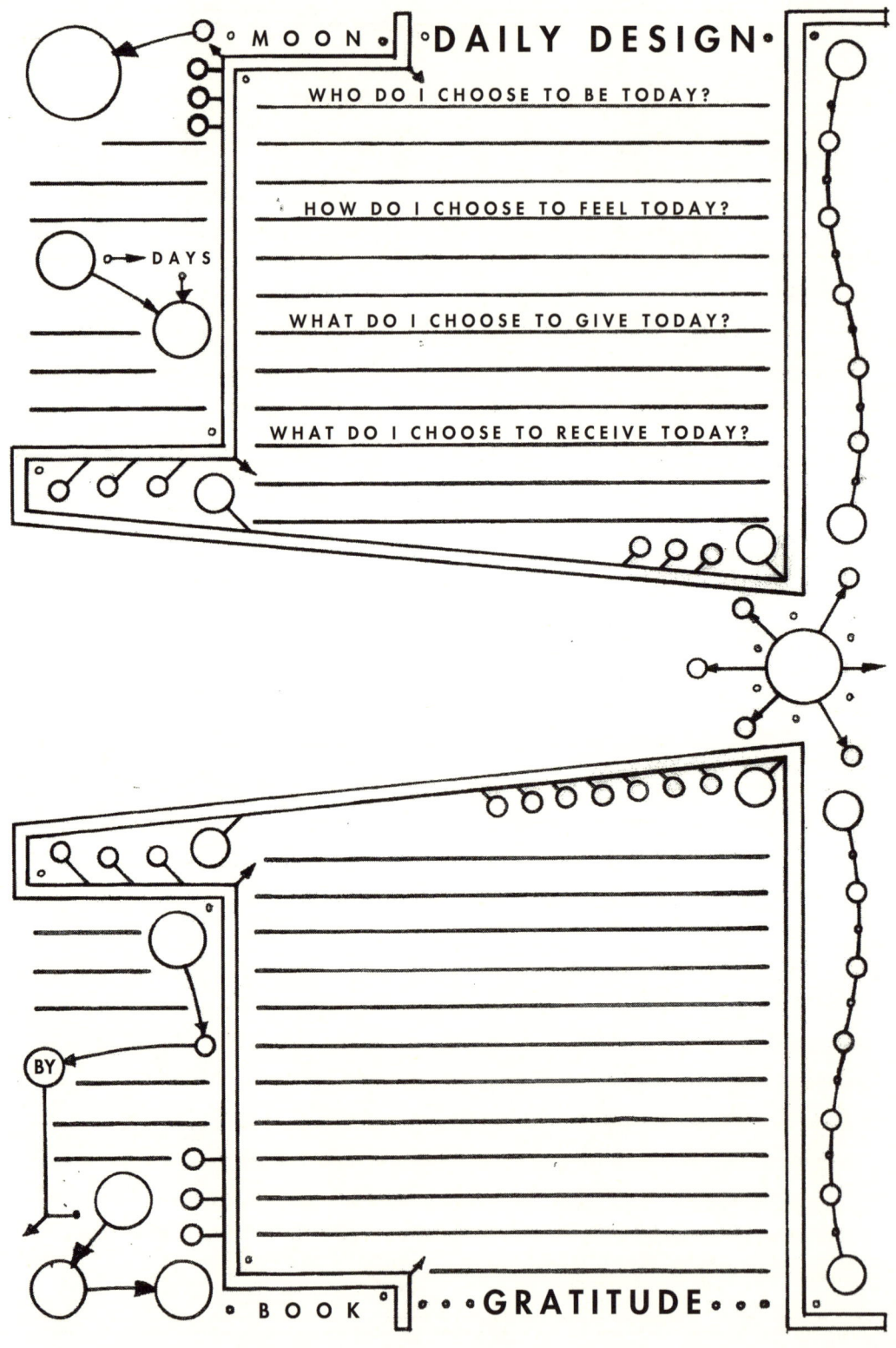

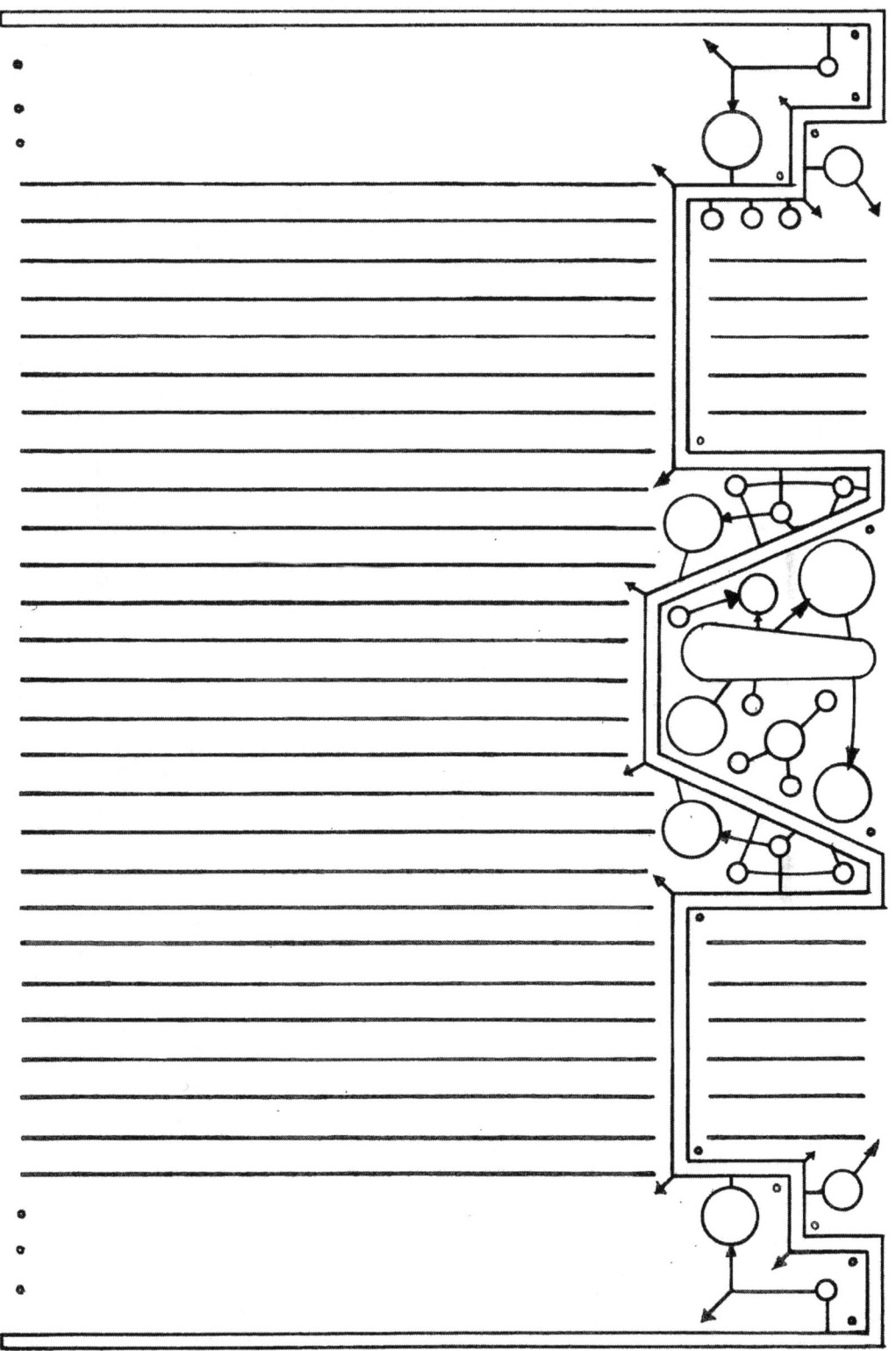

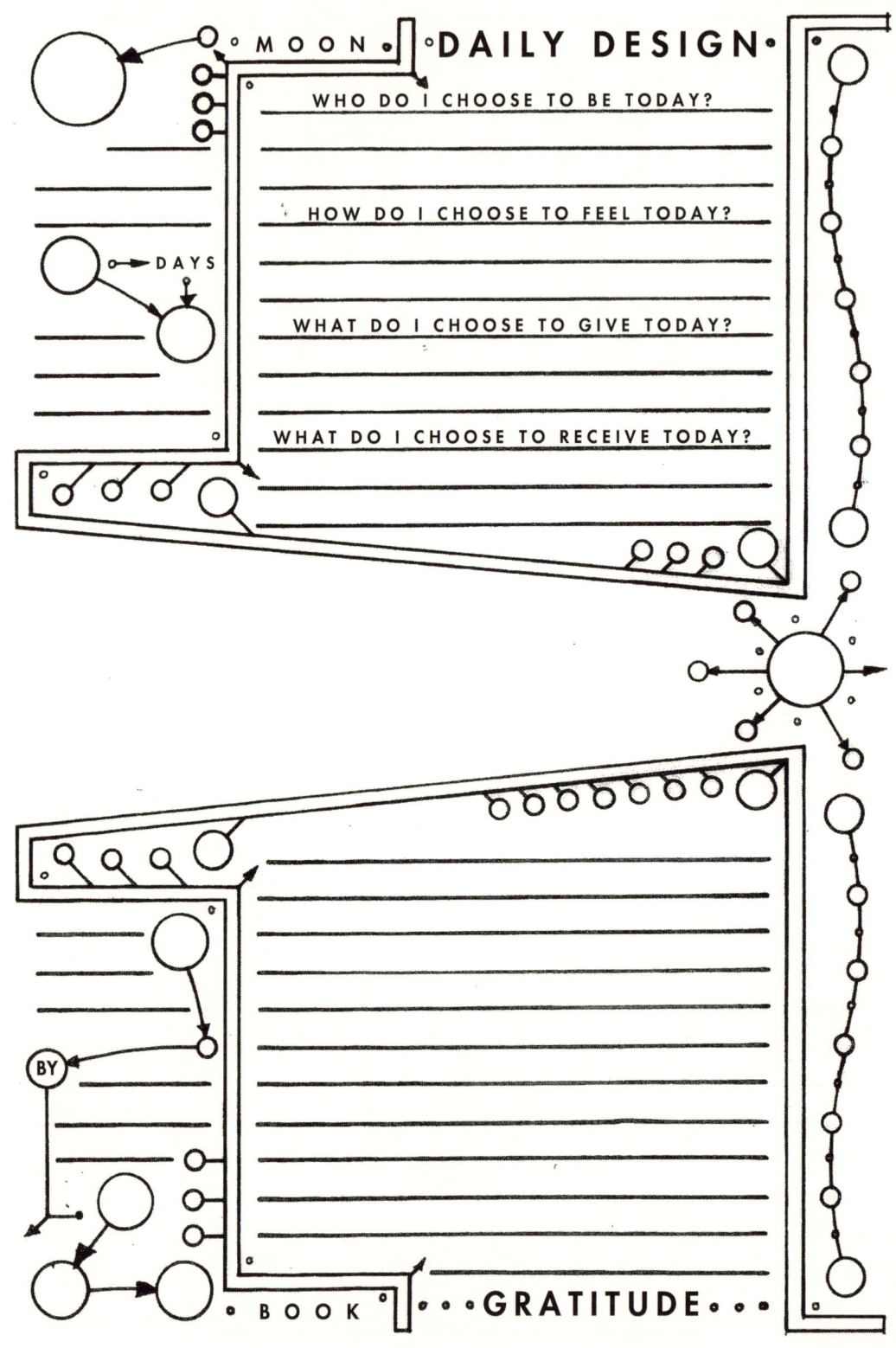

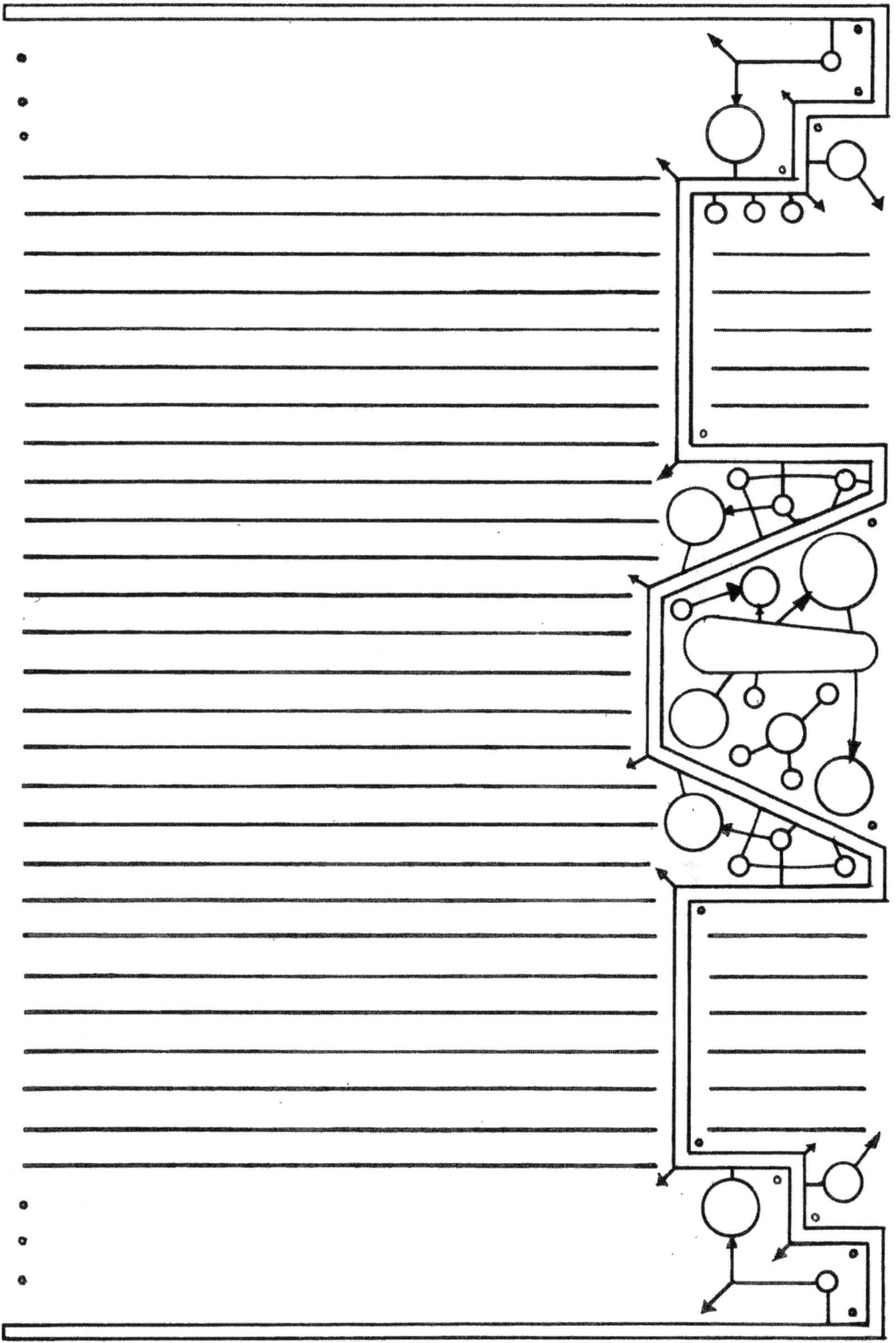

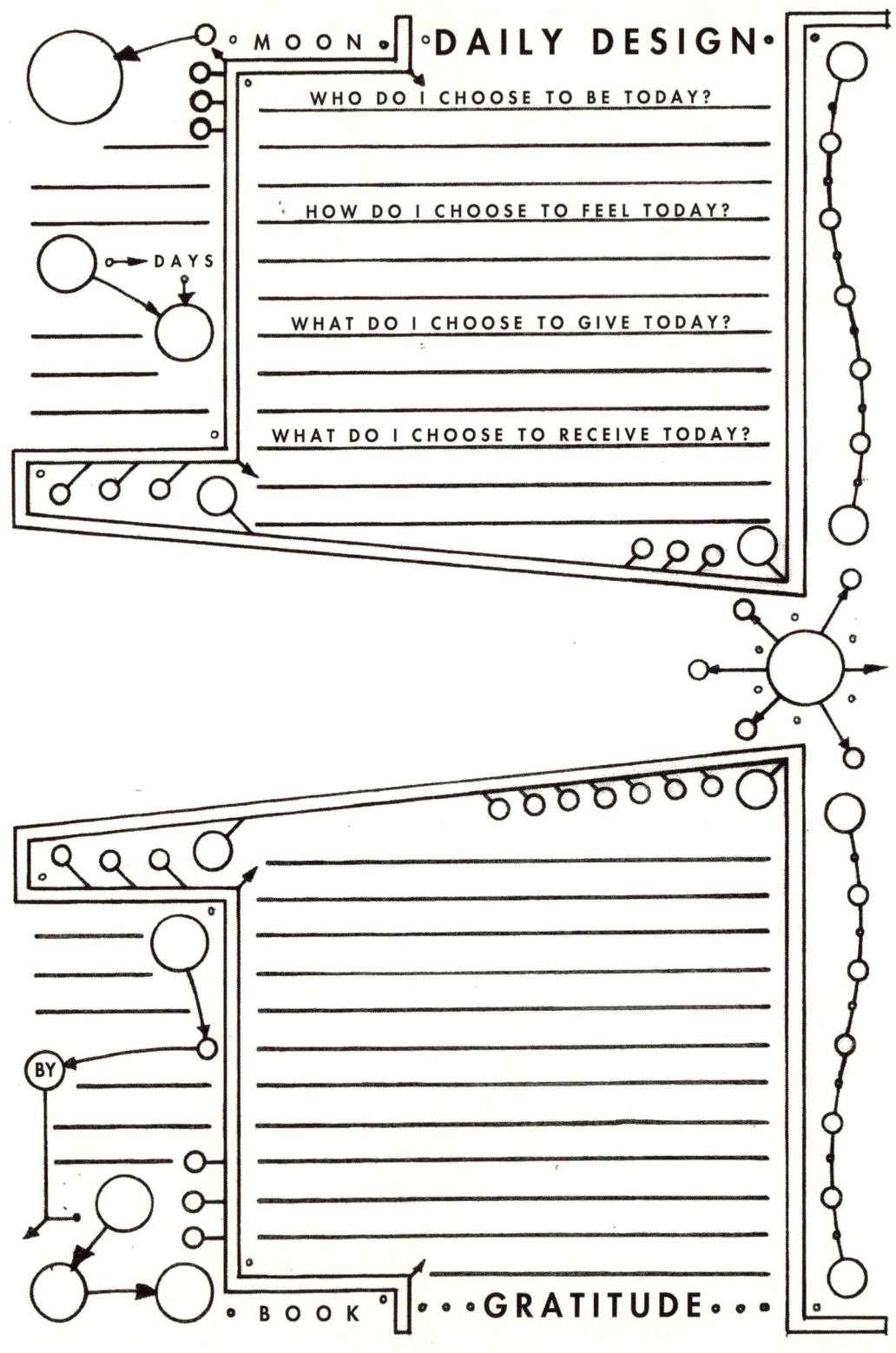

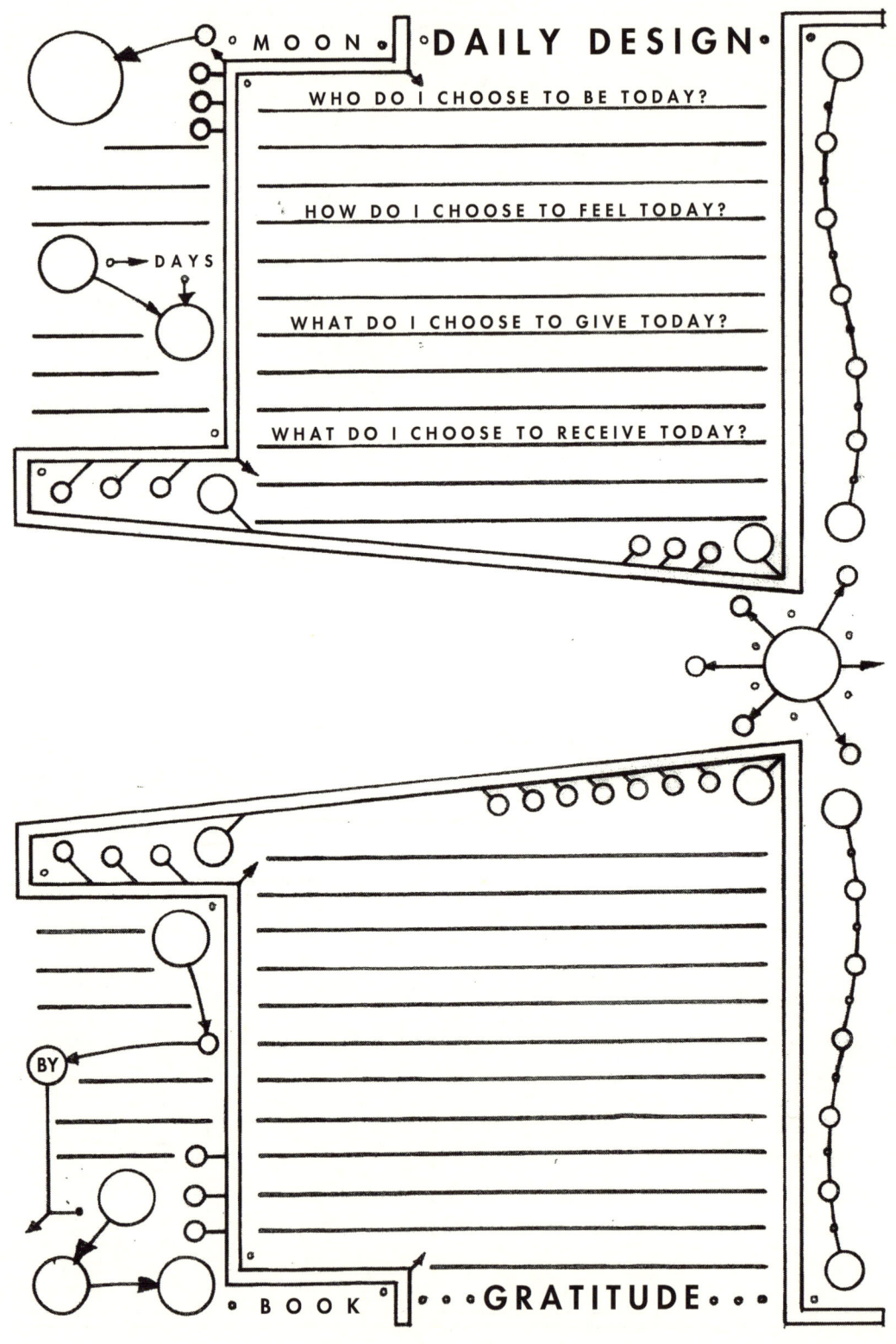

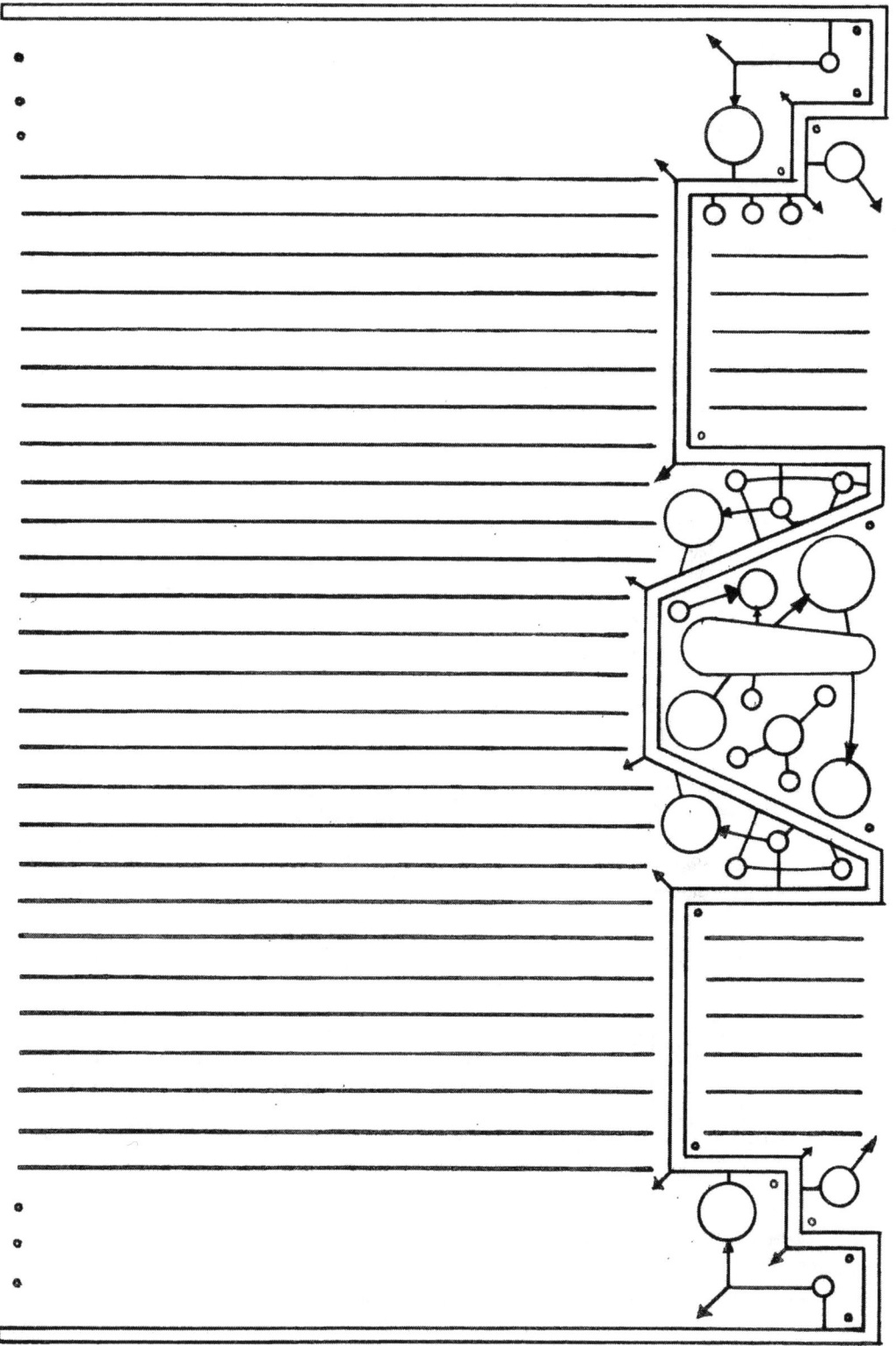

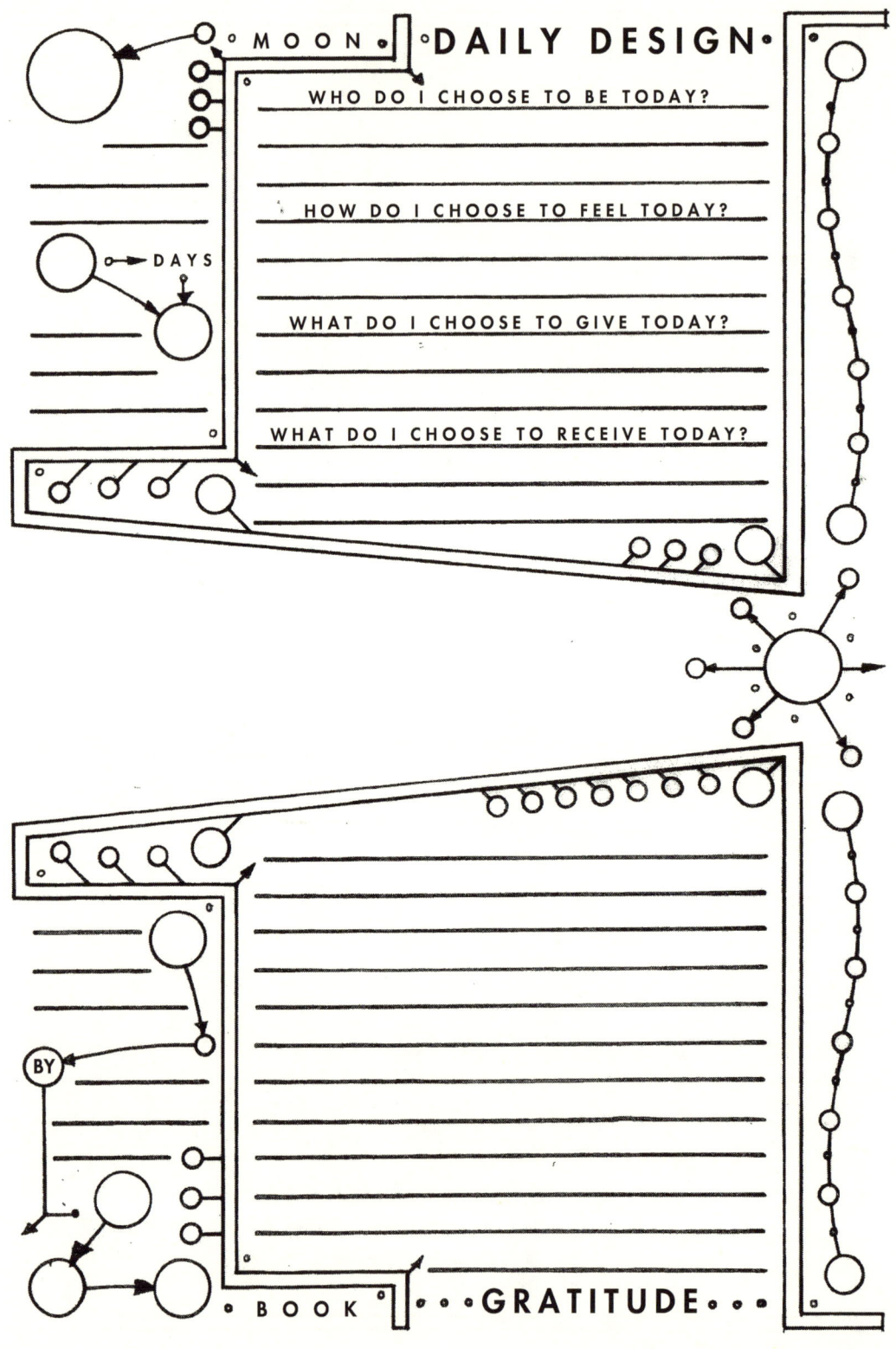

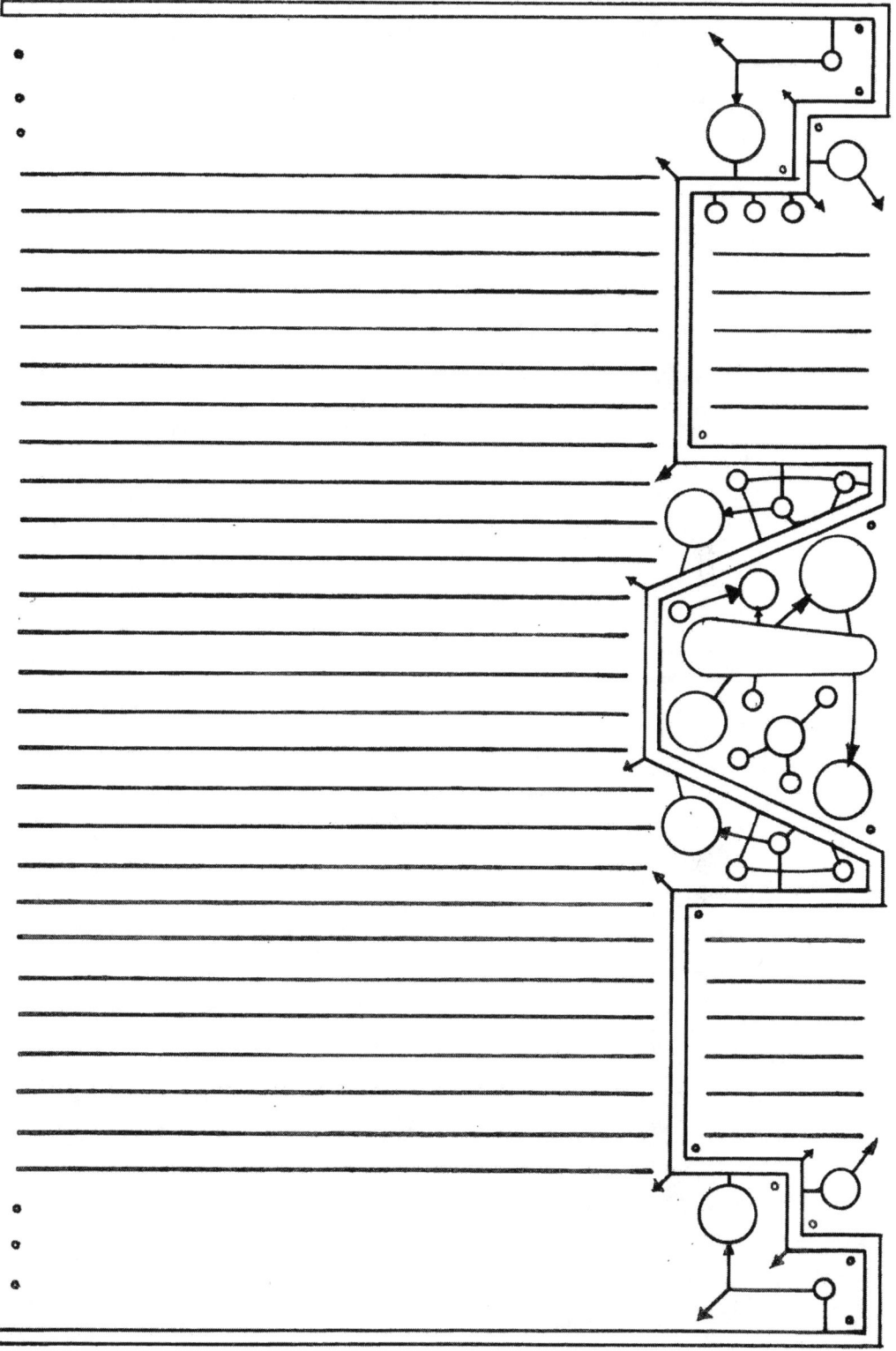

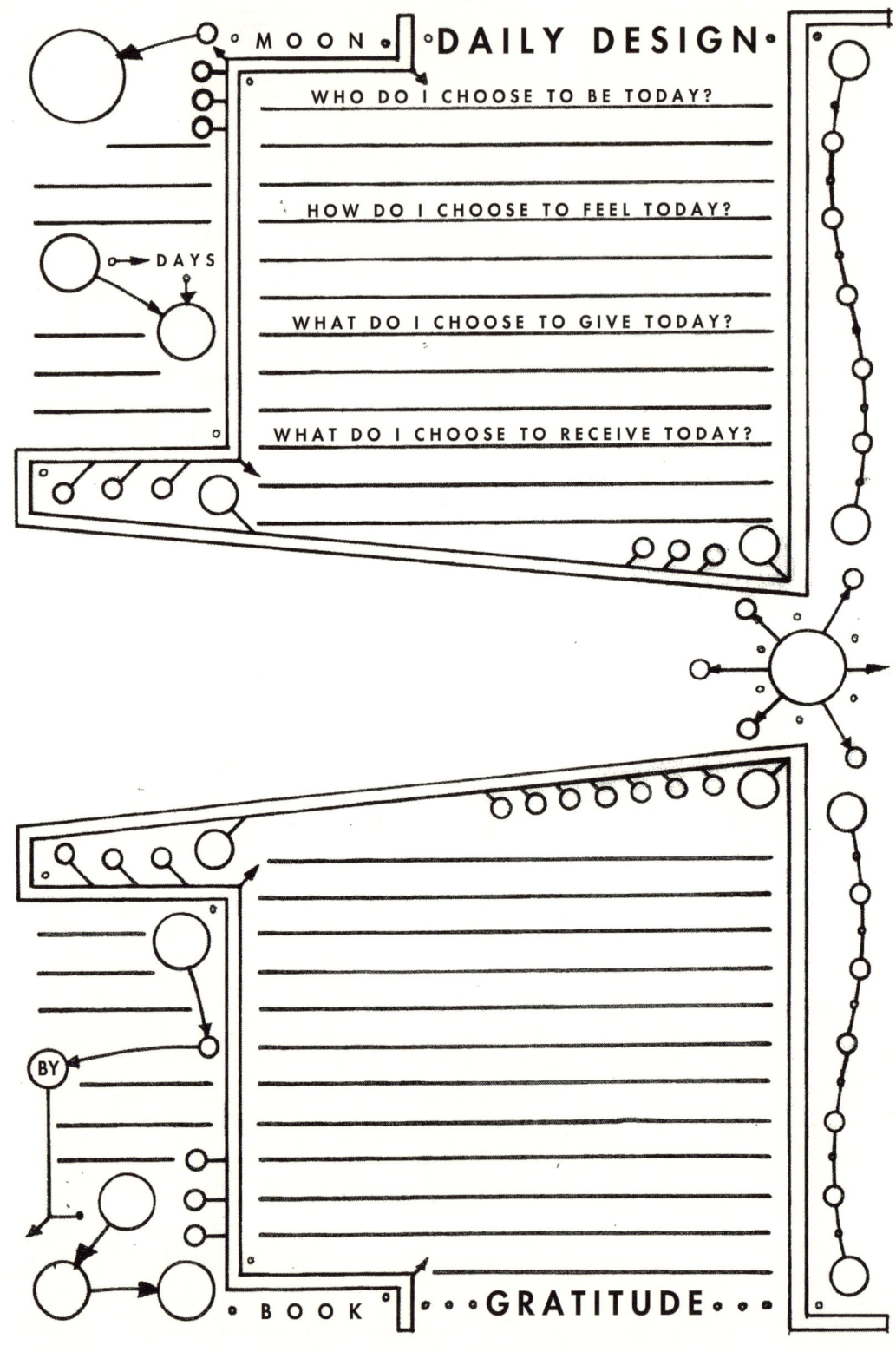

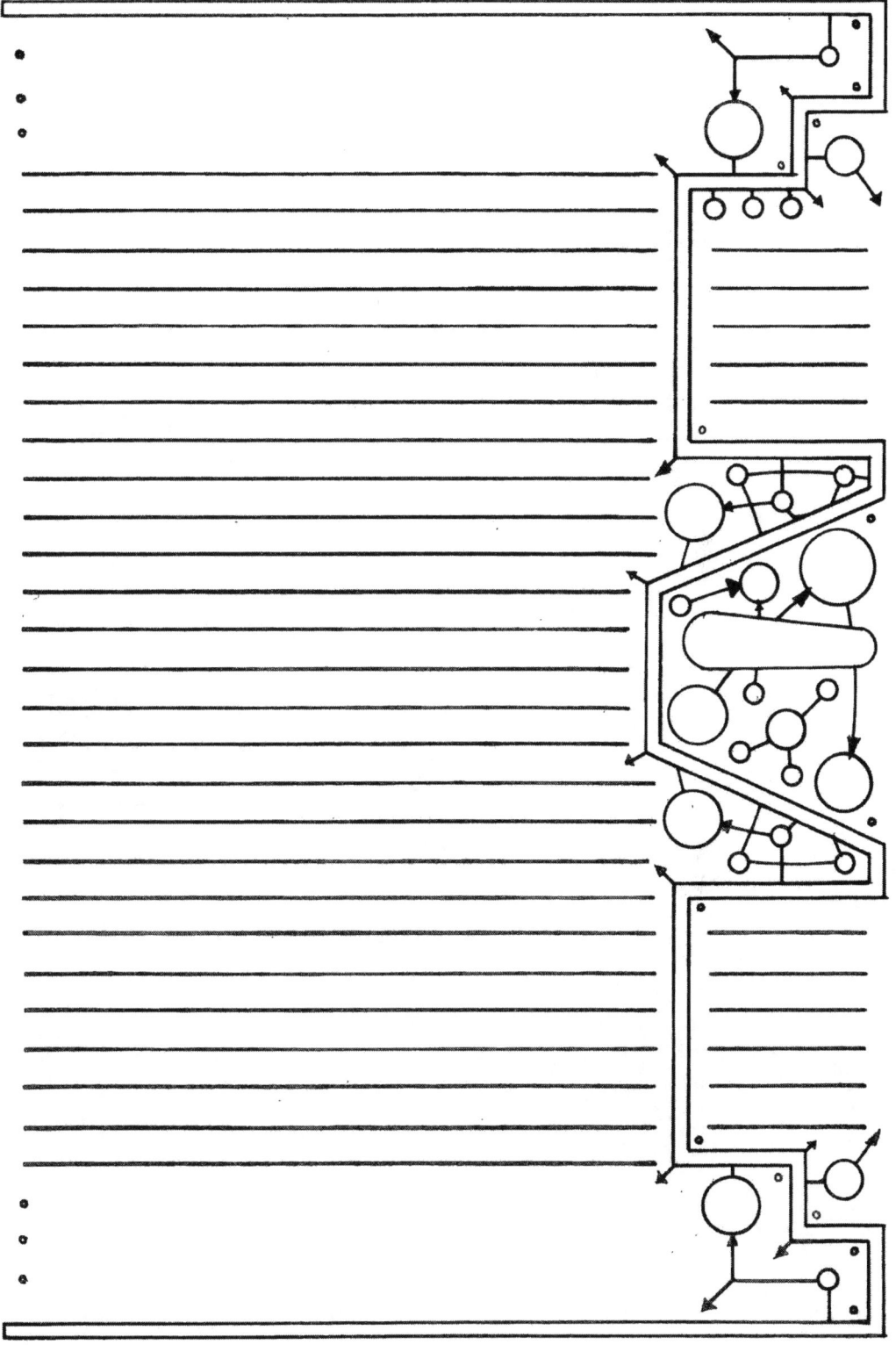

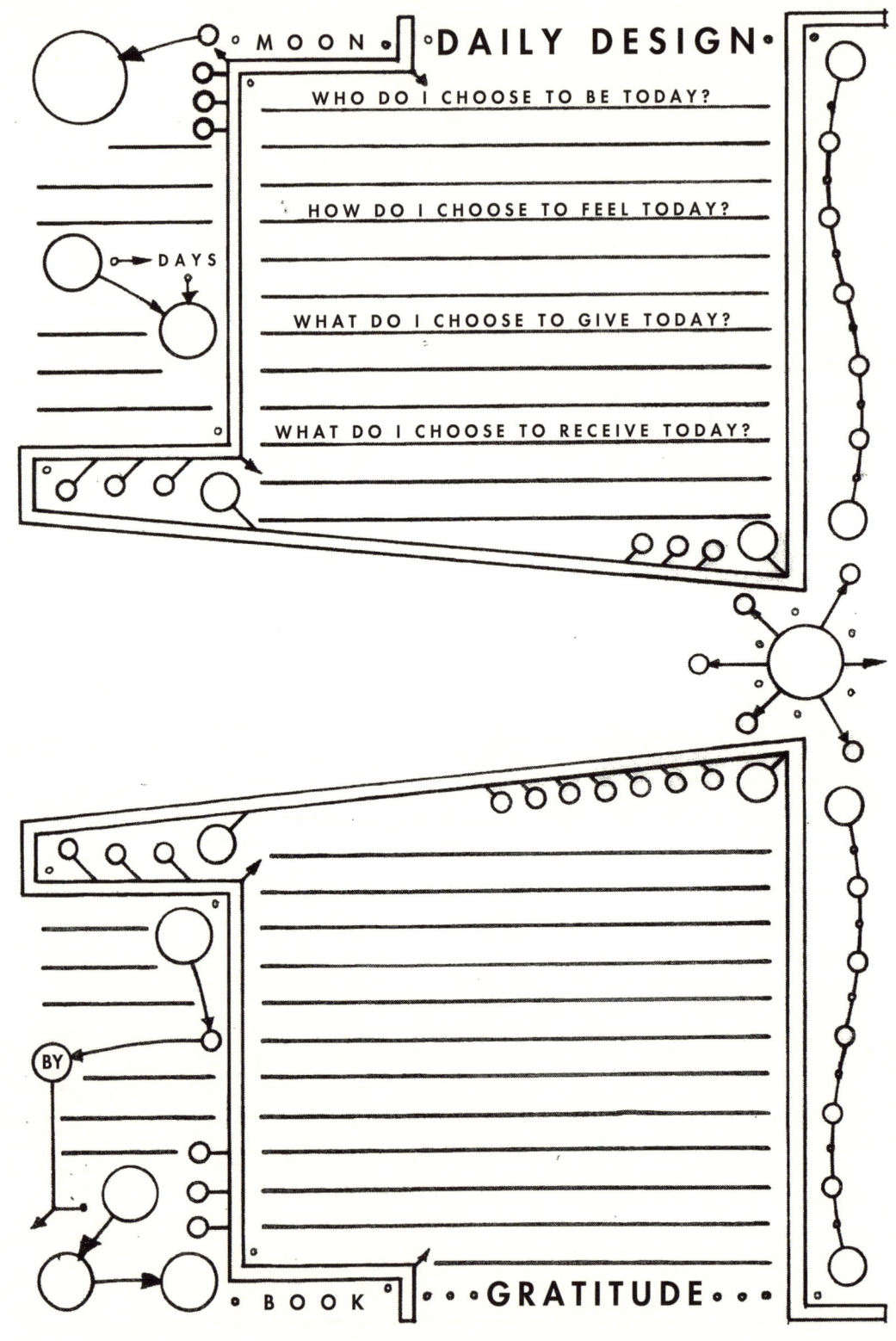

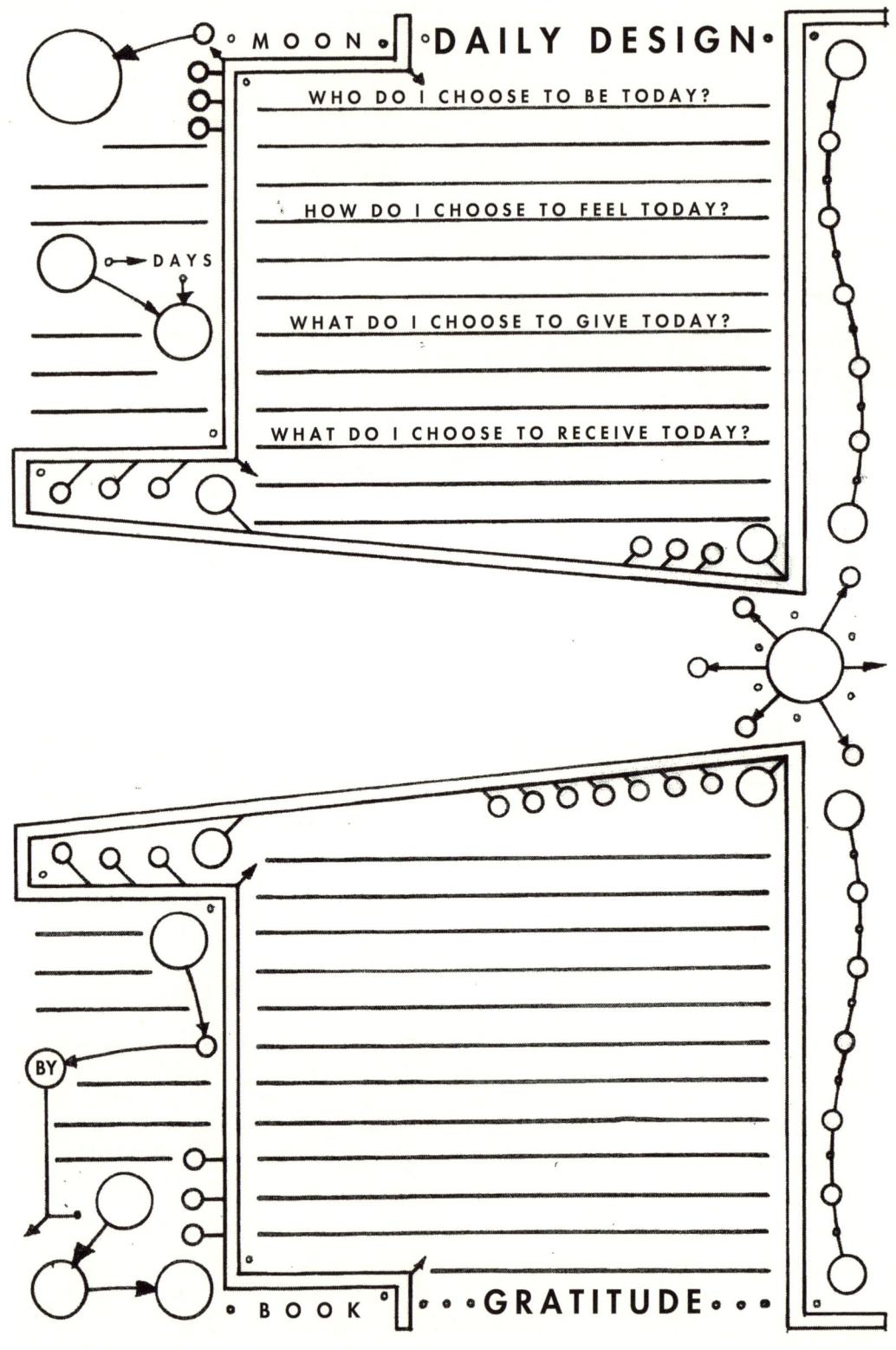

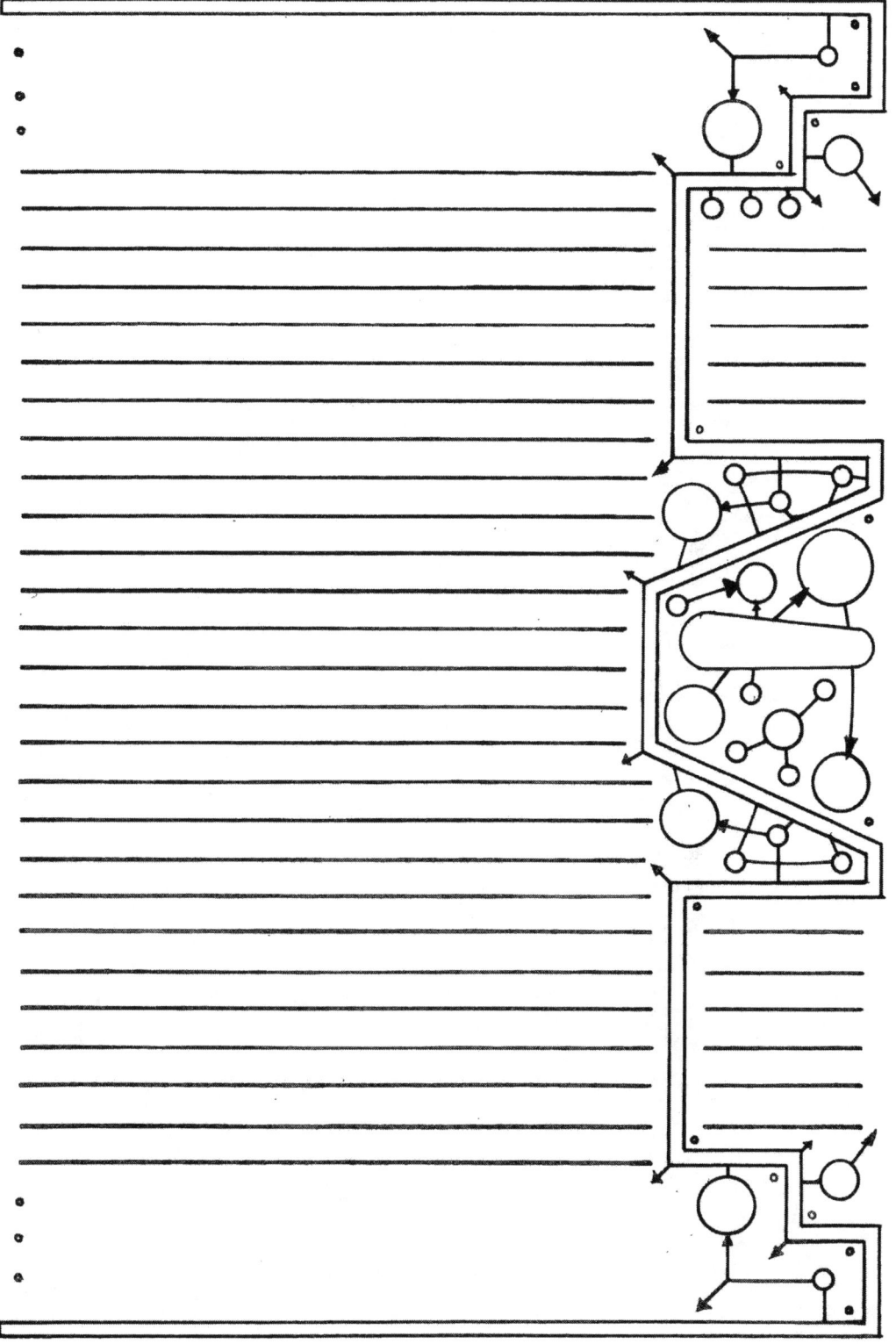

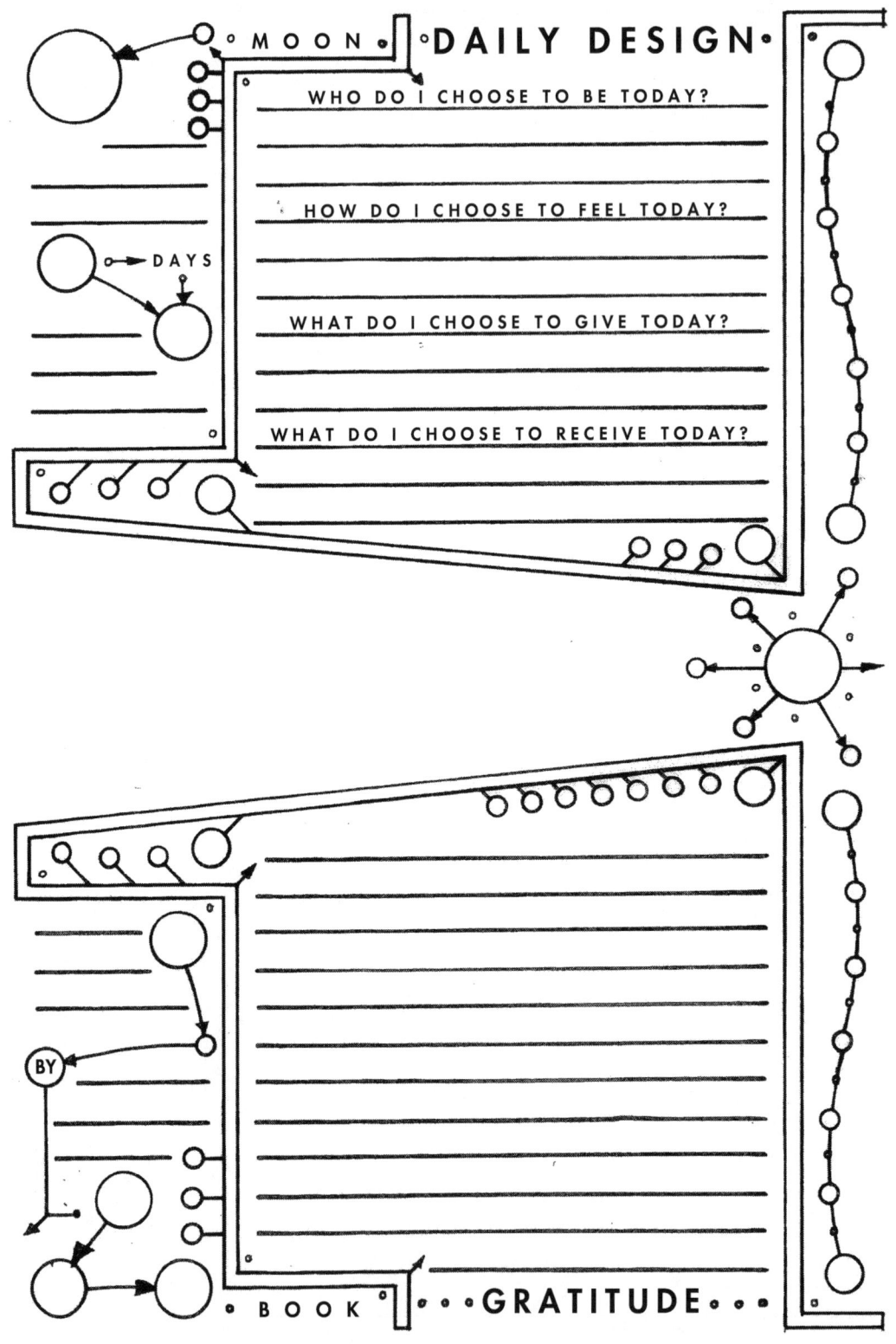

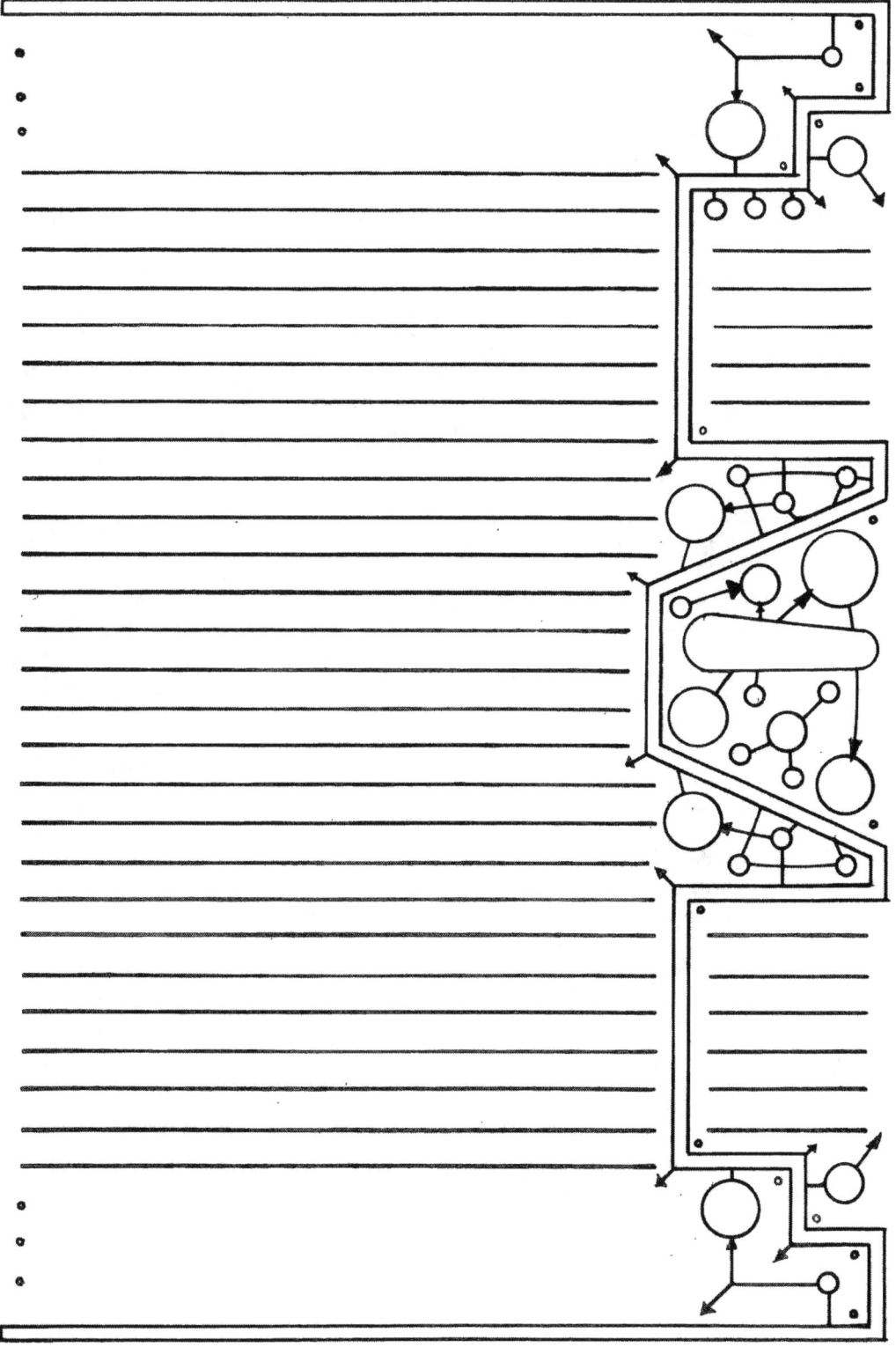

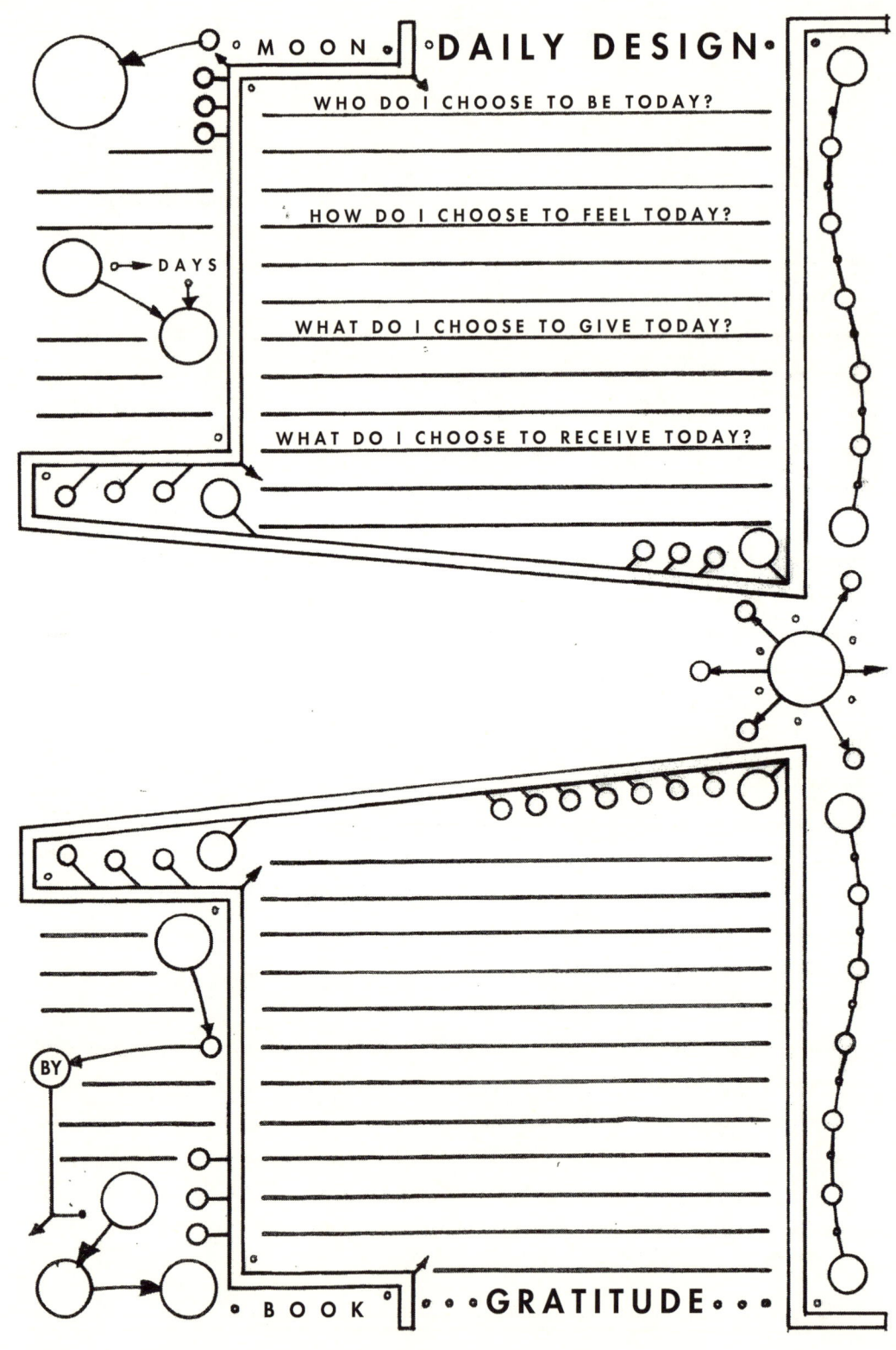

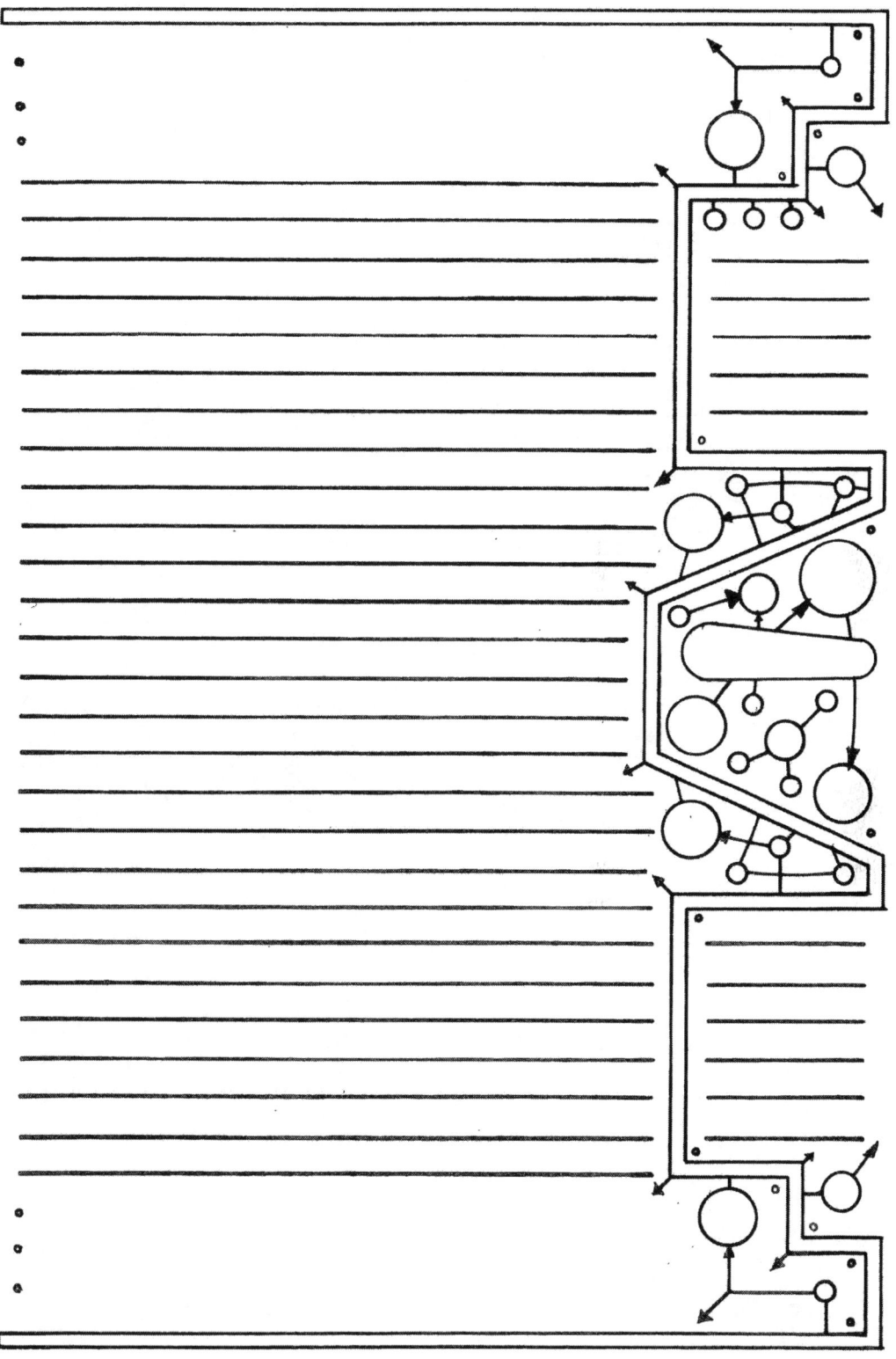

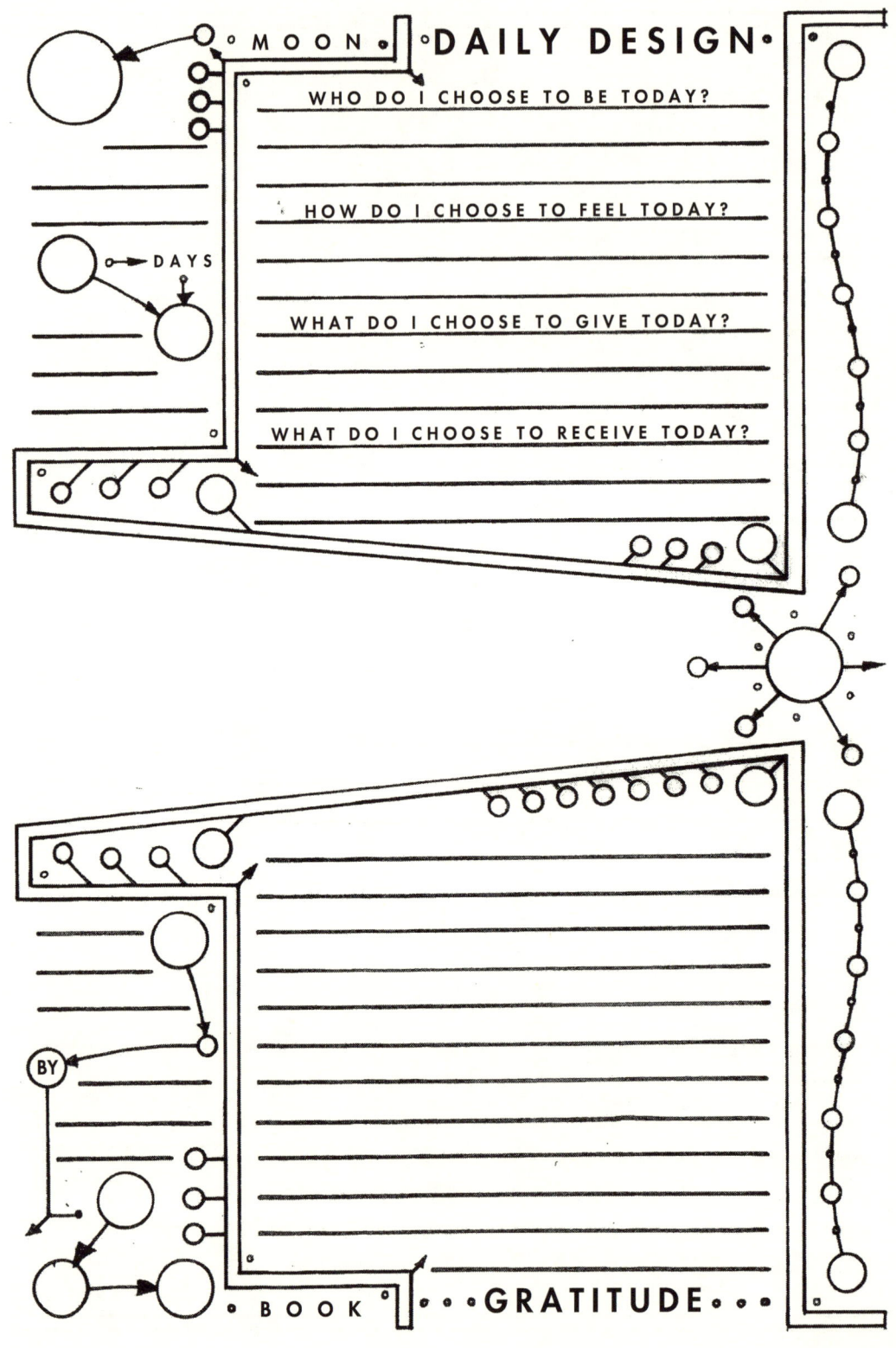

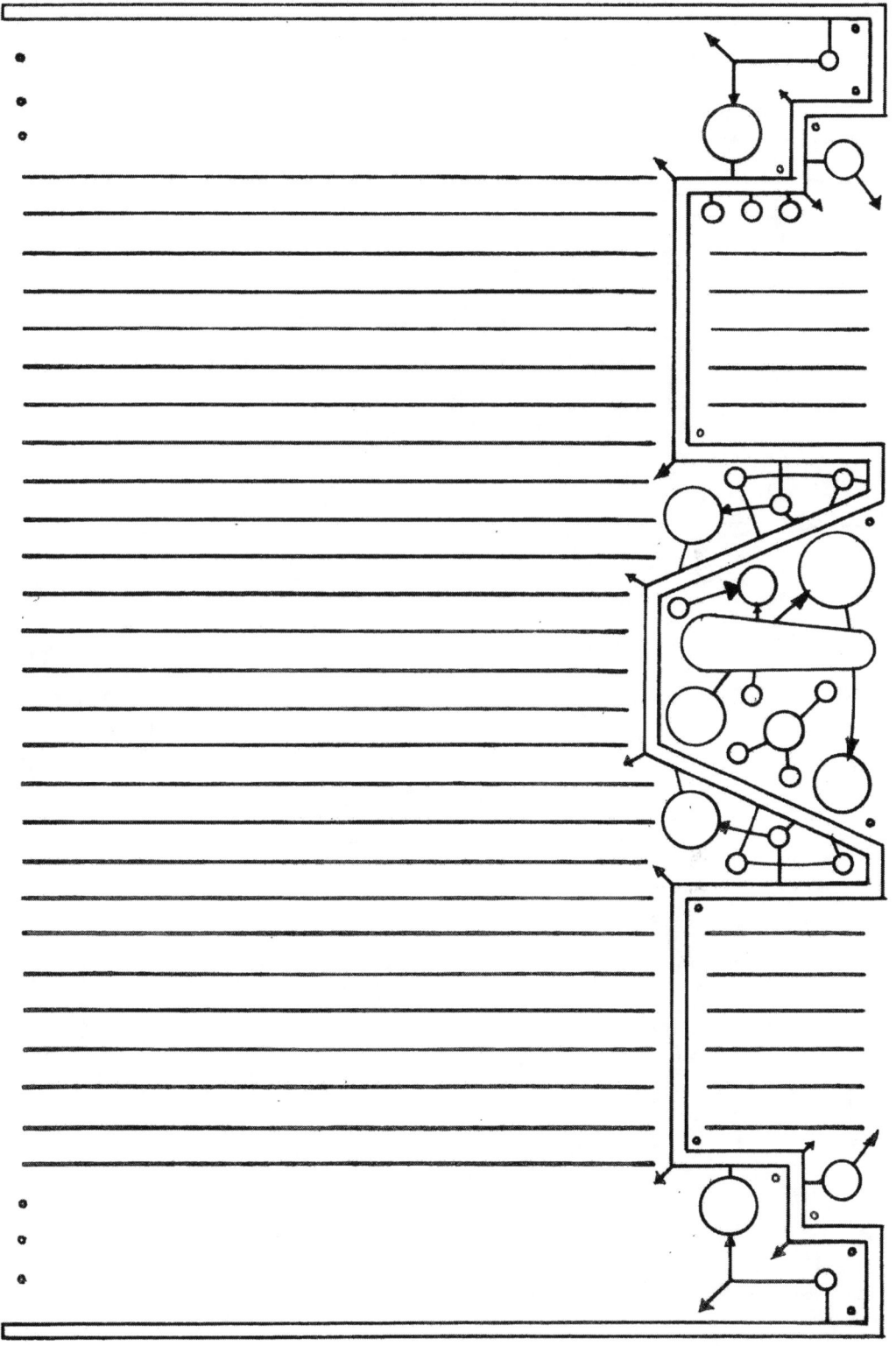

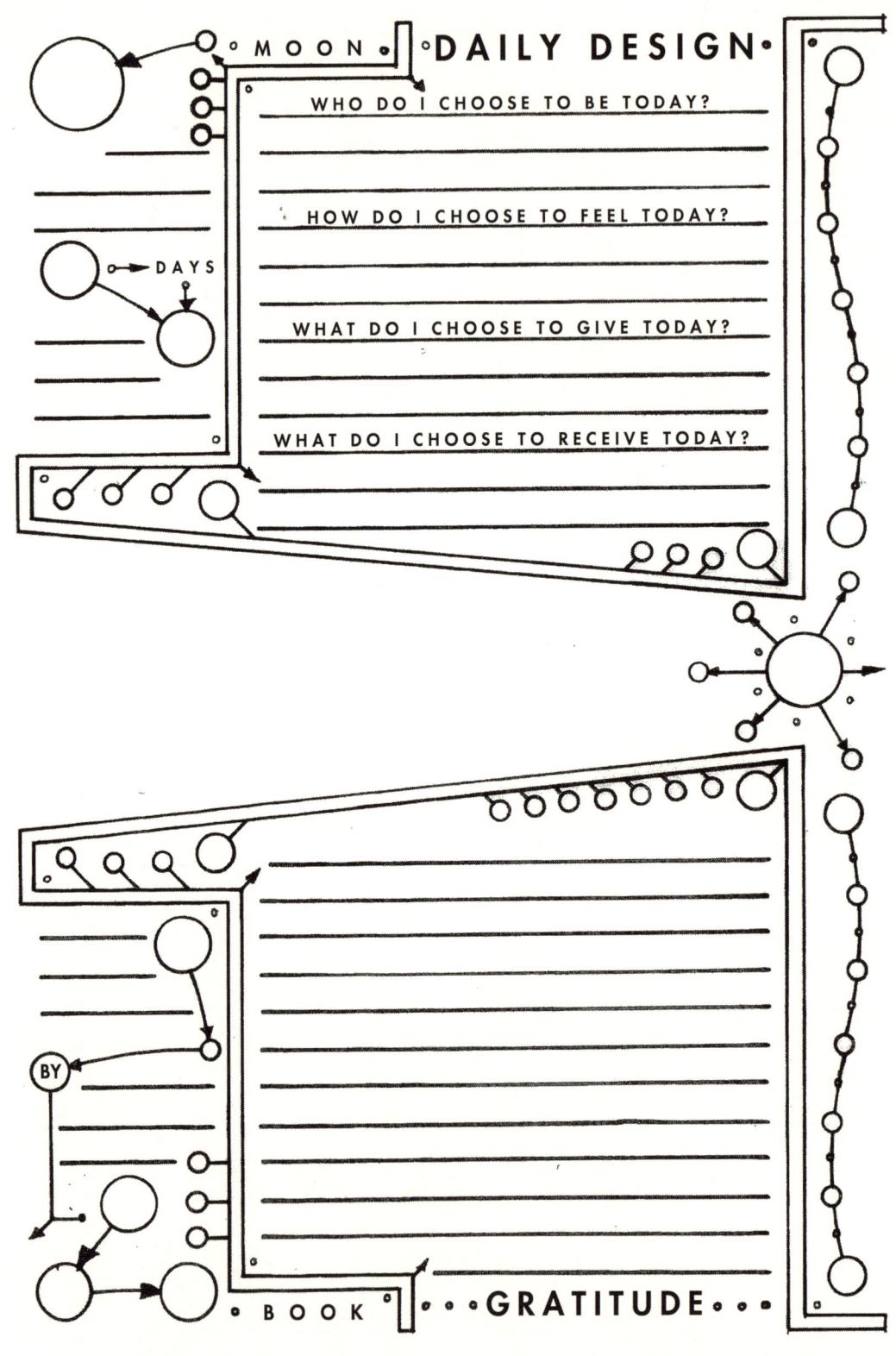

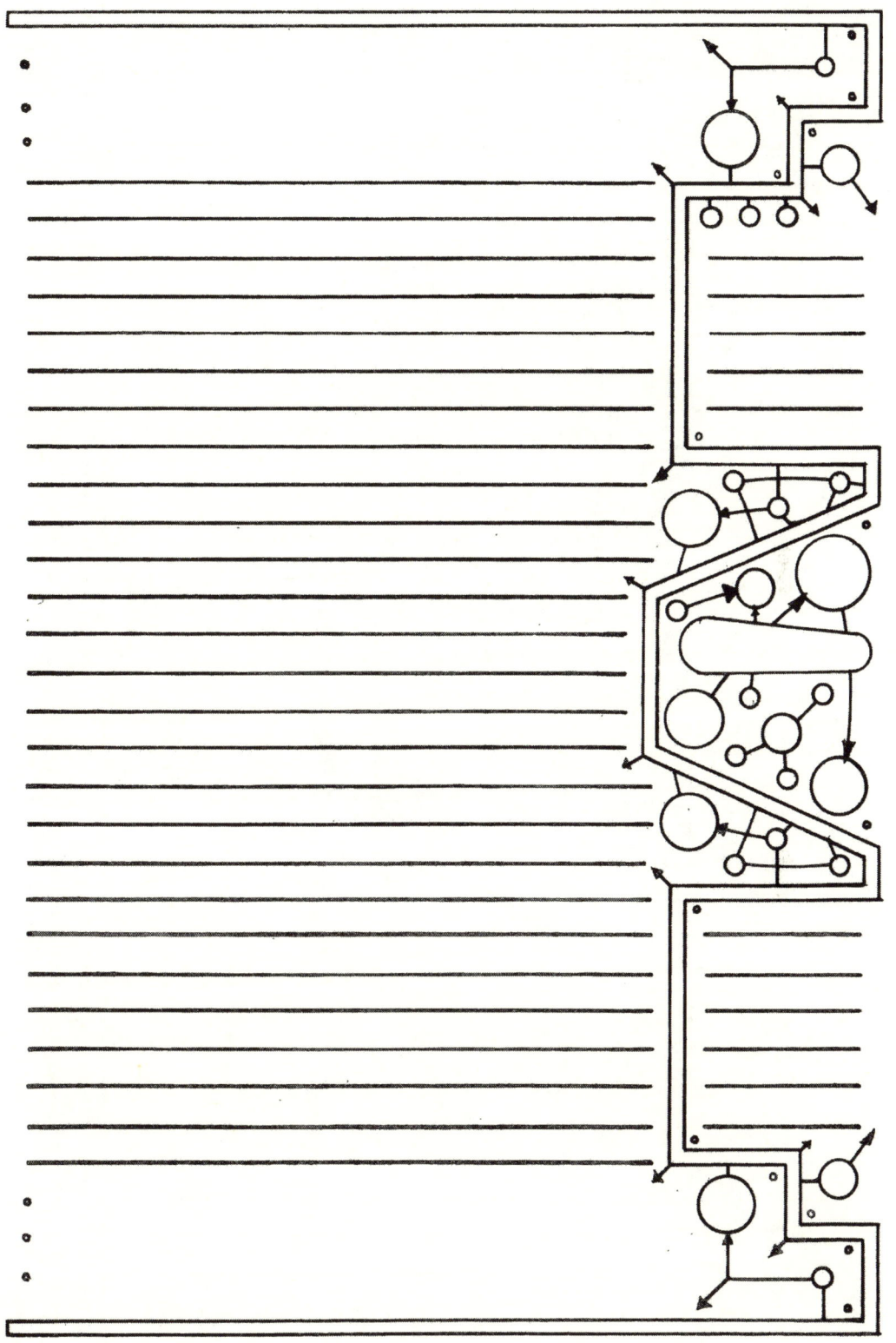

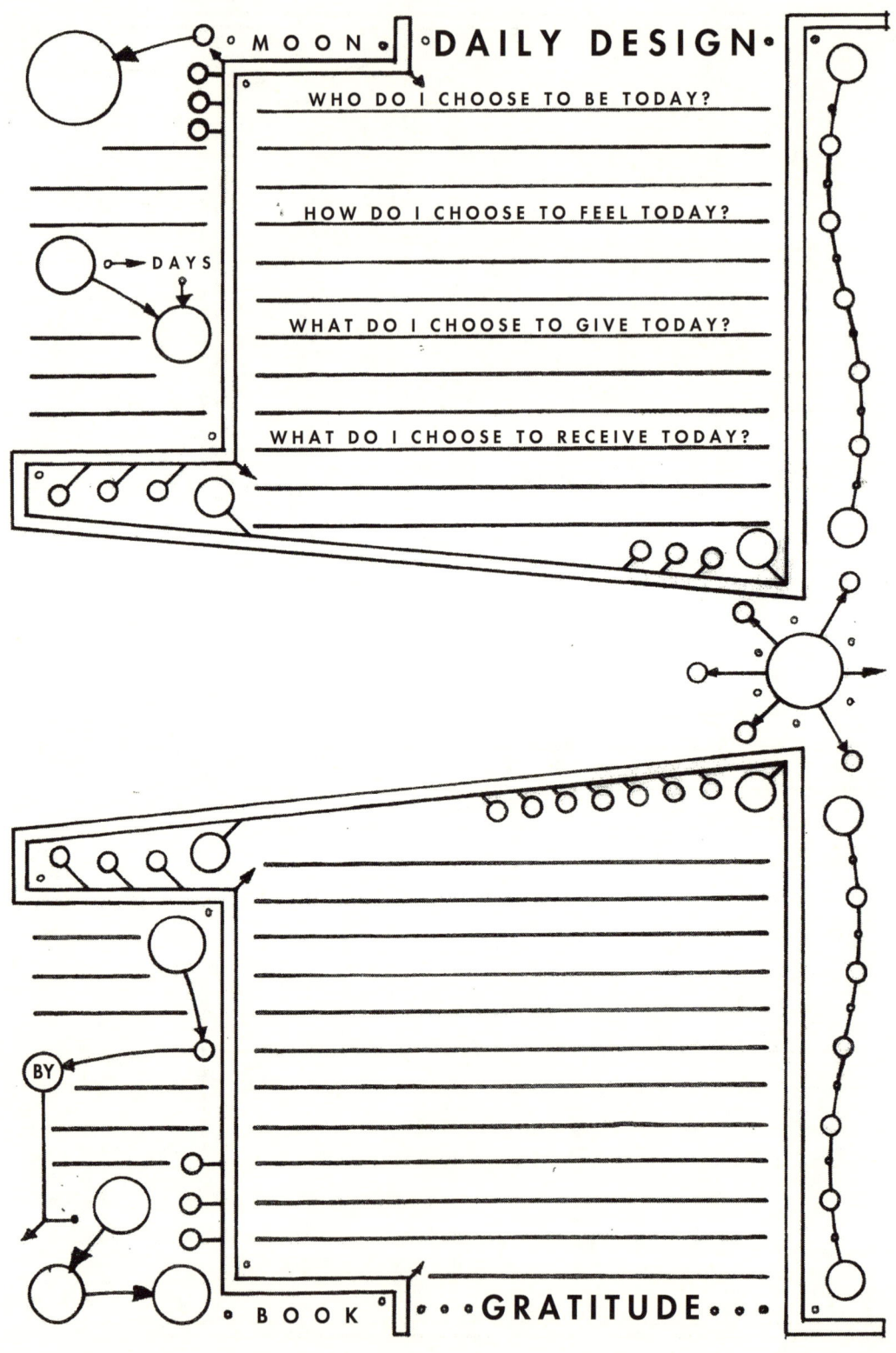

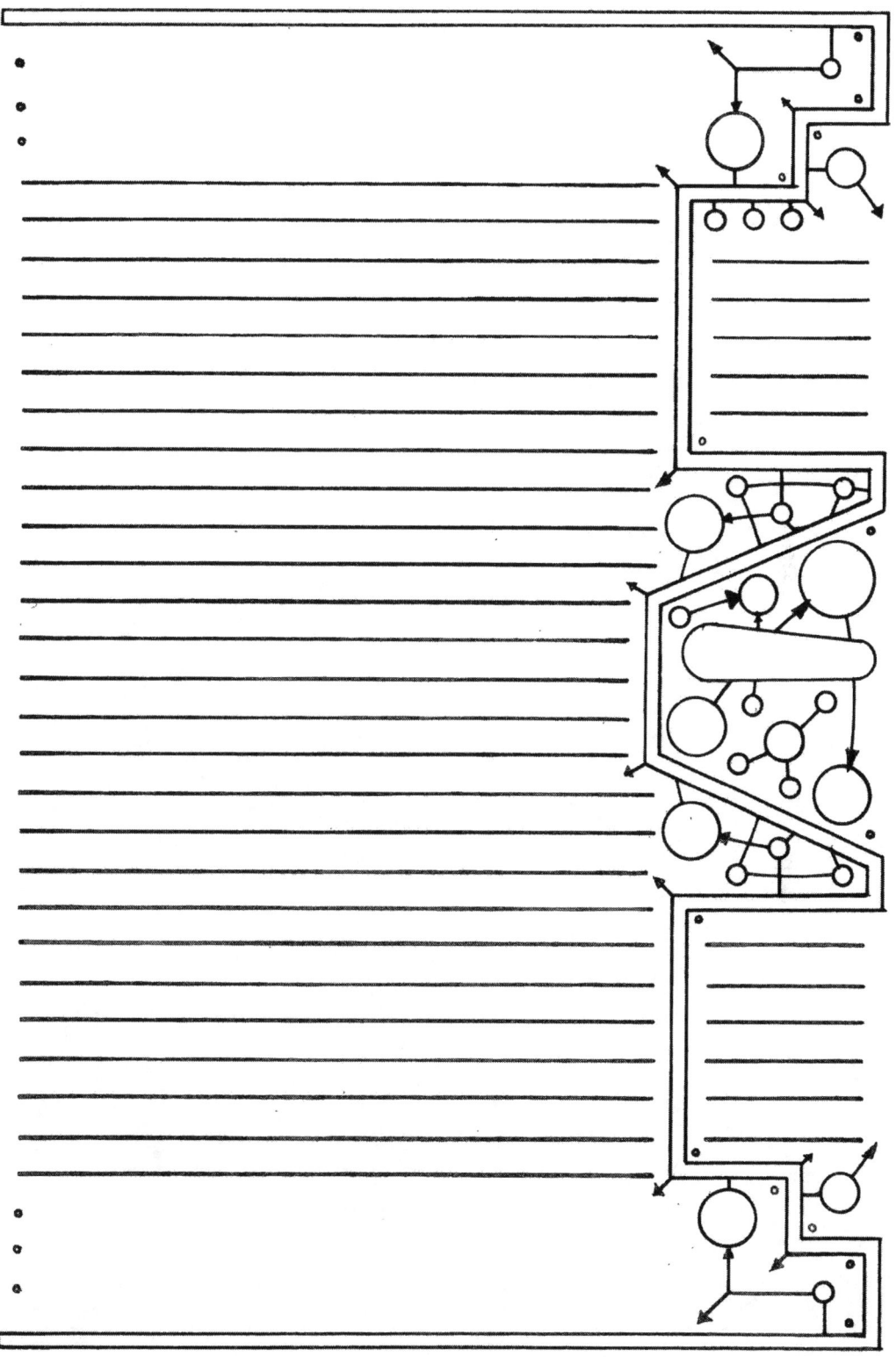

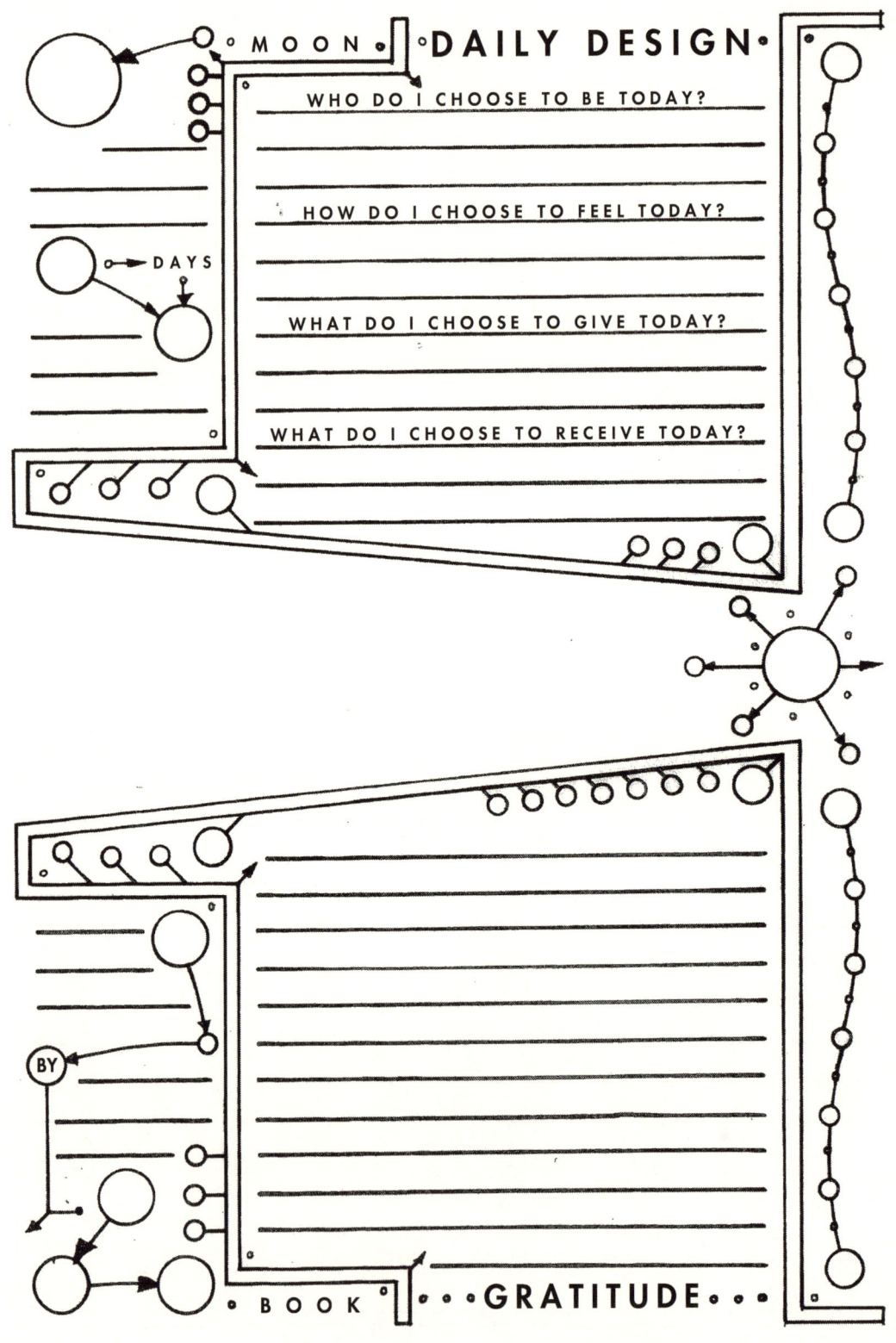

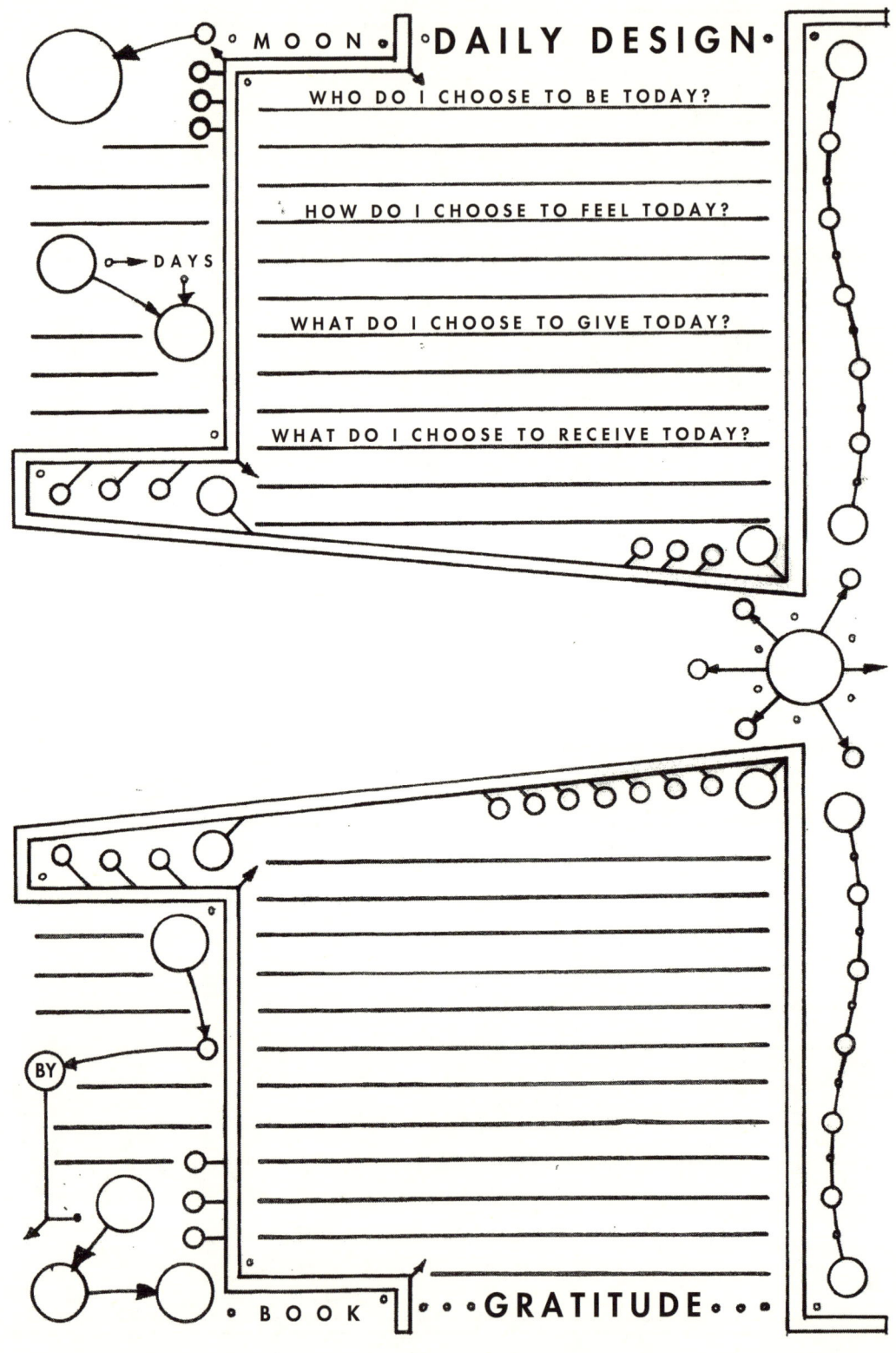

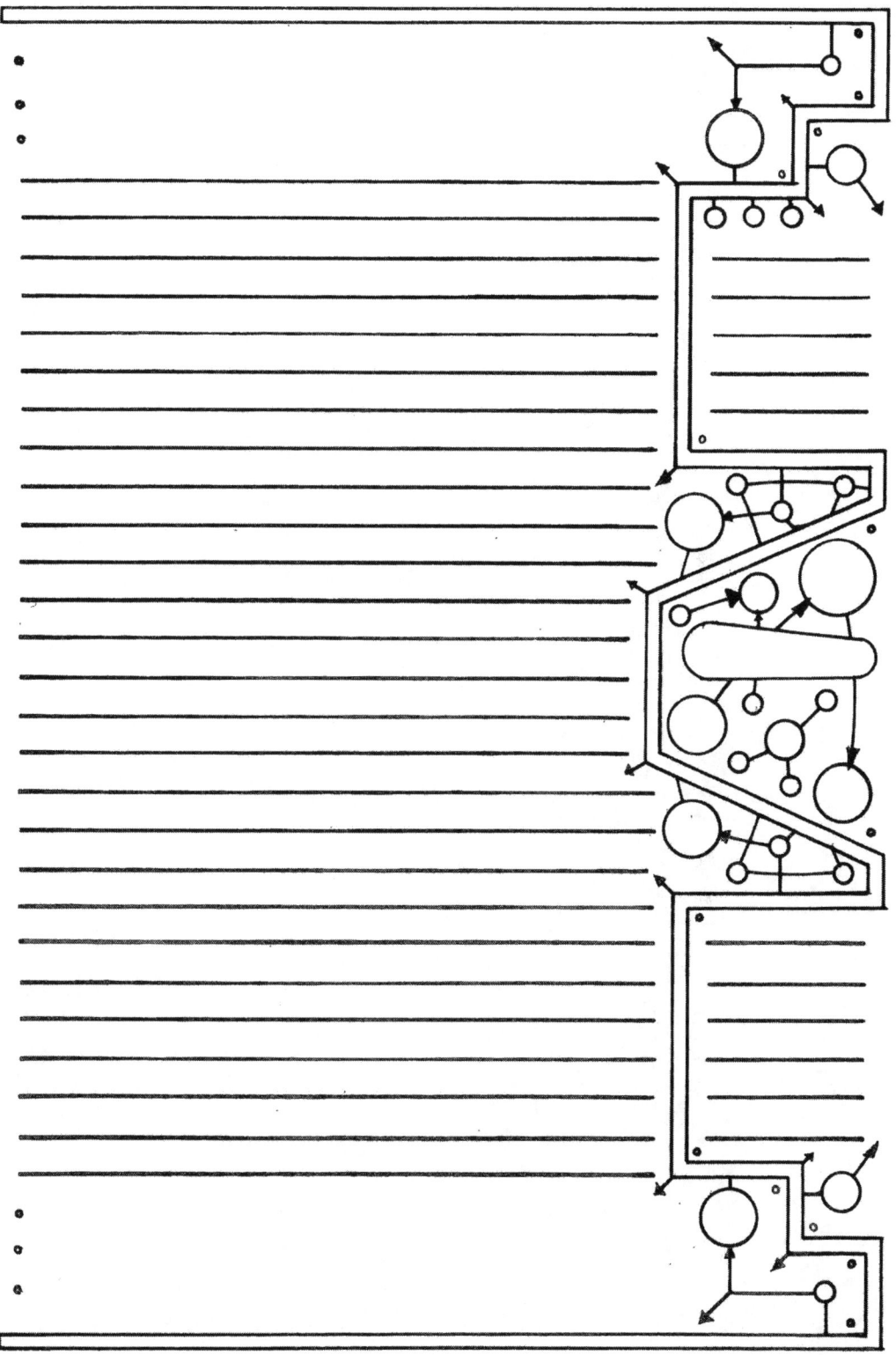

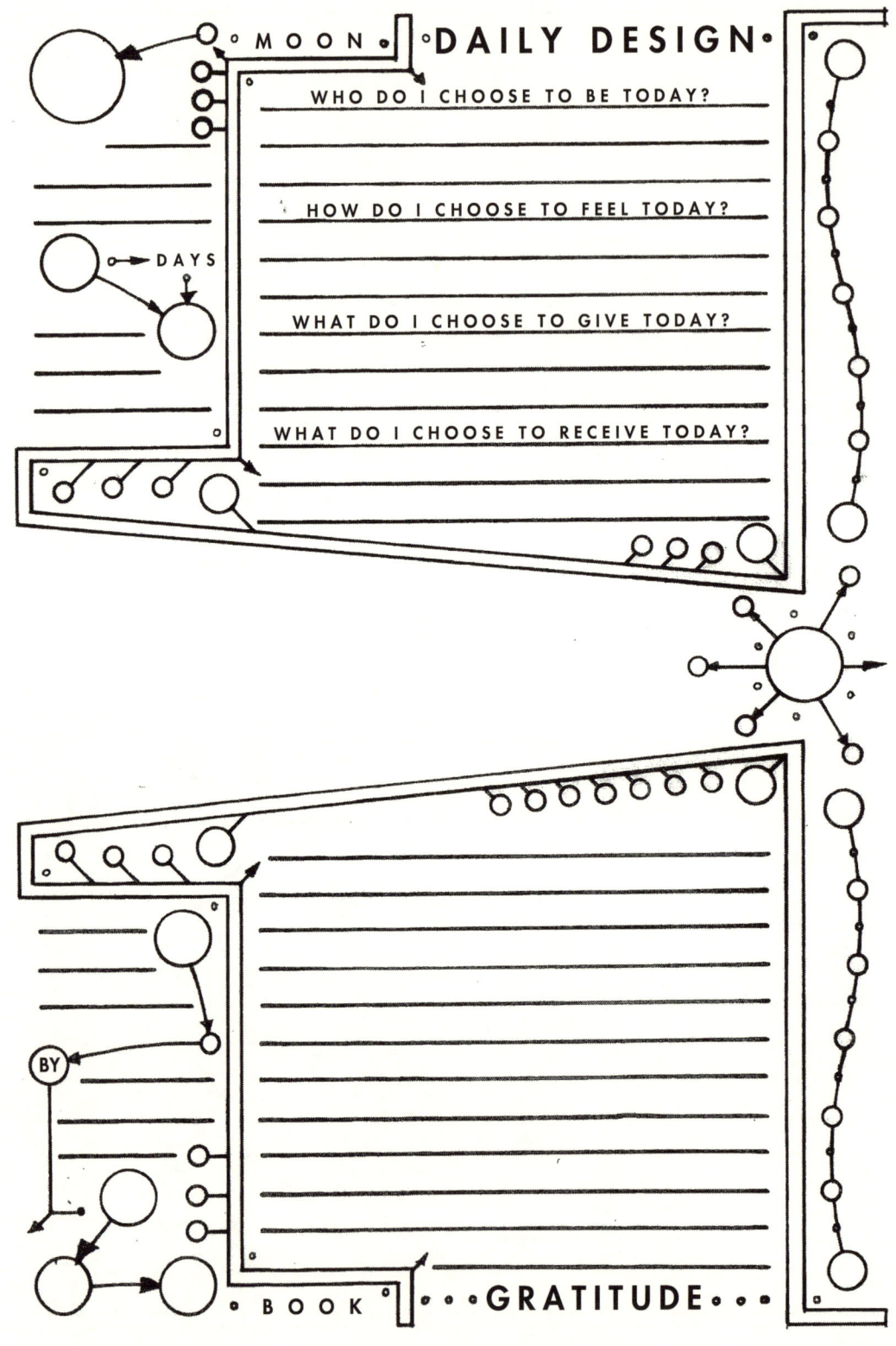

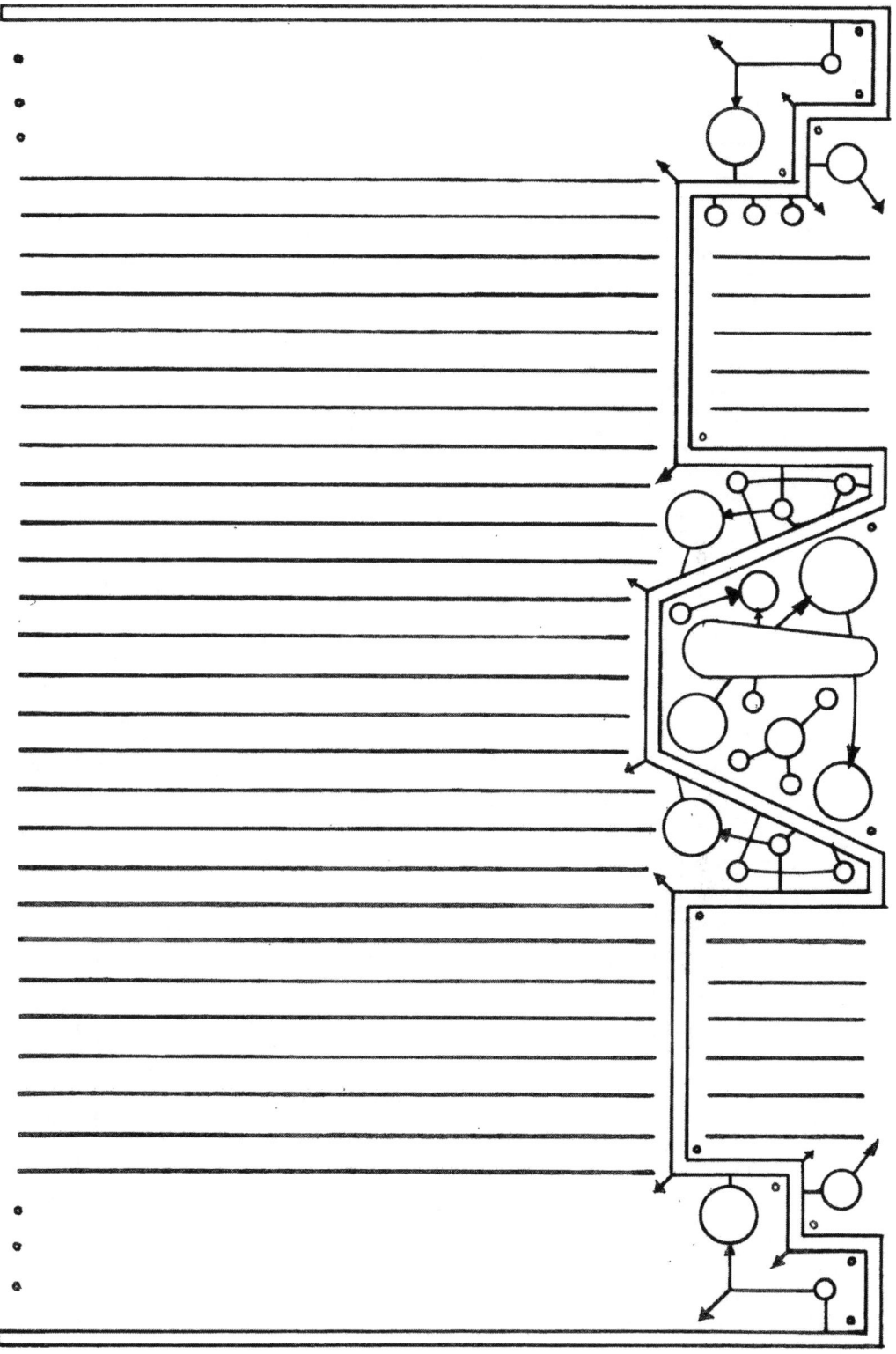

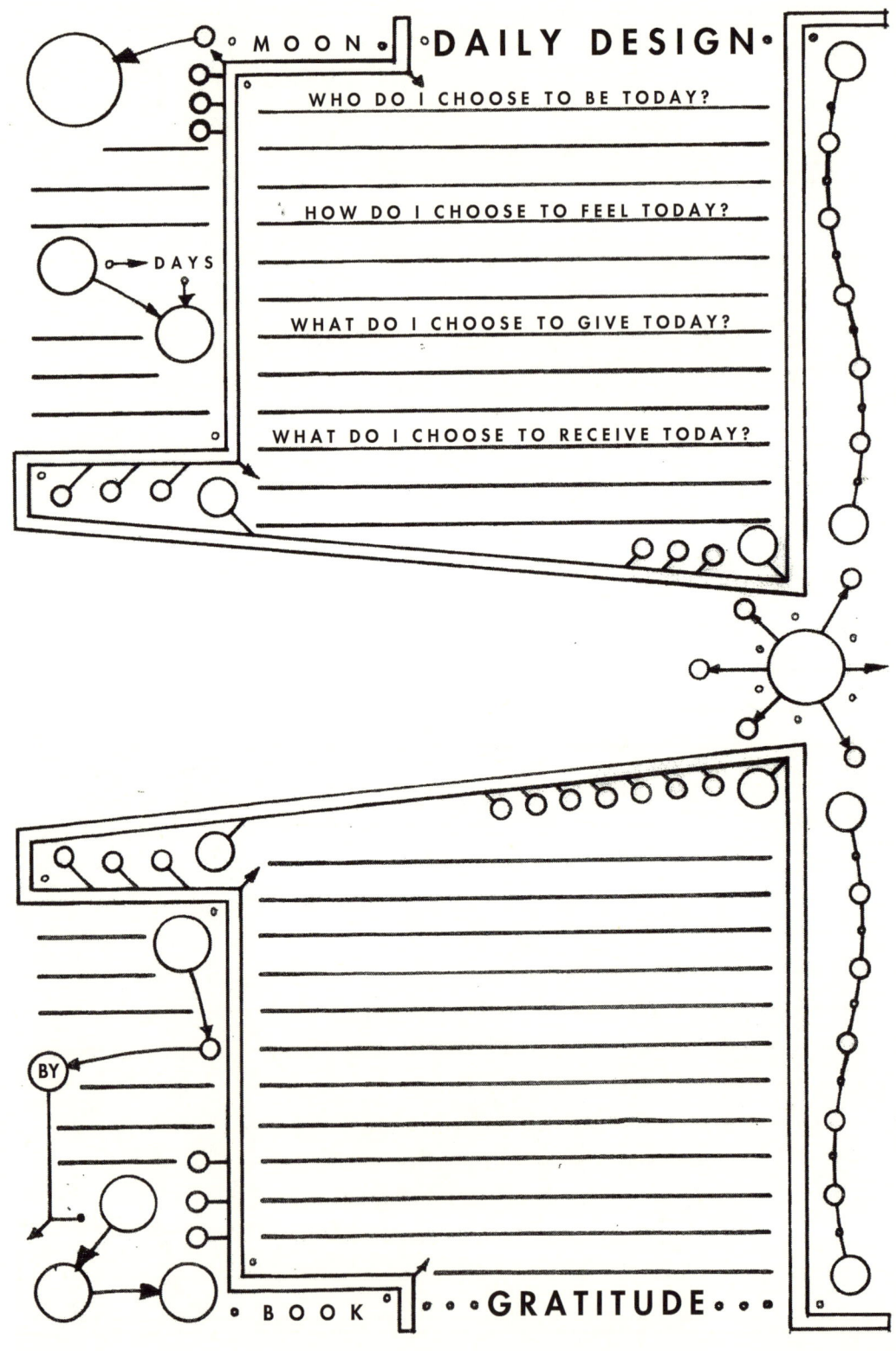

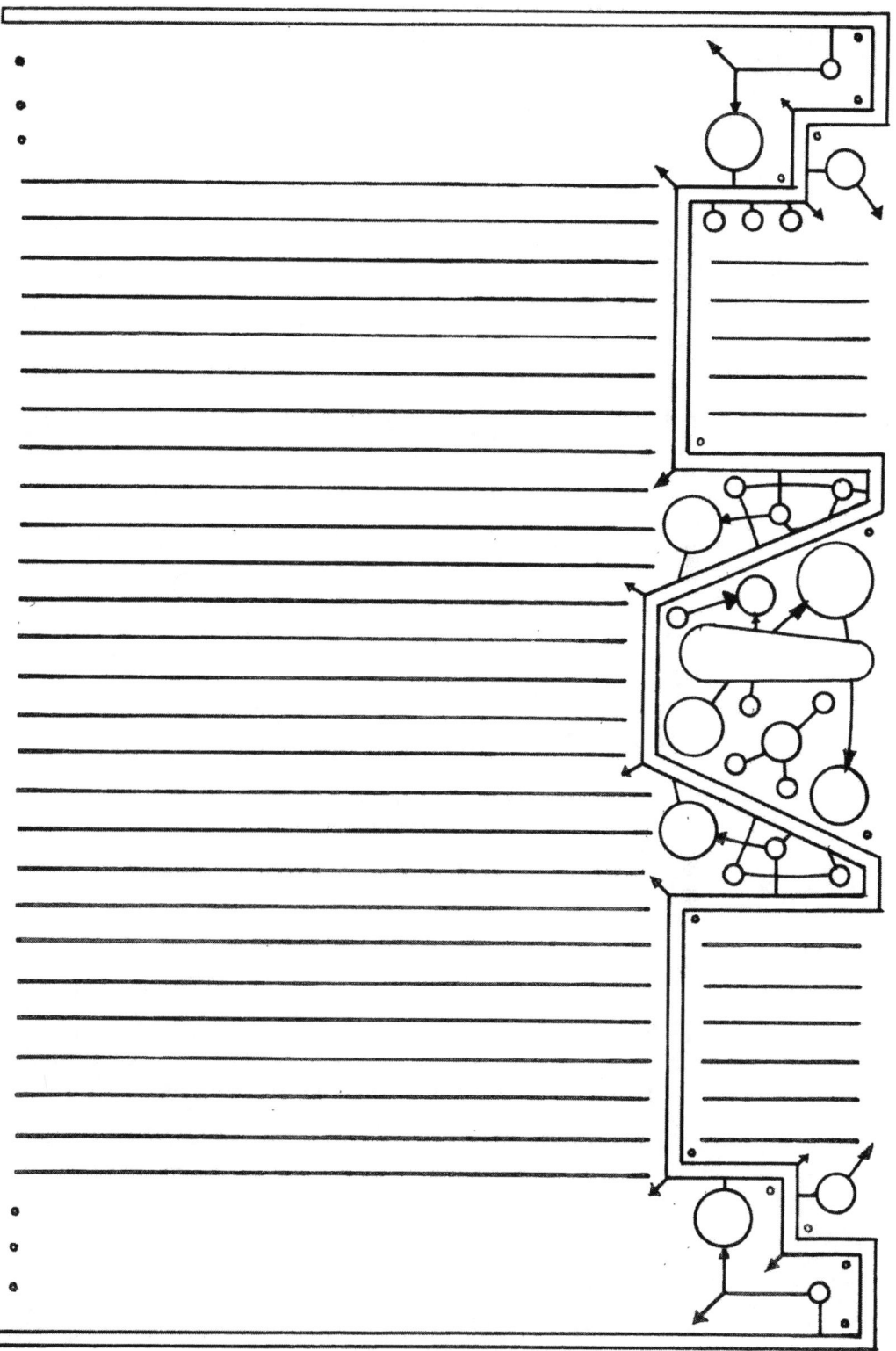

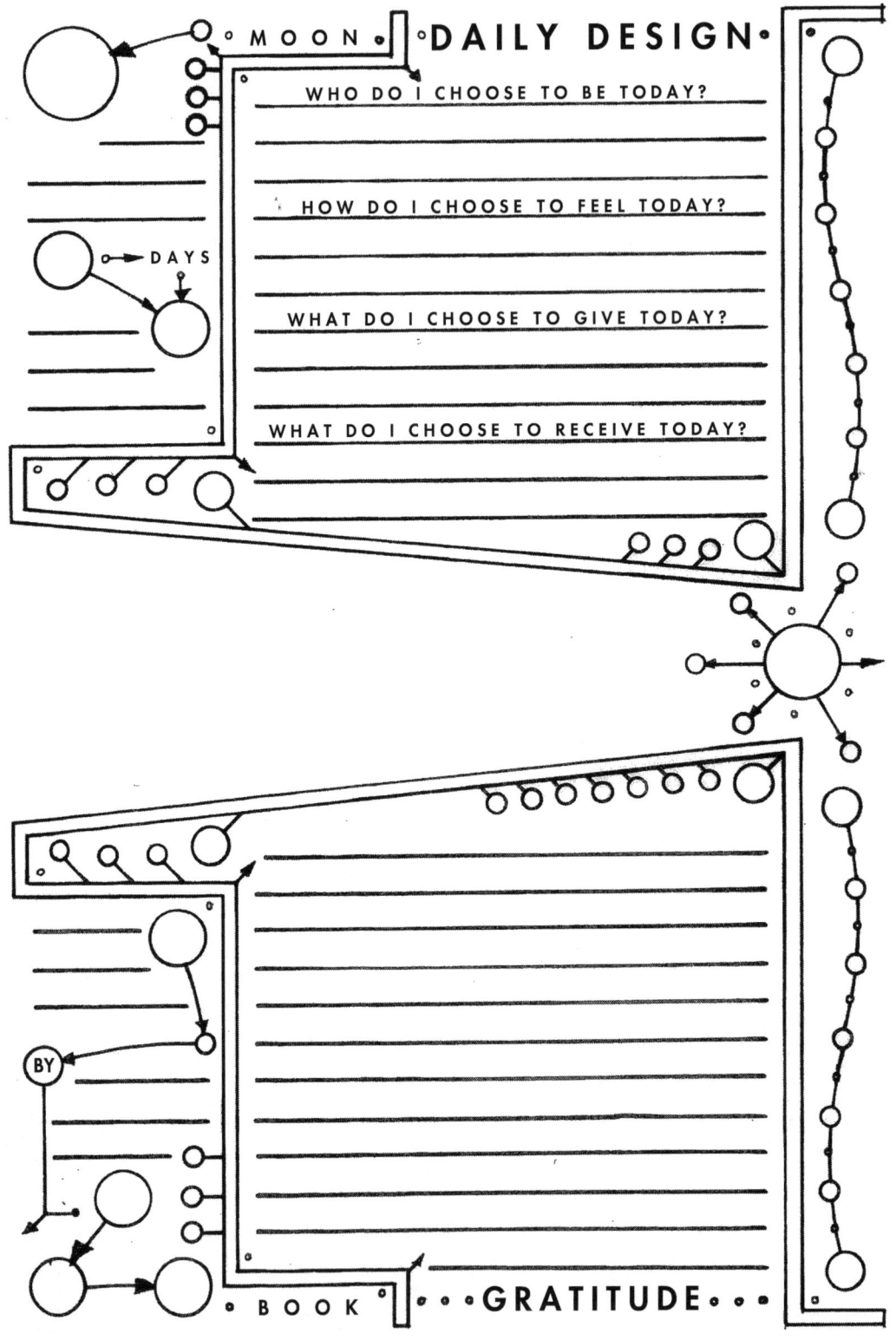

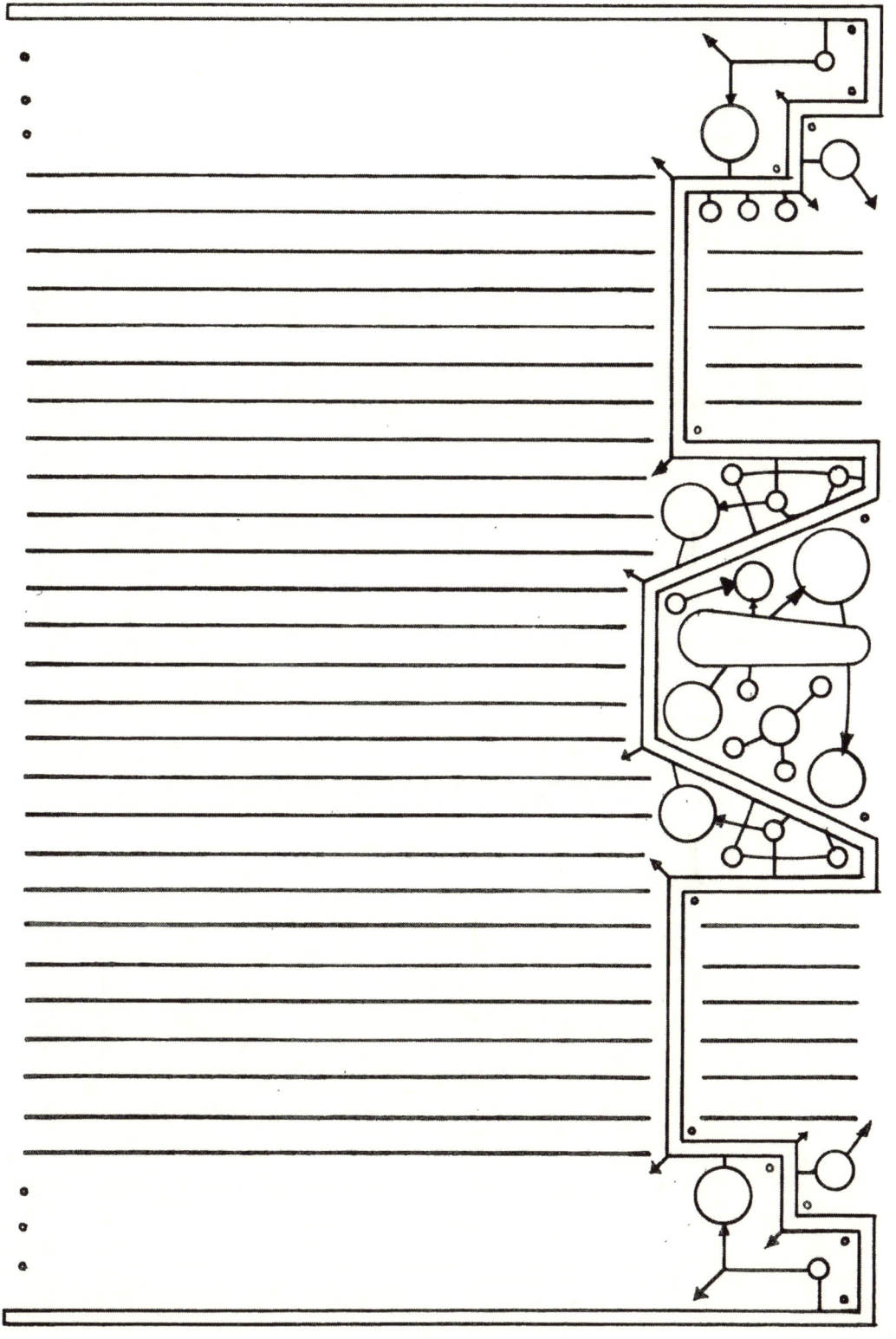

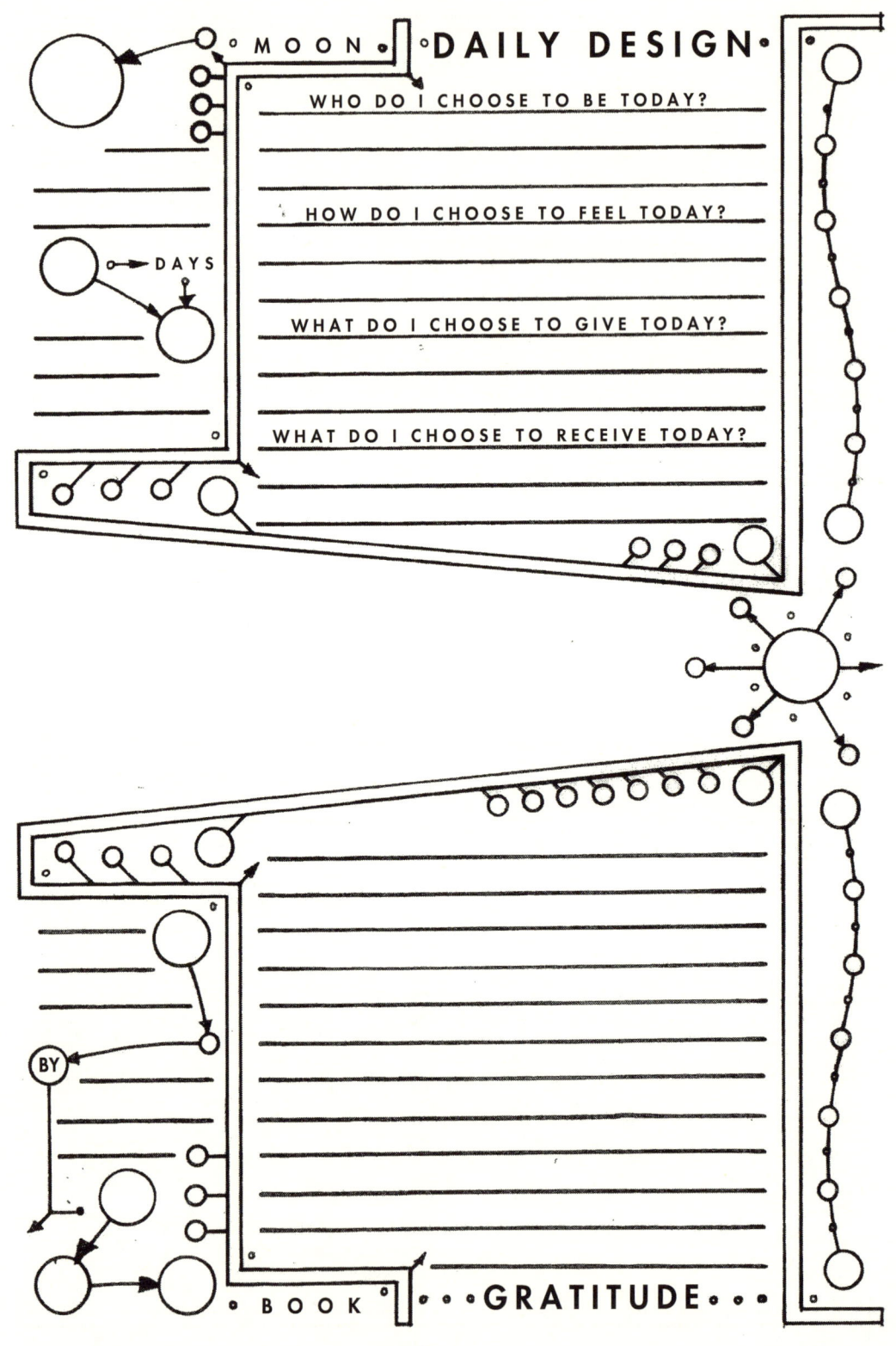

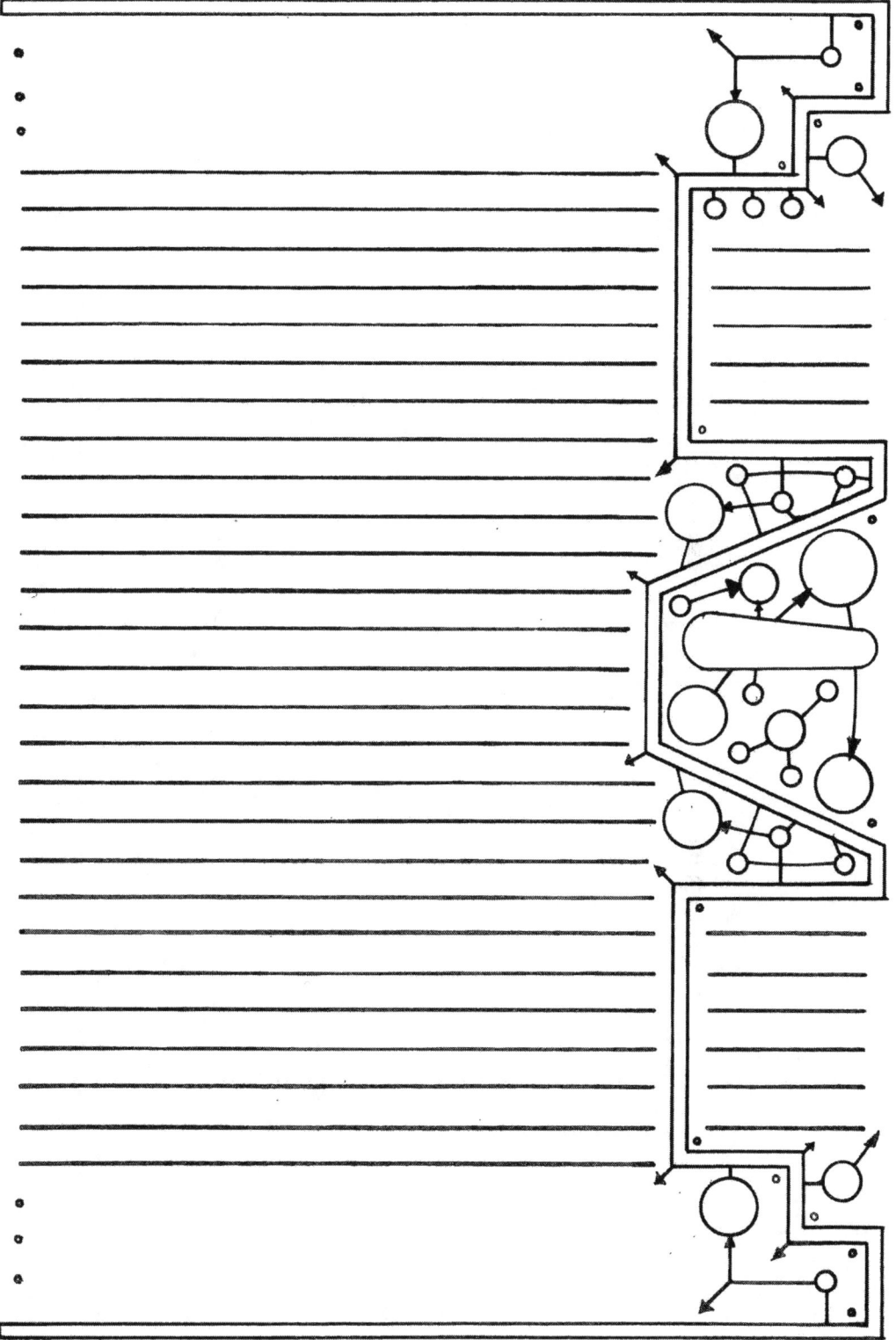

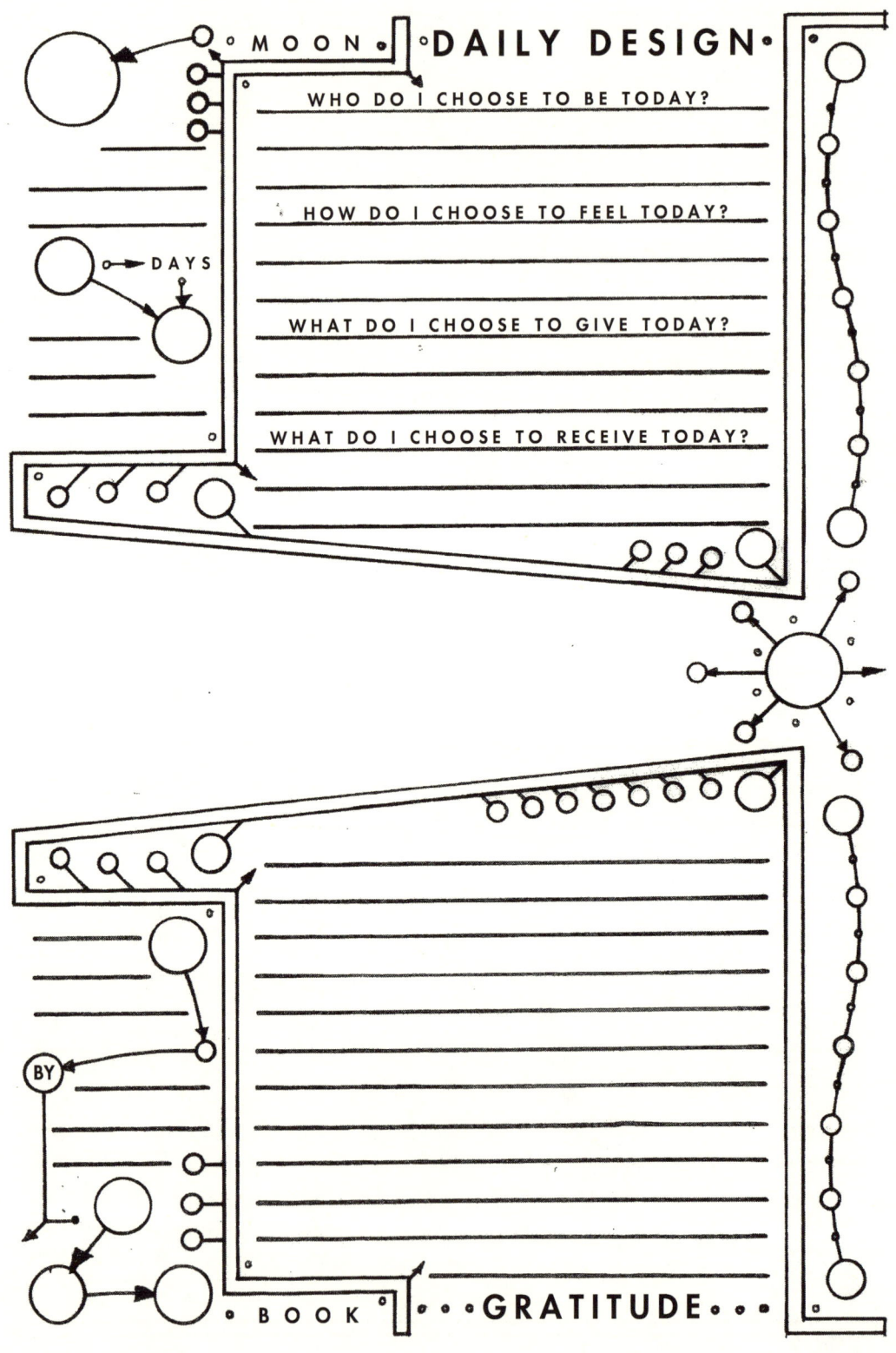

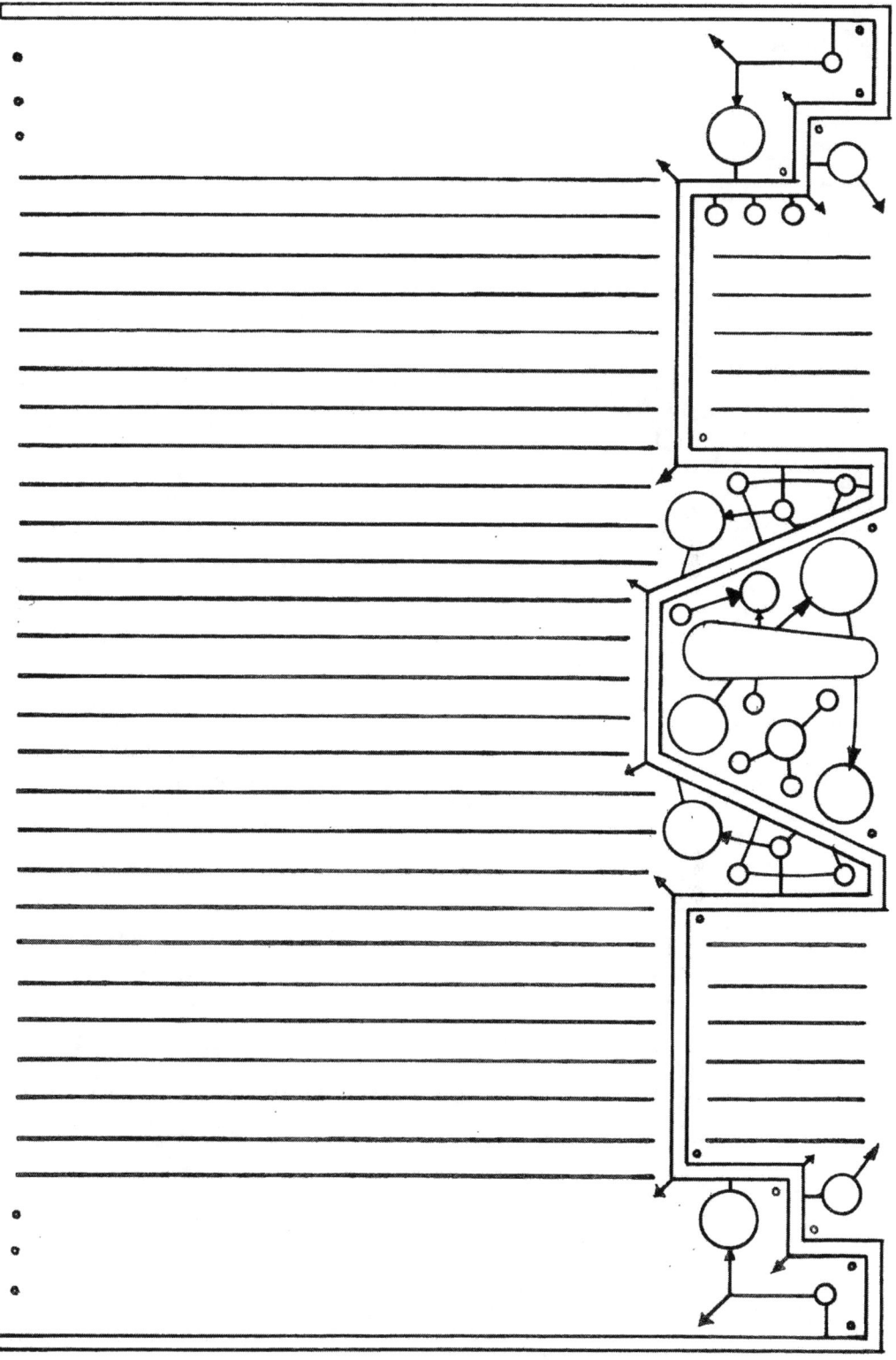

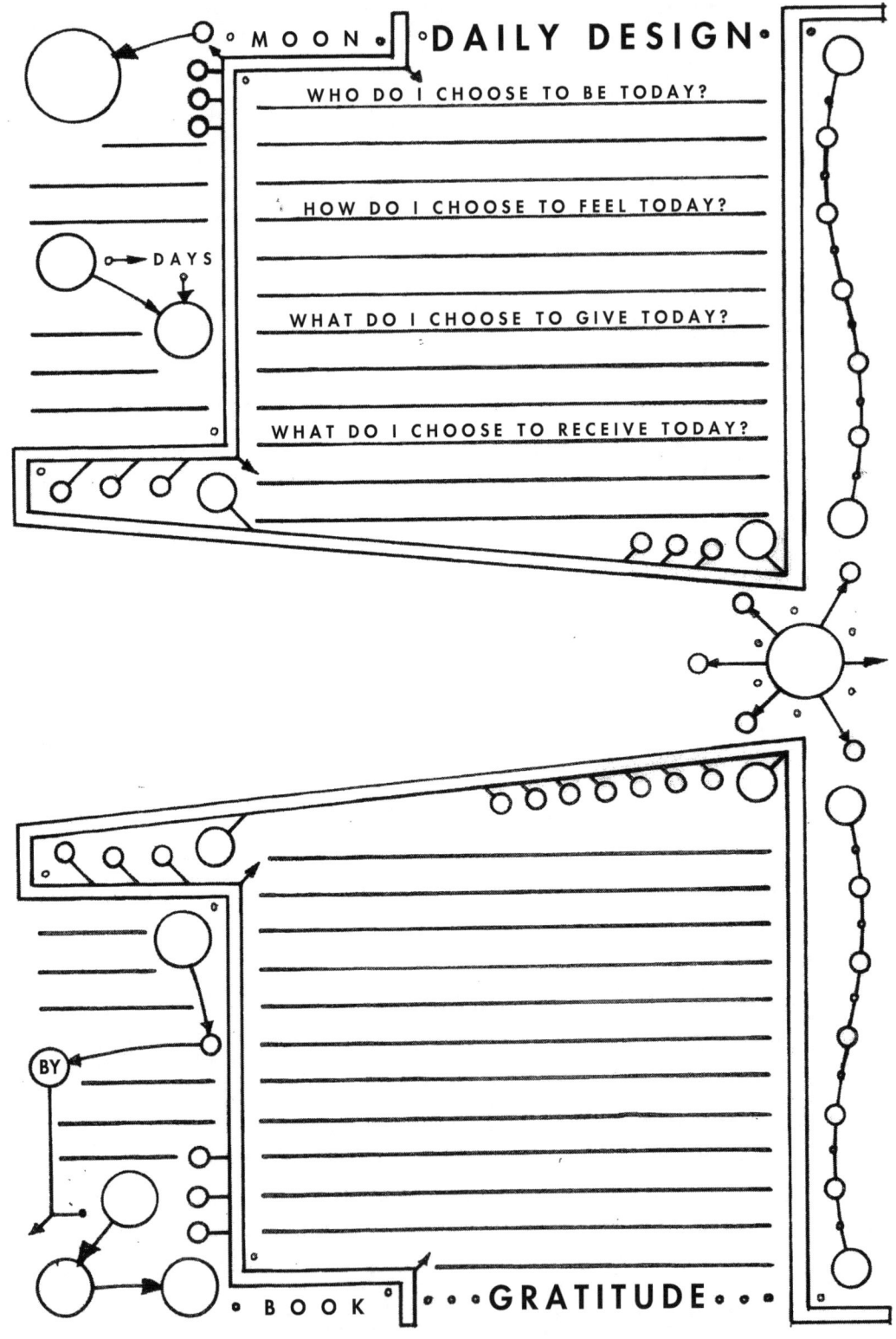

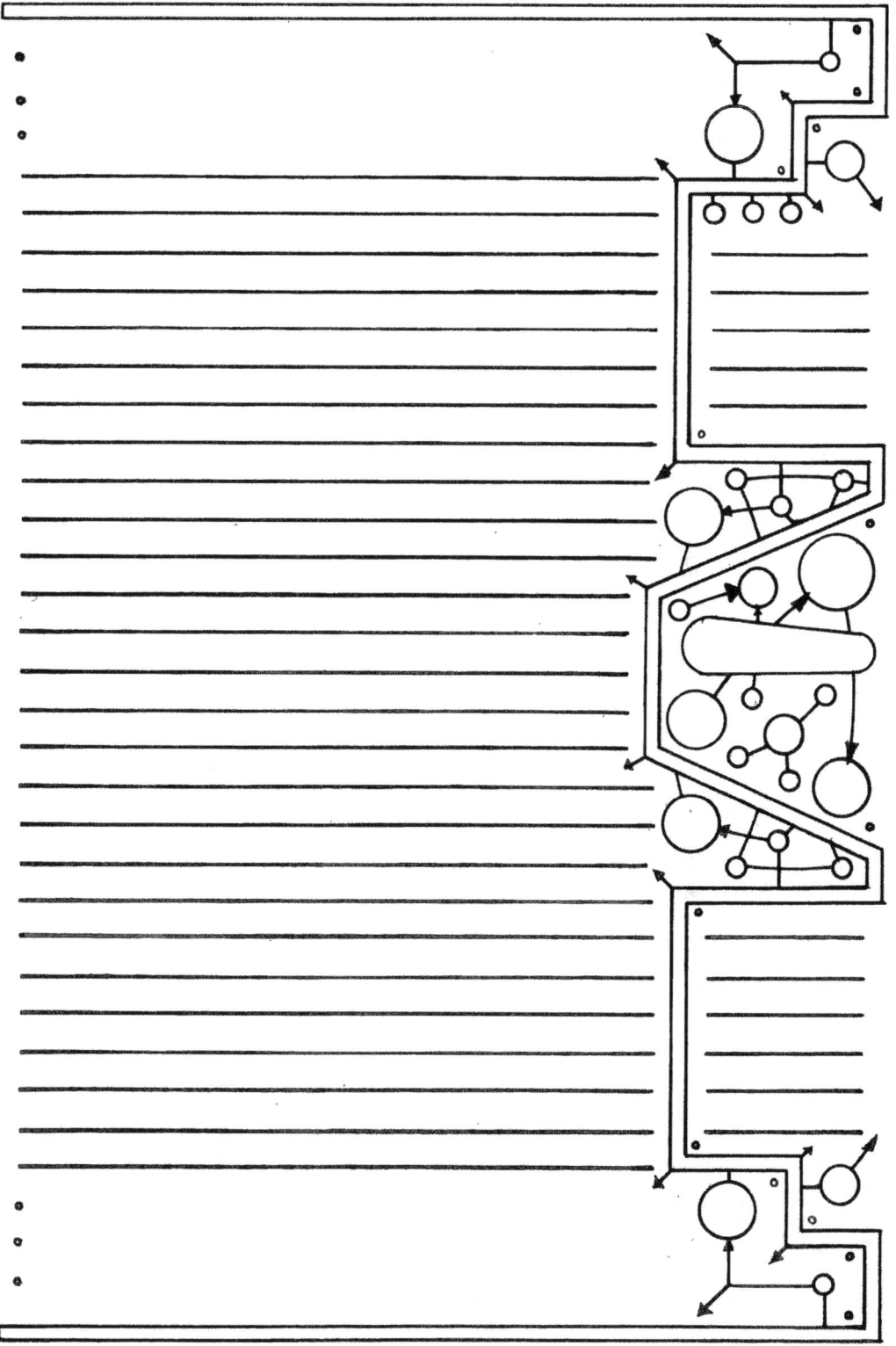

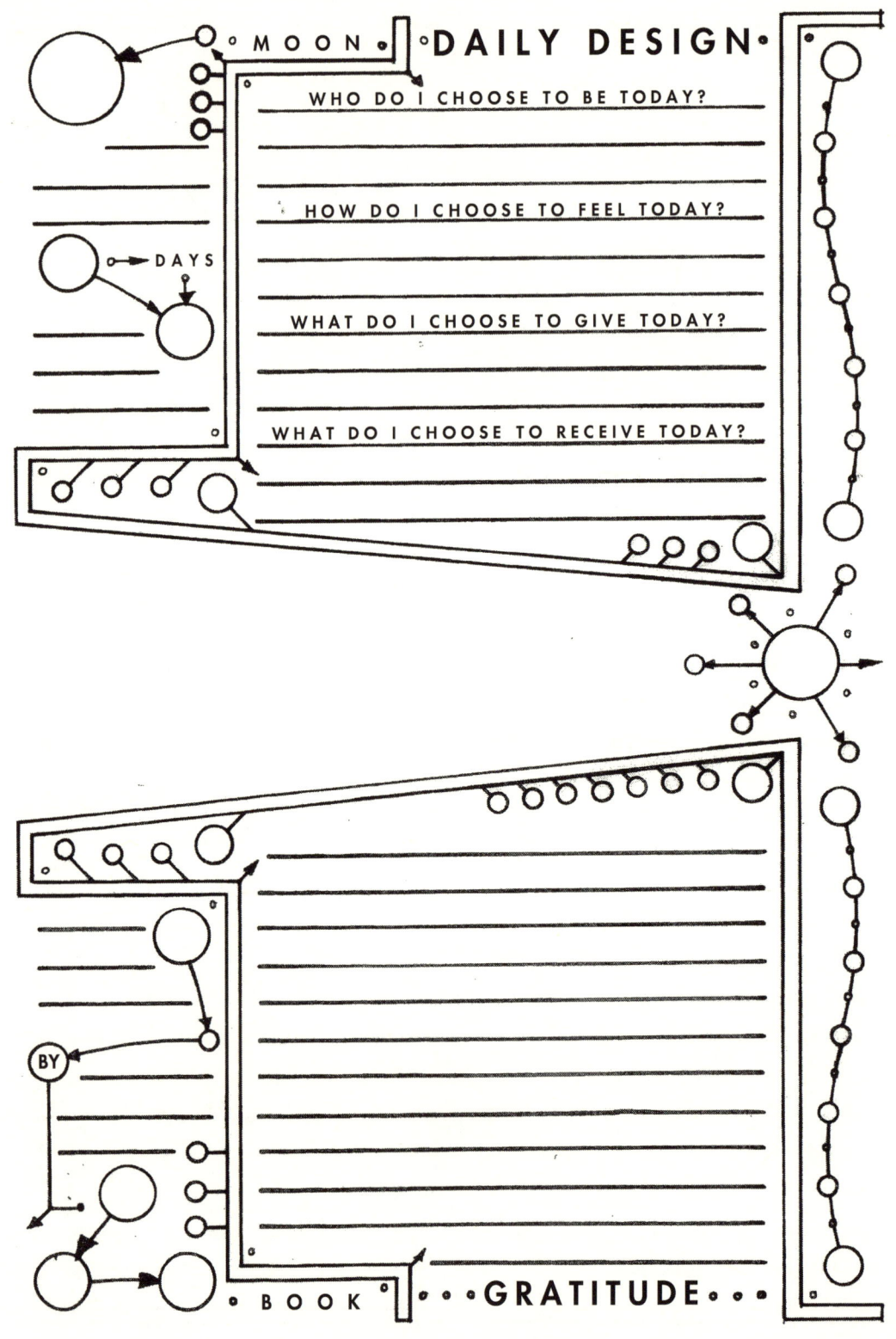

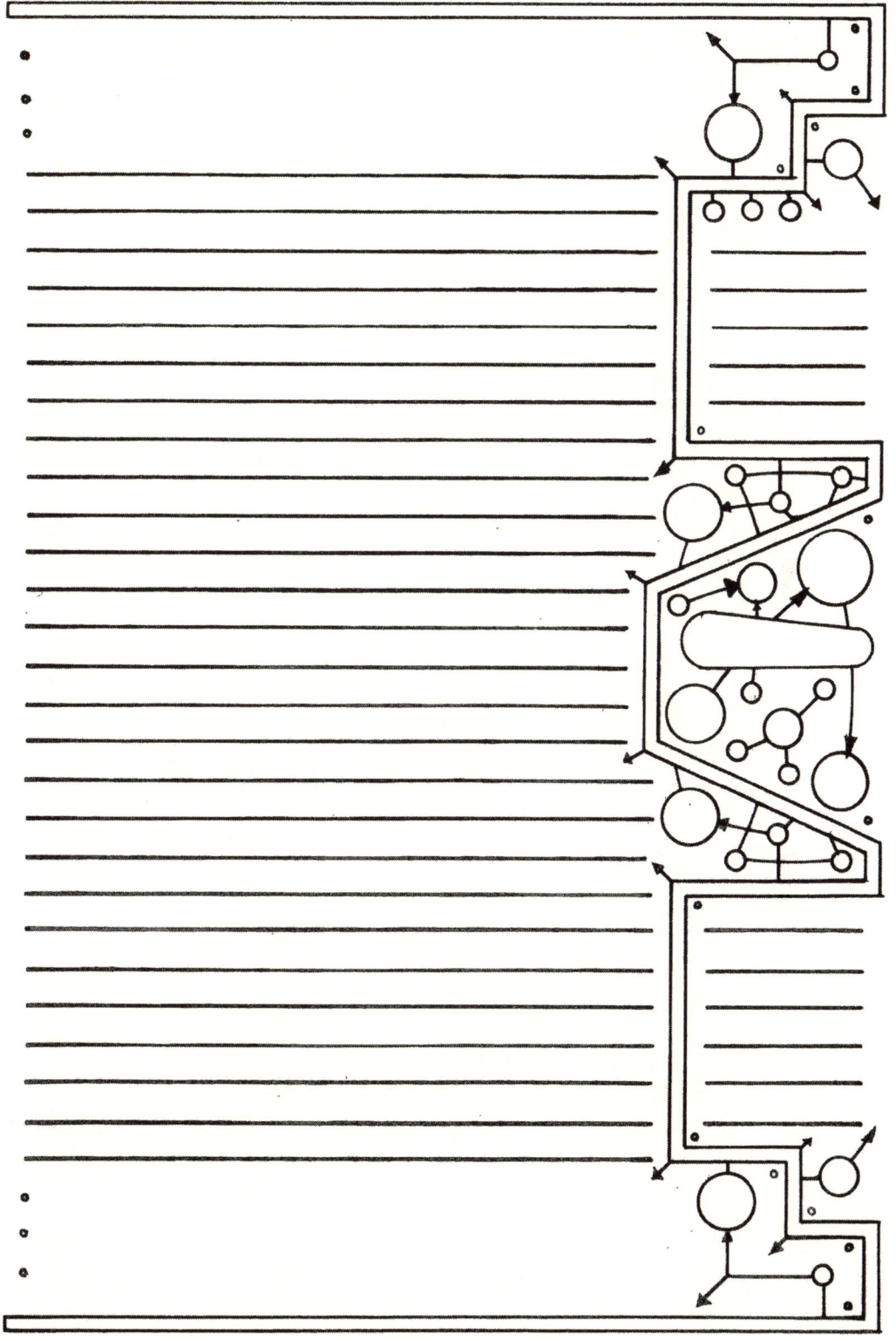

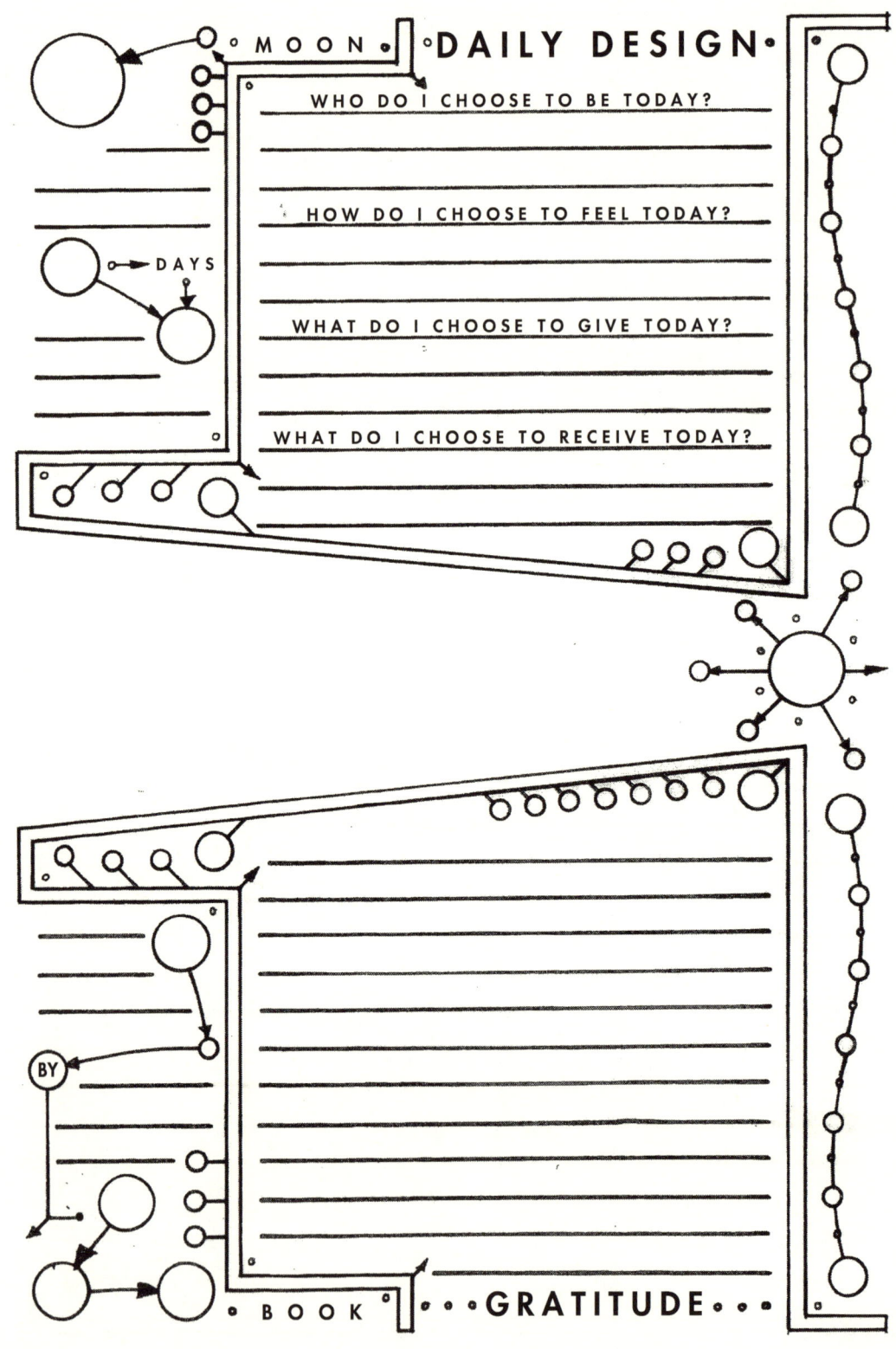

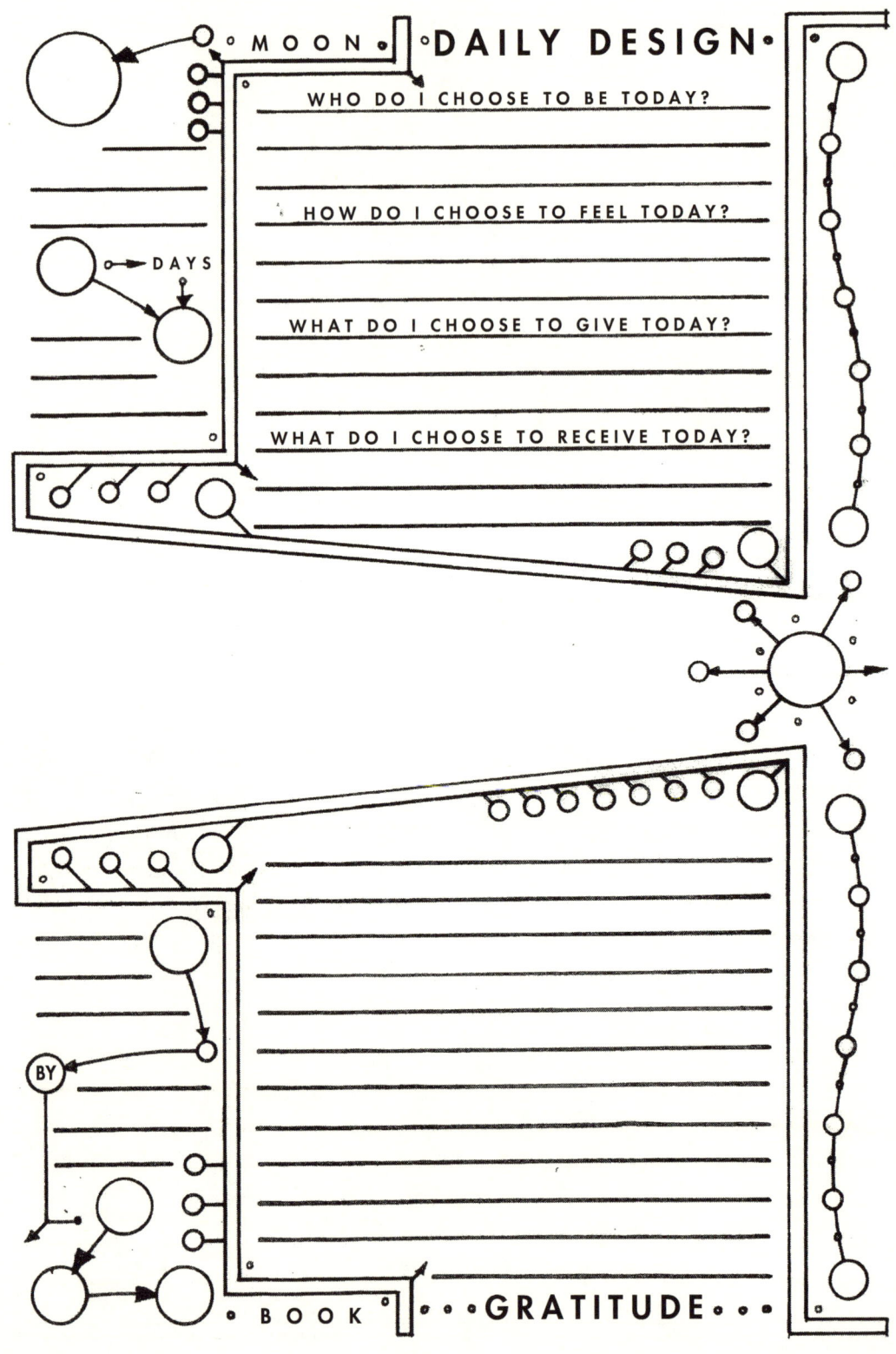

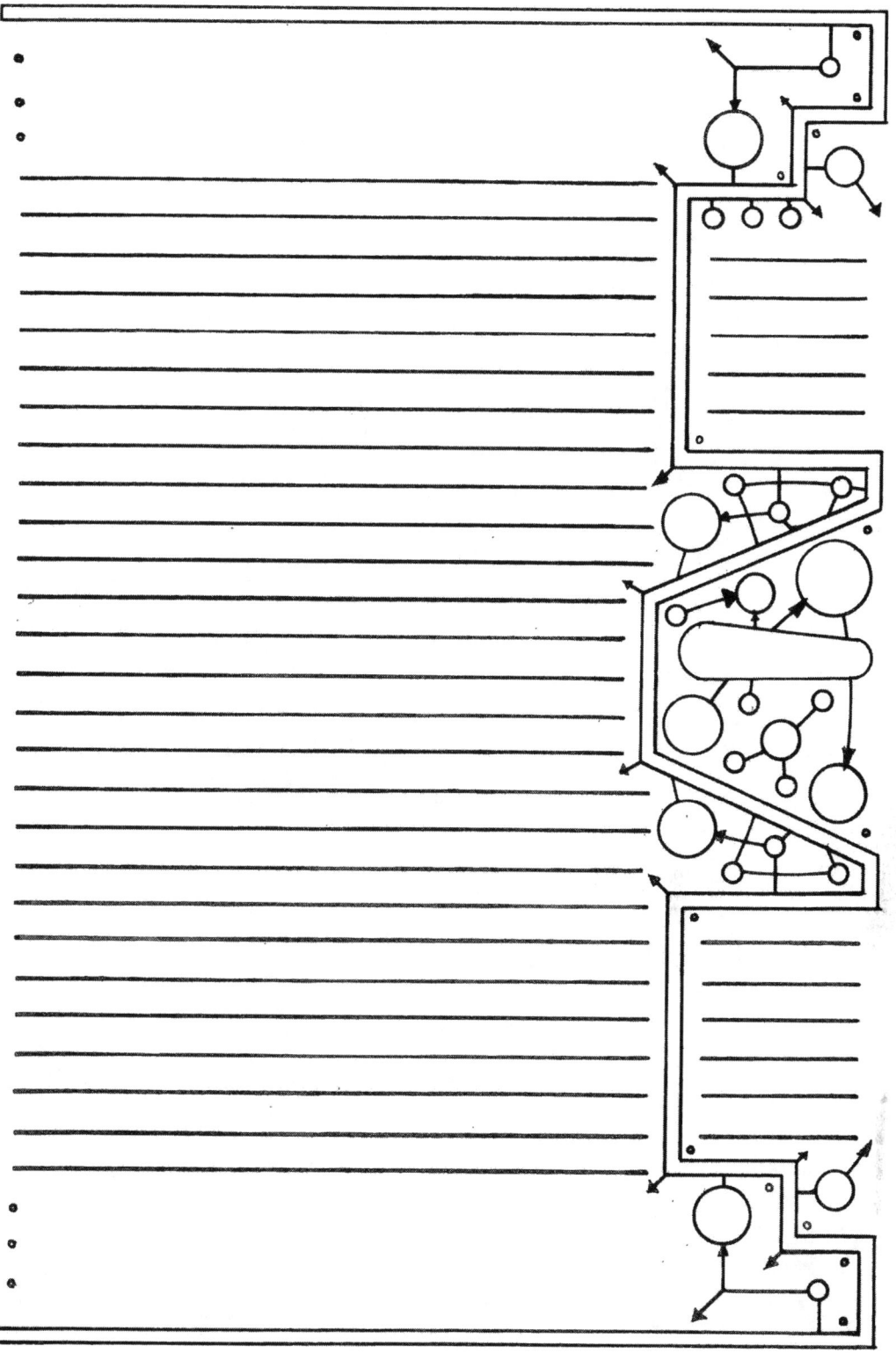

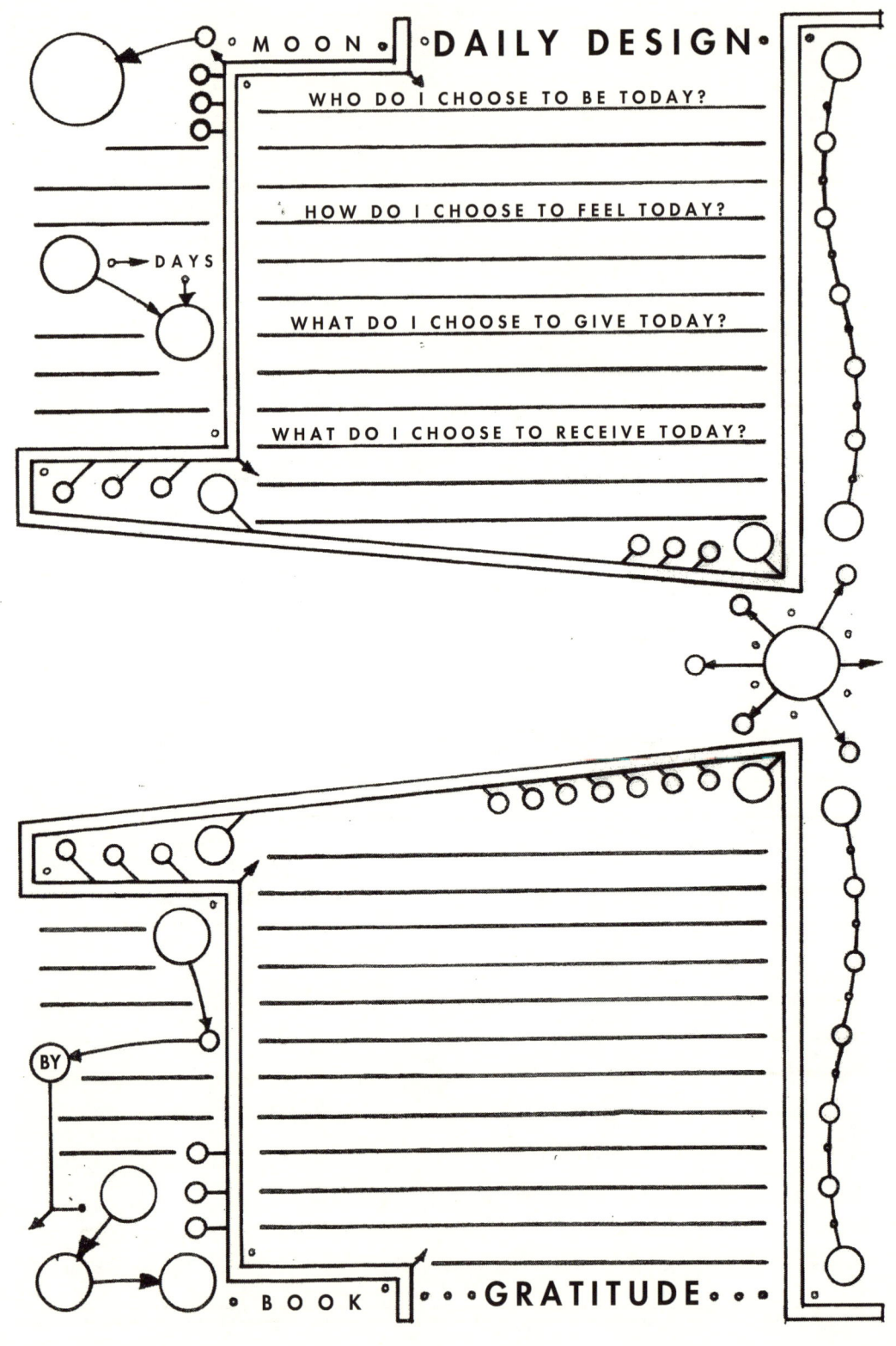

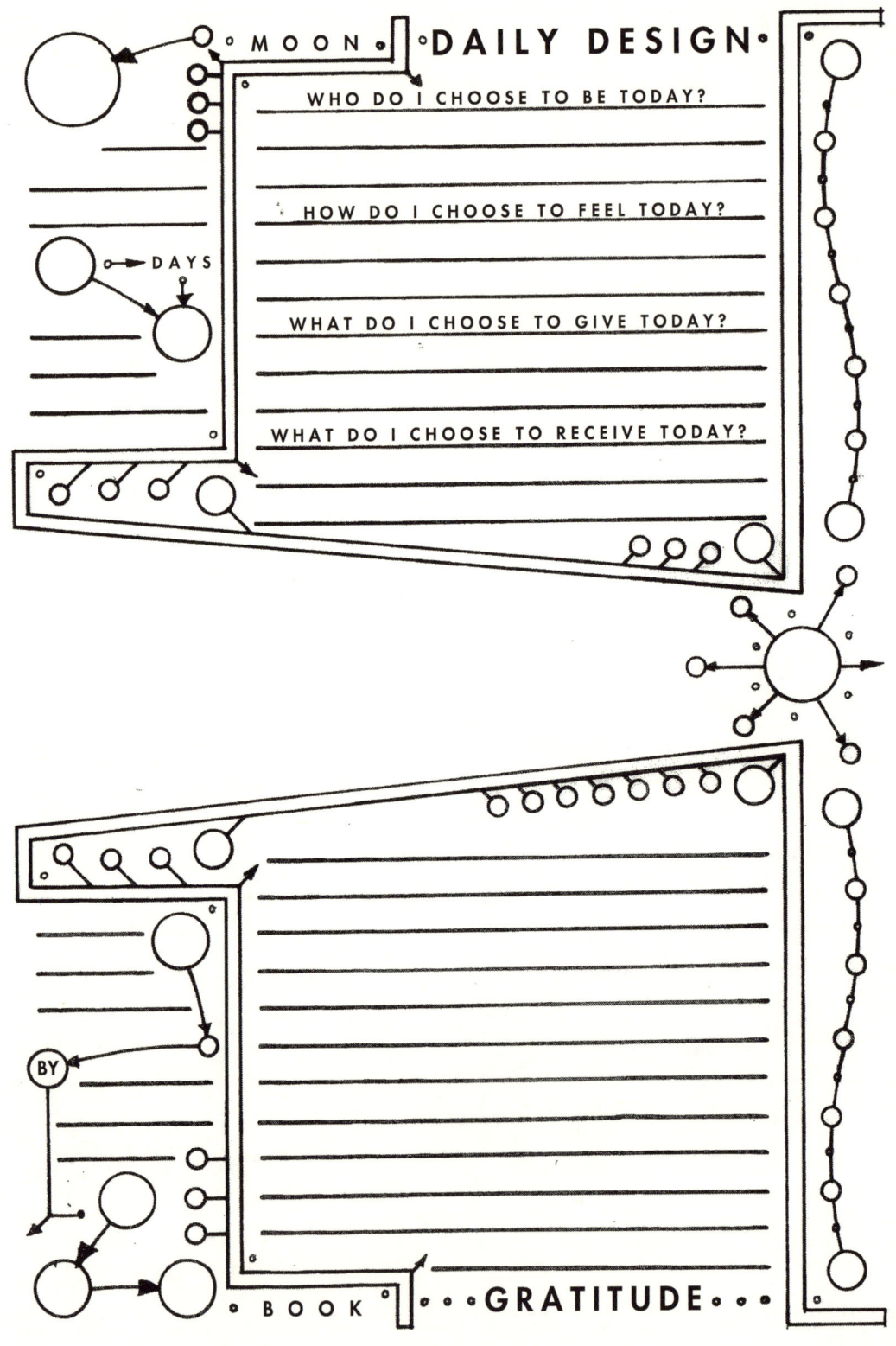

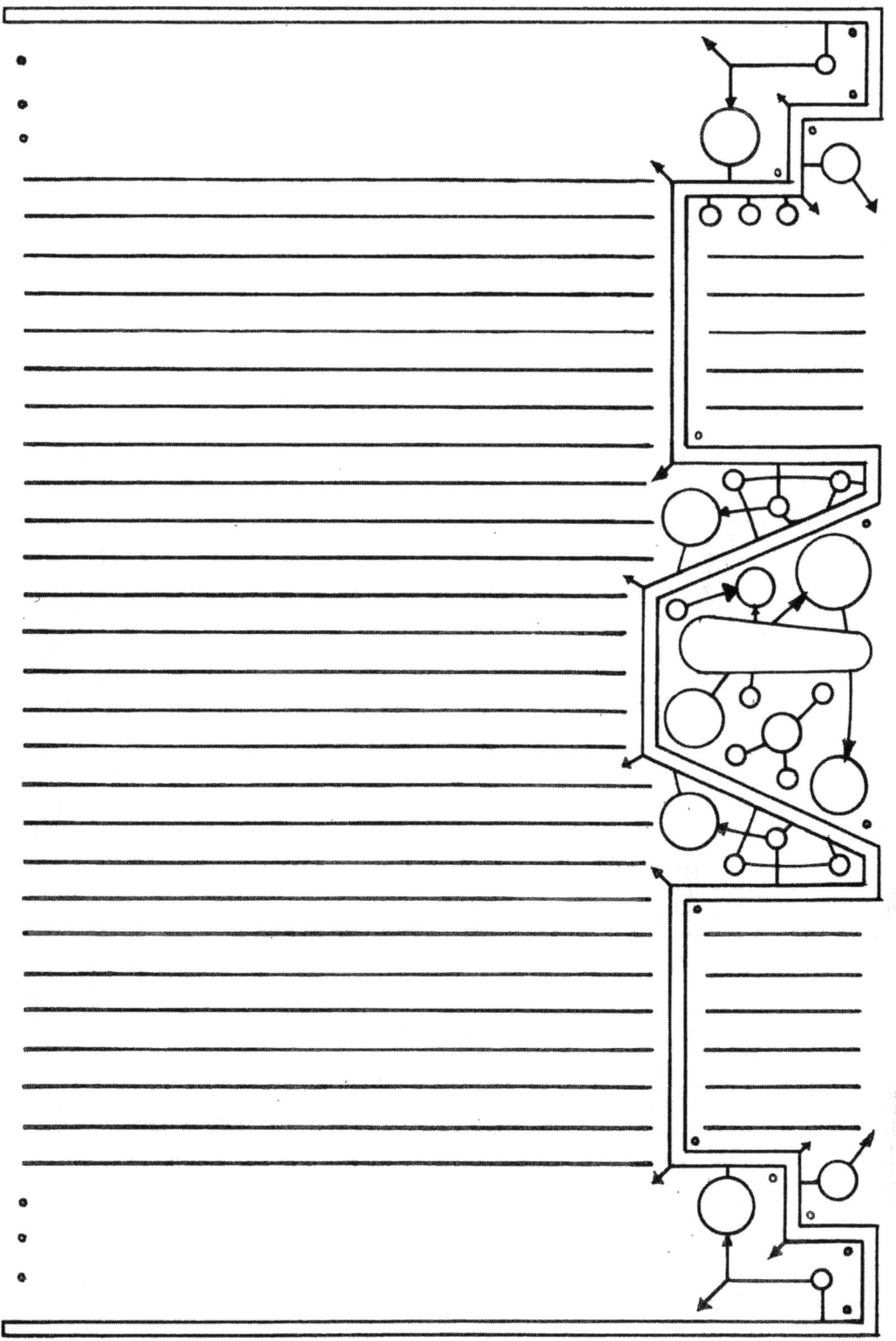

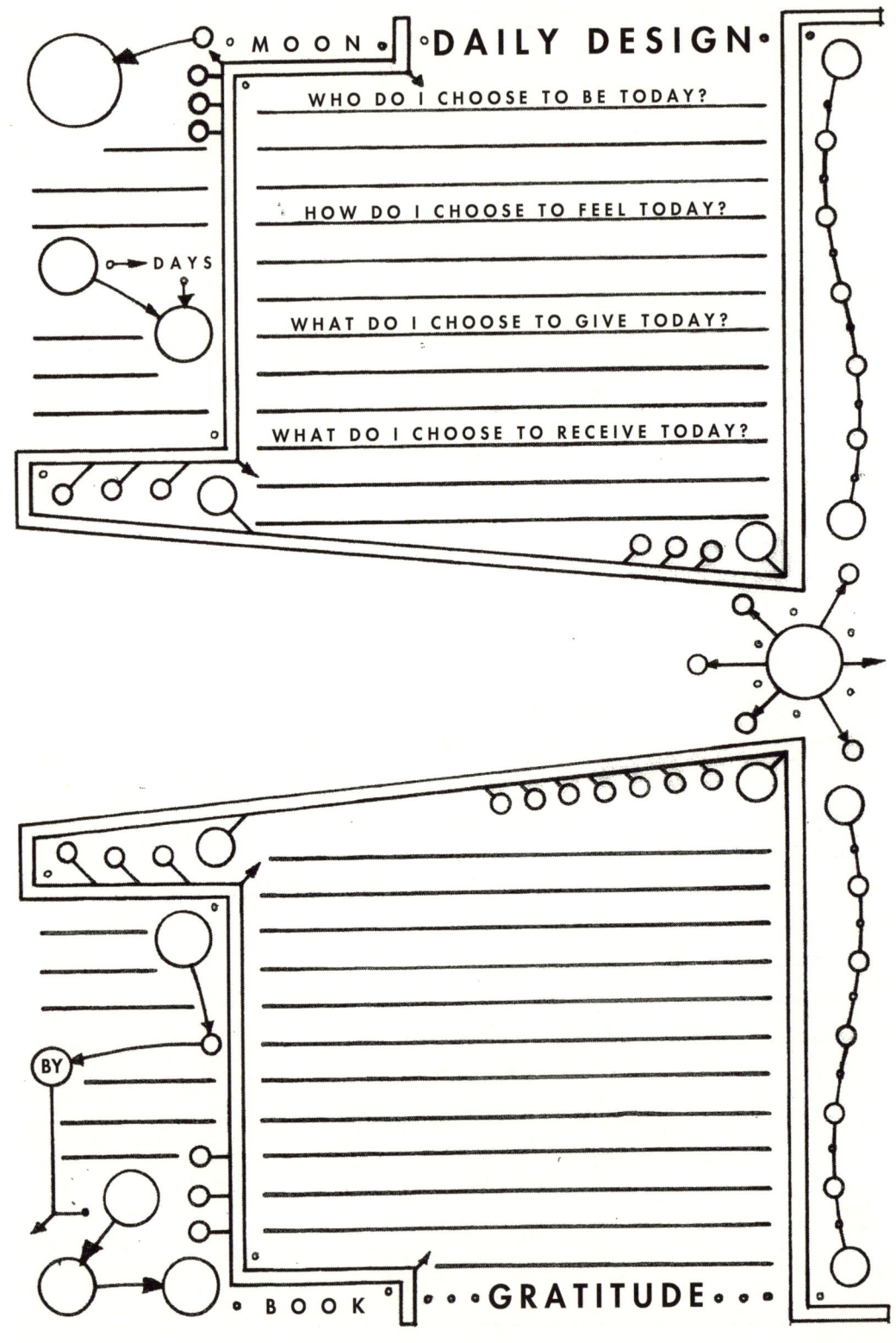

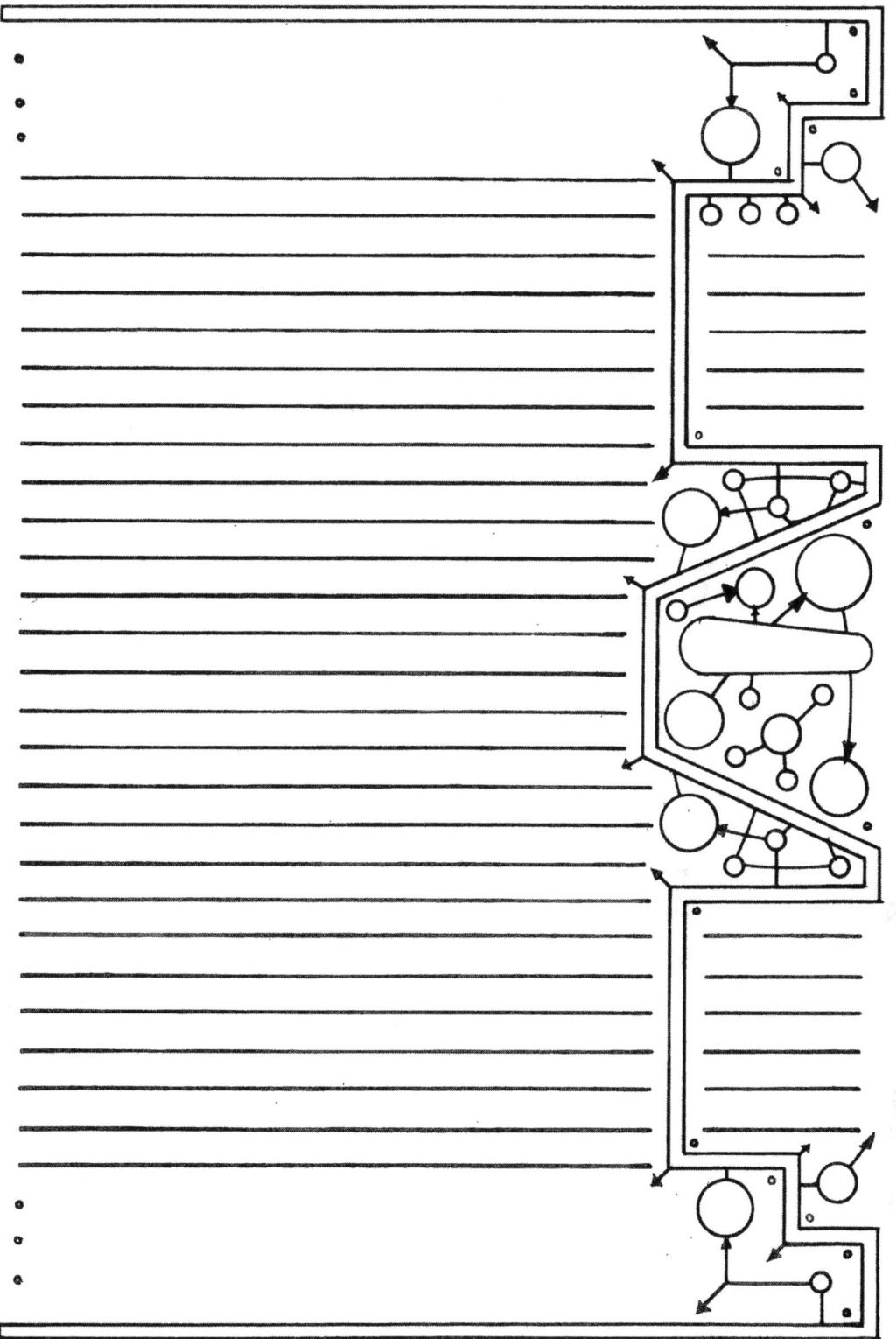

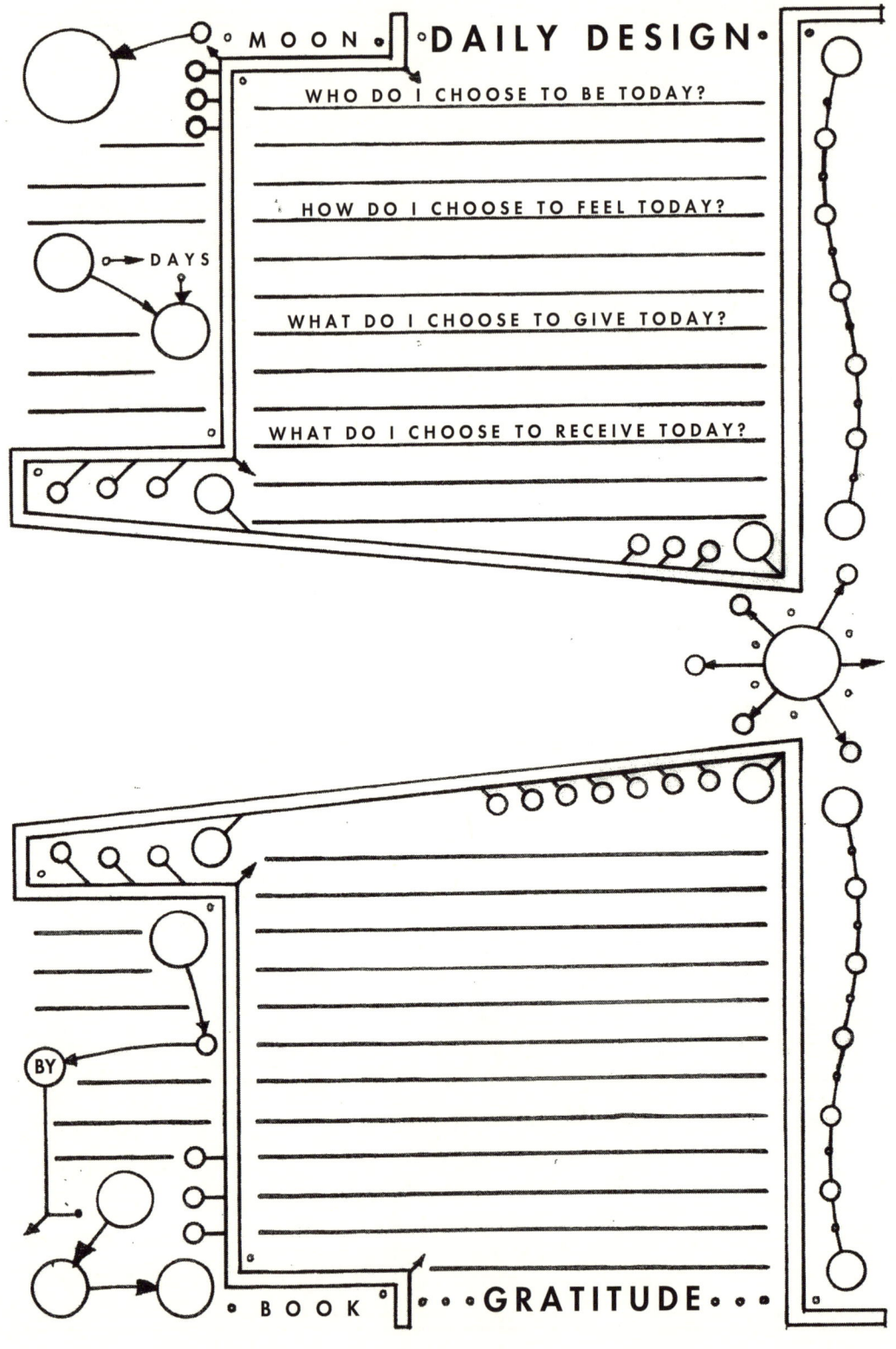

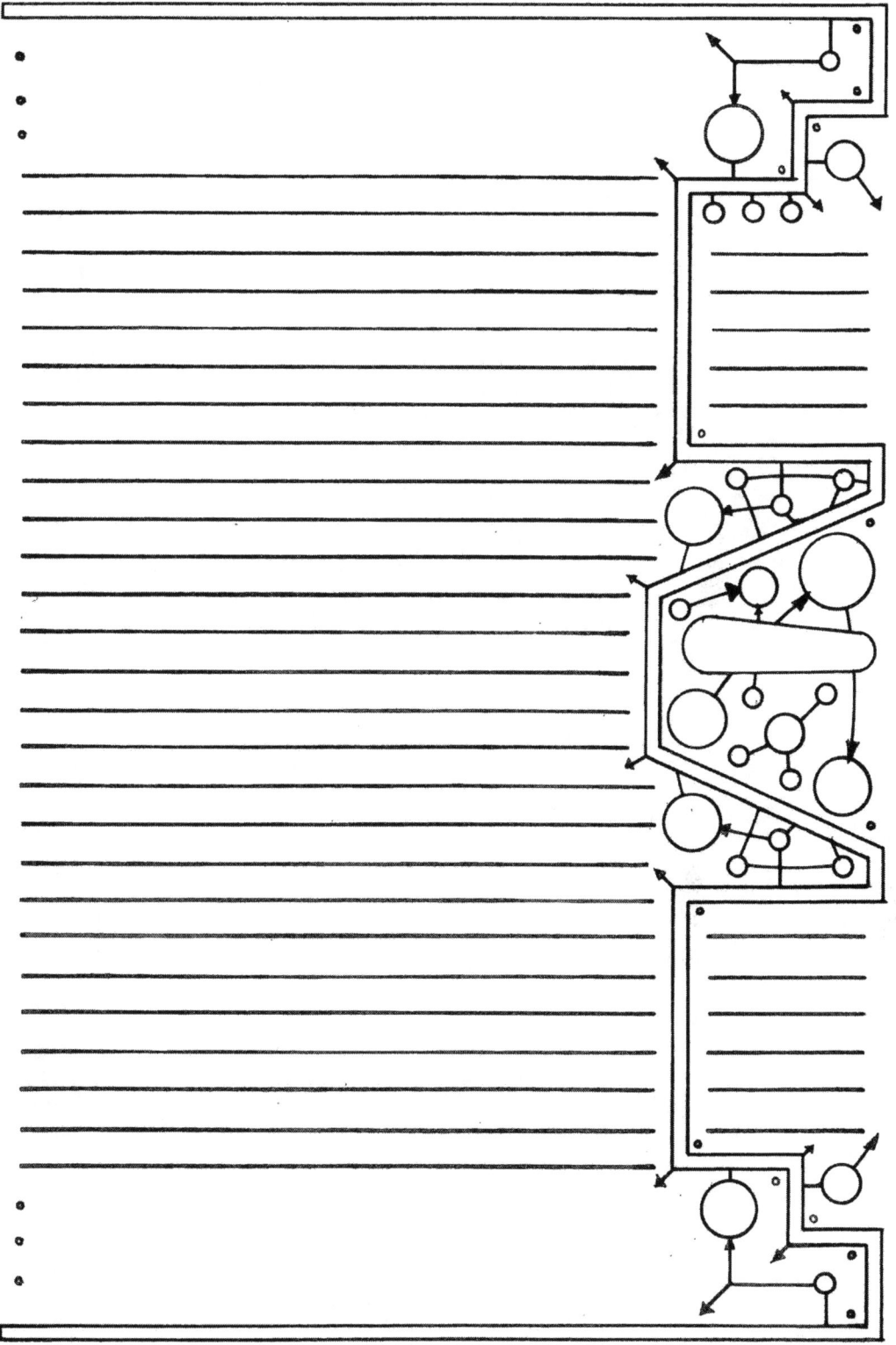

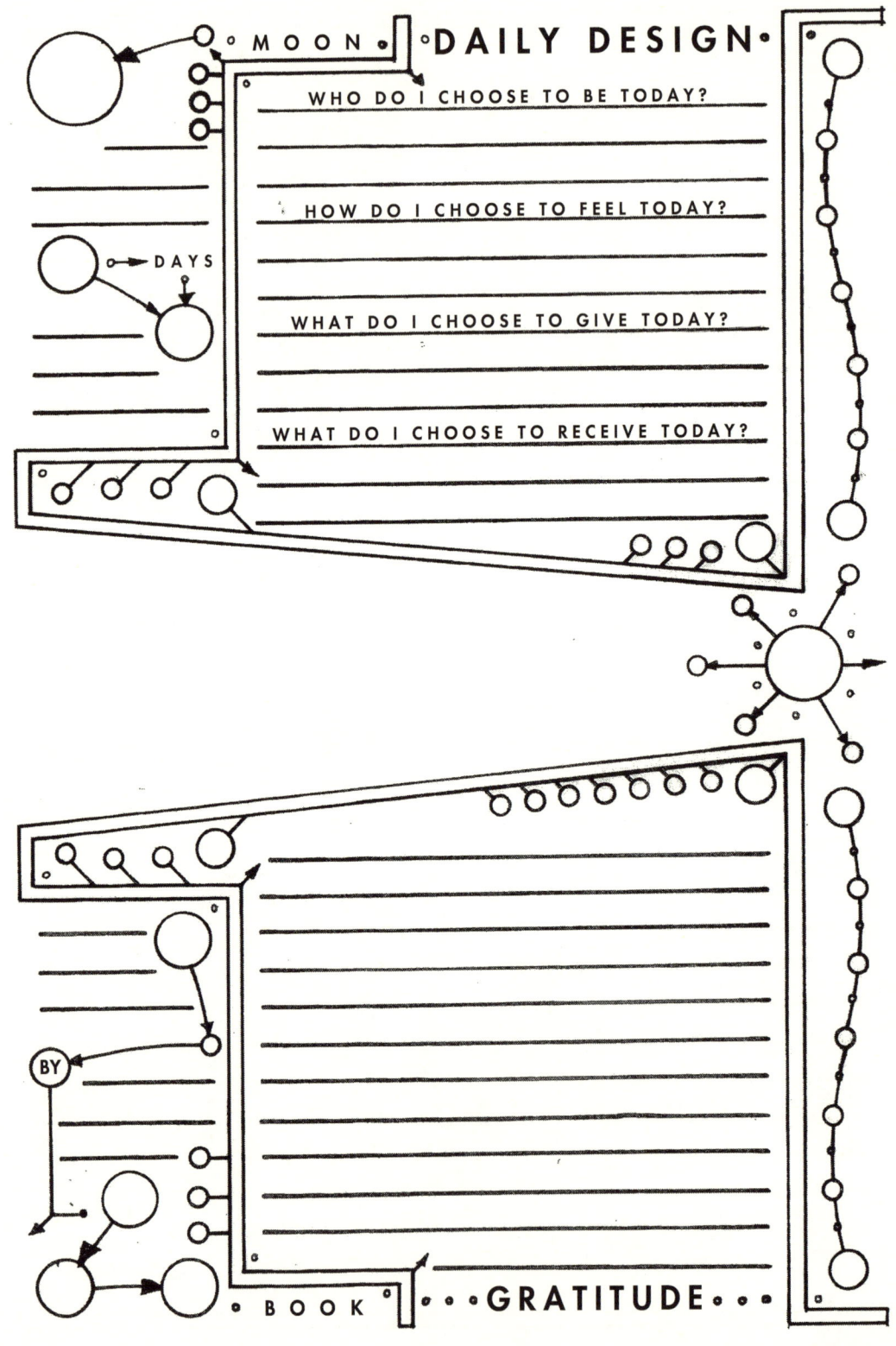

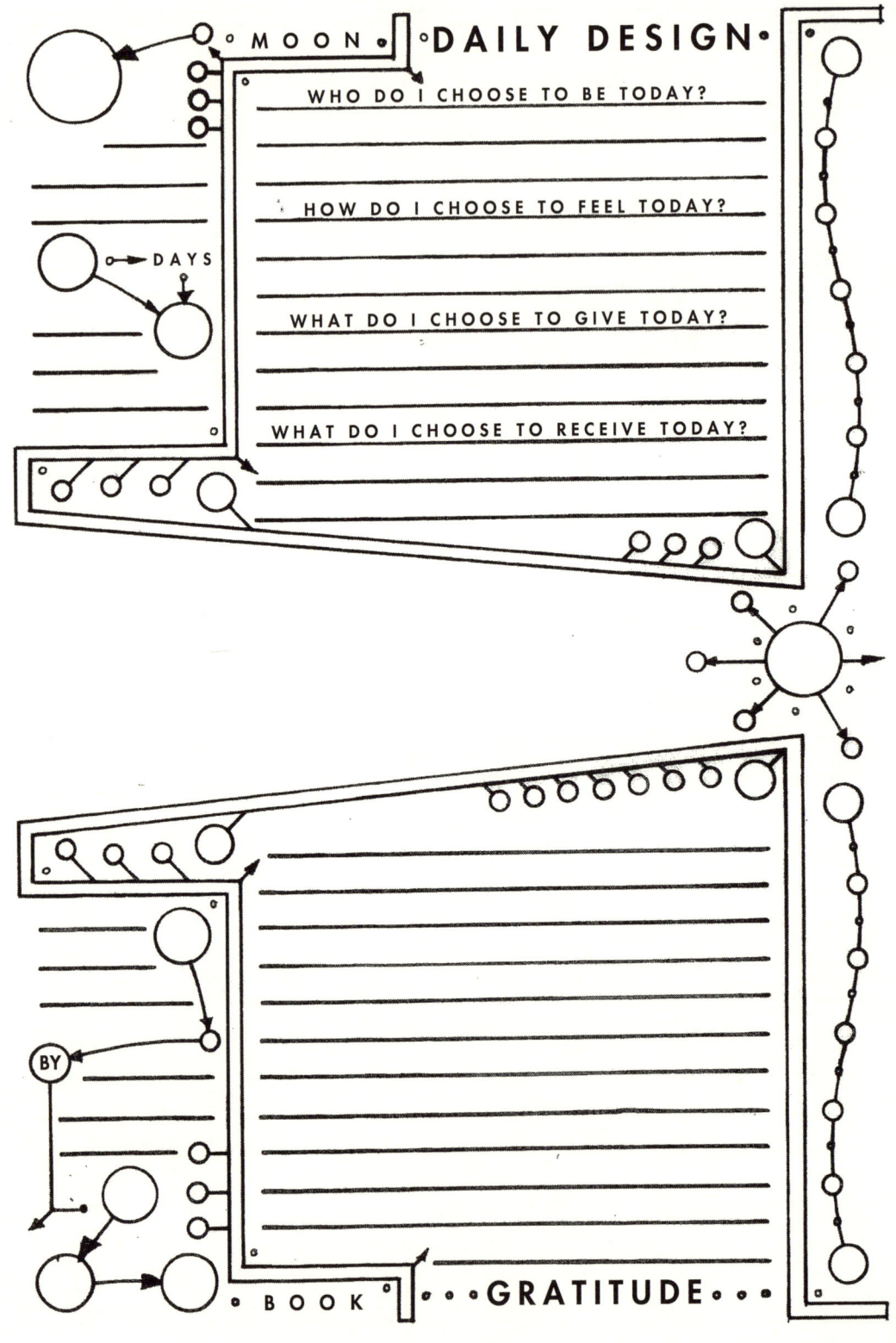

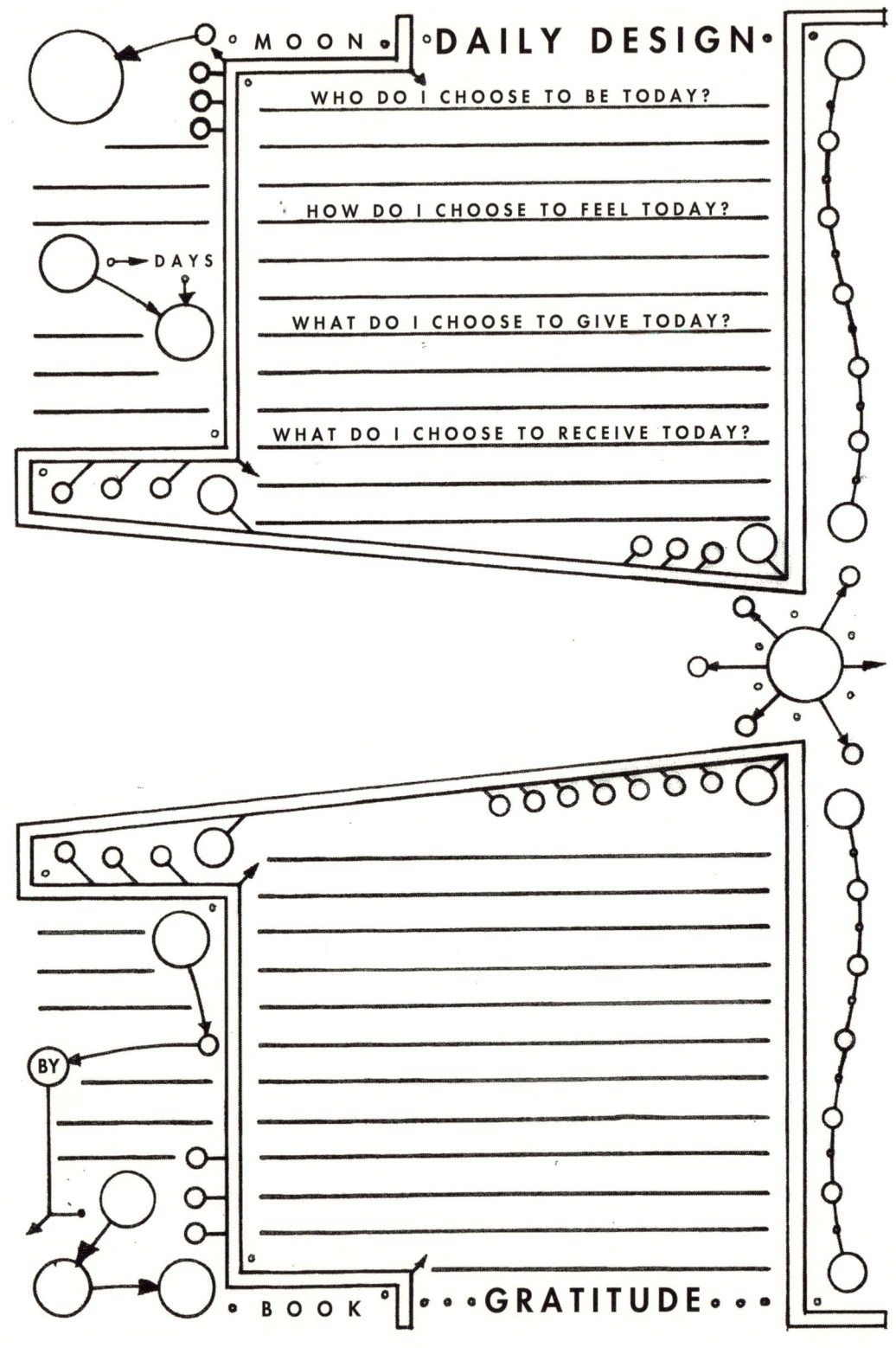

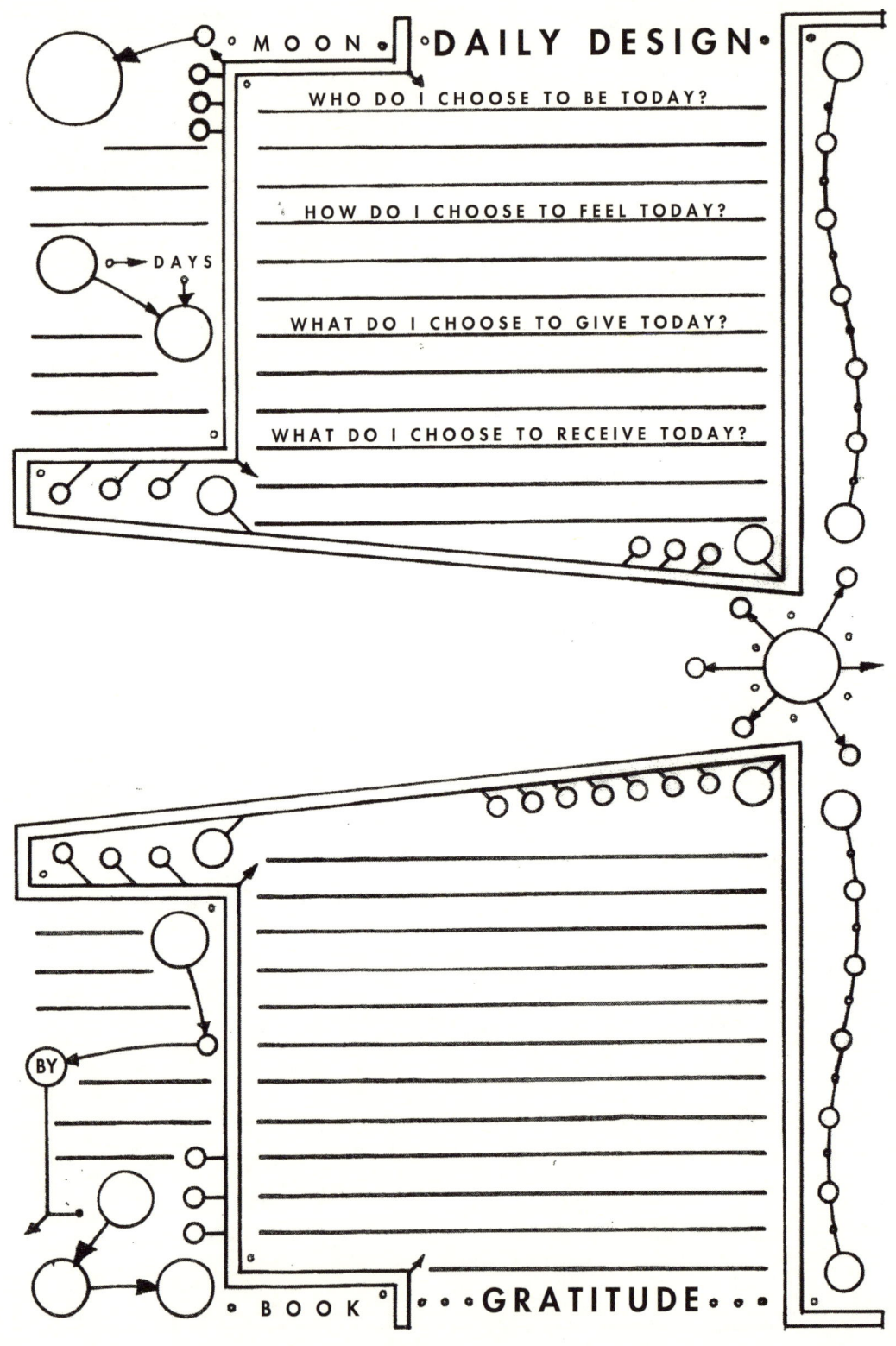

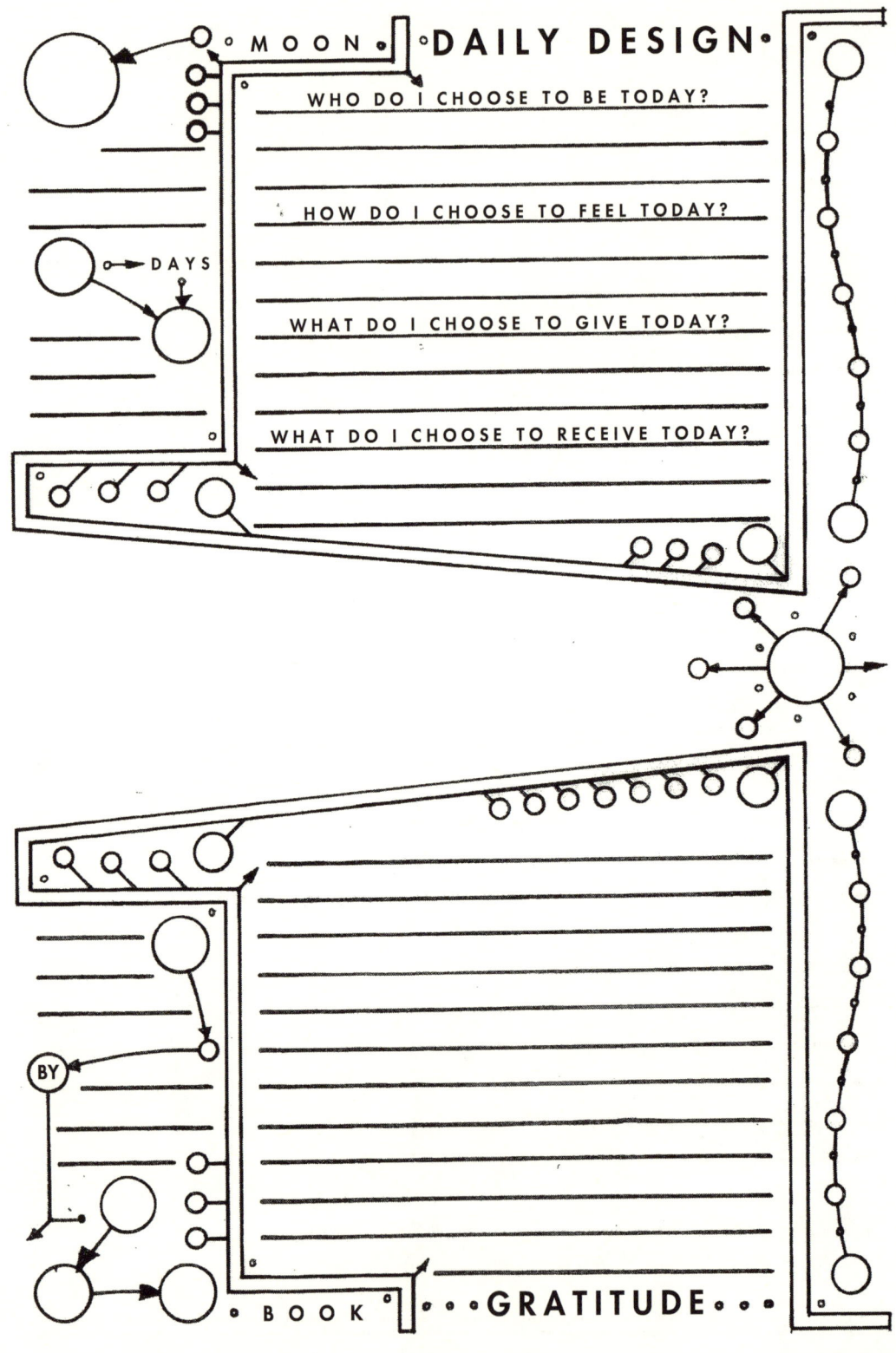

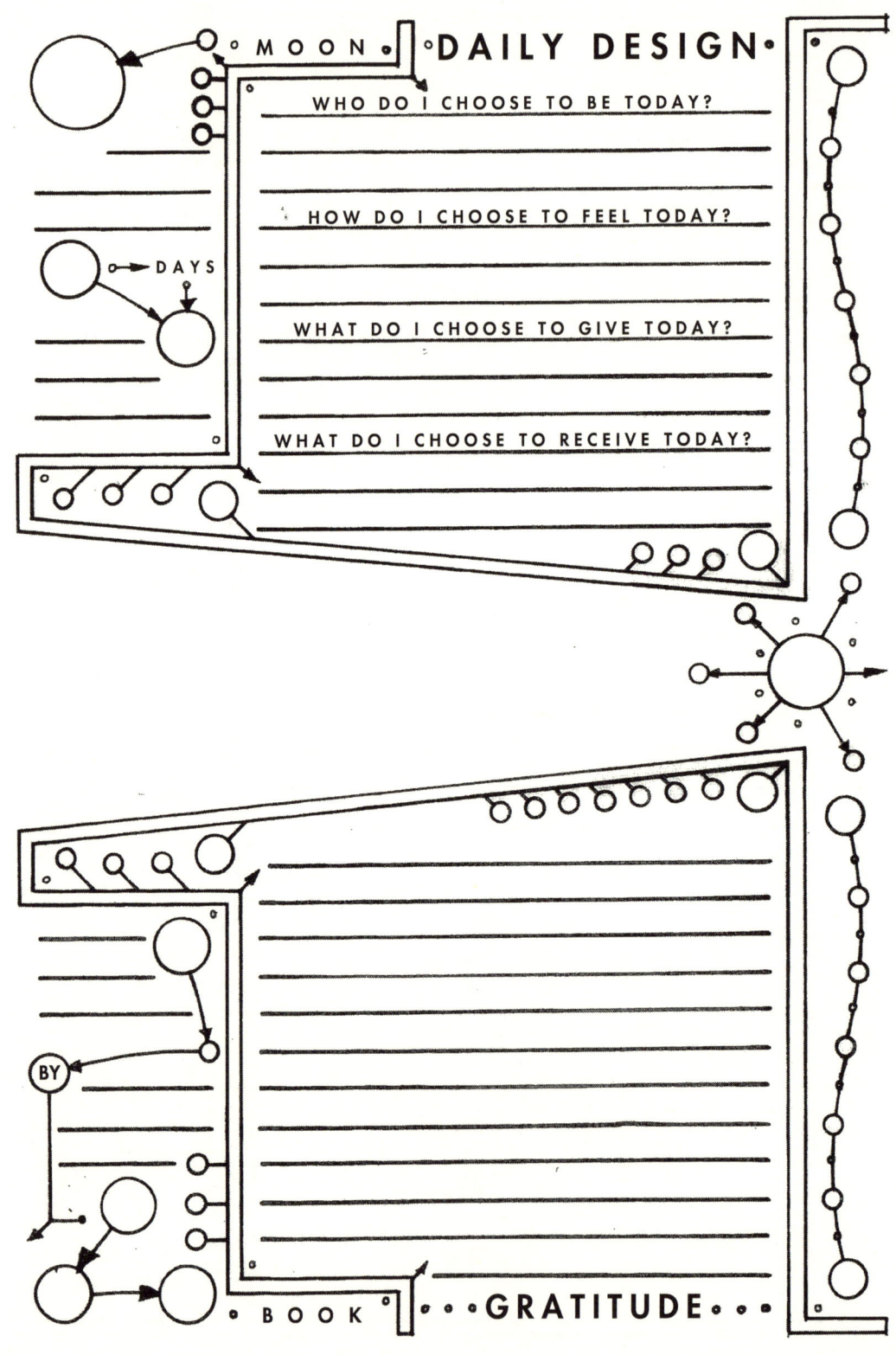

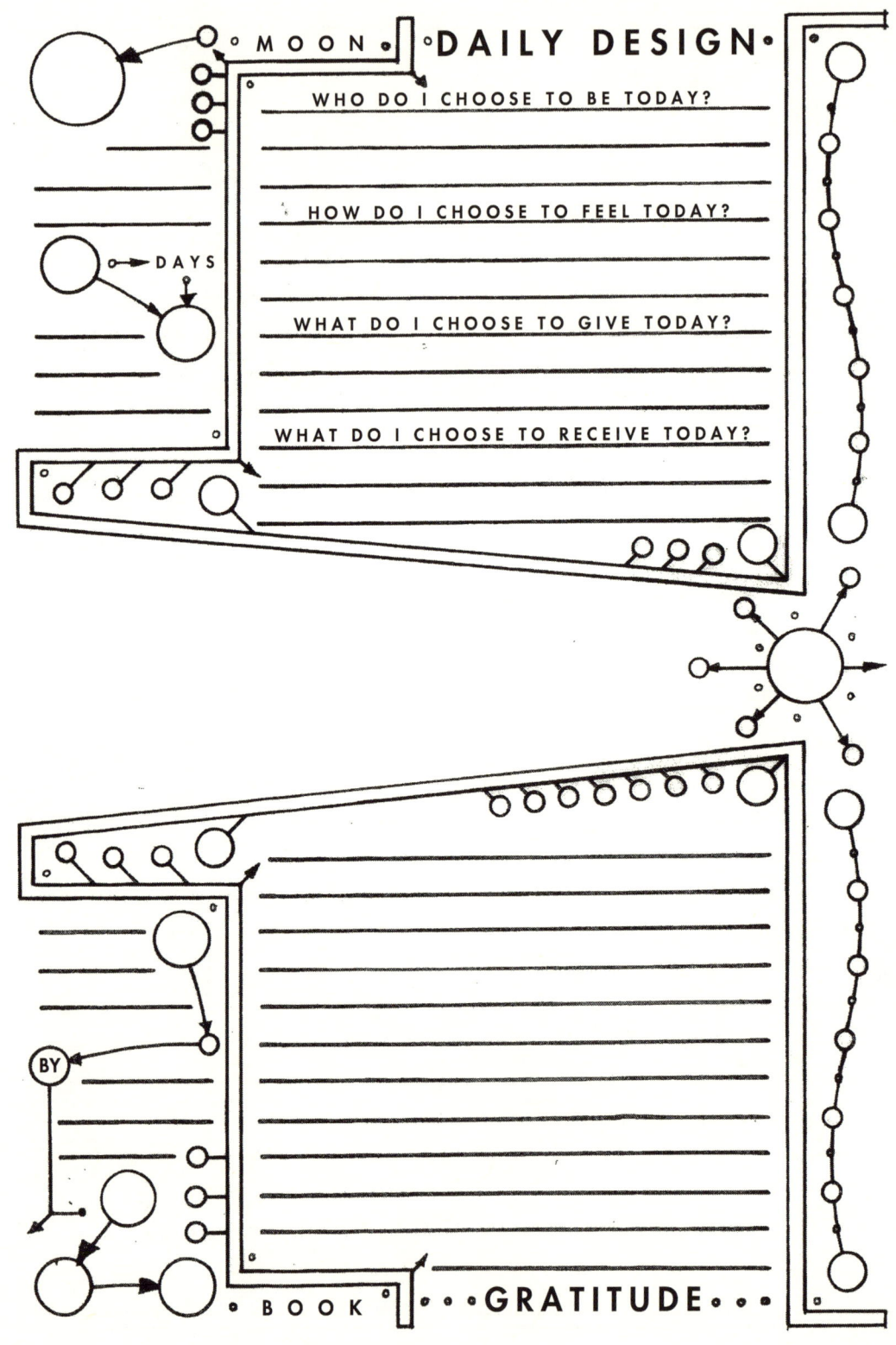

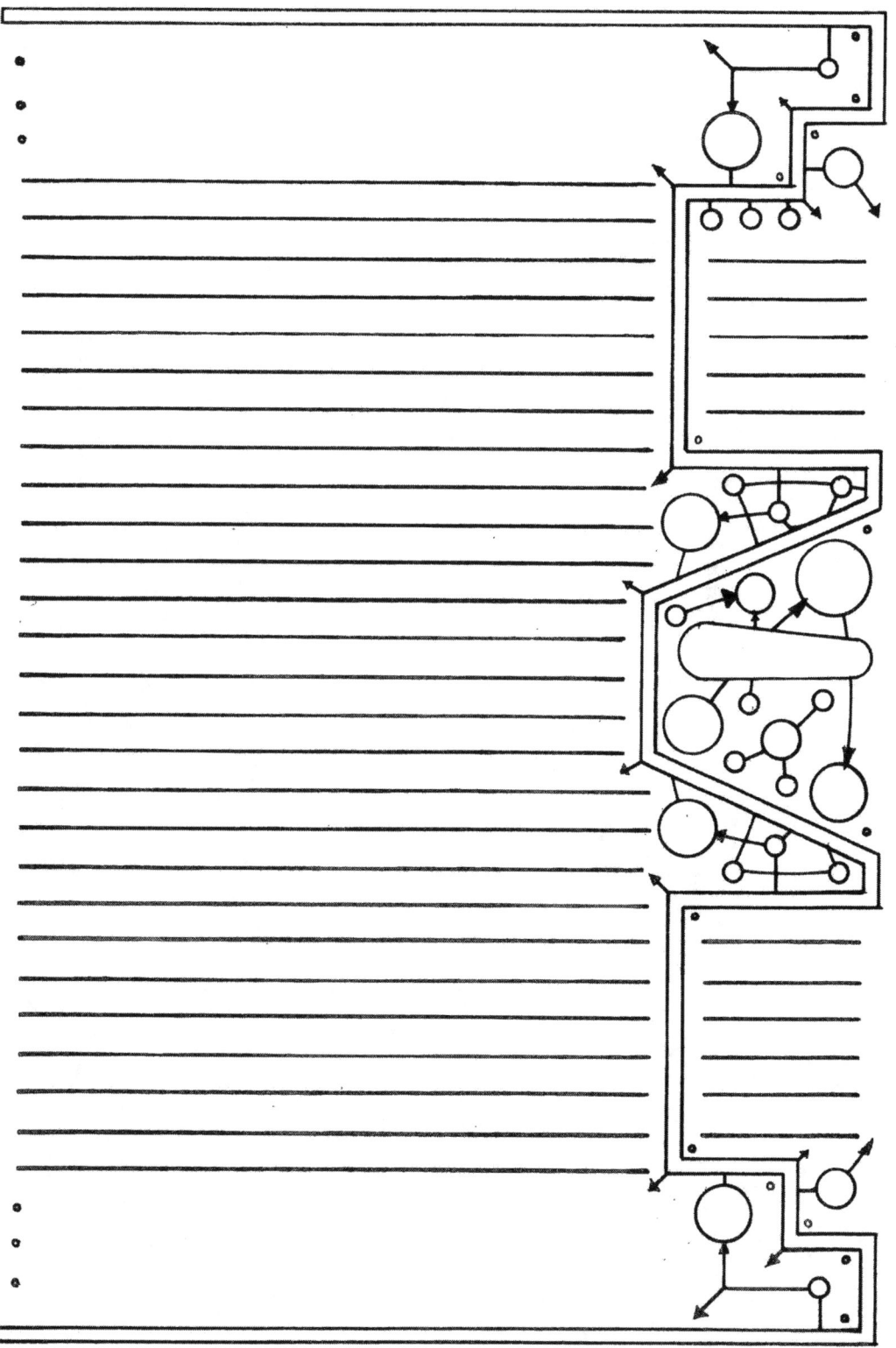

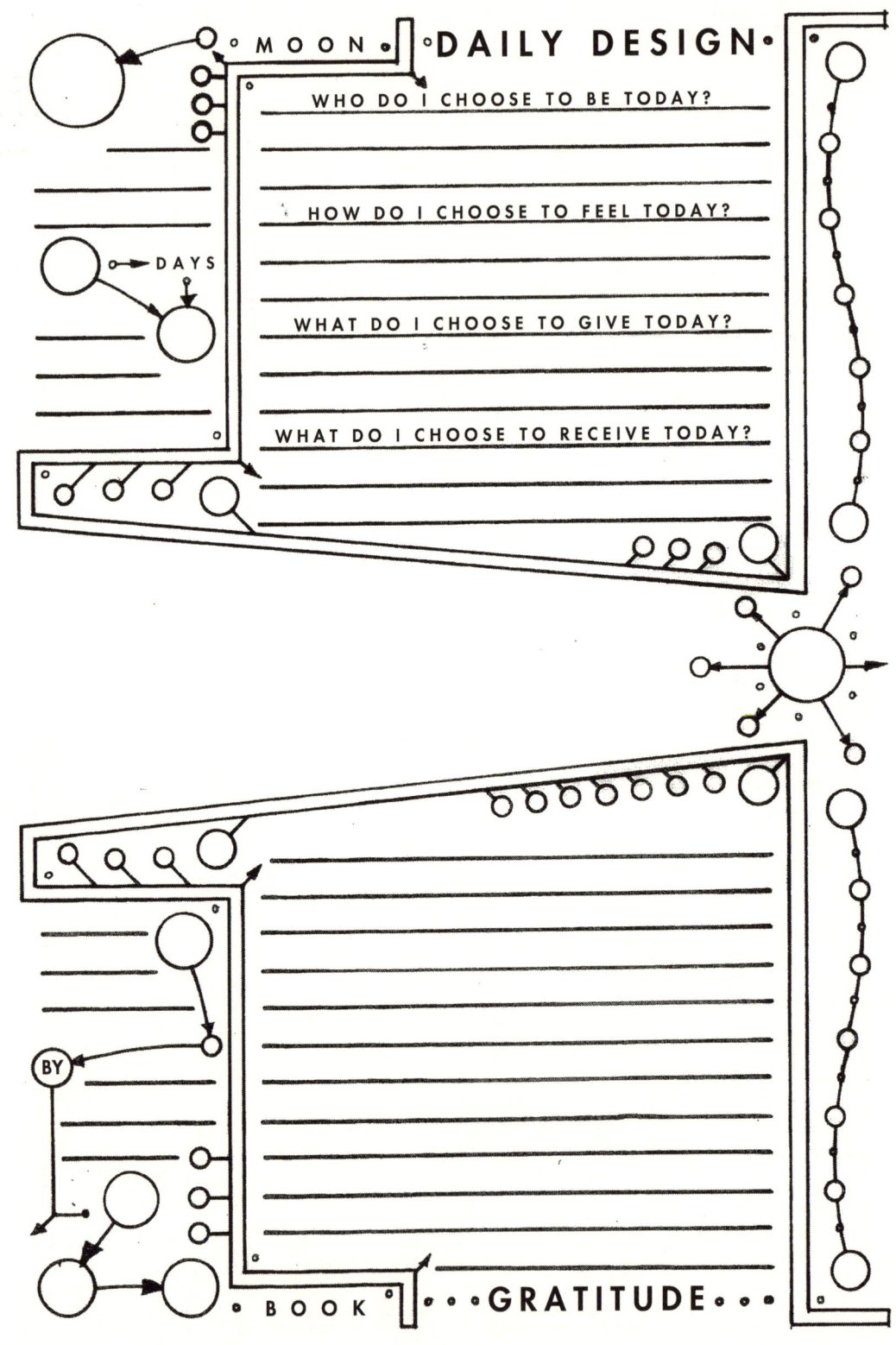

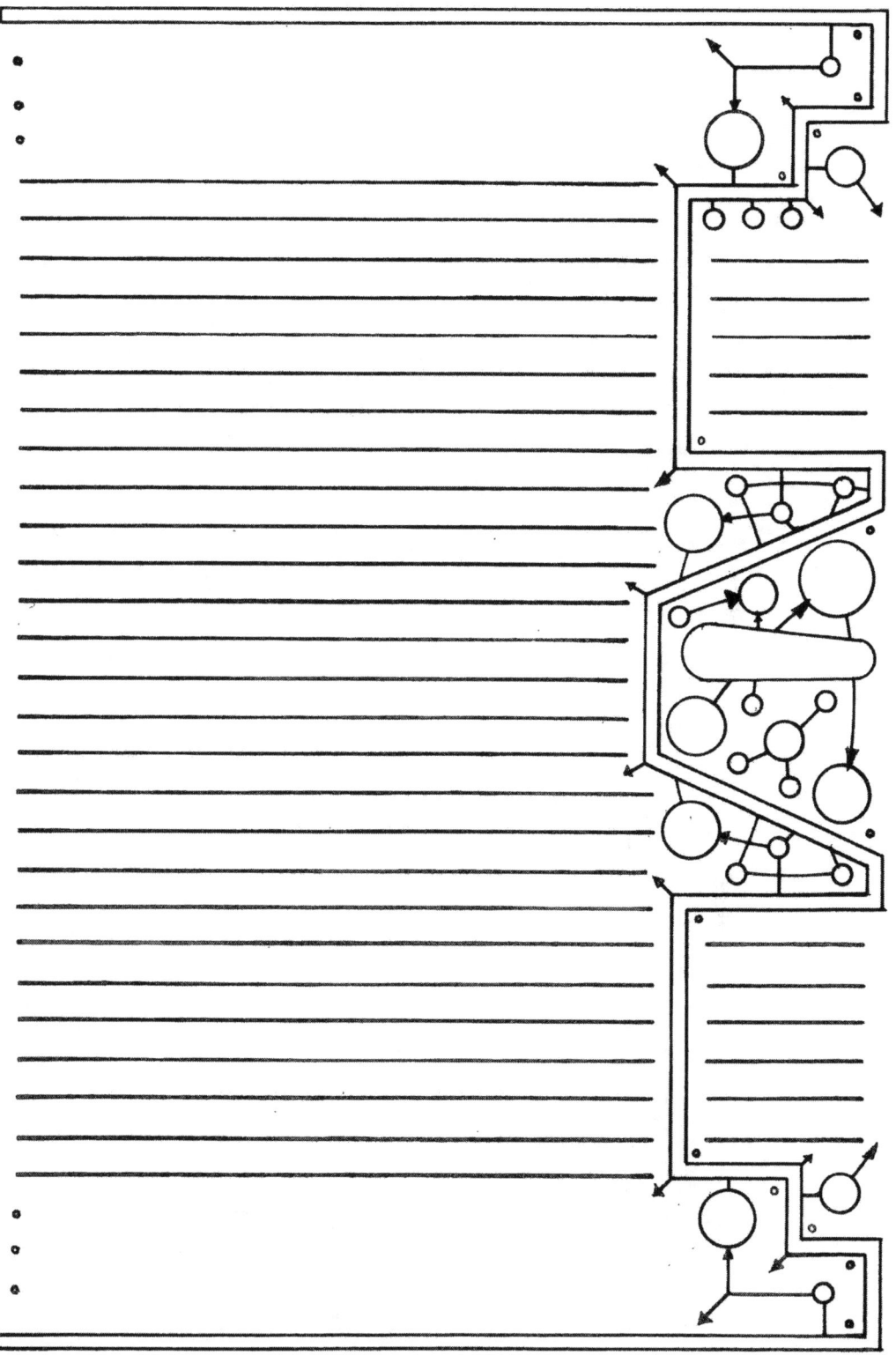

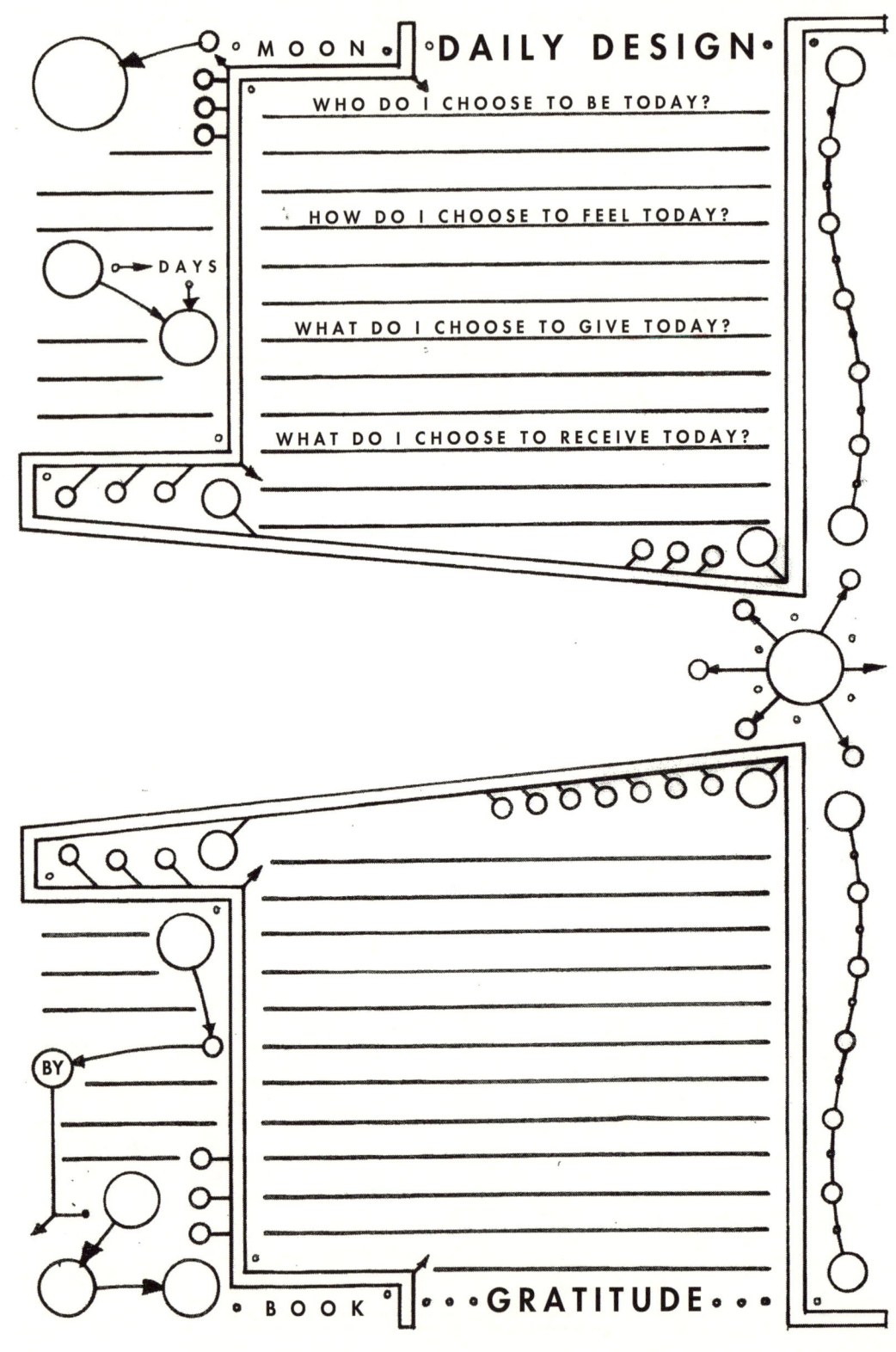

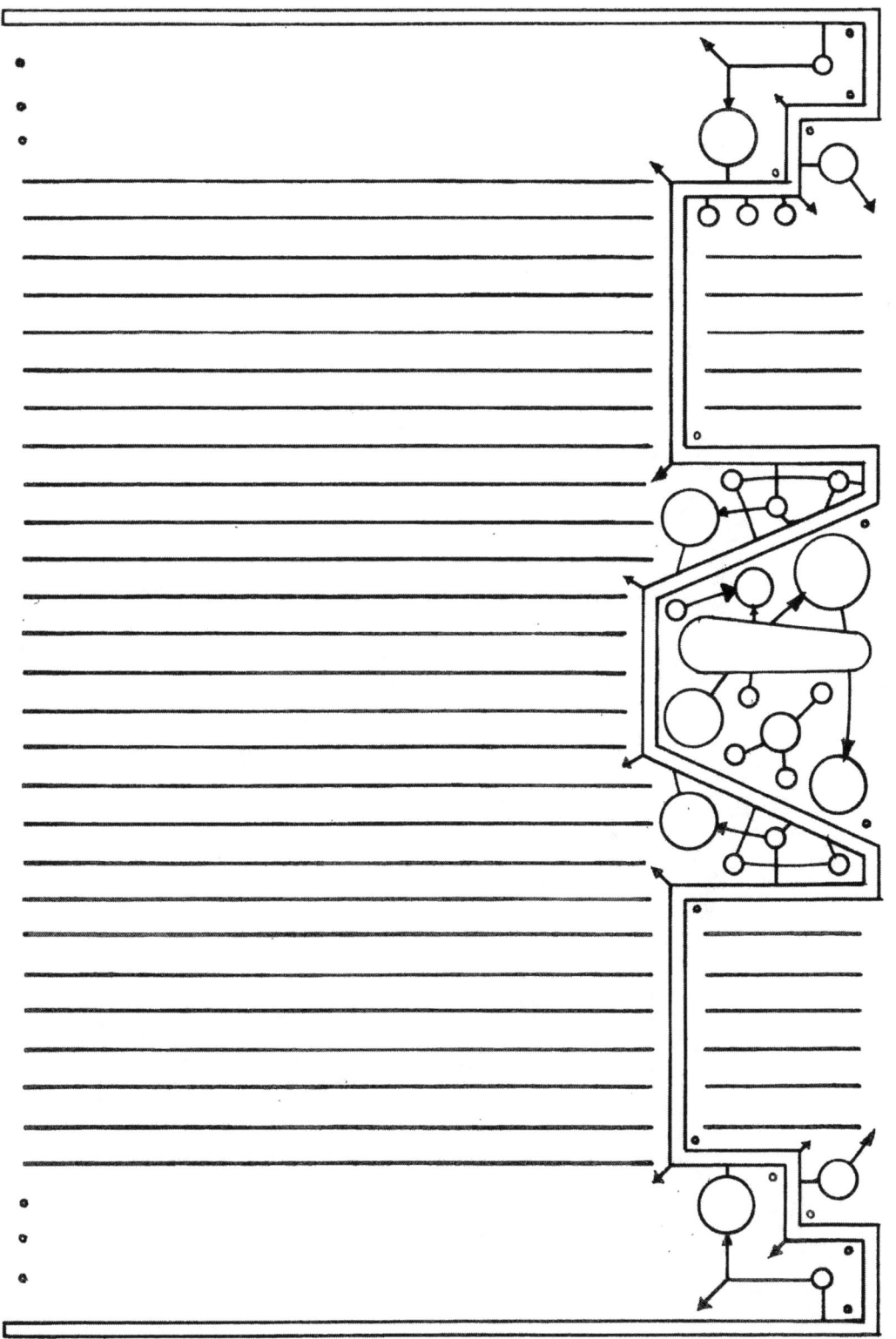

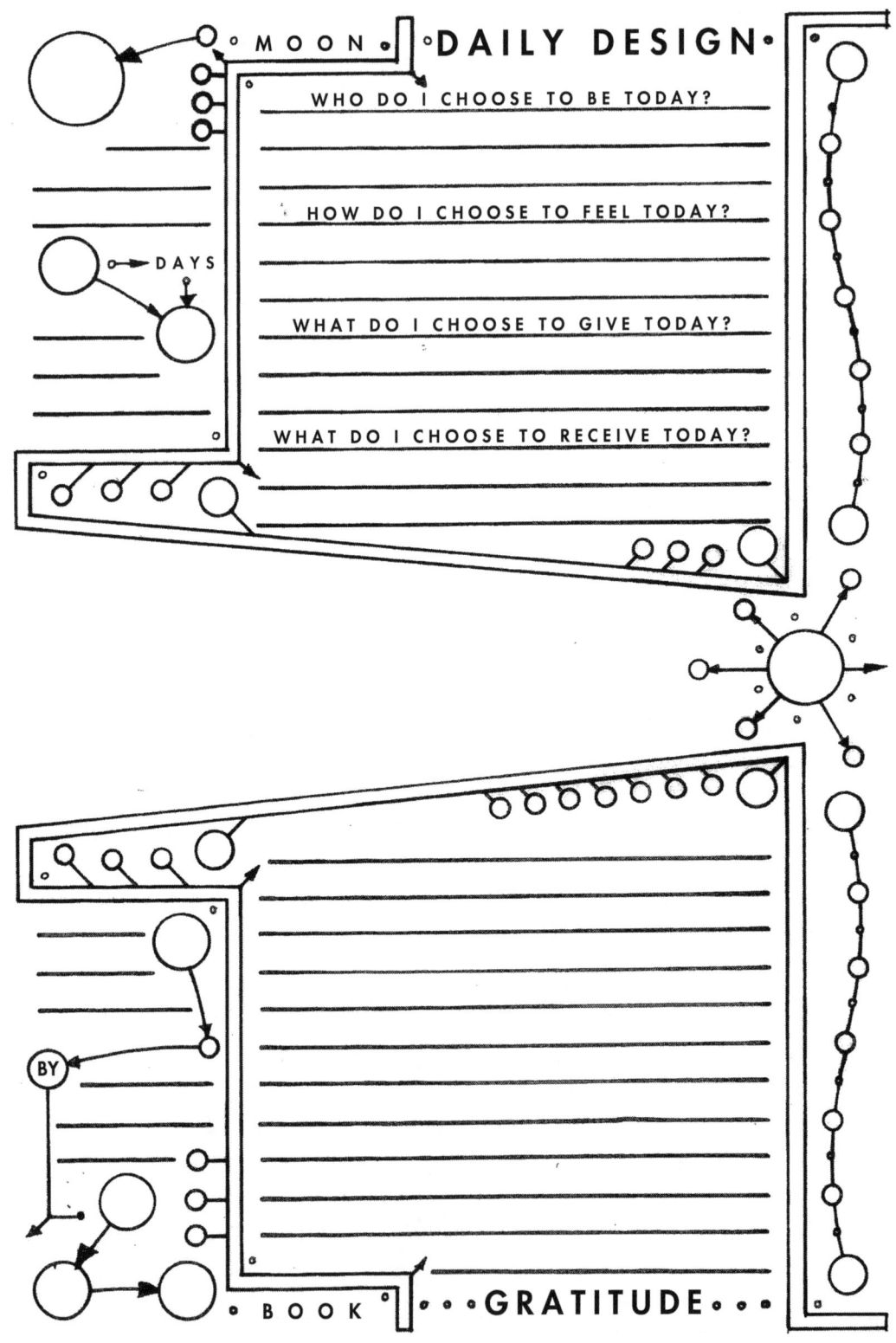

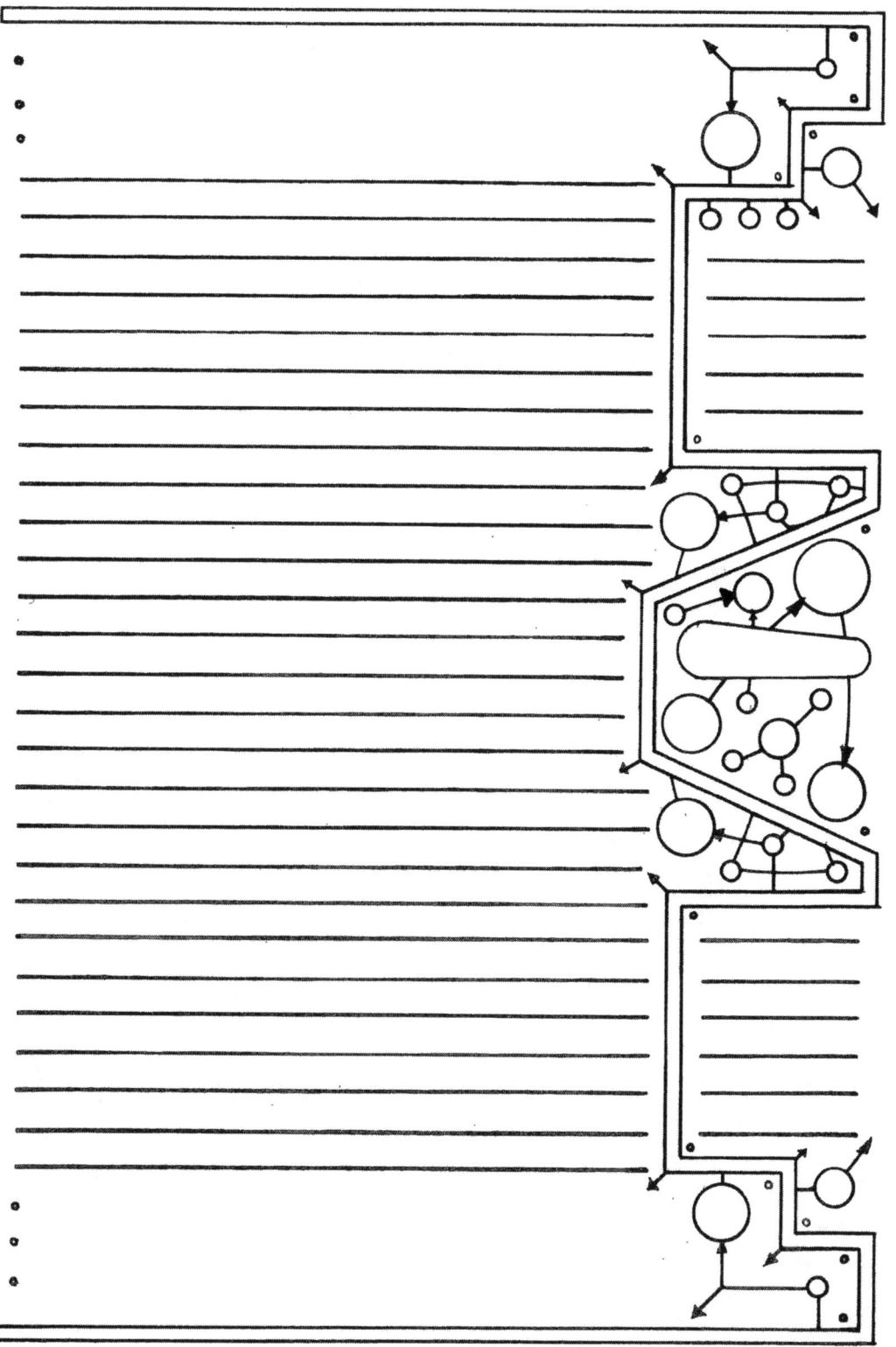

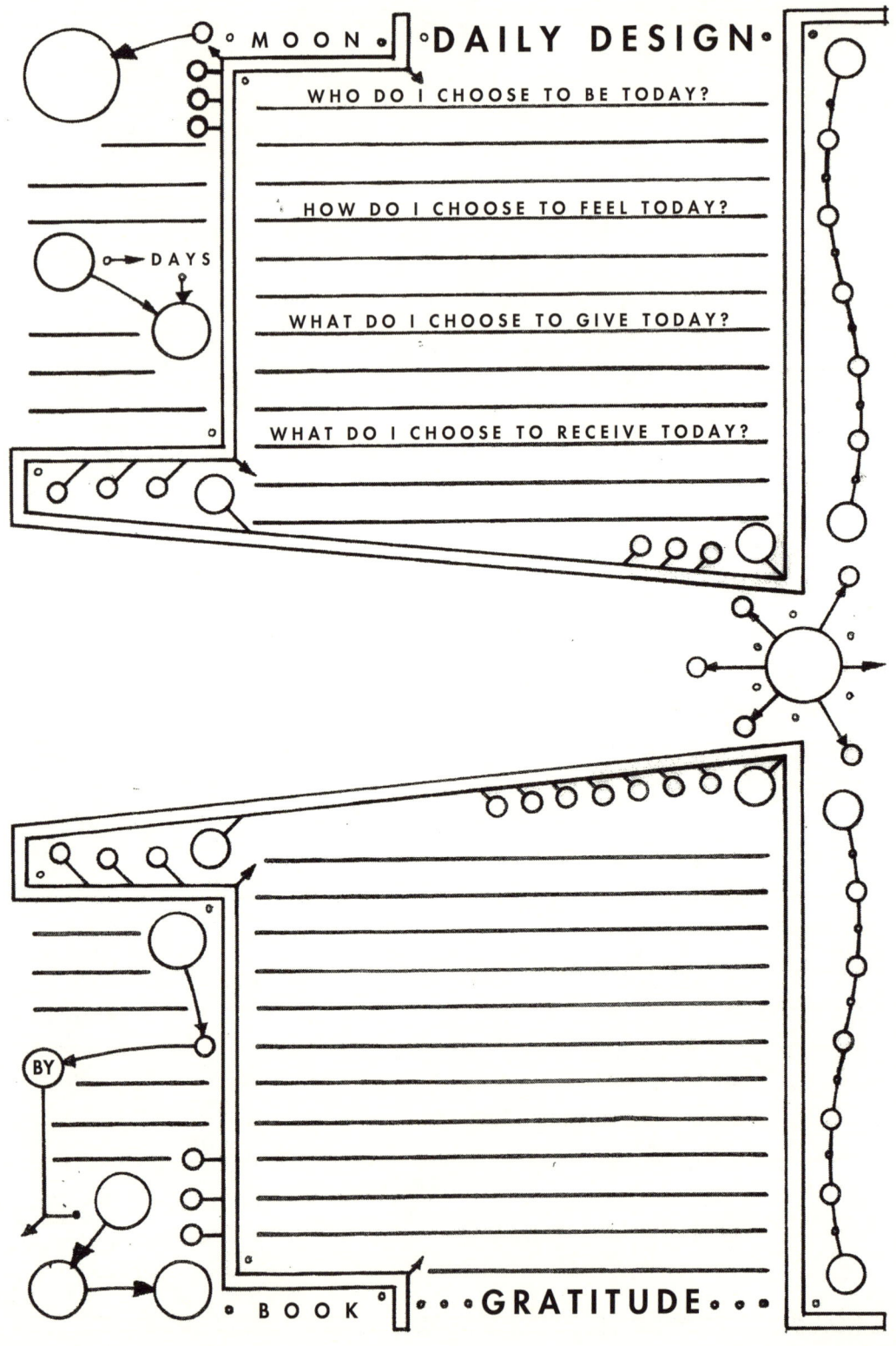

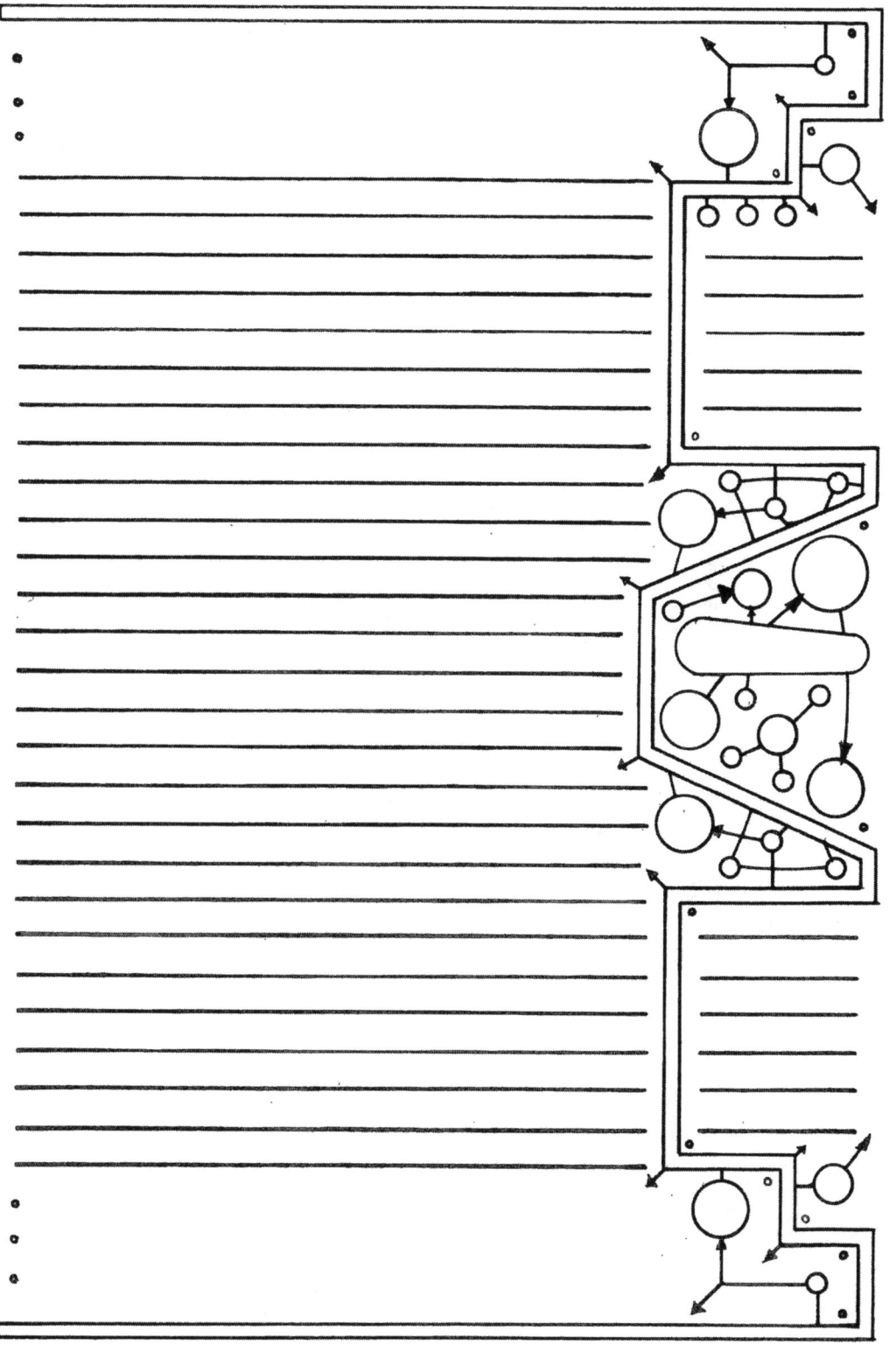

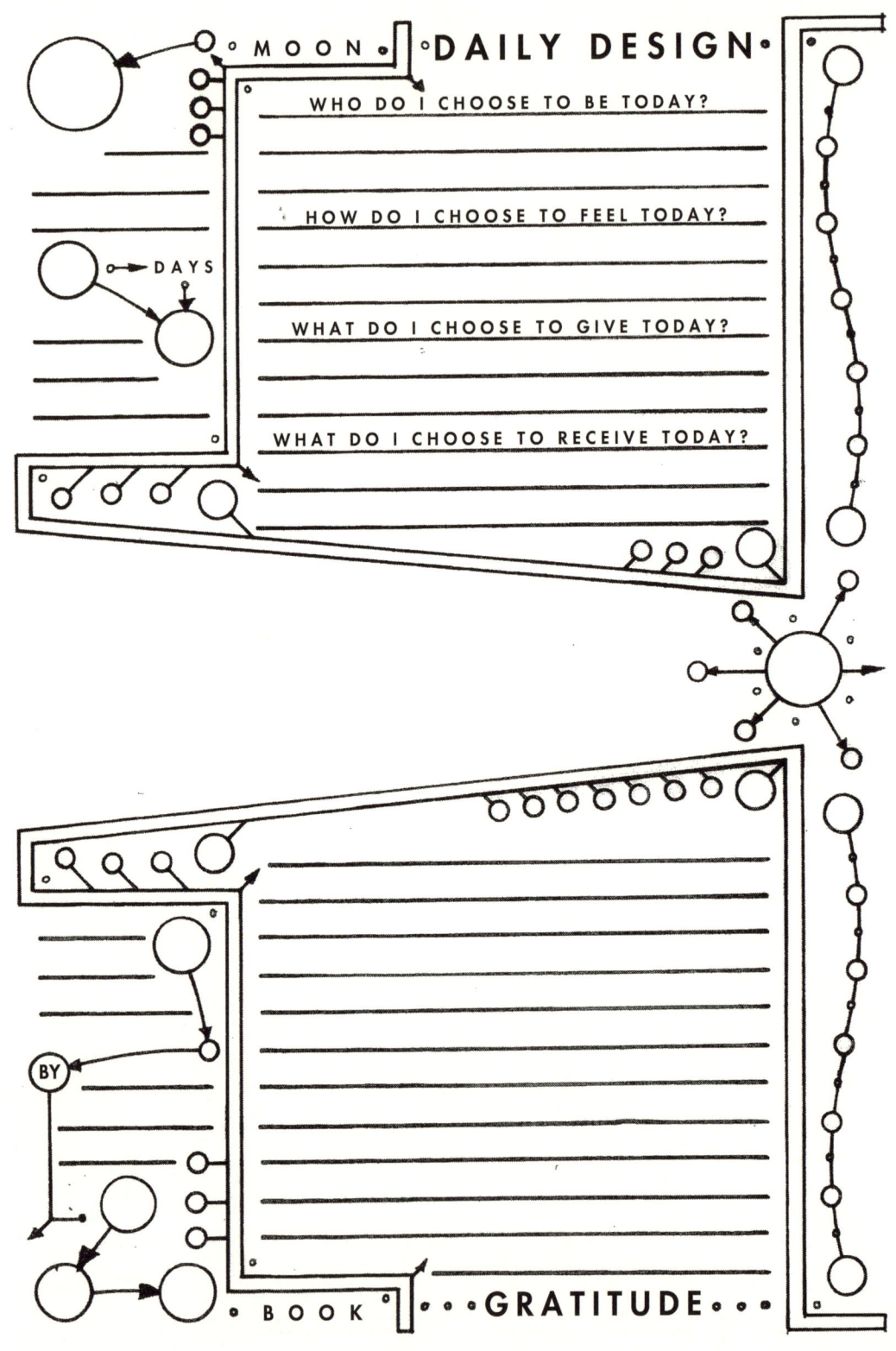

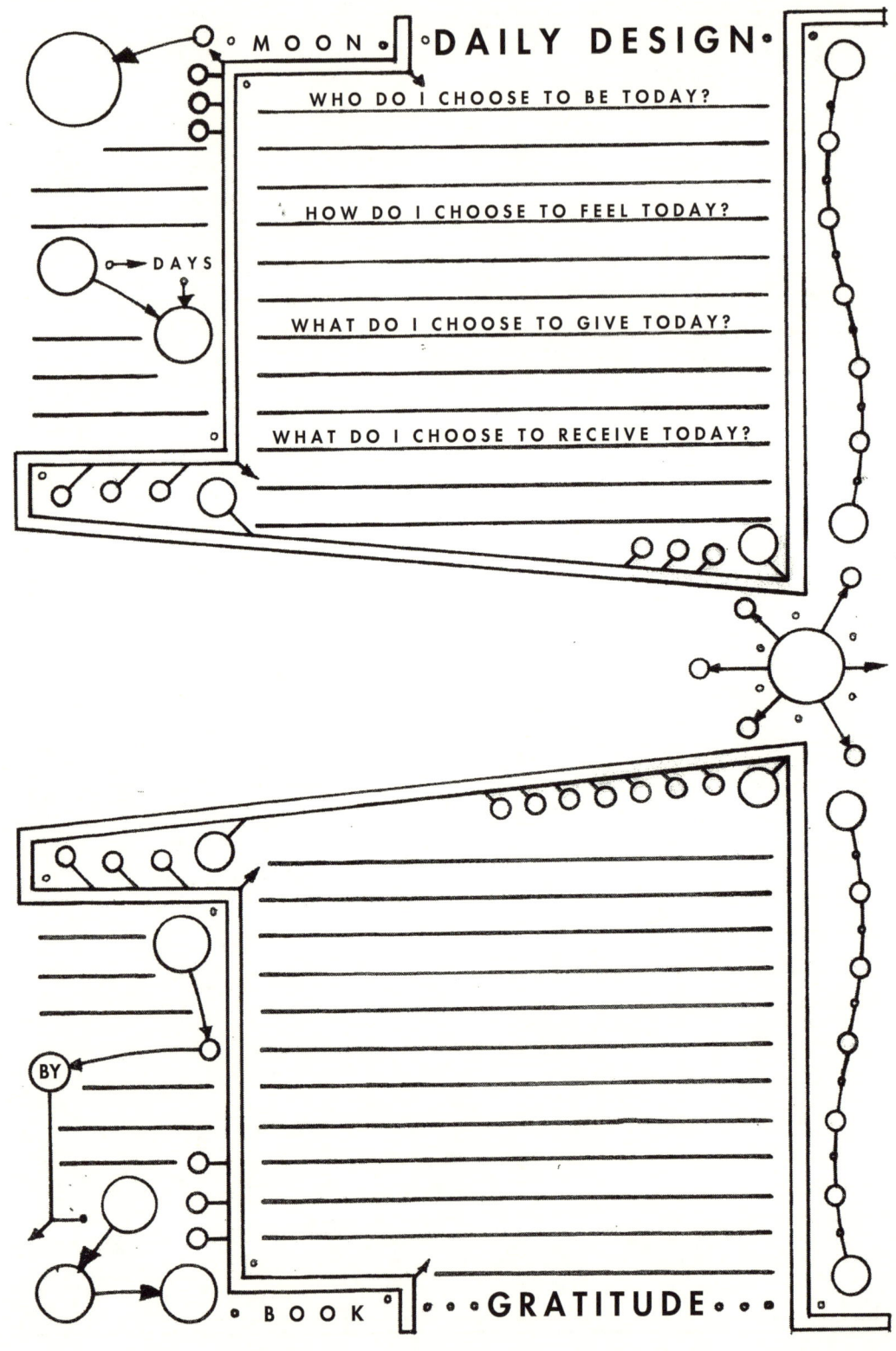

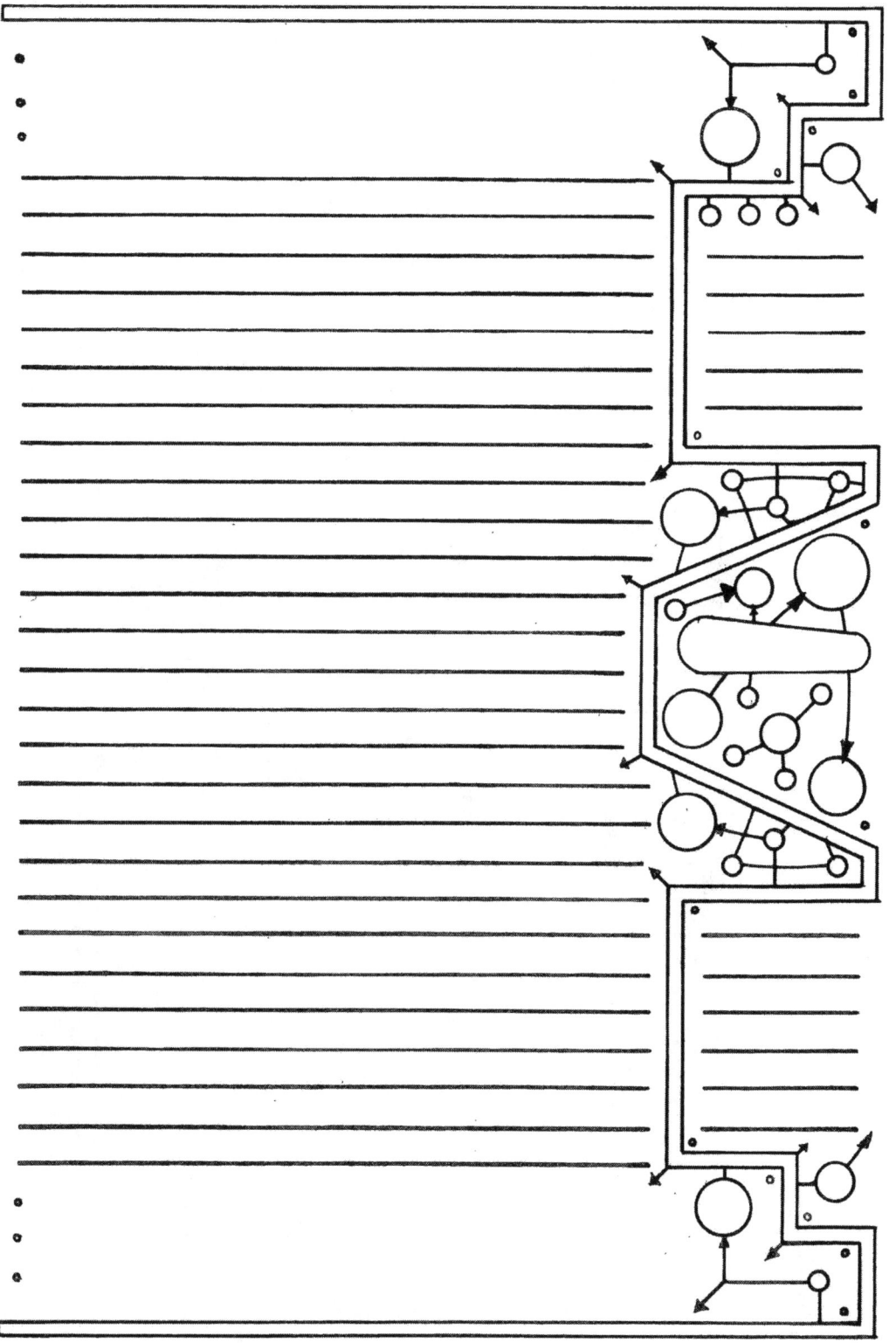

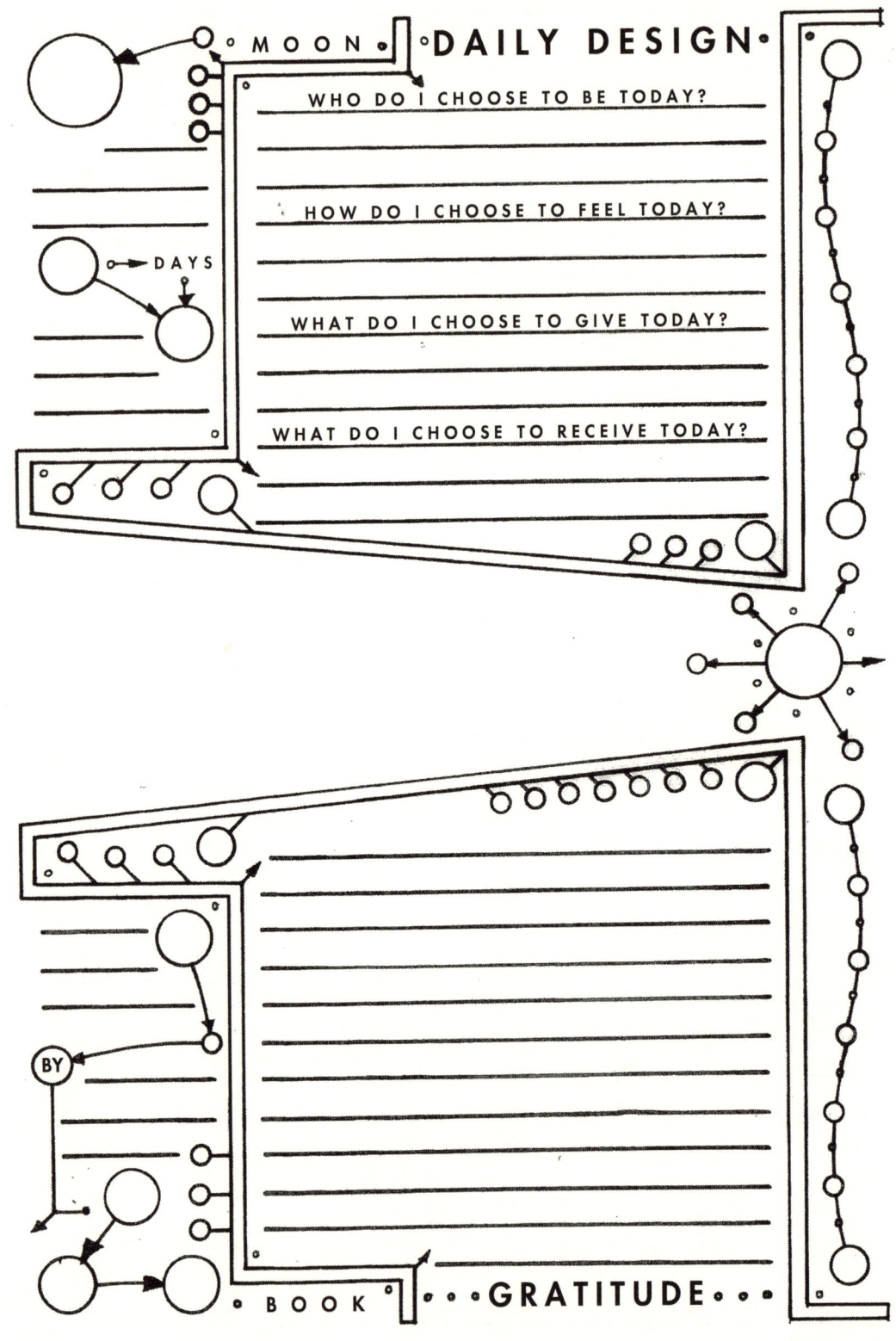

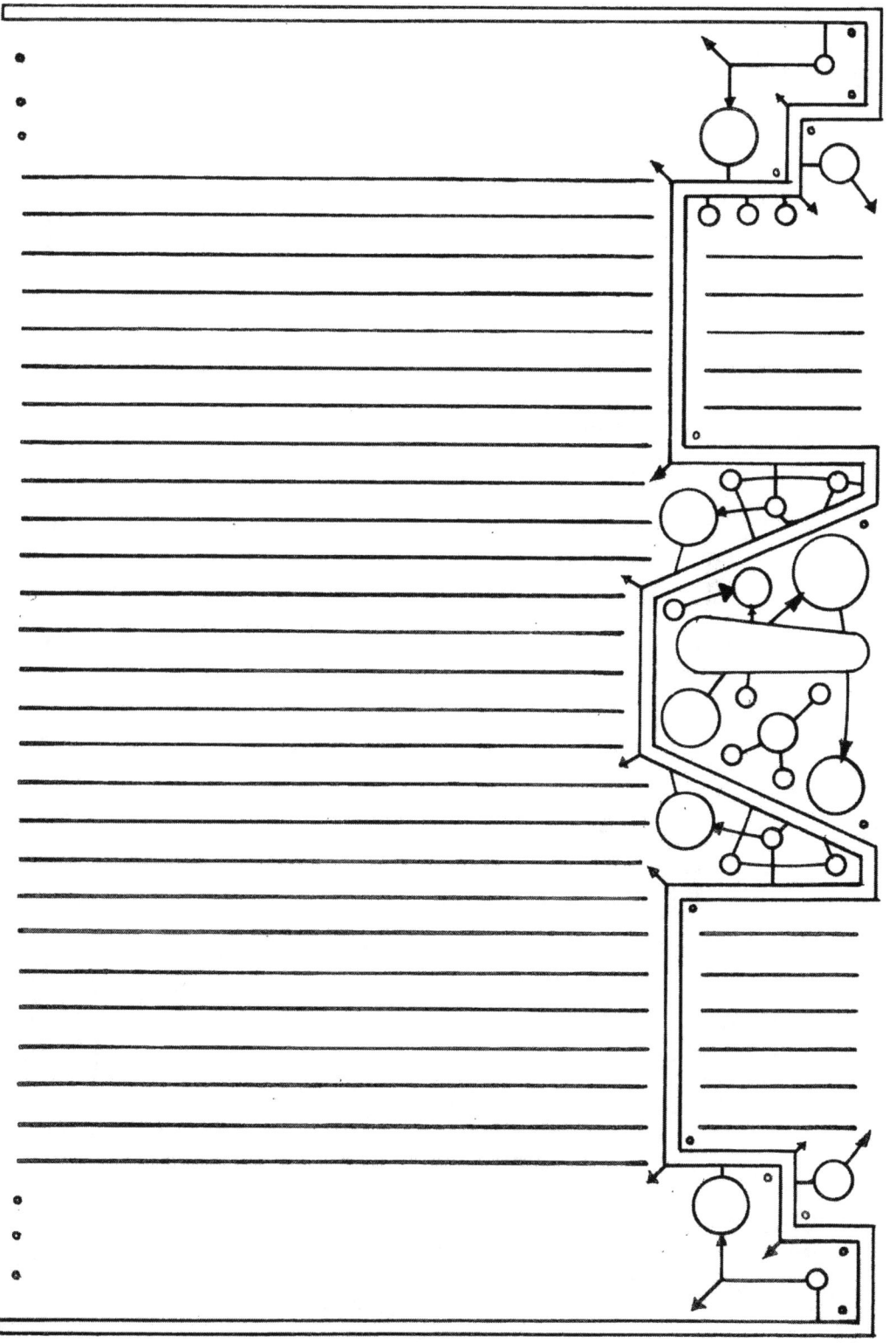

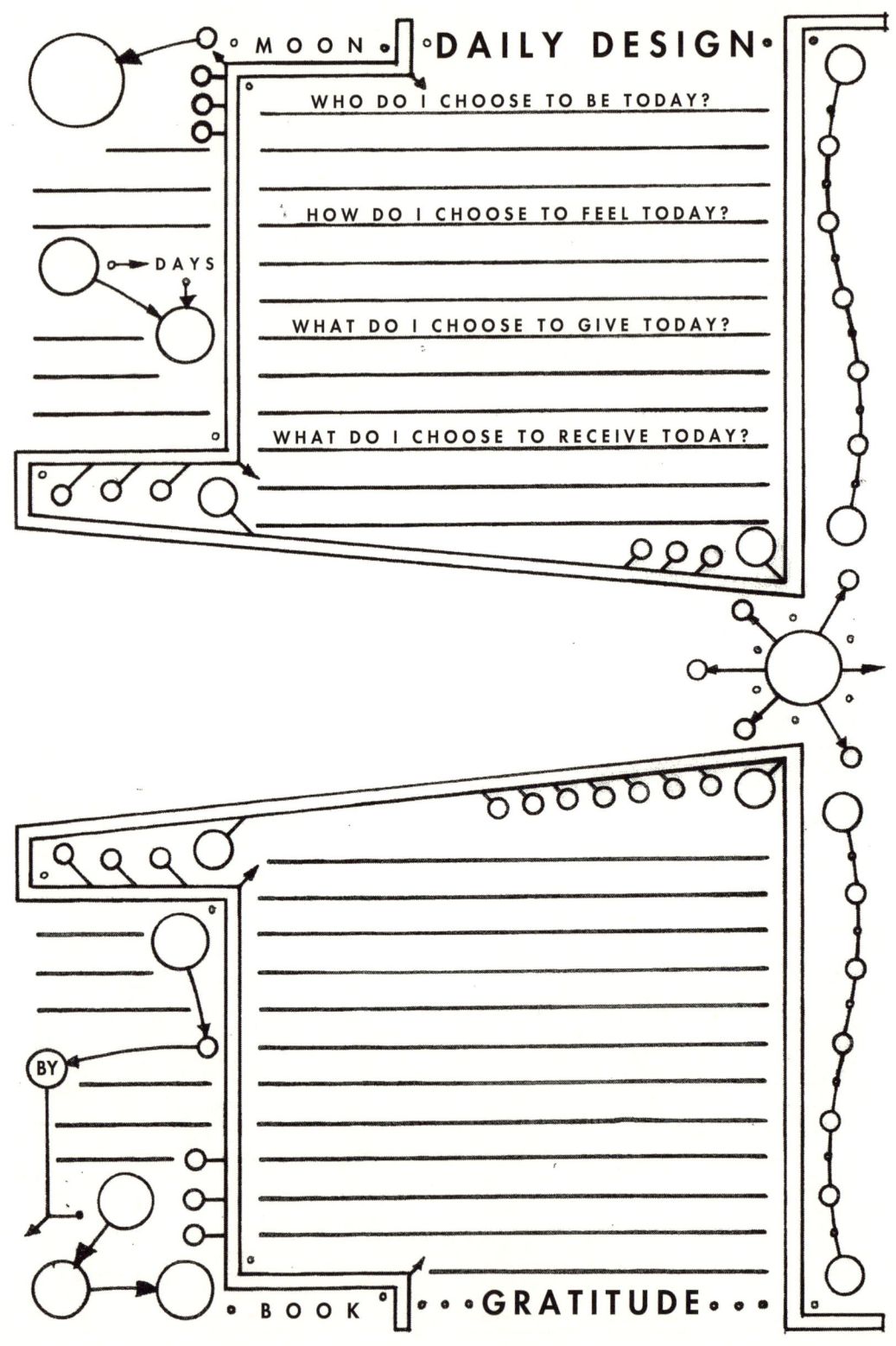

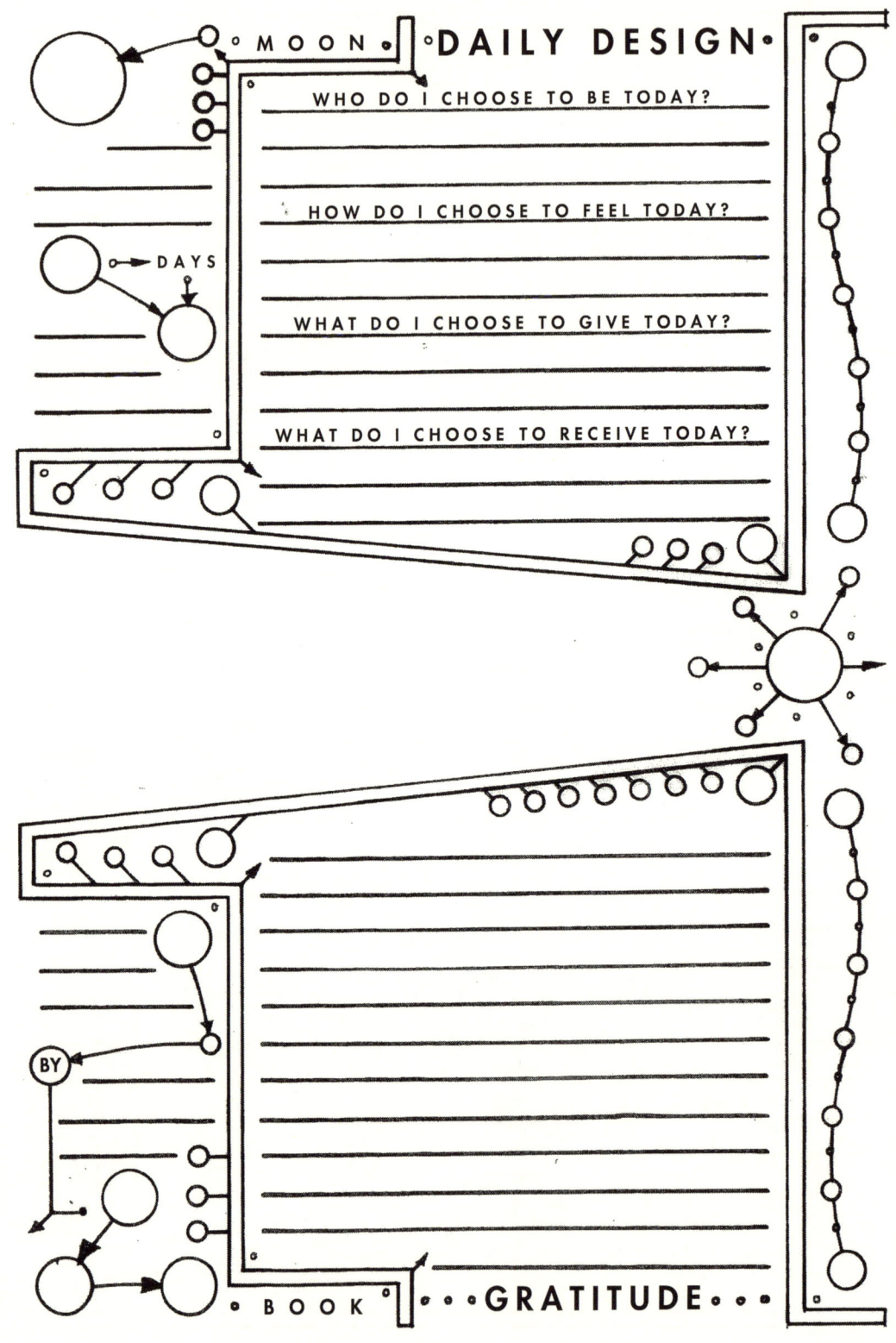

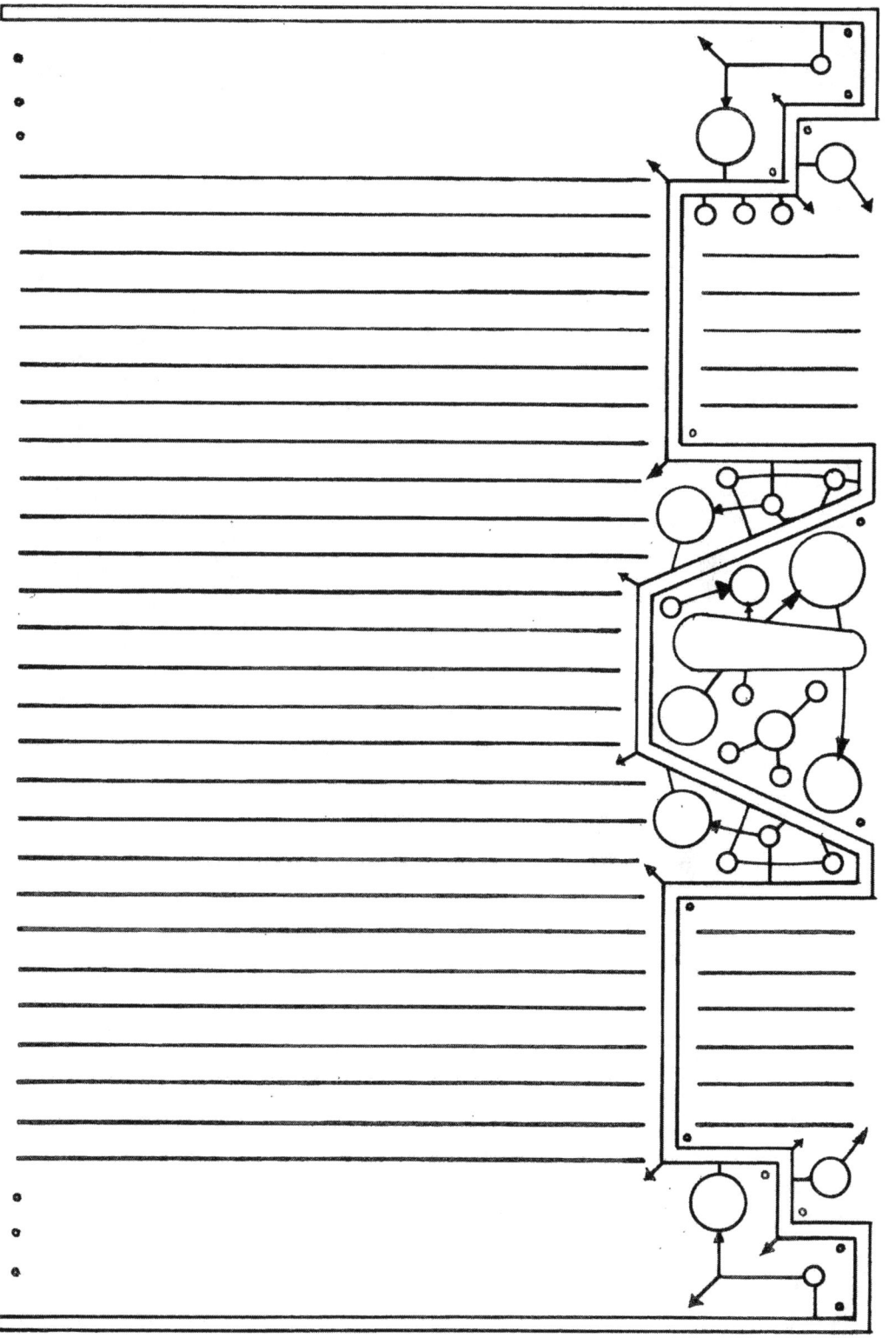

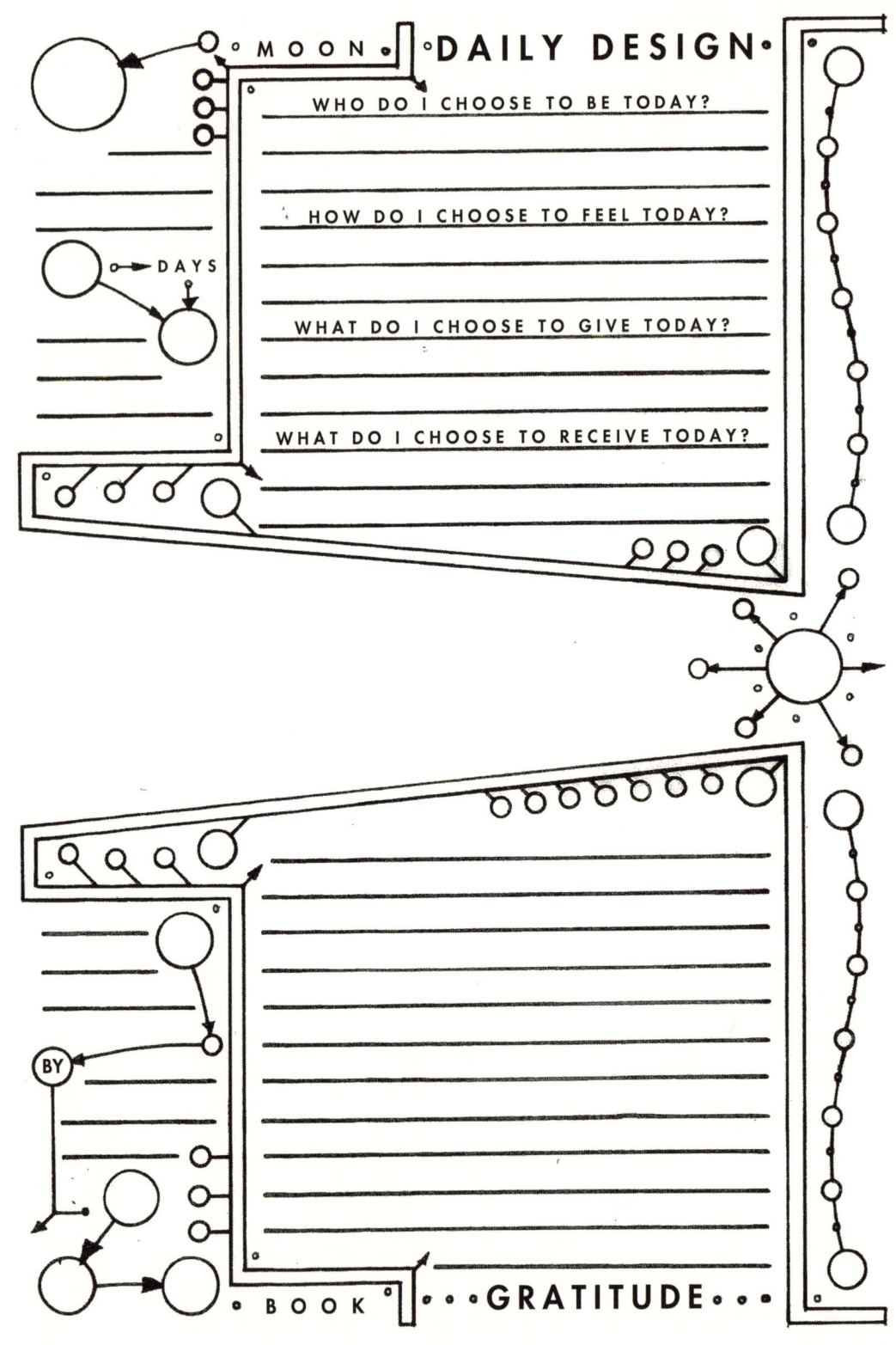

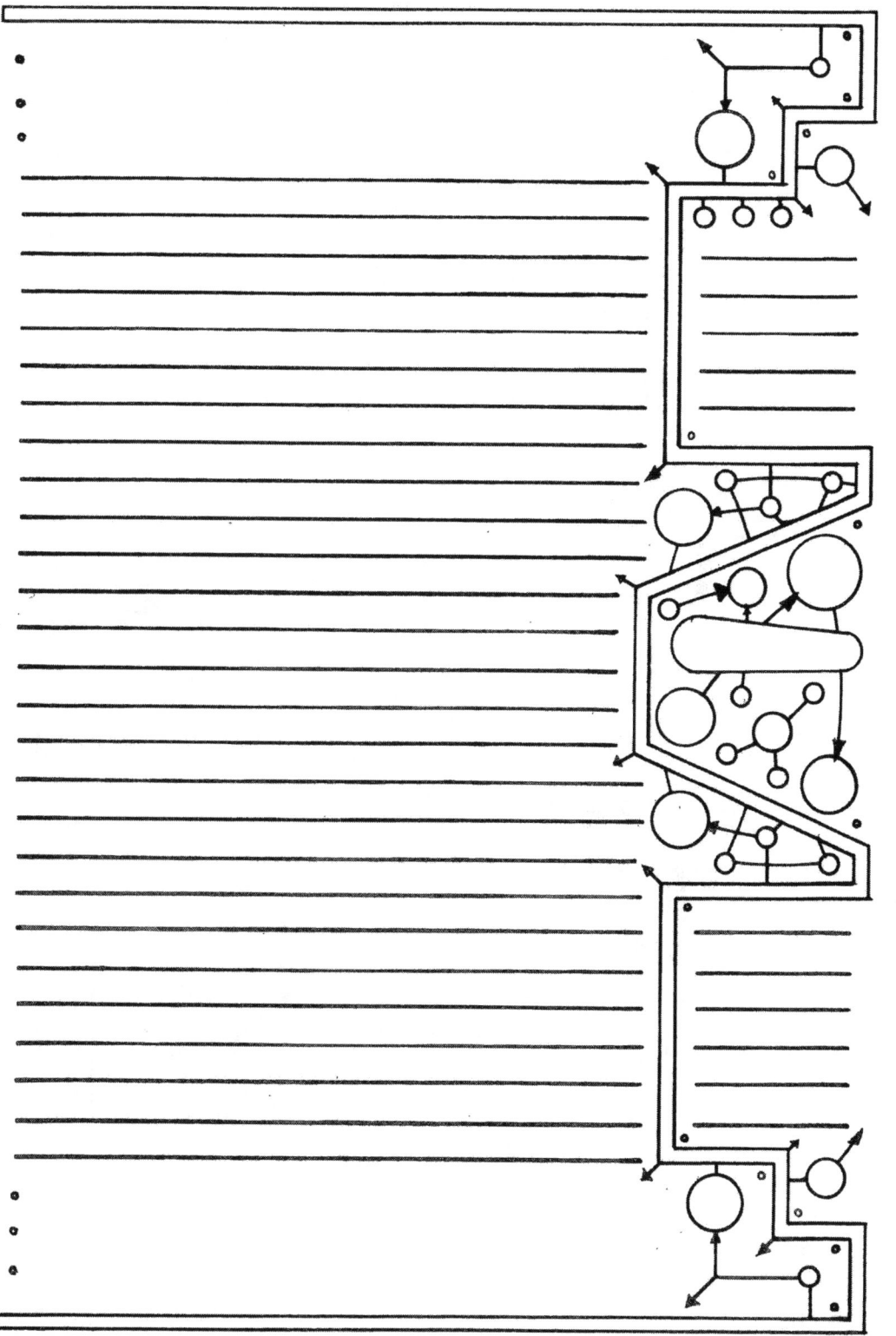

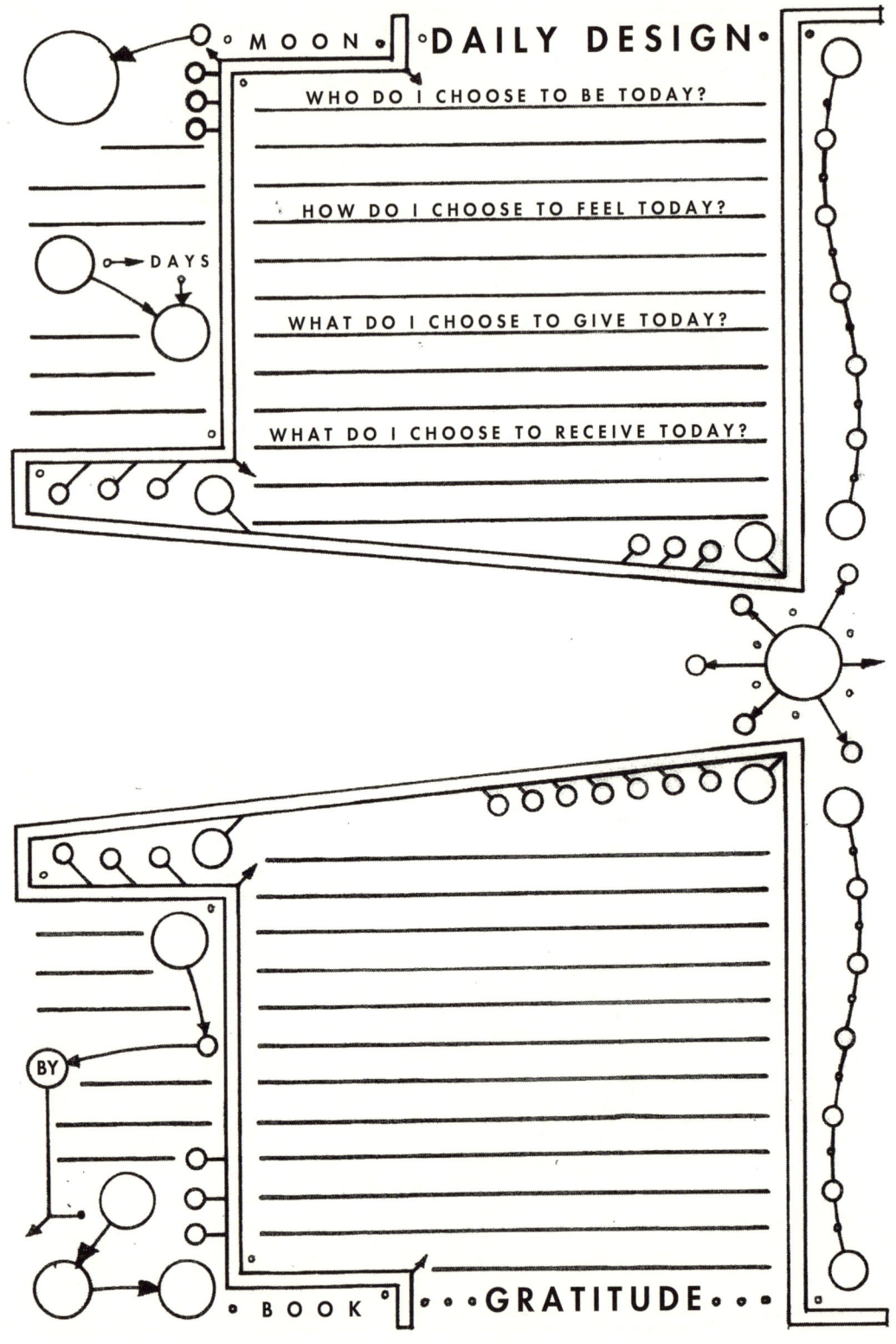

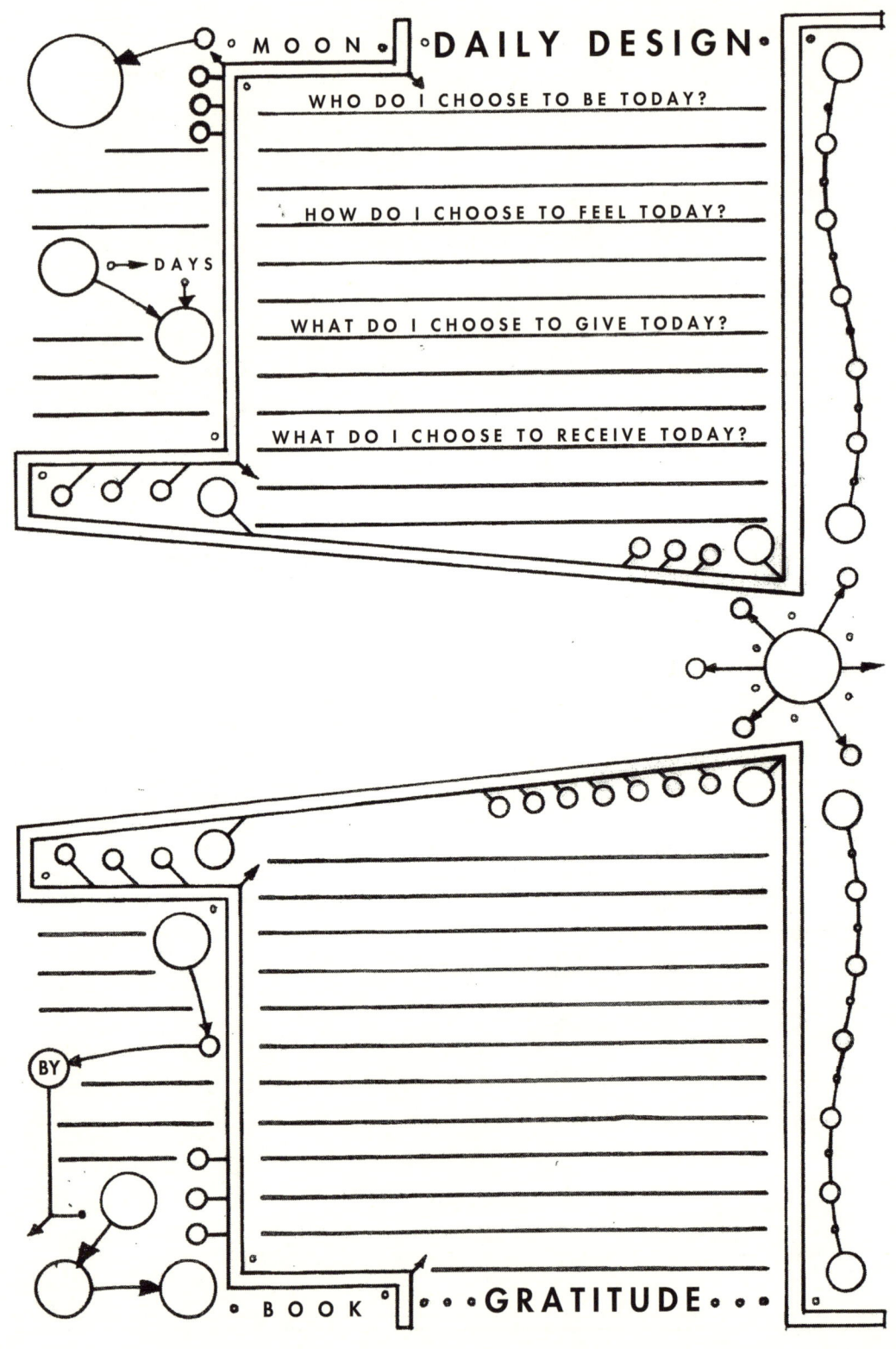

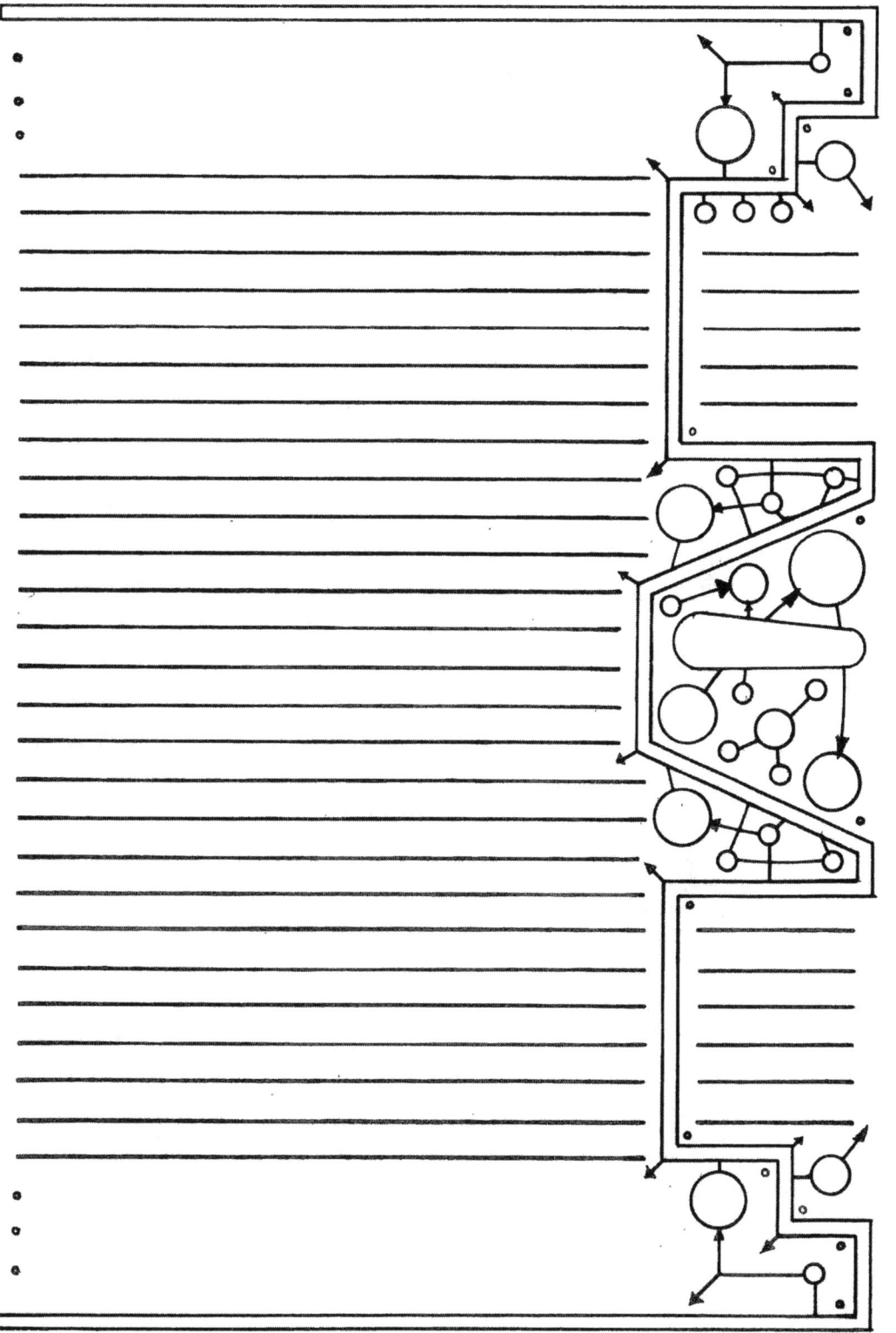

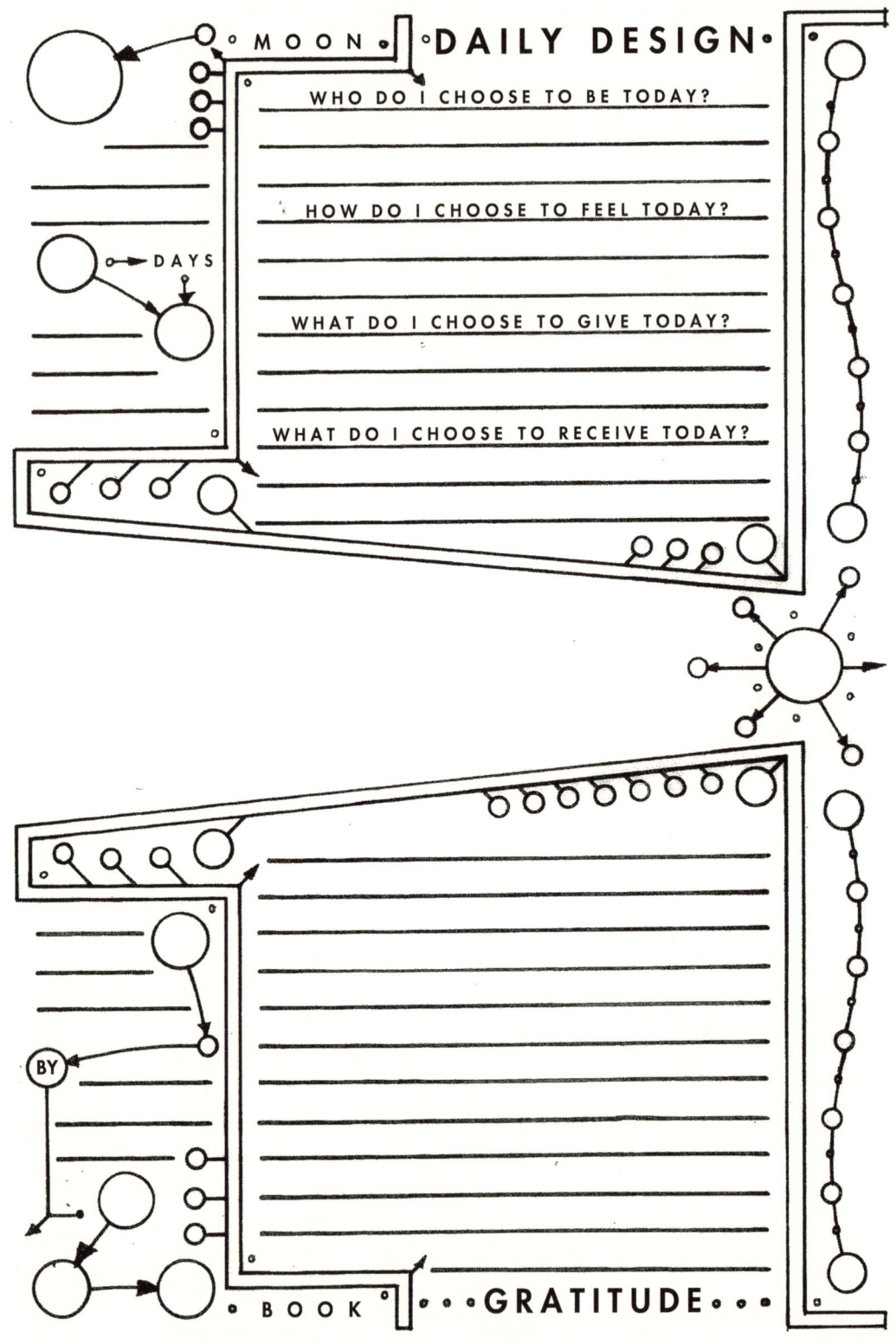

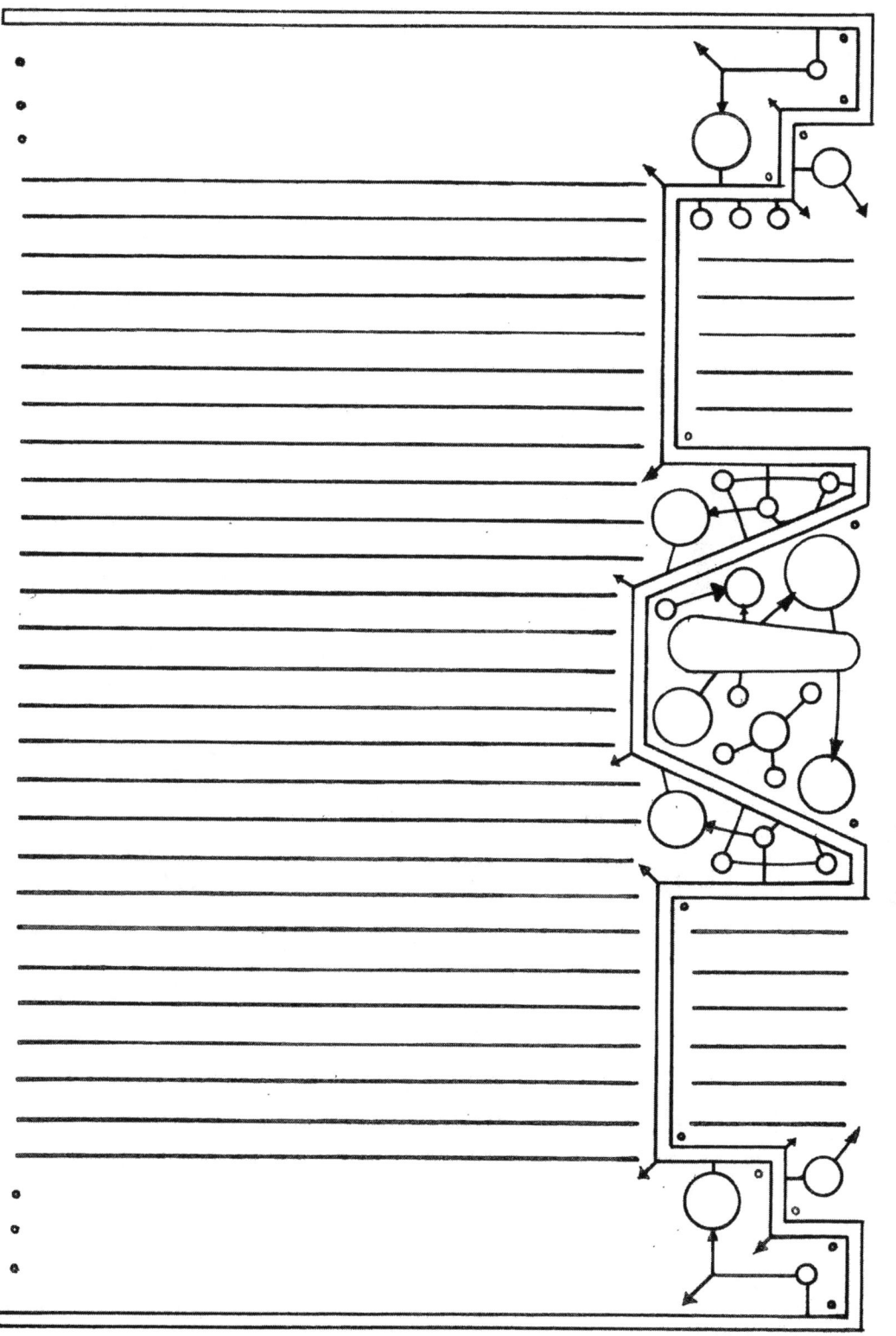

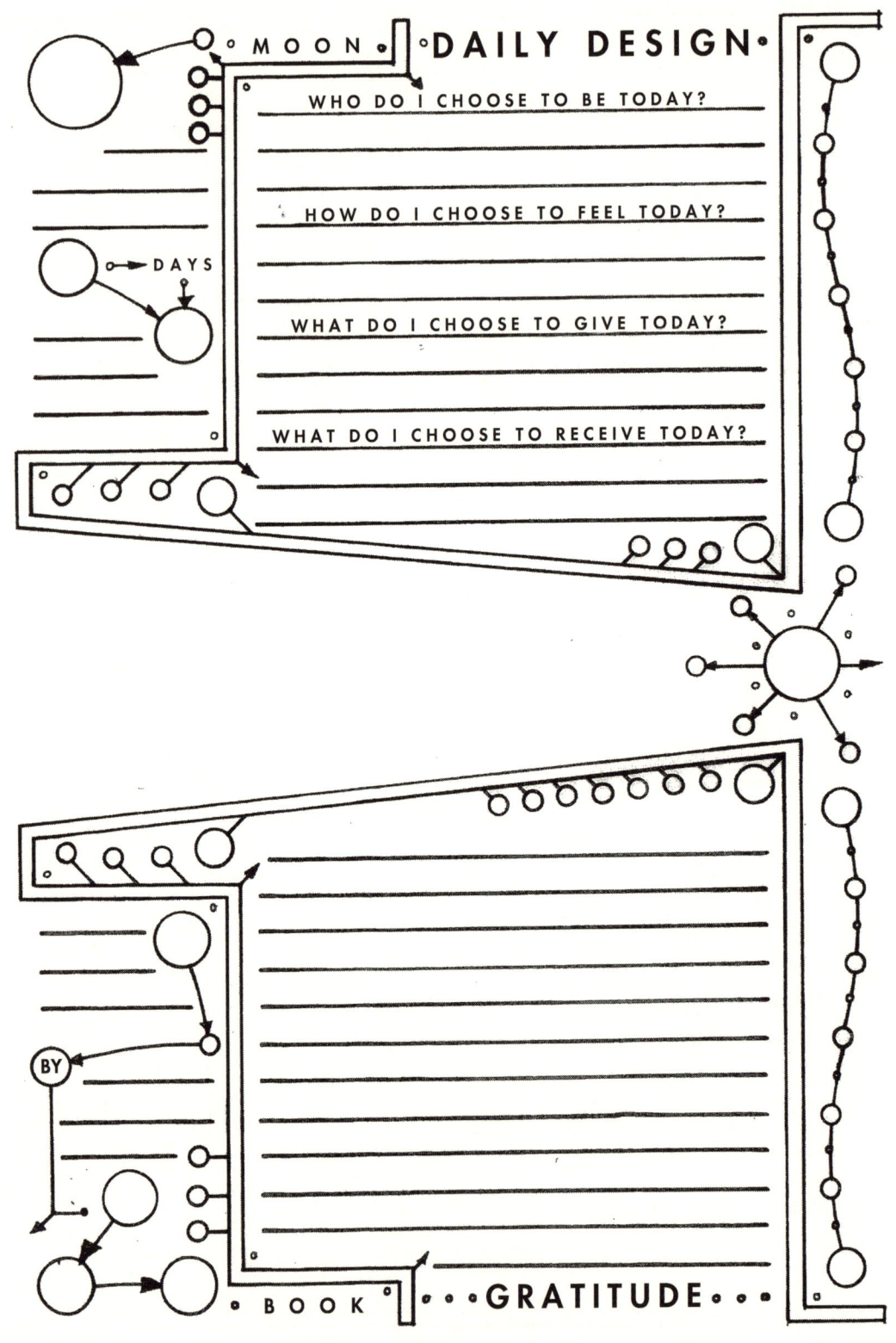

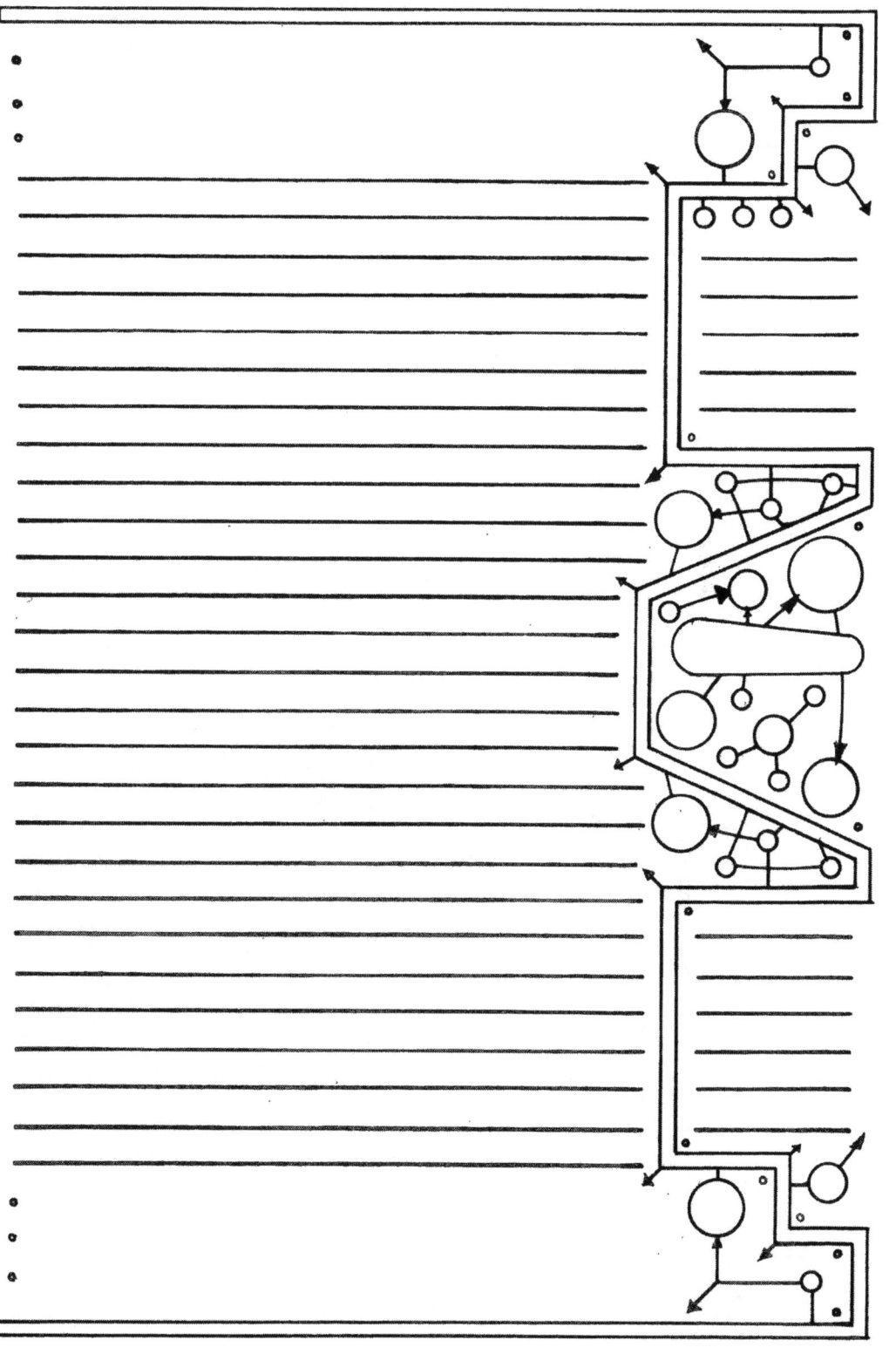

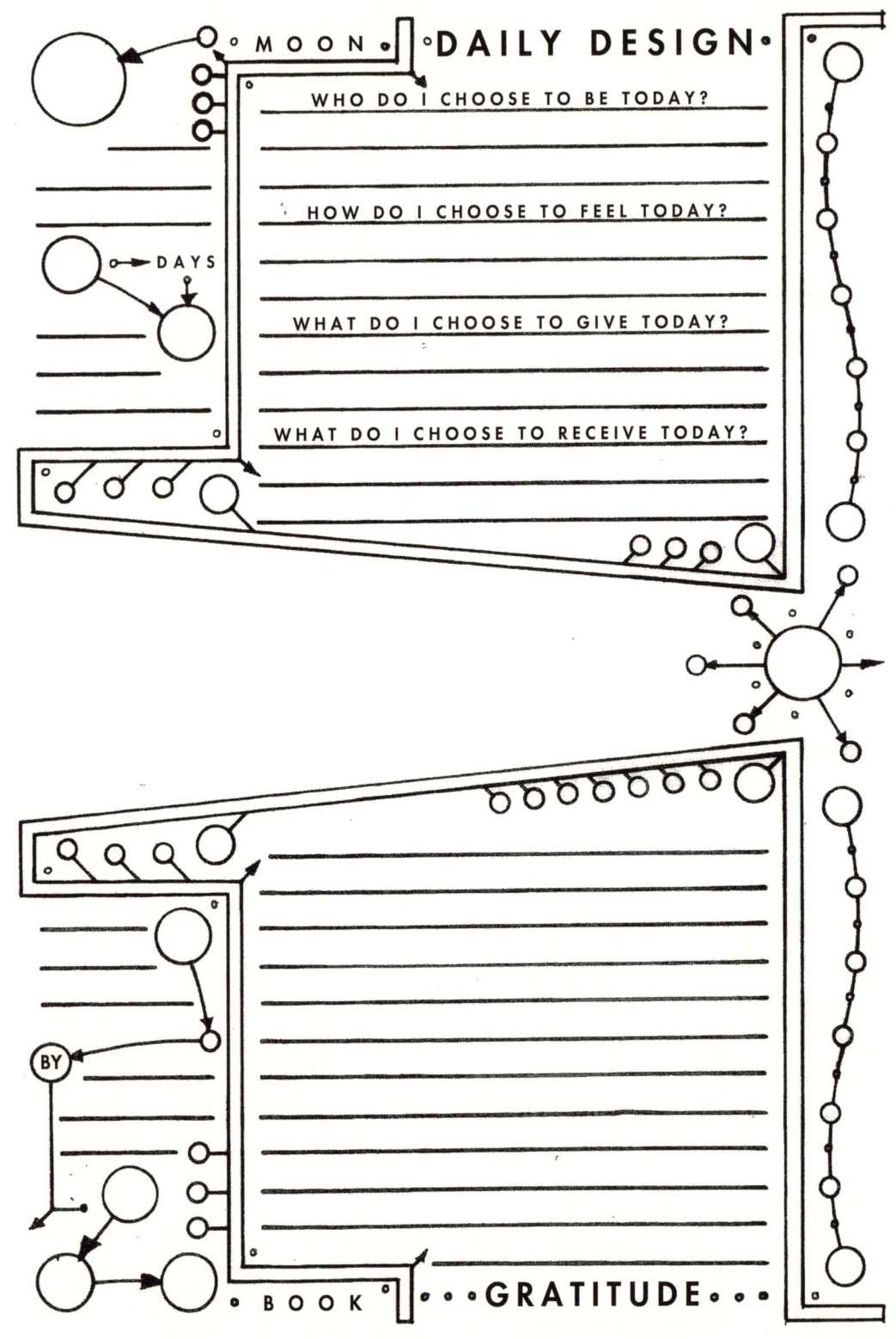

·MOON· ·DAILY DESIGN·

WHO DO I CHOOSE TO BE TODAY?

HOW DO I CHOOSE TO FEEL TODAY?

DAYS

WHAT DO I CHOOSE TO GIVE TODAY?

WHAT DO I CHOOSE TO RECEIVE TODAY?

BY

·BOOK· ·GRATITUDE·

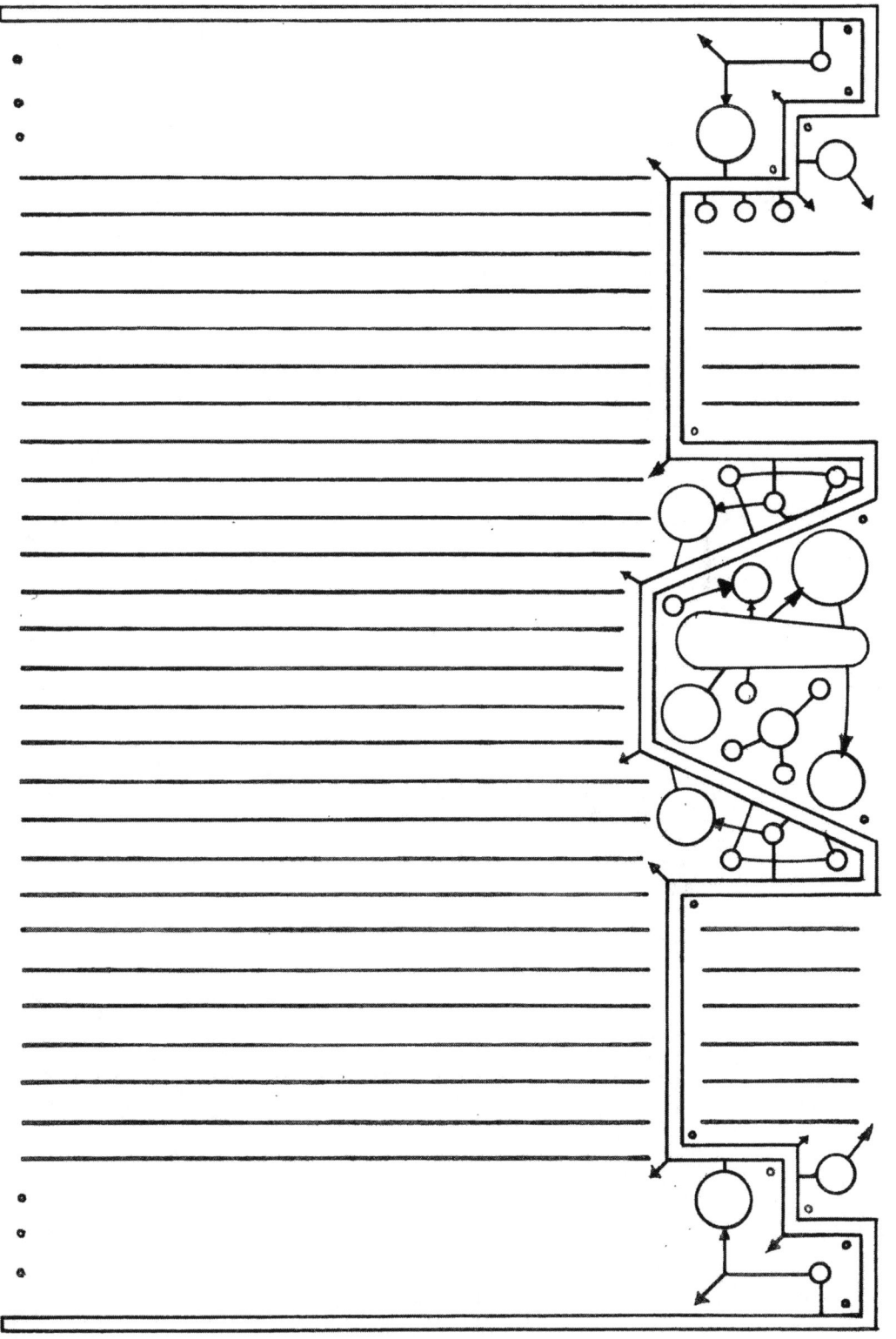

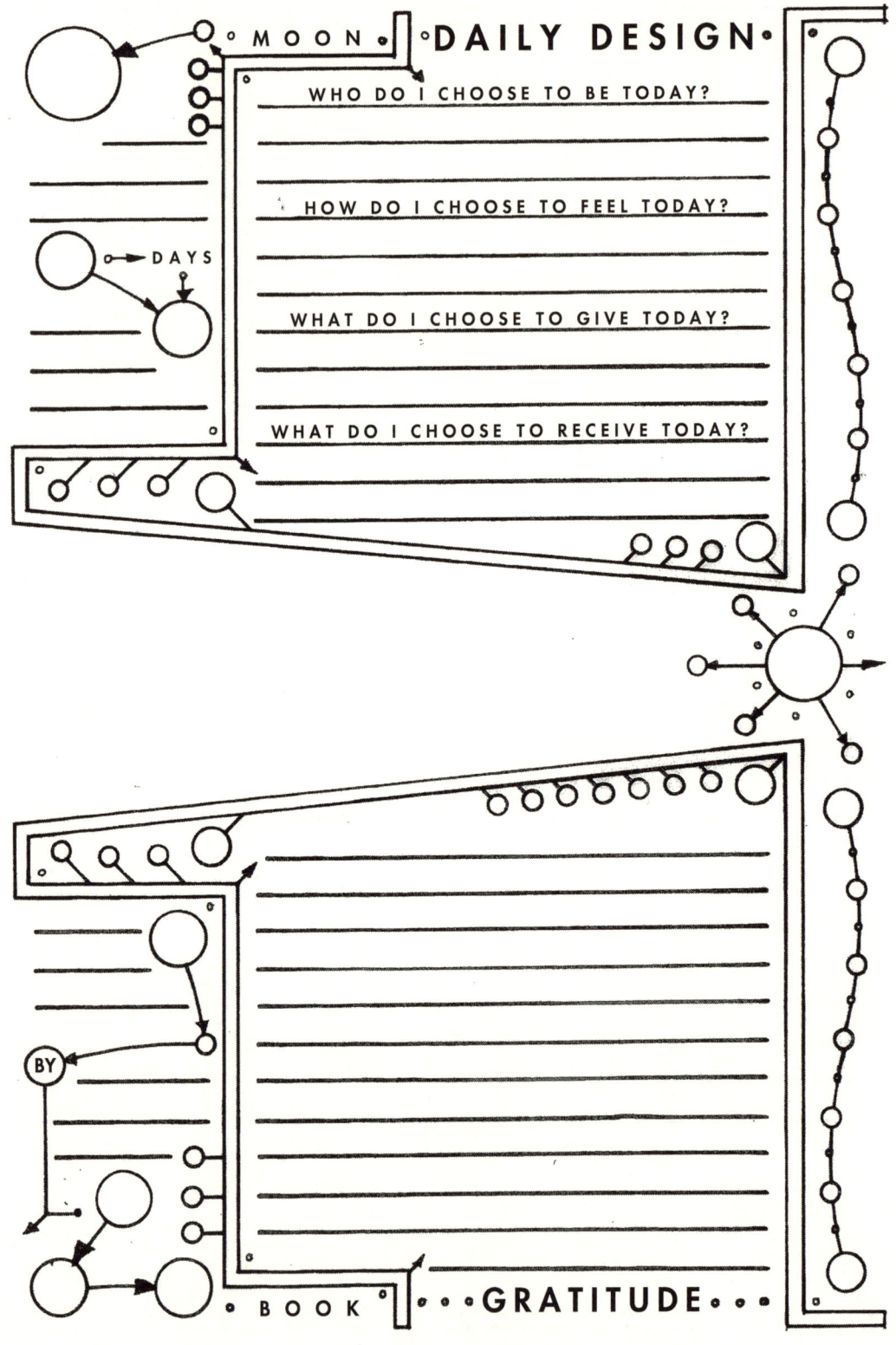

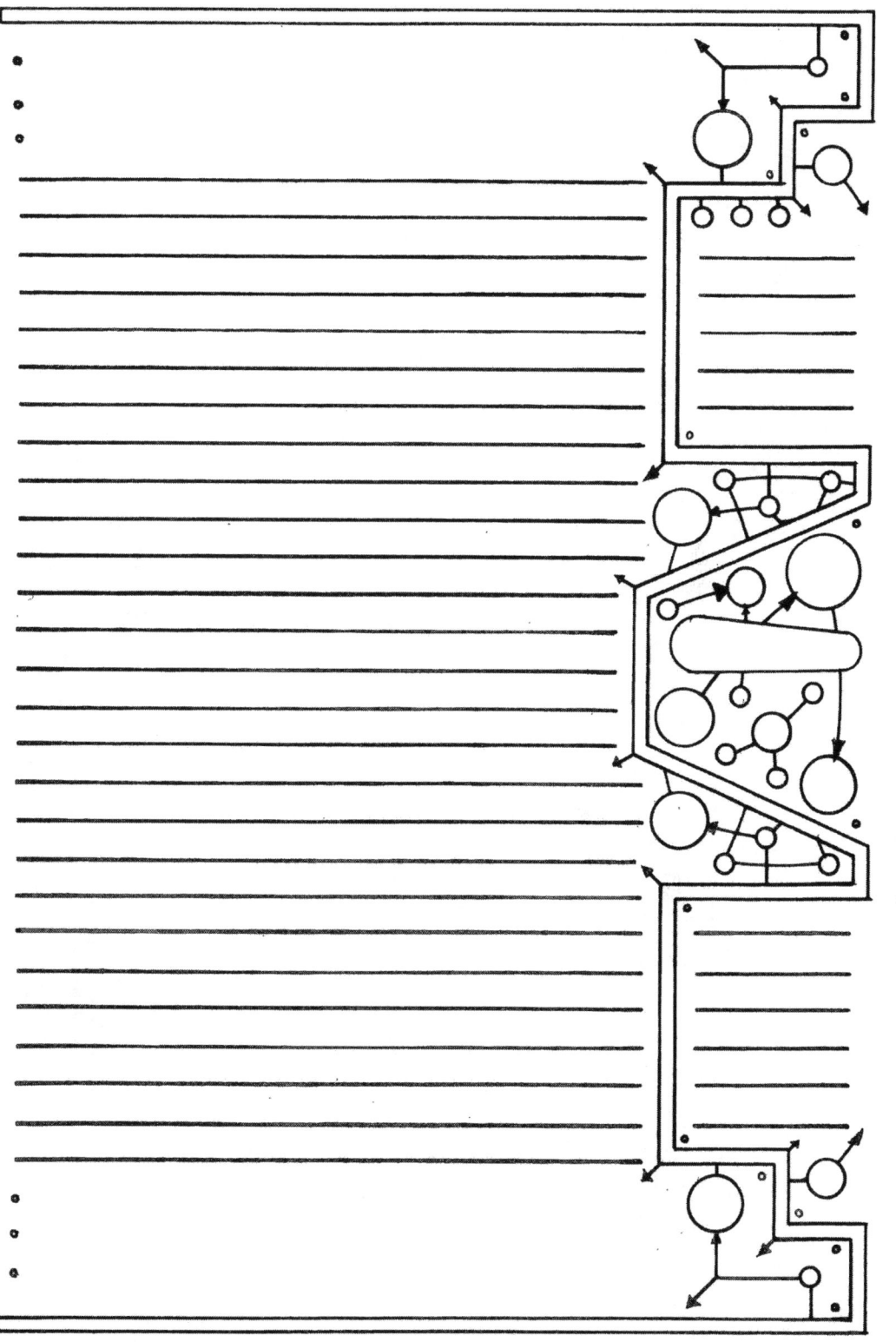

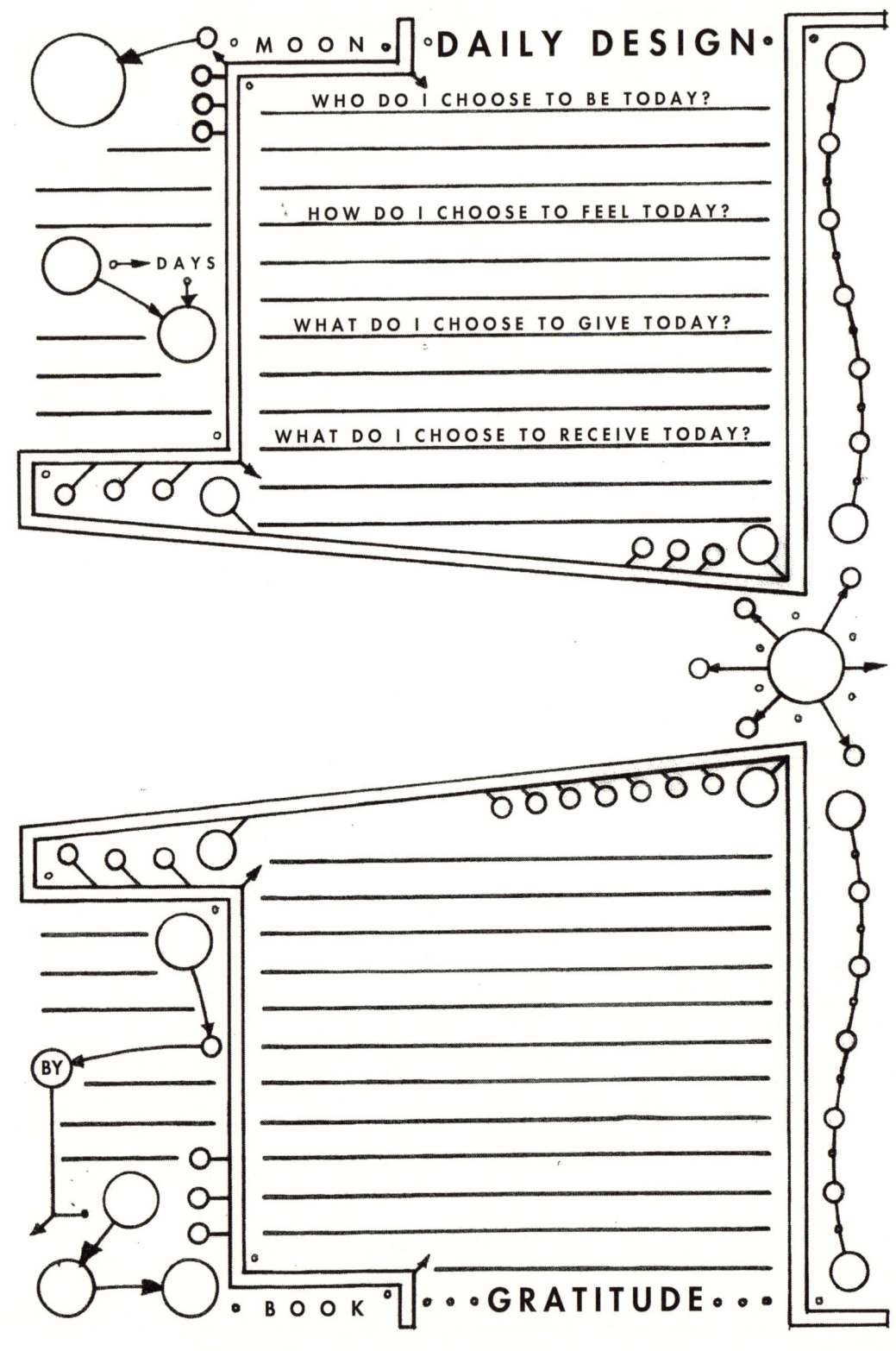

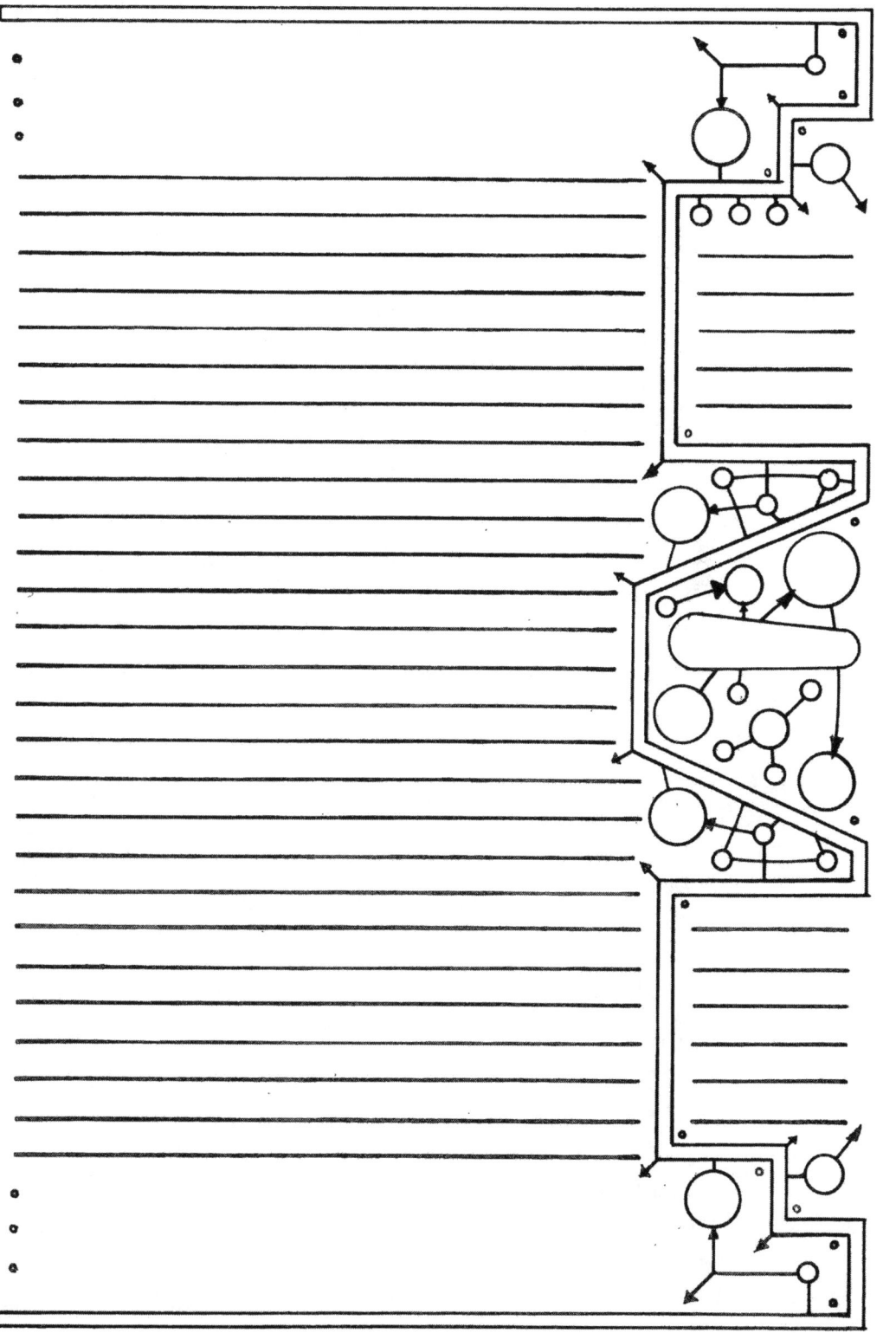

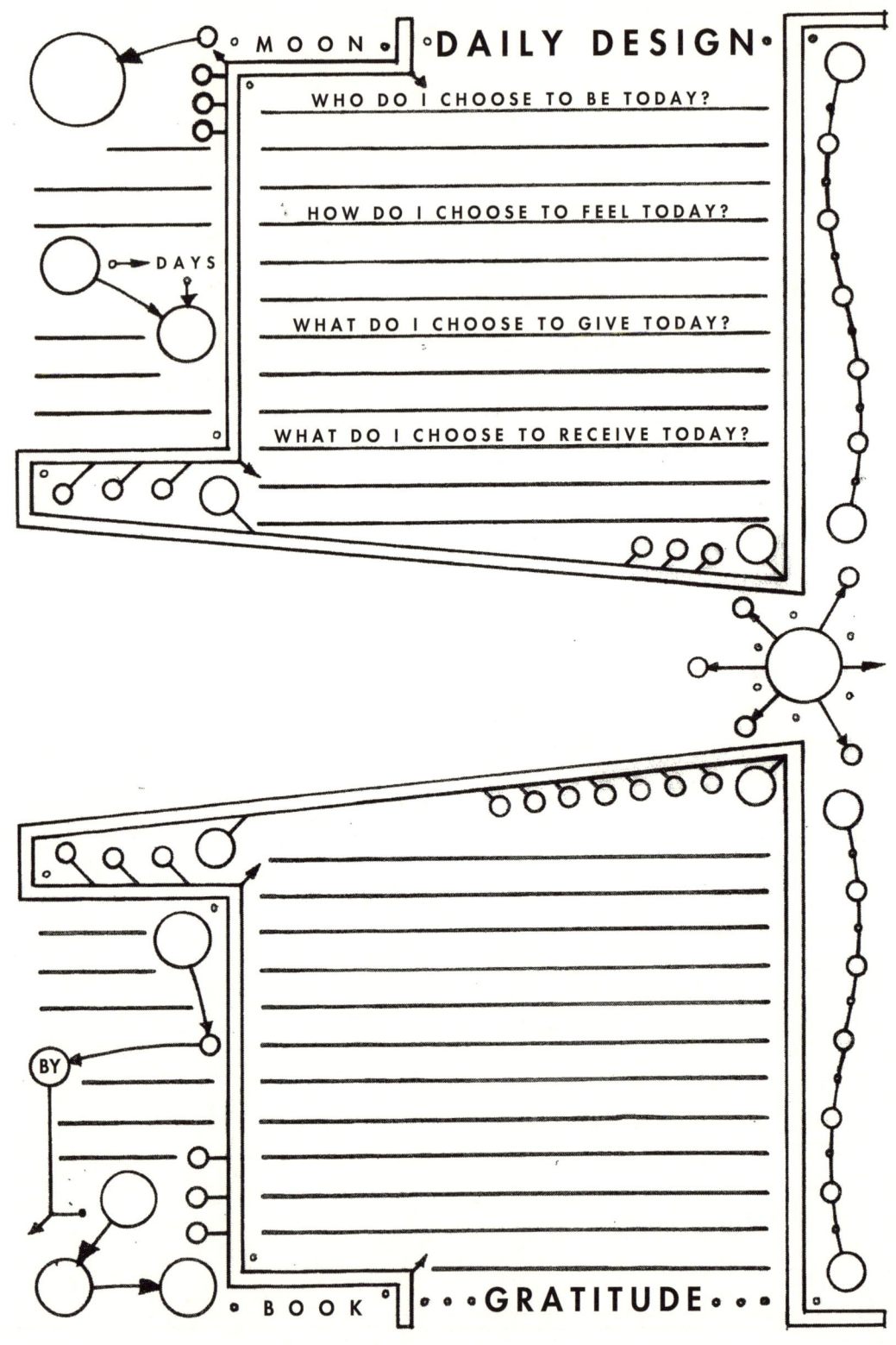

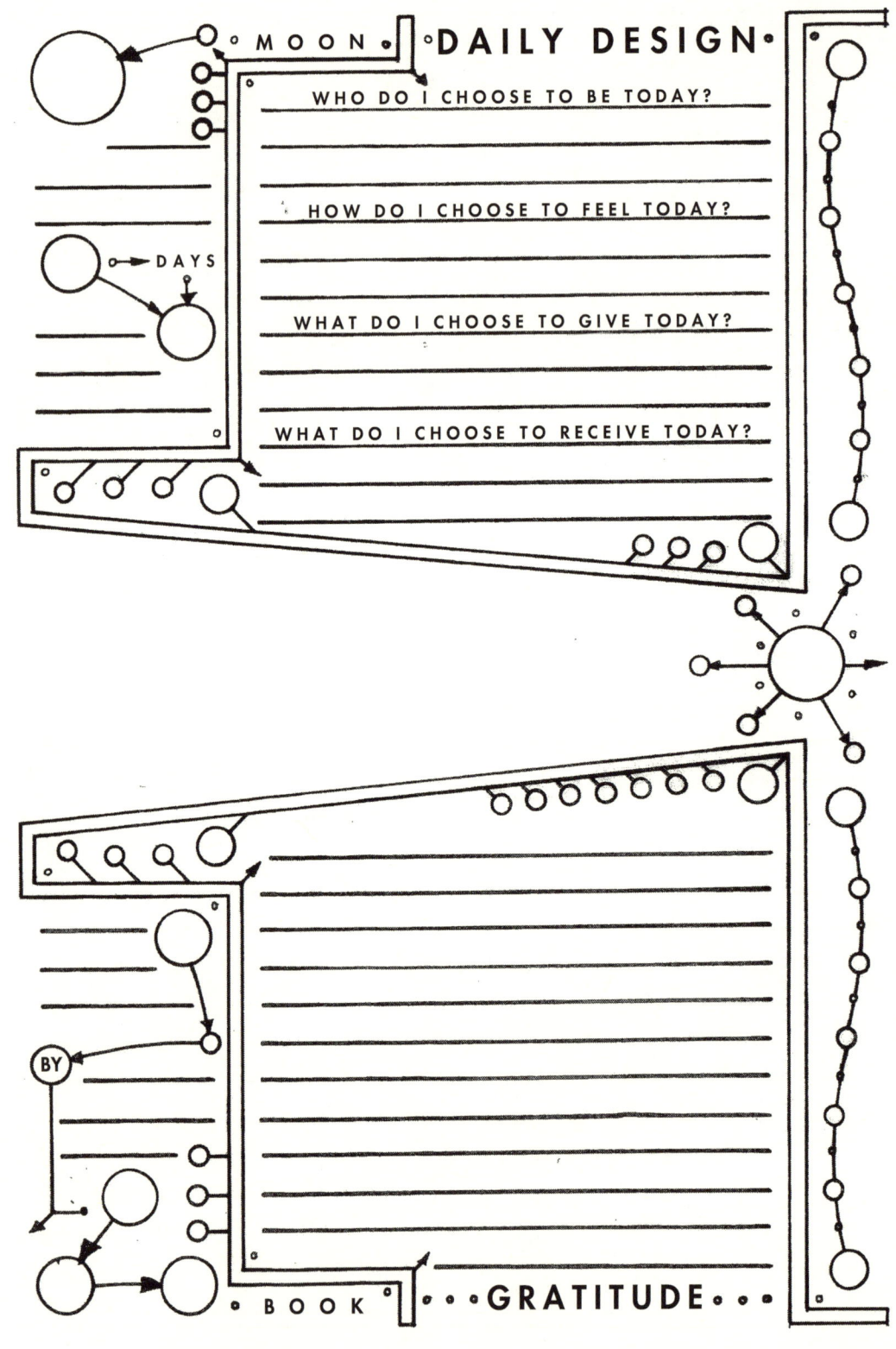

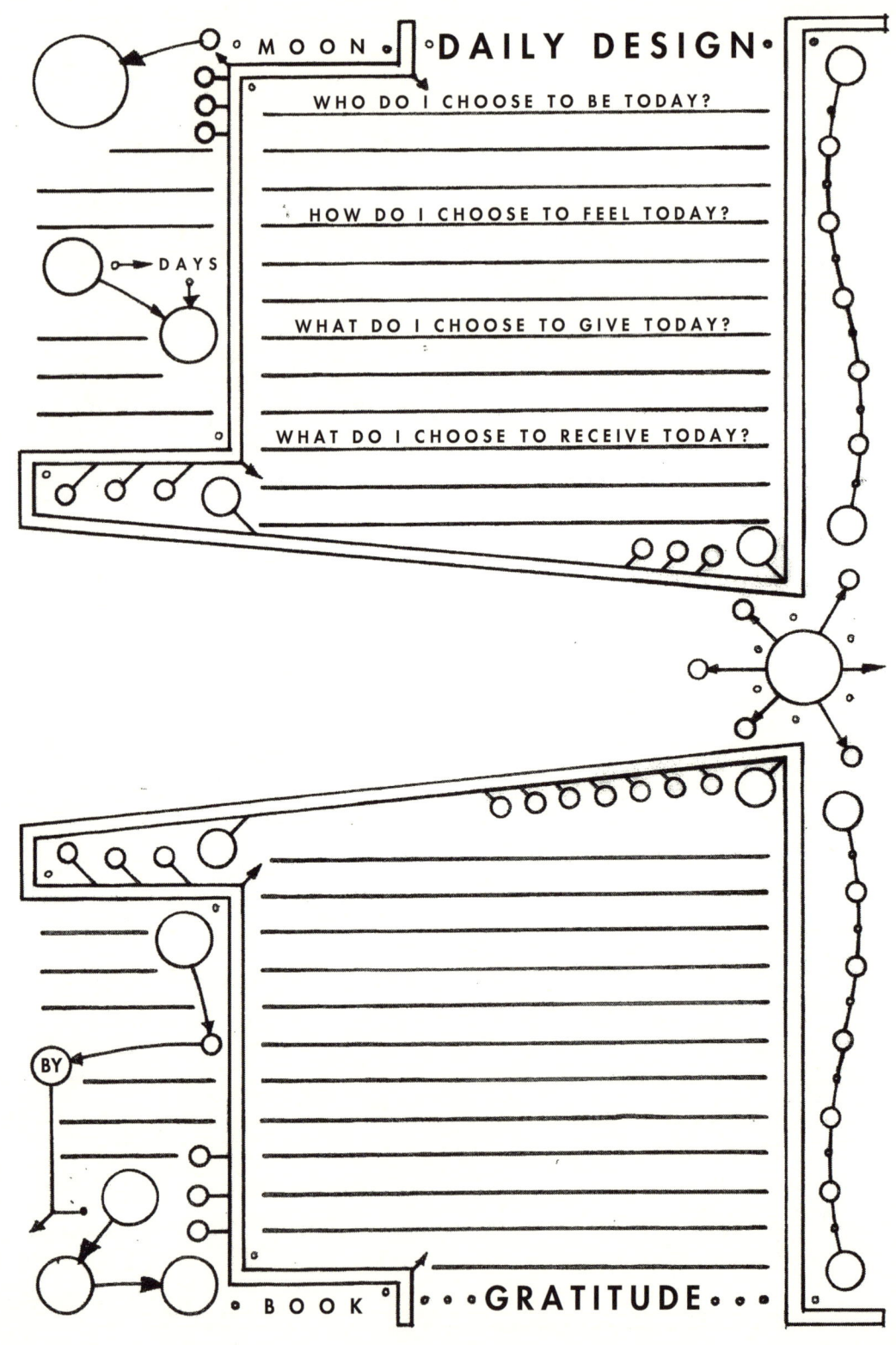

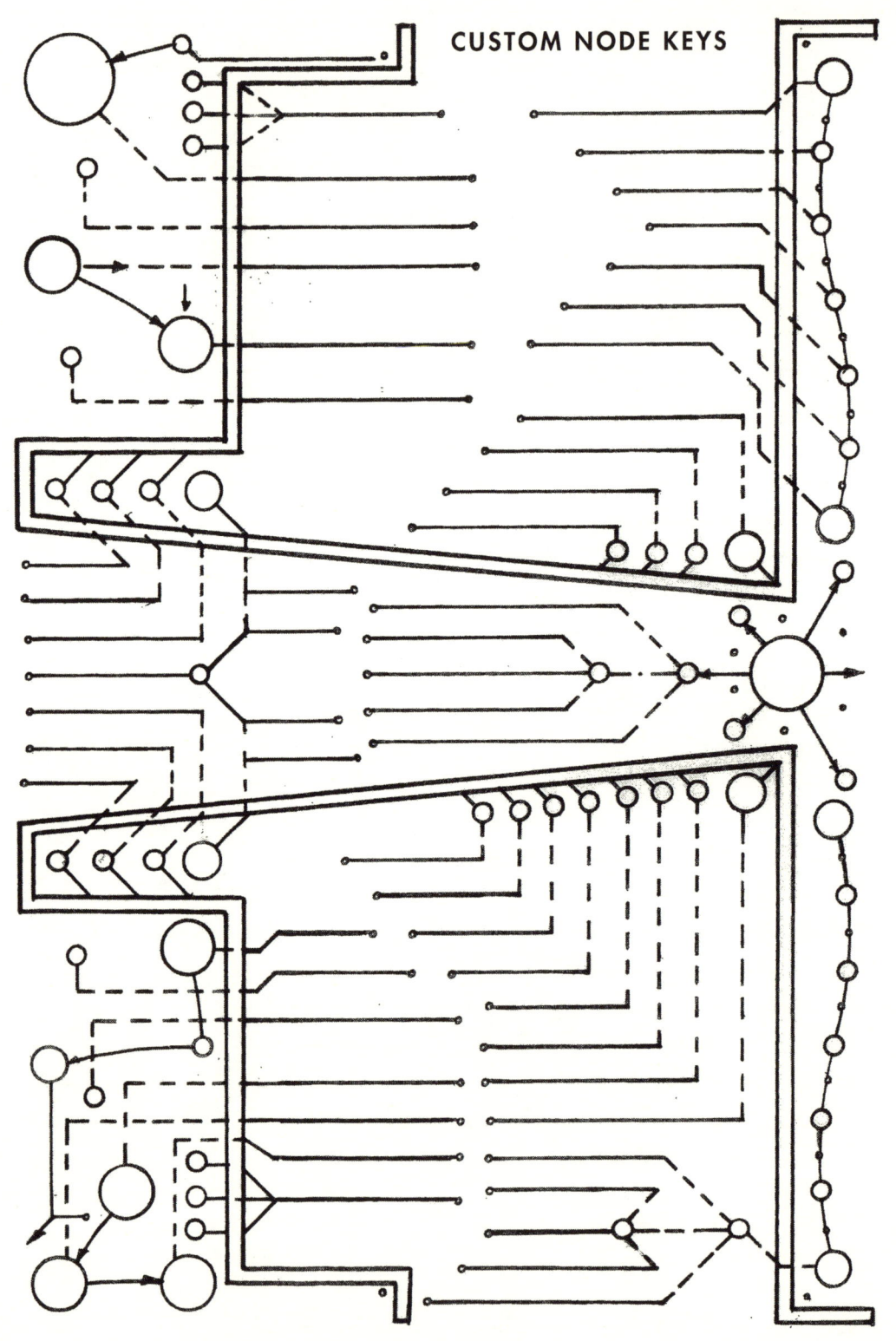

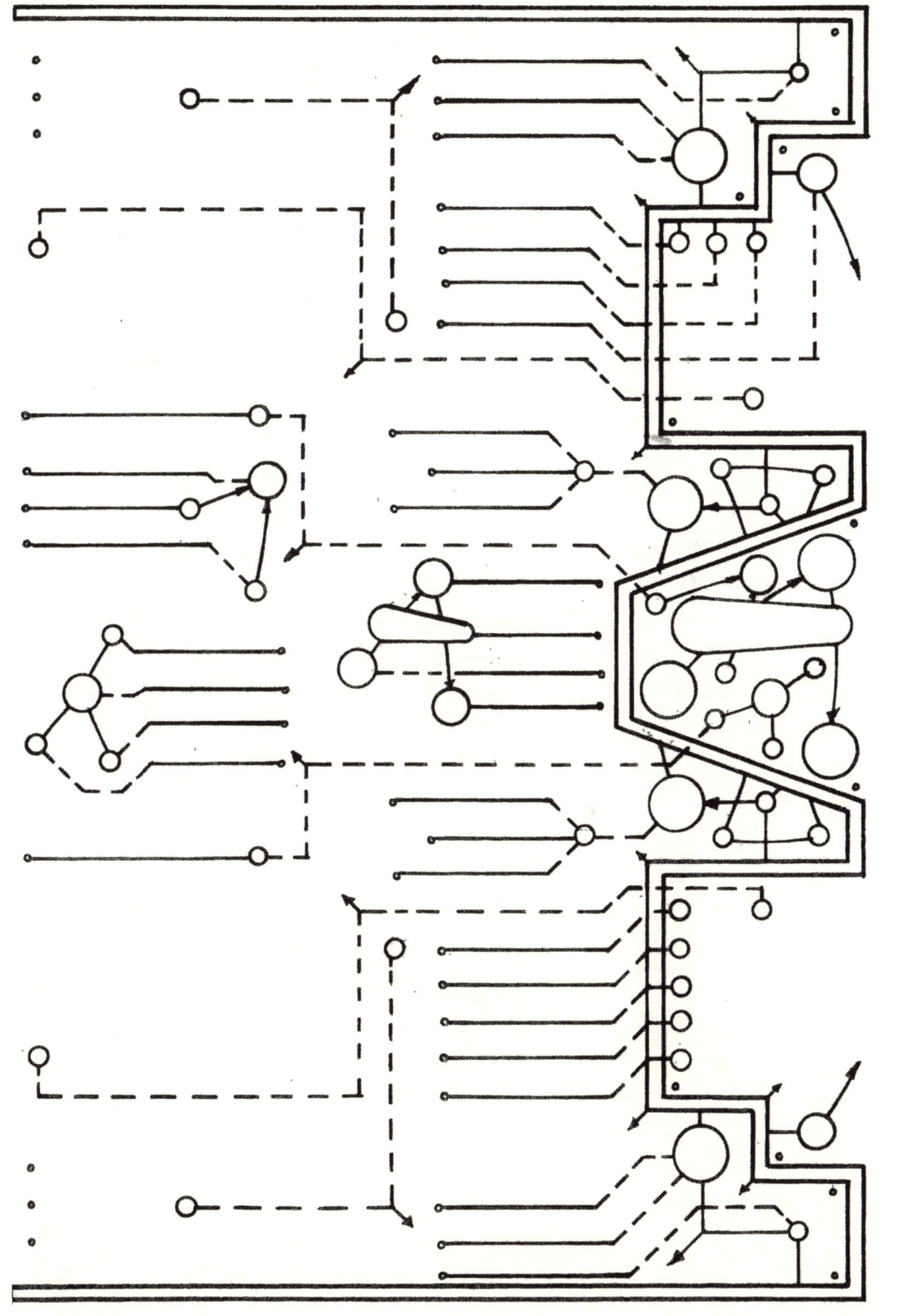

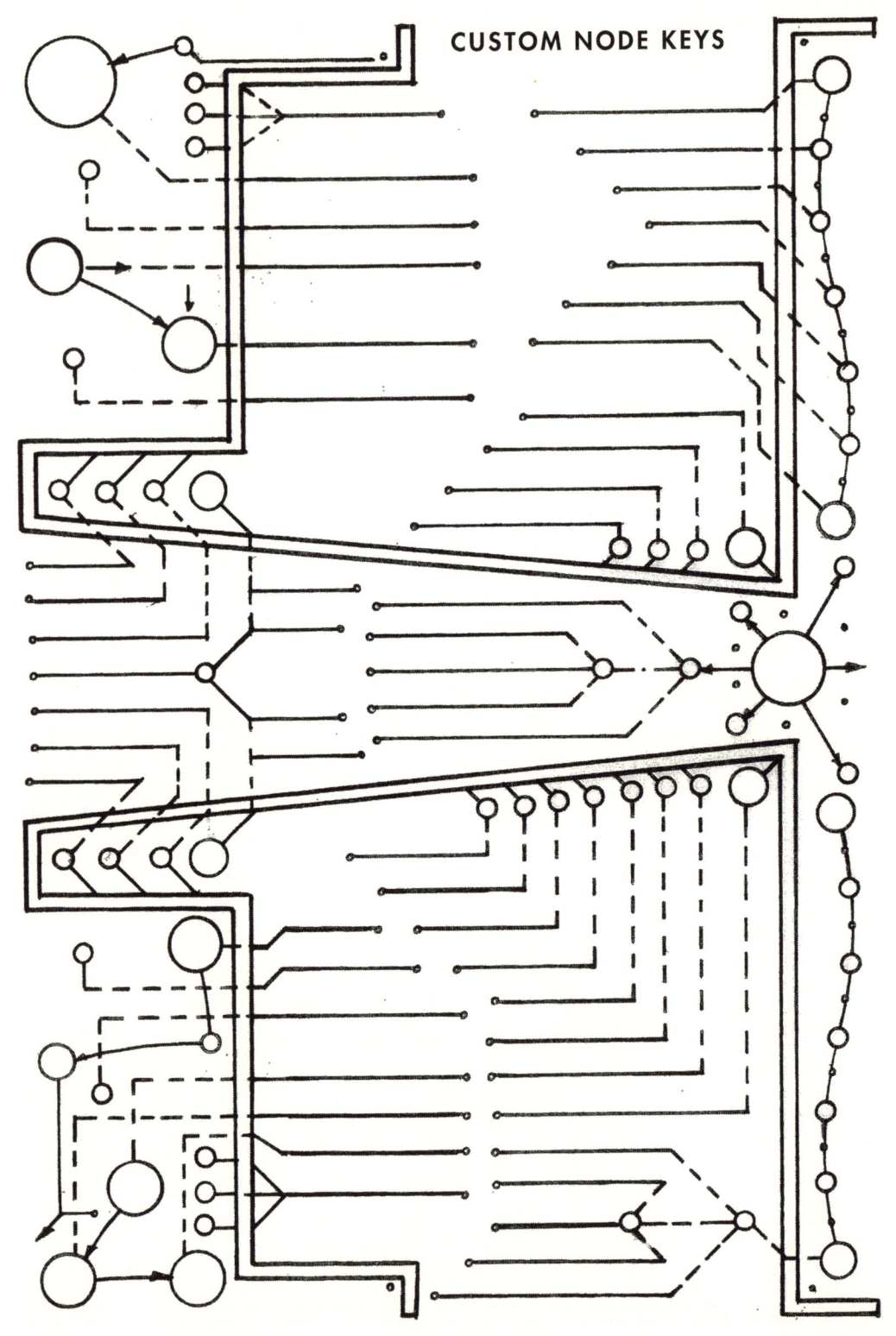

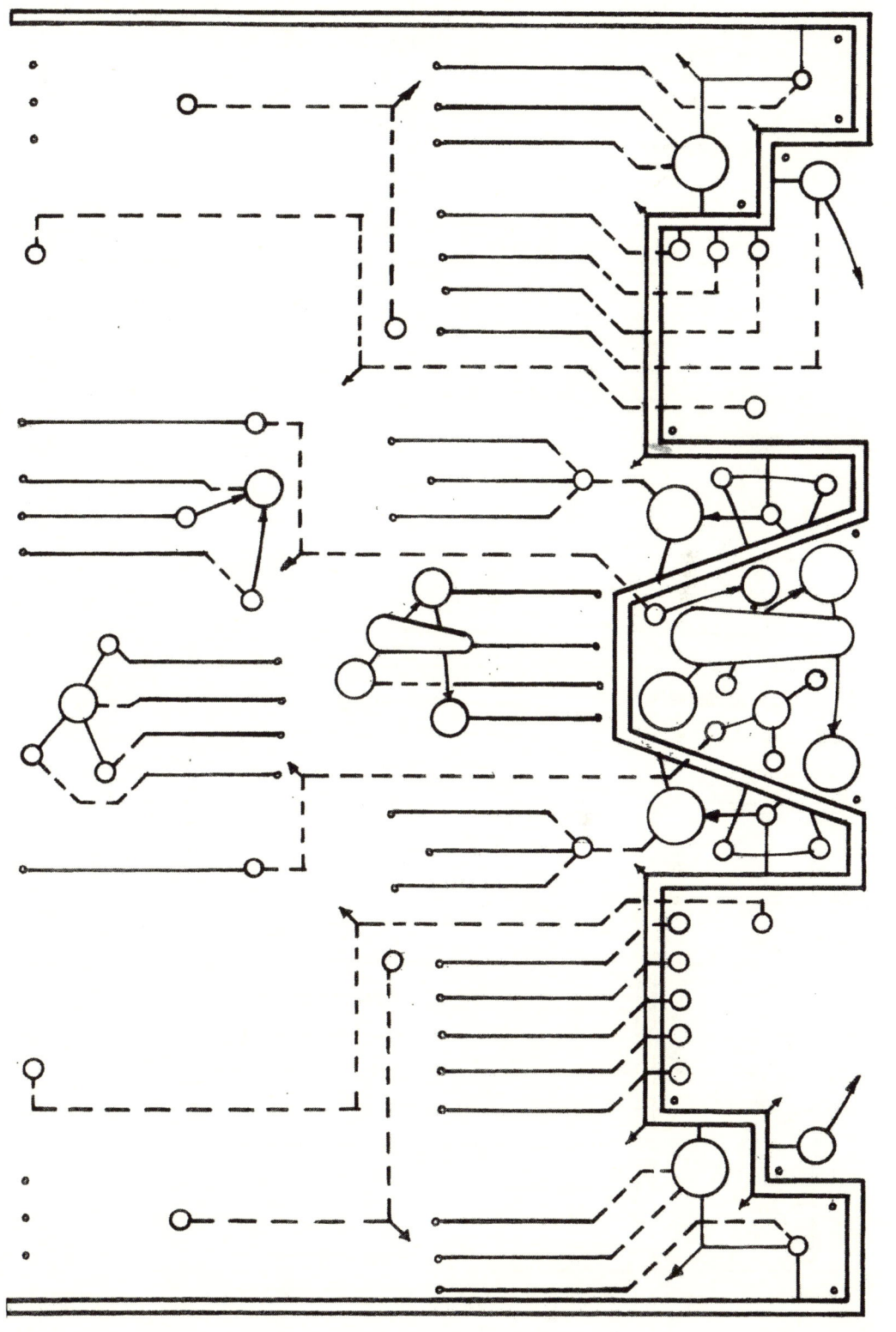

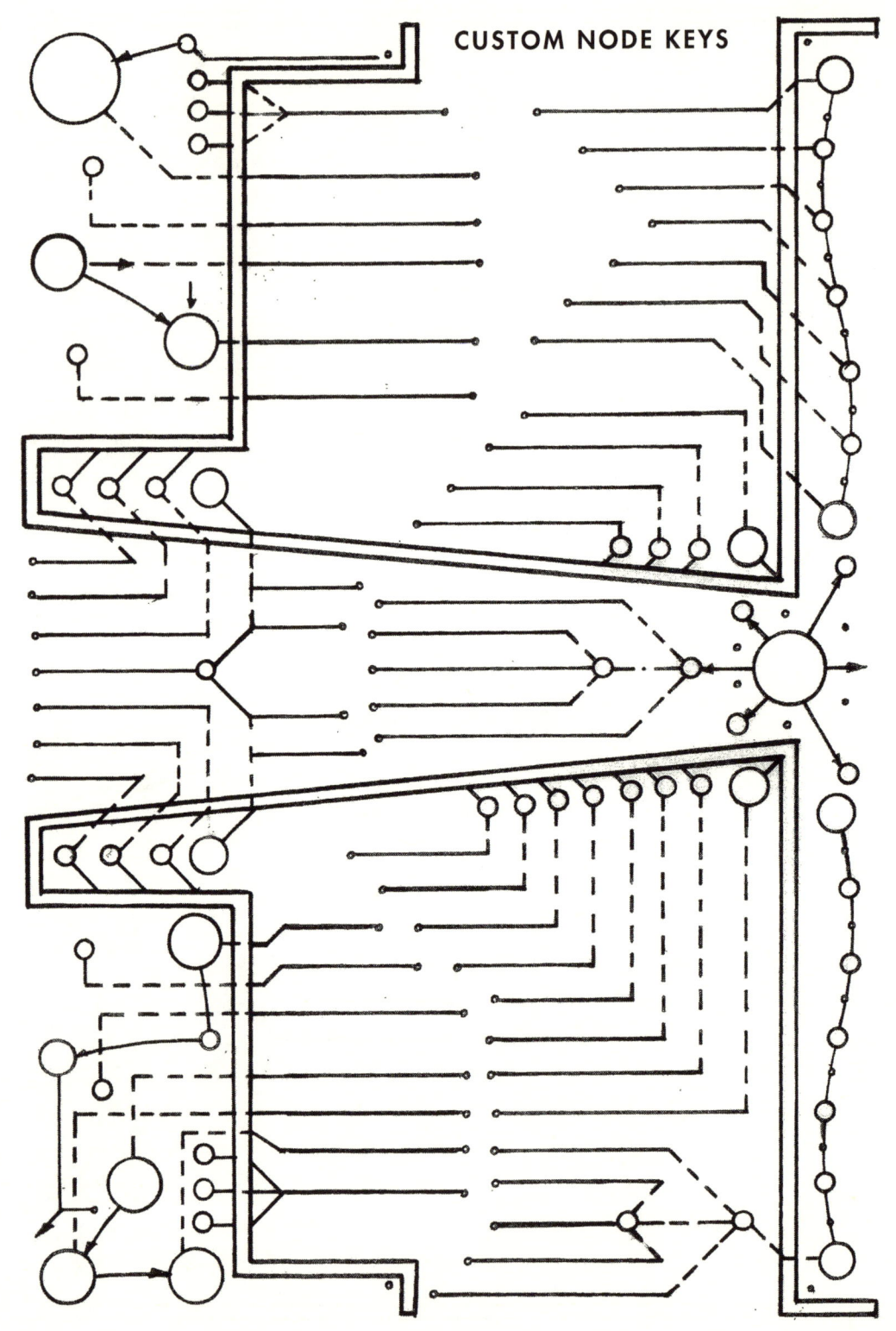

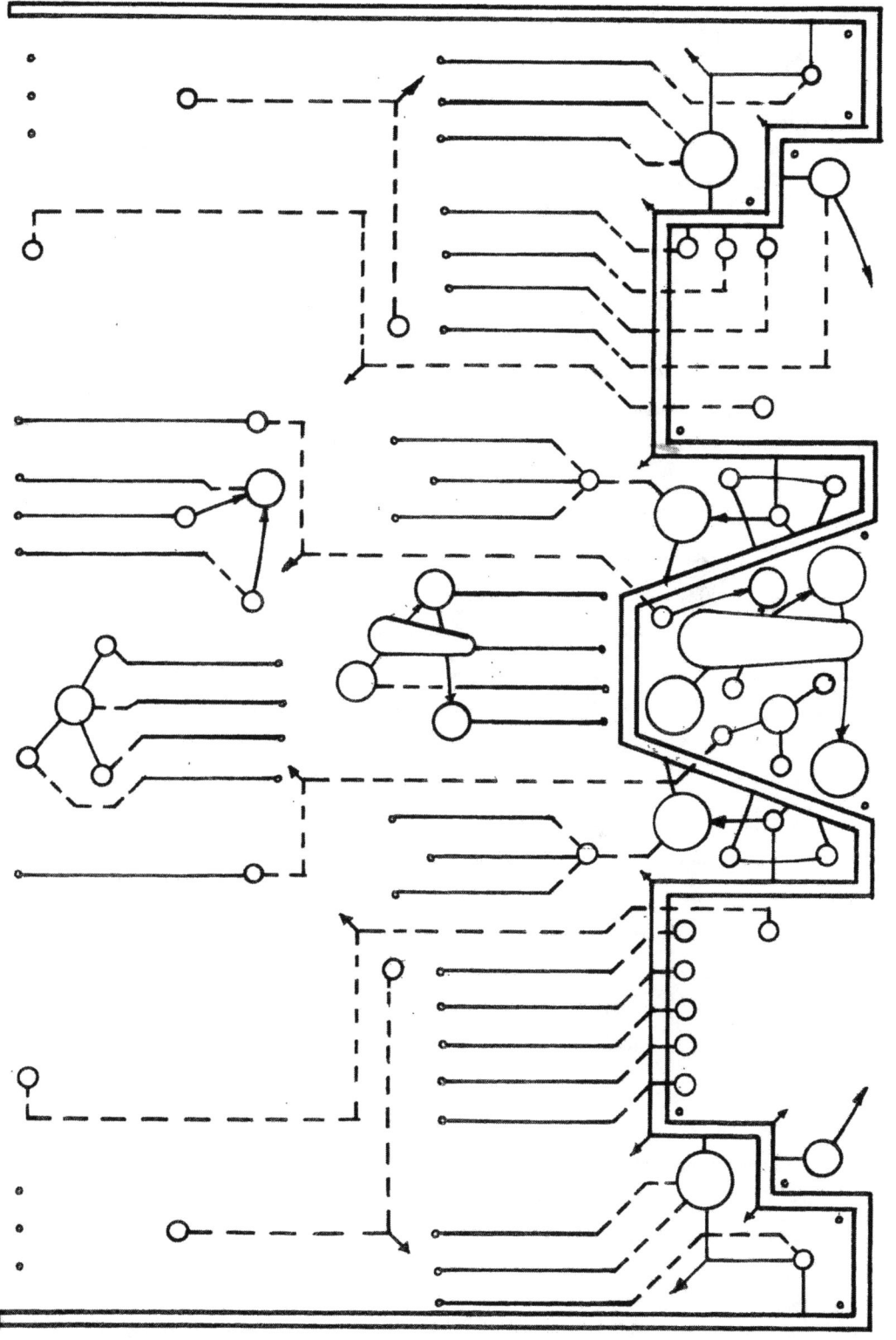

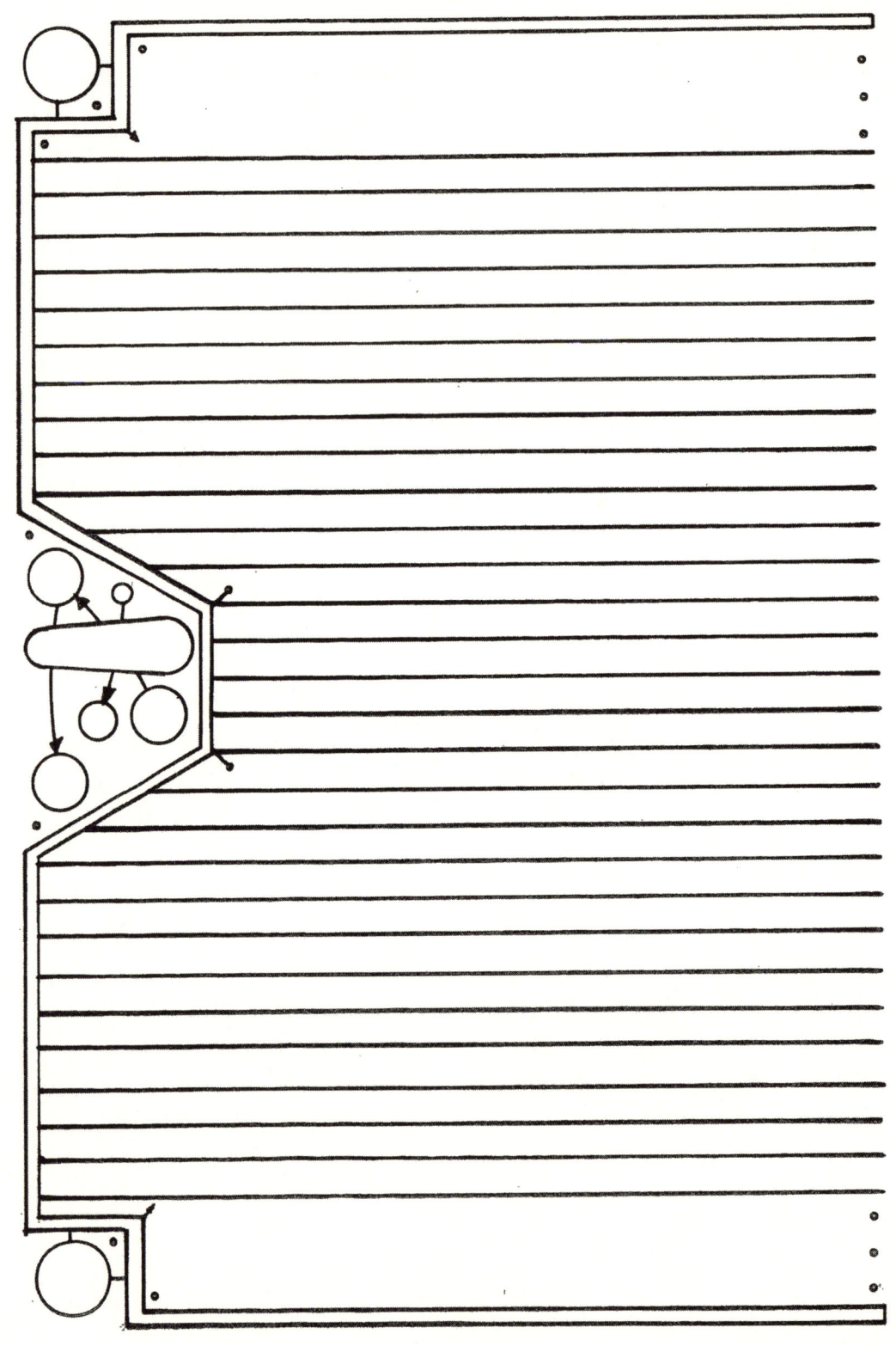

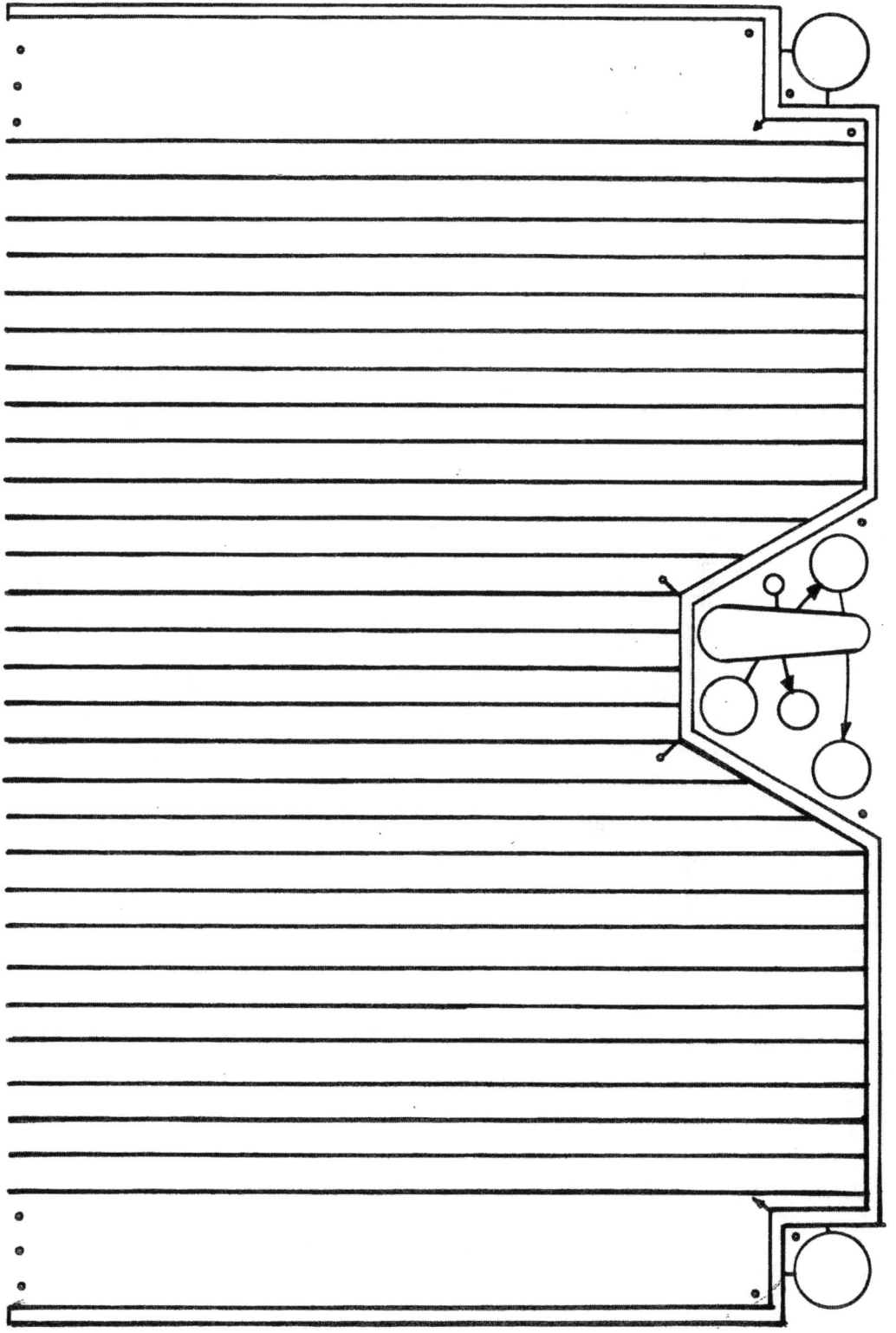

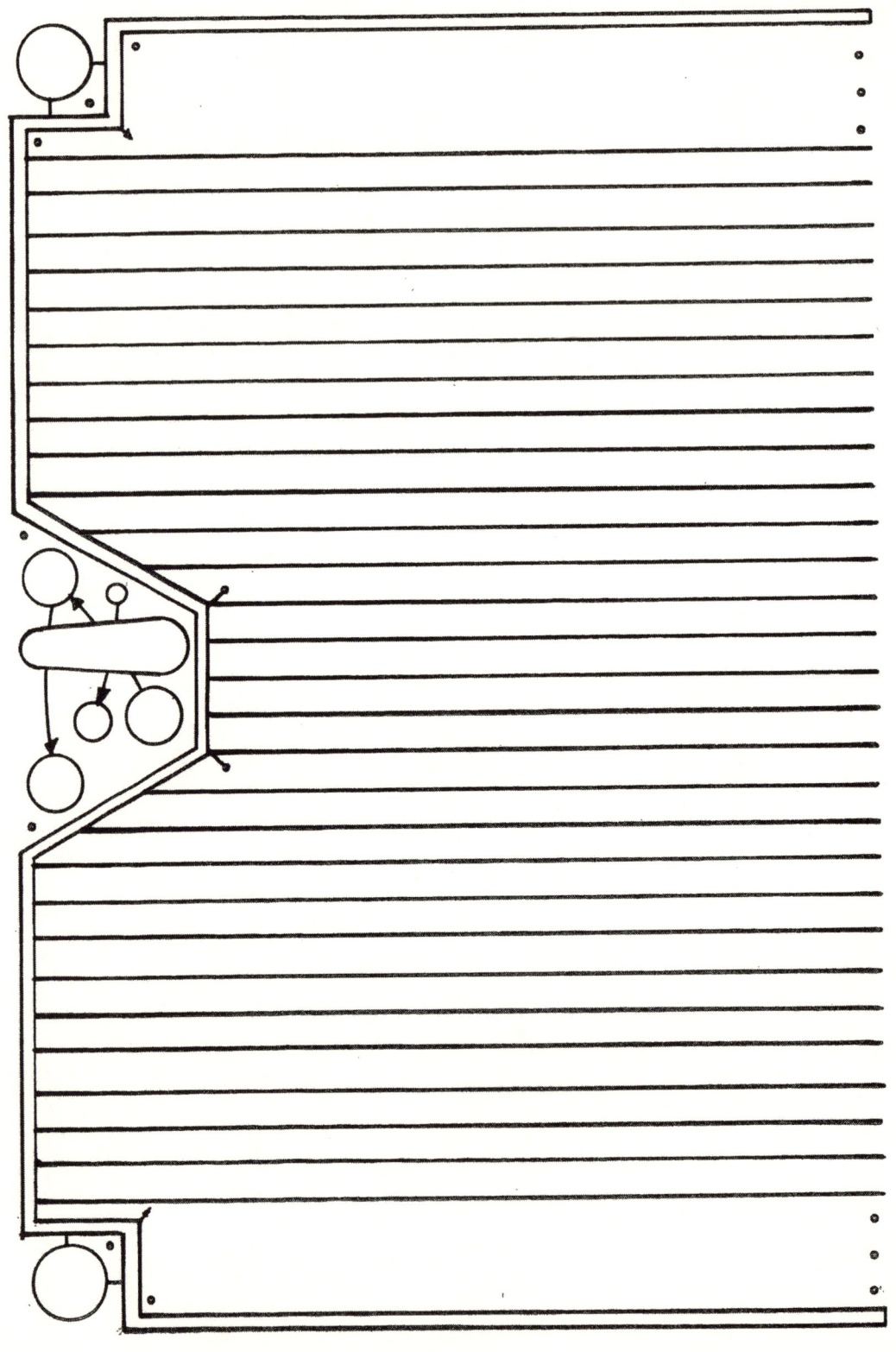

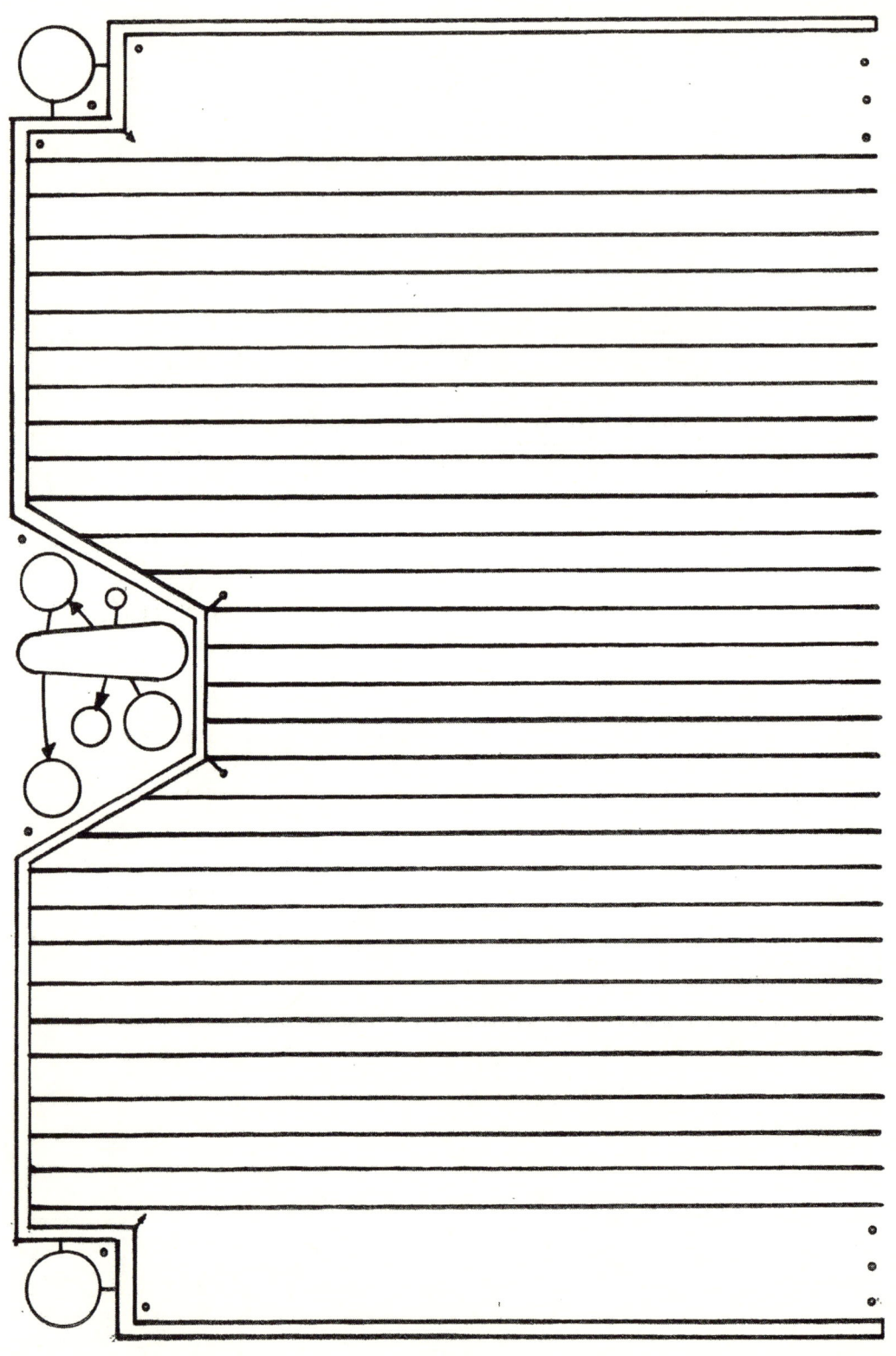

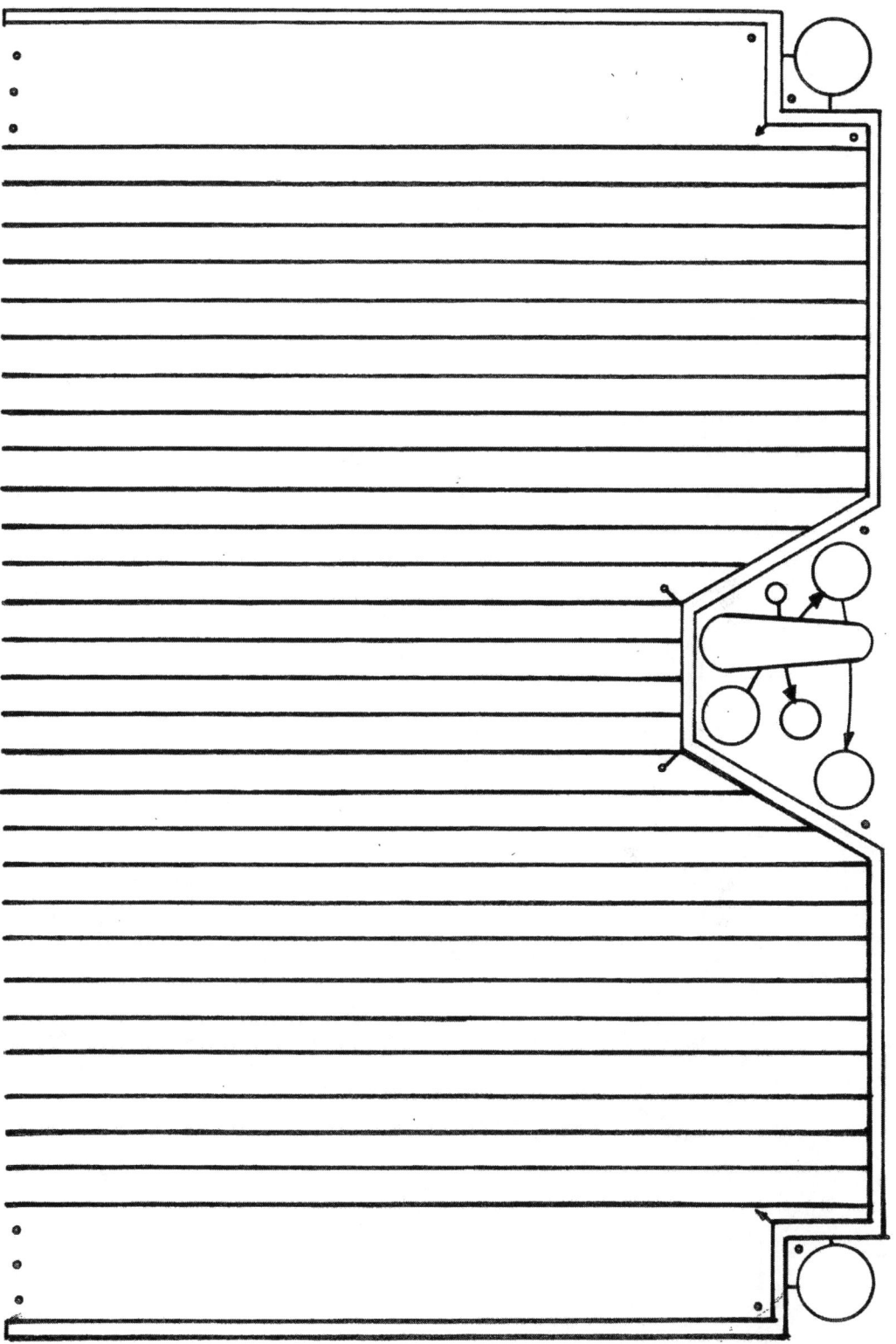

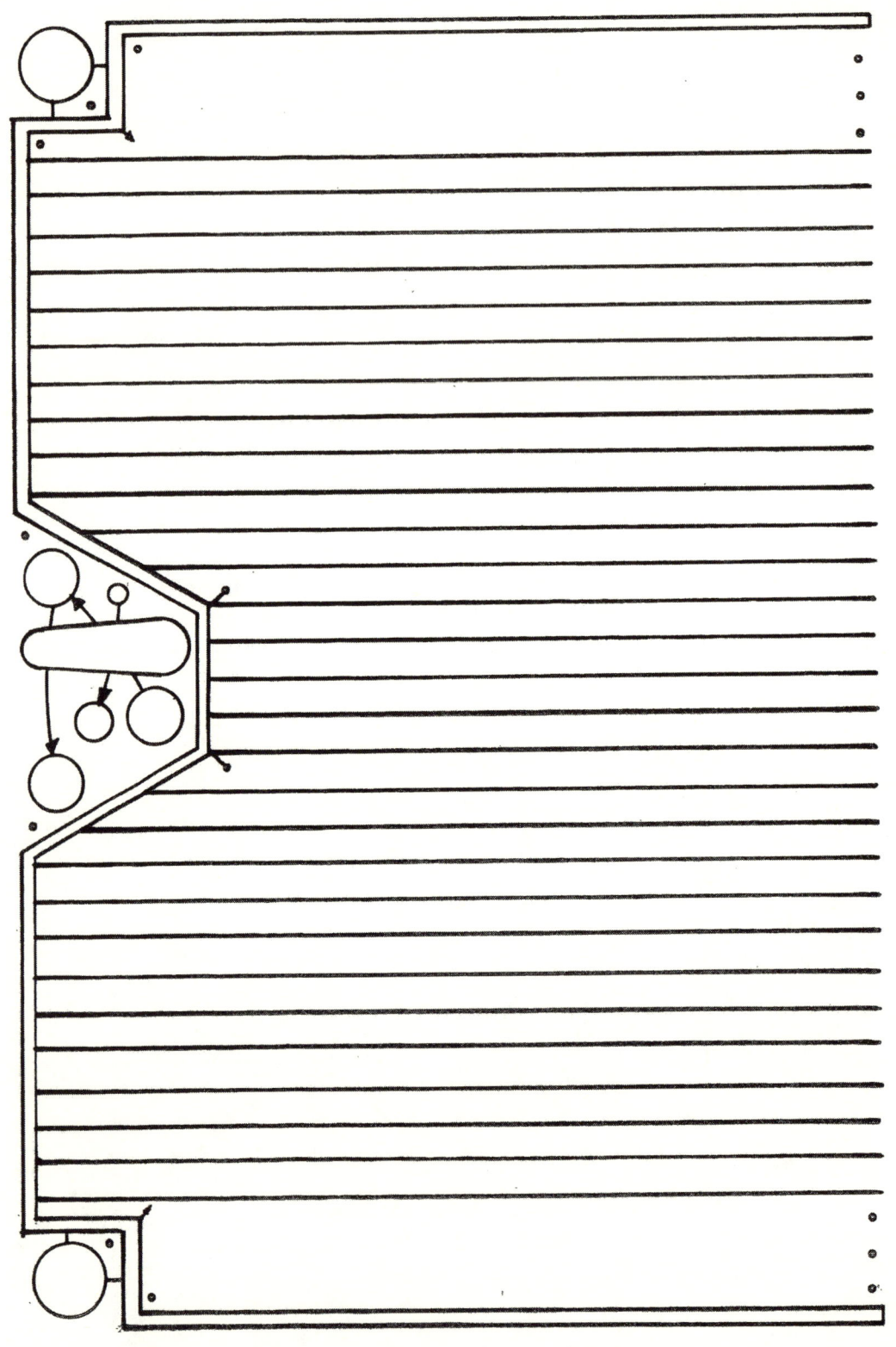

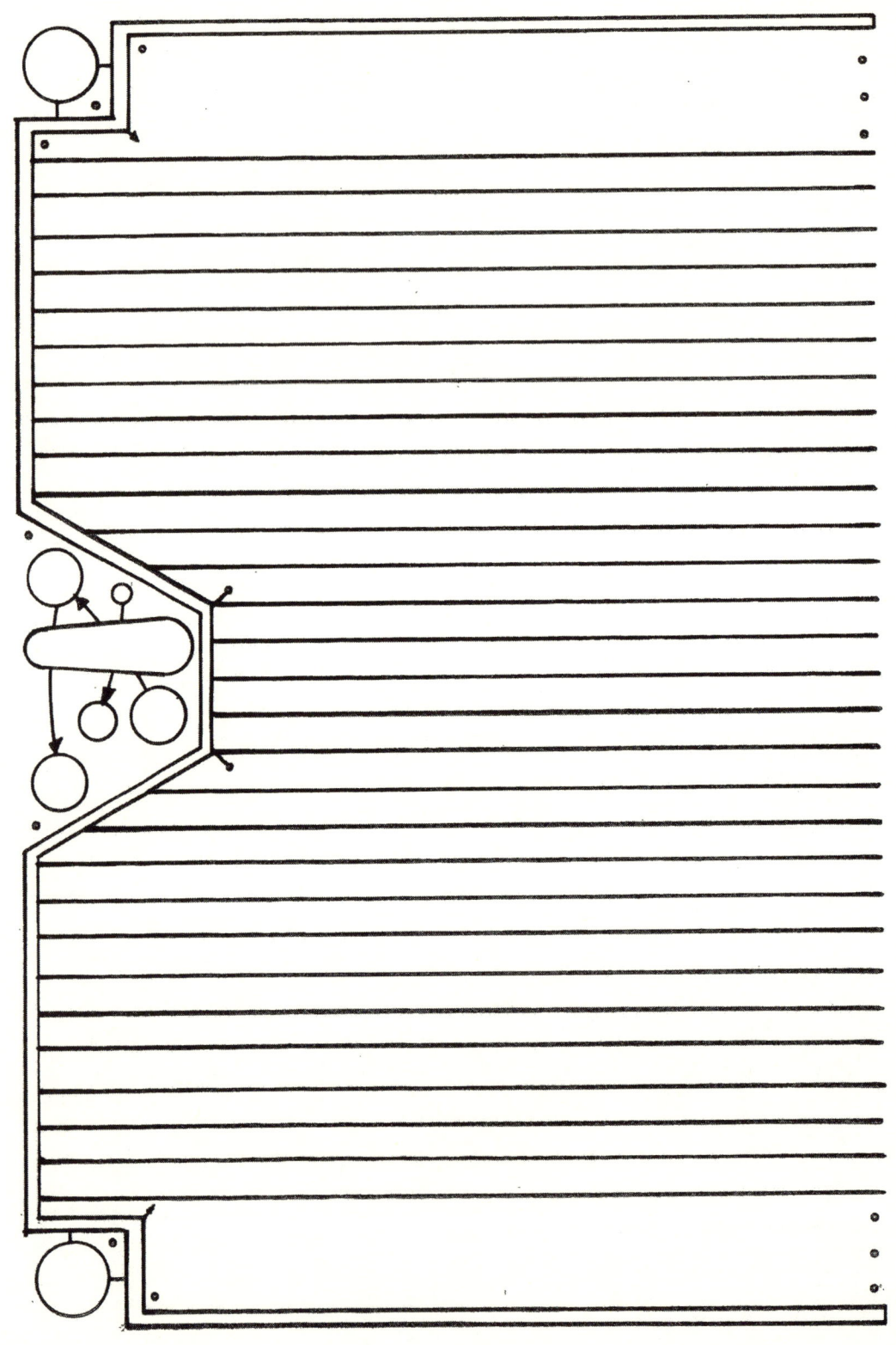

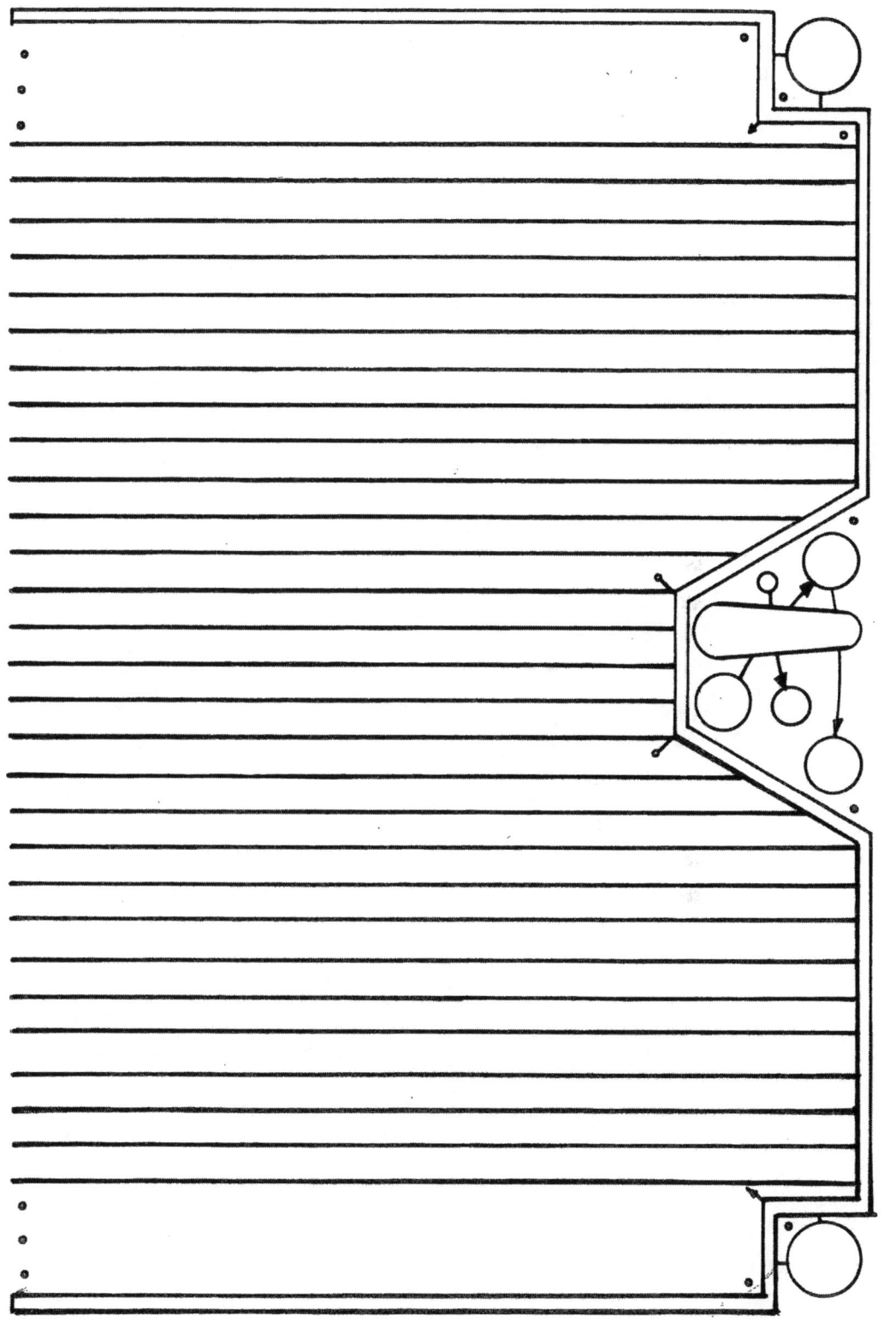

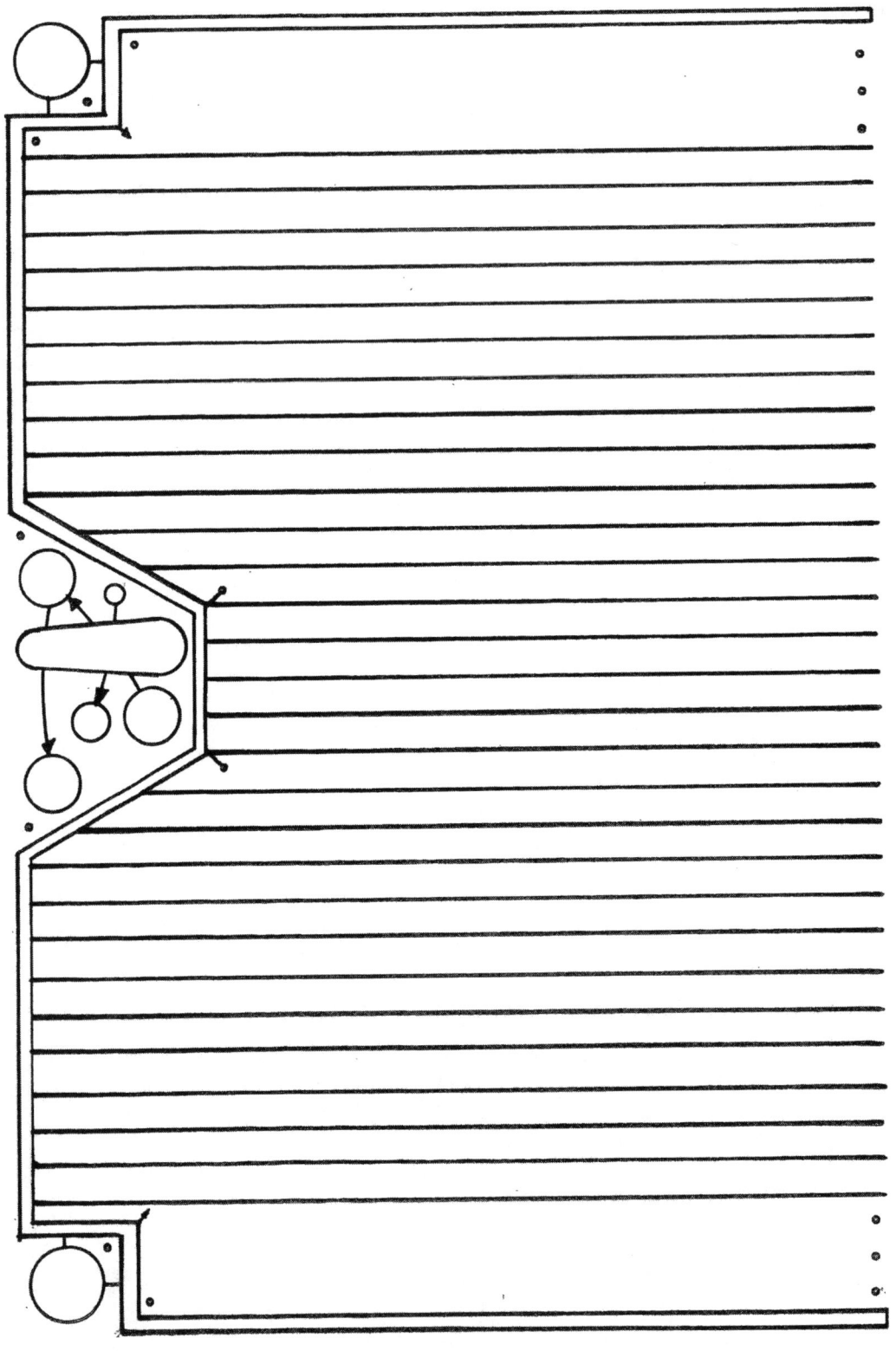

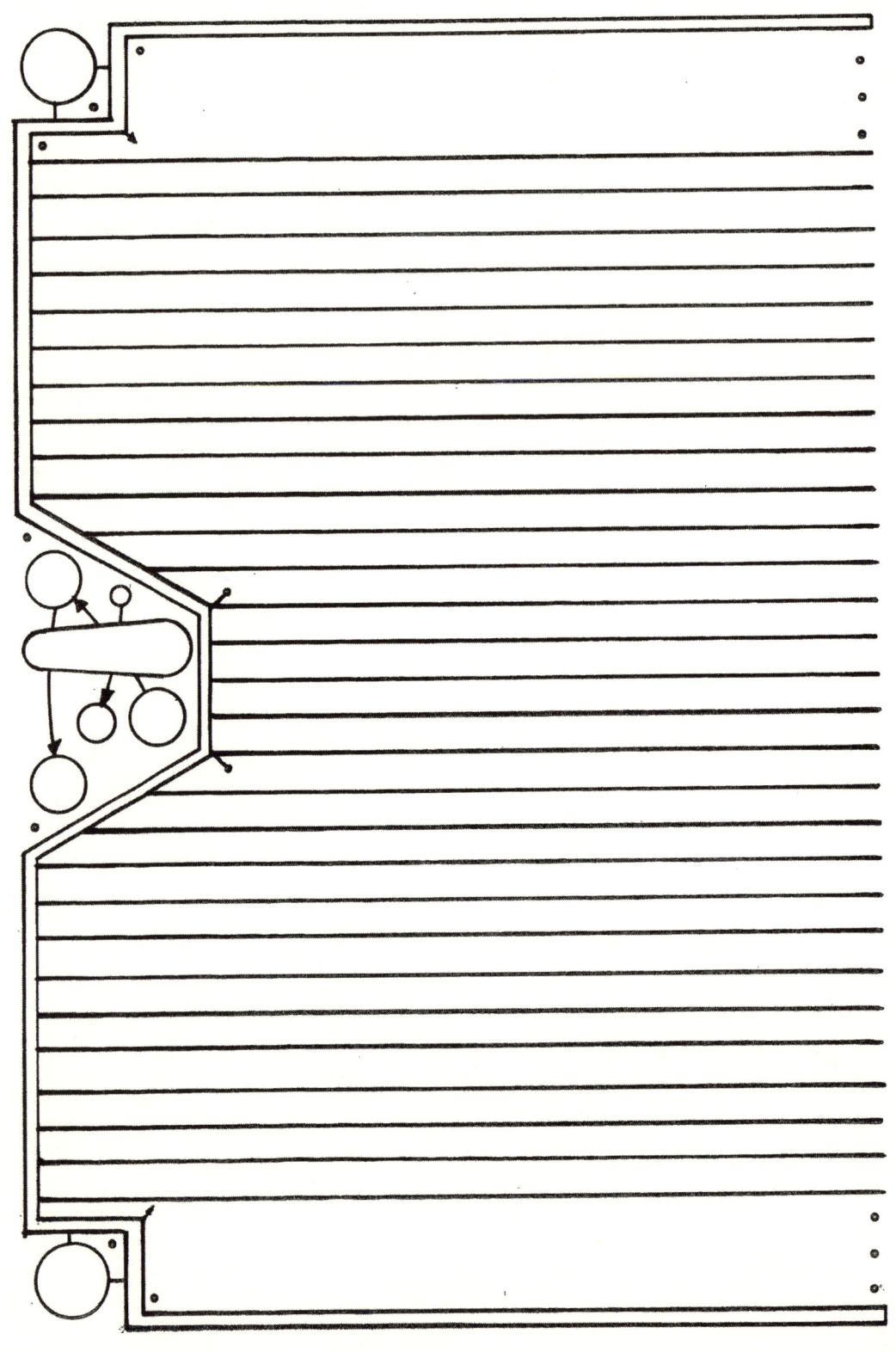

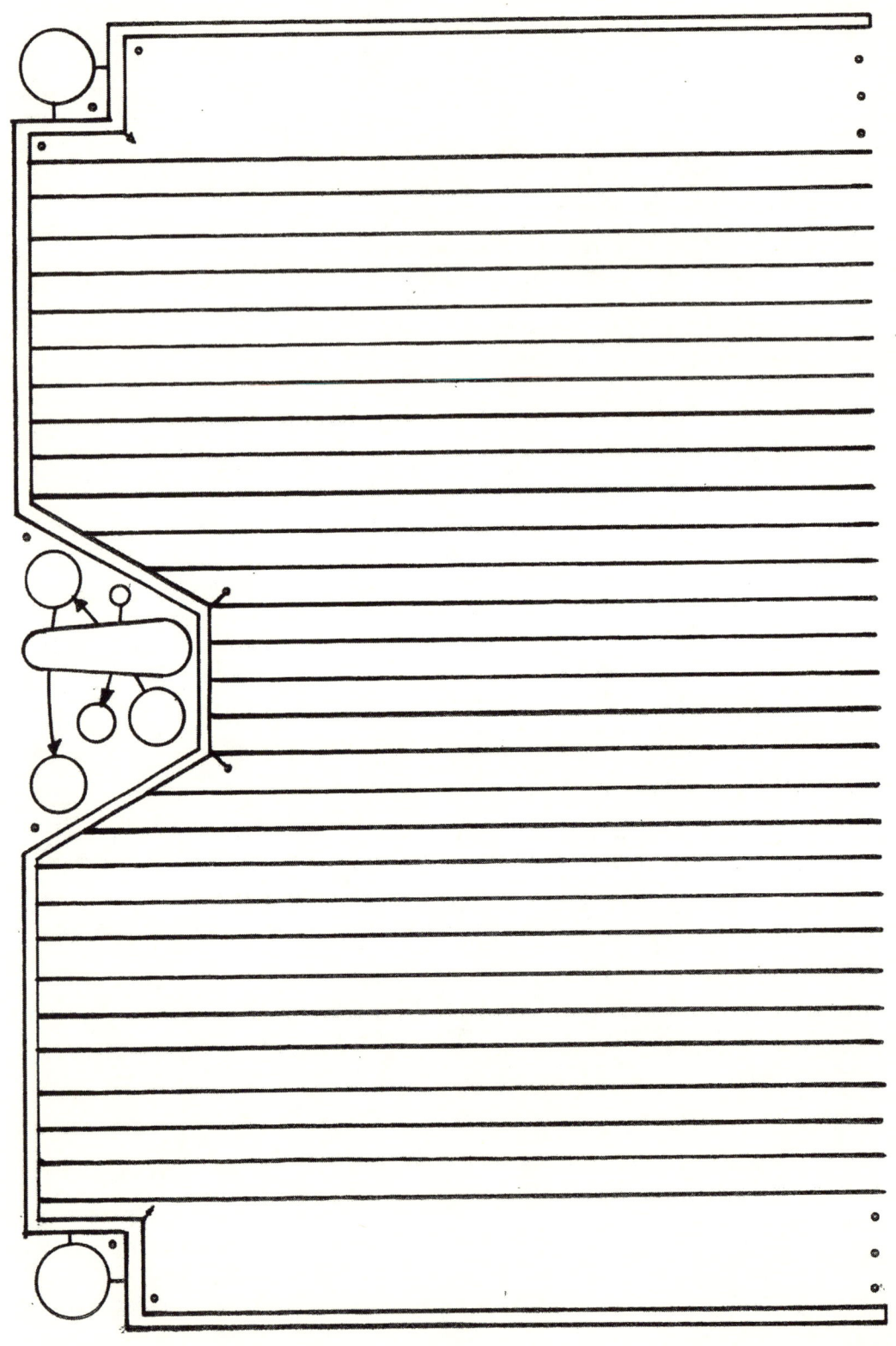

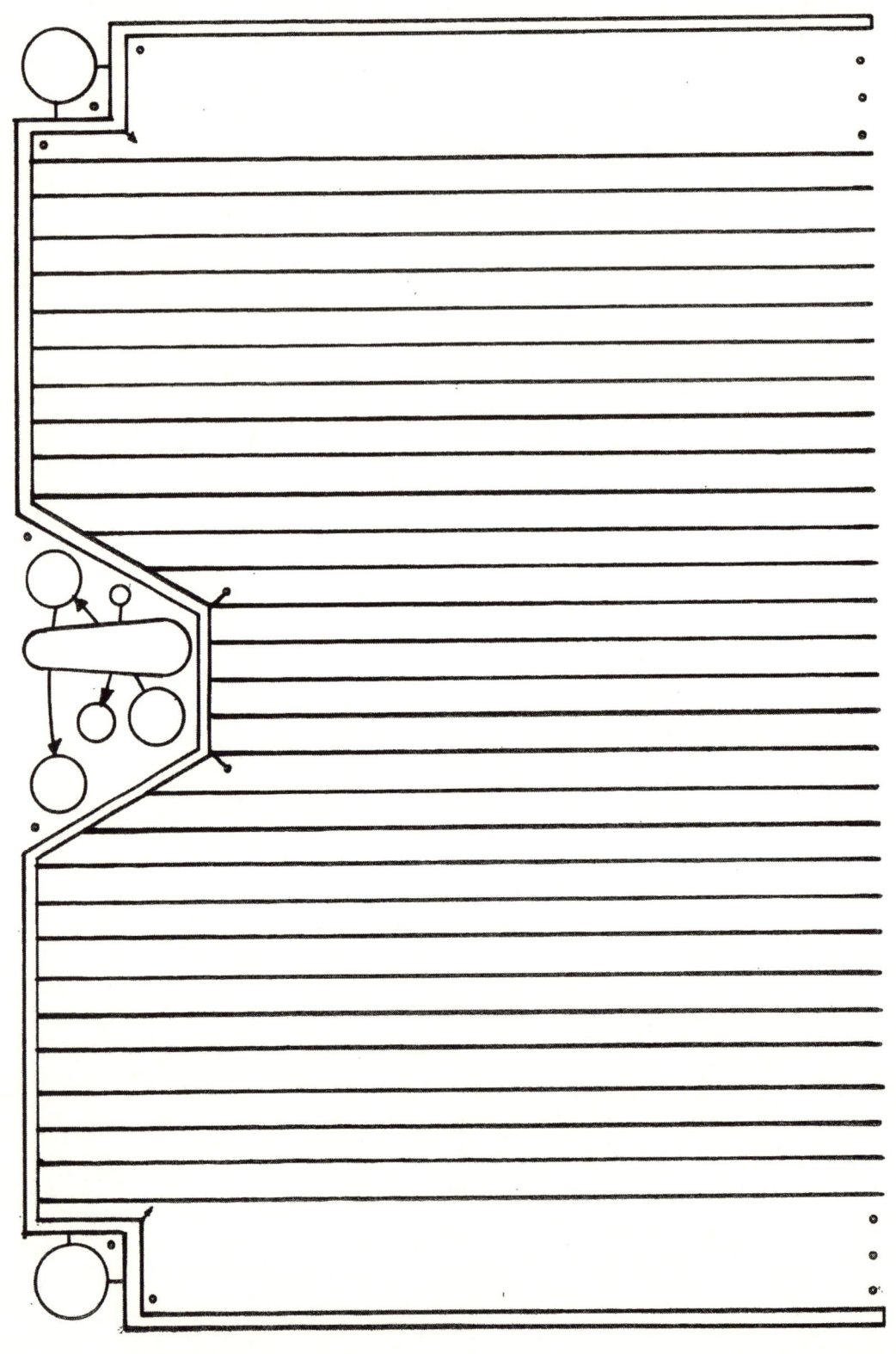

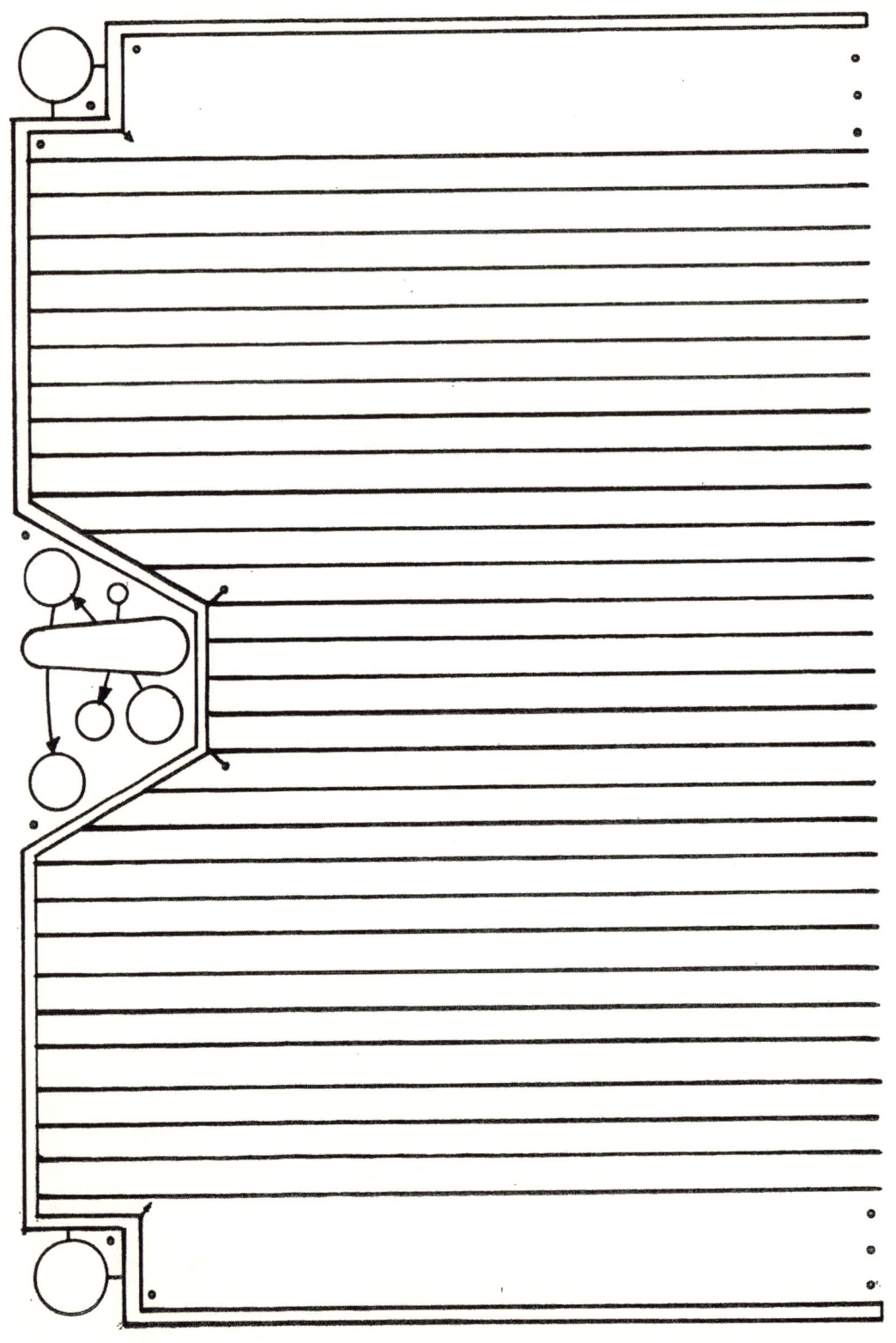

Thank you to all of the truly remarkable deliberate creators who mindfully contributed their love, intention and positive energy to this expansive project.

This realm is far more enjoyable with you in it.

WITH GRATITUDE

THANKS GOES TO YOU AS WELL, FELLOW TRAVELER, FOR EXPANDING YOUR REALITY INTO GREATER AND GRANDER POSSIBILITIES OF EXPERIENCE.
WELL DONE.

BEEAUTIFUL COVER ART BY
| JEANNINE BURGUESS |
jeannineburgess.com

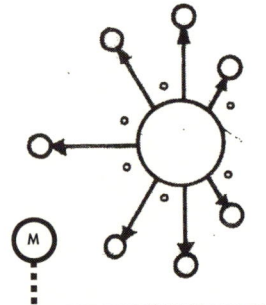

QUOTES, MANTRS AND ADDITIONAL ENERGETIC ACCOMPANIMENT CONTRIBUTED WITH LOVE BY...

RYAN COOK | the13podcast.com
BEC MYLONAS | becmylonas.com
MARK GOBER | markgober.com
BEN CARROLL | soundheals.us
AMY BELAIR | amybelair.com
NICHOLE EATON | nicholeeaton.com
BRITTANY RENEE | theebrittanyrenee.com
JESSTON WILLIAMS | thehiddengateway.com
DAVE ZED | patreon.com/generationzed

MEGHAN KITTREDGE | meghankittredge.com
SERENA FAITH MASTERSON | iamserena.net
CHARLIE ROBINSON | theoctopusofglobalcontrol.com
CHRYSTOPER KYNG | theastromedium.com
PAUL CLIFFORD | facebook.com/paul.clifford.397
PAT MAHAN | likeattractslikeevolution.com
MARISA LOVE | Instagram.com/the_ladybug_line
RYAN SPRAGUE | highlyoptimized.me
LEWIS SNOOKES | Instagram.com/lewis.snookes
HEATHER THOMAS | instagram.com/fullcircleawakening

Thank you as well to Cam Karri for his gift in the form of the words that look .
| CAM KARRI | cameron@masuyodigital.com

FEEL EMPOWERED TO REACH OUT AND SHOW THEM SOME LOVE.

Made in the USA
Middletown, DE
23 November 2023